The Heston Model and Its Extensions in VBA

Founded in 1807, John Wiley & Sons is the oldest independent publishing company in the United States. With offices in North America, Europe, Australia, and Asia, Wiley is globally committed to developing and marketing print and electronic products and services for our customers' professional and personal knowledge and understanding.

The Wiley Finance series contains books written specifically for finance and investment professionals as well as sophisticated individual investors and their financial advisors. Book topics range from portfolio management to e-commerce, risk management, financial engineering, valuation and financial instrument analysis, as well as much more.

For a list of available titles, visit our website at www.WileyFinance.com.

The Heston Model and Its Extensions in VBA

FABRICE DOUGLAS ROUAH

WILEY

Cover image: © Gilles Gheerbrant (1 2 3 4 au hasard)
Cover design: © Gilles Gheerbrant

Published by John Wiley & Sons, Inc., Hoboken, New Jersey.
Published simultaneously in Canada.

Library of Congress Cataloging-in-Publication Data:

Rouah, Fabrice, 1964–
The Heston model and its extensions in VBA + website / Fabrice D. Rouah.
pages cm. – (Wiley finance)
Includes bibliographical references and index.
ISBN 978-1-119-00330-4 (paperback) – ISBN 978-1-119-00332-8 (ePDF) – ISBN 978-1-119-00331-1 (ePub) 1. Options (Finance)–Mathematical models. 2. Options (Finance)–Prices. 3. Finance–Mathematical models. 4. Visual Basic for Applications (Computer program language) I. Title.
HG6024.A3R6778 2015
332.64′5302855133–dc23

2014043249

10 9 8 7 6 5 4 3 2 1

TO GIOVANNA

Contents

Foreword xi

Preface xiii

Acknowledgments xv

About This Book xvii

VBA Library for Complex Numbers xix

Chapter 1
The Heston Model for European Options 1
Model Dynamics 1
The Heston European Call Price 2
Dividend Yield and the Put Price 8
Consolidating the Integrals 9
Black-Scholes as a Special Case 10
Conclusion 12

Chapter 2
Integration Issues, Parameter Effects, and Variance Modeling 13
Remarks on the Characteristic Functions 14
Problems with the Integrand 16
The Little Heston Trap 18
Effect of the Heston Parameters 20
Variance Modeling in the Heston Model 26
Moment Explosions 38
Bounds on Implied Volatility Slope 40
Conclusion 42

Chapter 3
Derivations Using the Fourier Transform 45
Derivation of Gatheral (2006) 46
Attari (2004) Representation 47
Carr and Madan (1999) Representation 49
Conclusion 61

Chapter 4
The Fundamental Transform for Pricing Options **63**
The Payoff Transform 64
Option Prices Using Parseval's Identity 70
Volatility of Volatility Series Expansion 75
Conclusion 81

Chapter 5
Numerical Integration Schemes **83**
The Integrand in Numerical Integration 84
Newton-Cotes Formulas 85
Gaussian Quadrature 90
Integration Limits, Multidomain Integration, and Kahl and Jäckel Transformation 98
Illustration of Numerical Integration 103
Fast Fourier Transform 106
Fractional Fast Fourier Transform 108
Conclusion 114

Chapter 6
Parameter Estimation **115**
Estimation Using Loss Functions 116
Speeding Up the Estimation 126
Differential Evolution 128
Maximum Likelihood Estimation 132
Risk-Neutral Density and Arbitrage-Free Volatility Surface 135
Conclusion 140

Chapter 7
Simulation in the Heston Model **143**
General Setup 144
Euler Scheme 146
Milstein Scheme 147
Implicit Milstein Scheme 149
Transformed Volatility Scheme 152
Balanced, Pathwise, and IJK Schemes 155
Quadratic-Exponential Scheme 157
Alfonsi Scheme for the Variance 161
Moment-Matching Scheme 165
Conclusion 167

Chapter 8
American Options 169
Least-Squares Monte Carlo 169
The Explicit Method 174
Beliaeva-Nawalkha Bivariate Tree 178
Medvedev-Scaillet Expansion 191
Chiarella and Ziogas American Call 200
Conclusion 208

Chapter 9
Time-Dependent Heston Models 209
Generalization of the Riccati Equation 209
Bivariate Characteristic Function 210
Linking the Bivariate CF and the General Riccati Equation 212
Mikhailov and Nögel Model 214
Elices Model 219
Benhamou-Miri-Gobet Model 223
Black-Scholes Derivatives 231
Conclusion 232

Chapter 10
Methods for Finite Differences 235
The PDE in Terms of an Operator 236
Building Grids 236
Finite Difference Approximation of Derivatives 239
Boundary Conditions for the PDE 240
The Weighted Method 241
Explicit Scheme 248
ADI Schemes 251
Conclusion 256

Chapter 11
The Heston Greeks 257
Analytic Expressions for European Greeks 258
Finite Differences for the Greeks 263
Numerical Implementation of the Greeks 264
Greeks under the Attari and Carr-Madan Formulations 267
Greeks under the Lewis Formulations 273
Greeks Using the FFT and FRFT 276
American Greeks Using Simulation 279
American Greeks Using the Explicit Method 281
American Greeks from Medvedev and Scaillet 284
Conclusion 285

Chapter 12
The Double Heston Model **287**
Multidimensional Feynman-Kac Theorem 288
Double Heston Call Price 288
Double Heston Greeks 292
Parameter Estimation 297
Simulation in the Double Heston Model 301
American Options in the Double Heston Model 306
Conclusion 308

Bibliography **309**

About the Website **317**

Index **319**

Foreword

I am pleased to write this forward for Fabrice Rouah's final book on the "Heston Model." He had previously written an excellent book entitled *Option Pricing Models and Volatility Using Excel/VBA*, surveying a variety of modern models. He had also written the comprehensive book *The Heston Model and Its Extensions in Matlab and C#*. While these languages are widely used in large-scale econometric and commercial applications, there is conspicuous gap for people who want to implement stochastic volatility models in VBA. This present book fills that gap.

This book should interest a broad audience of practitioners and academics, including graduate students, quants on trading desks and in risk management, and researchers in option pricing and financial engineering. In the spirit of the classic *Numerical Recipes* books, the present book explains a variety of numerical methods and illustrates them with VBA routines. It includes numerical integration, the calculation of Greeks, American options, many simulation-based methods for valuation, finite difference numerical schemes, and subsequent developments such as the introduction of time-dependent parameters and the double version of the model. There is an old saying: "Teach a man to fish, and you will feed him for a lifetime." In a similar spirit, this book will support students, researchers, and practitioners who need to understand their computations for a lifetime of implementation.

Professor Steven L. Heston
Robert H. Smith School of Business
University of Maryland
January 15, 2015

Preface

In 20 years, since its introduction in 1993, the Heston model has become one of the most important models, if not the single most important model, in a then-revolutionary approach for pricing options known as stochastic volatility modeling. To understand why this model has become so important, we must revisit an event that shook financial markets around the world: the stock market crash of October 1987 and its subsequent impact on mathematical models to price options.

The exacerbation of smiles and skews in the implied volatility surface that resulted from the crash brought into question the ability of the Black-Scholes model to provide adequate prices in a new regime of volatility skews, and served to highlight the restrictive assumptions underlying the model. The most tenuous of these assumptions is that of continuously compounded stock returns being normally distributed with constant volatility. An abundance of empirical studies, since the 1987 crash, have shown that this assumption does not hold in equity markets. It is now a stylized fact in these markets that returns distribution is not normal. Returns exhibit skewness and kurtosis—fat tails—that normality cannot account for. Volatility is not constant in time, but tends to be inversely related to price, with high stock prices usually showing lower volatility than low stock prices. A number of researchers have sought to eliminate this assumption in their models, by allowing volatility to be time varying.

One popular approach for allowing time-varying volatility is to specify that volatility can be driven by its own stochastic process. The models that use this approach, including the Heston (1993) model, are known as stochastic volatility models. The models of Hull and White (1987), Scott (1987), Wiggins (1987), Chensey and Scott (1989), and Stein and Stein (1991) are among the most significant stochastic volatility models that predate Steve Heston's model. The Heston model was not the first stochastic volatility model to be introduced to the problem of pricing options, but it has emerged as the most important and now serves as a benchmark against which many other stochastic volatility models are compared.

Allowing for non-normality can be done by introducing skewness and kurtosis in the option price directly, as done, for example, by Jarrow and Rudd (1982); Corrado and Su (1997); and Backus, Foresi, and Wu (2004). In these models, skewness and kurtosis are specified in Edgeworth expansions or Gram-Charlier expansions. In stochastic volatility models, skewness can be induced by allowing correlation between the processes driving the stock price and the process driving its volatility. Alternatively, skewness can arise by introducing jumps into the stochastic process driving the underlying asset price.

The parameters of the Heston model are able to induce skewness and kurtosis, and produce a smile or skew in implied volatilities extracted from option prices generated by the model. The model easily allows for the inverse relationship between price level and volatility in a manner that is intuitive and easy to understand. Moreover, the call price in the Heston model is available in closed form, up to an integral that must be evaluated numerically. For these reasons, the Heston model has become the most popular stochastic volatility model for pricing equity options.

Another reason the Heston model is so important is that it is the first to exploit characteristic functions in option pricing, by recognizing that the terminal price density need not be known, only its characteristic function. This crucial line of reasoning was the genesis for a new approach for pricing options, known as pricing by characteristic functions. See Zhu (2010) for a discussion.

In this book, we present a treatment not only of the classical Heston model, but also of the many extensions that researchers from the academic and practitioner communities have contributed to this model since its inception. In Chapter 1, we present the characteristic function and call price of Heston's (1993) original derivation. Chapter 2 deals with some of the issues around the model such as integrand discontinuities, and also shows how to model implied and local volatility in the model. Chapter 3 presents several Fourier transform methods for the model, and Chapter 4 deals exclusively with Alan Lewis's (2000, 2001) approach to stochastic volatility modeling as it applies to the Heston model. Chapter 5 presents a variety of numerical integration schemes and explains how integration can be speeded up. Chapter 6 deals with parameter estimation, and Chapter 7 presents classical simulation schemes applied to the model and several simulation schemes designed specifically for the model. Chapter 8 deals with pricing American options in the Heston model. Chapter 9 presents models in which the parameters of the original Heston model are allowed to be piecewise constant. Chapter 10 presents methods for obtaining the call price that rely on solving the Heston partial differential equation with finite differences. Chapter 11 presents the Greeks in the Heston model. Finally, Chapter 12 presents the double Heston model, which introduces an additional stochastic process for variance and thus allows the model to provide a better fit to the volatility surface.

All of the models presented in this book have been coded in VBA.

Acknowledgments

I would like to thank Steve Heston not only for having bestowed his model to the financial engineering community, but also for contributing the Foreword to the original book on which this book is based. And to my team at Wiley—Bill Falloon, Meg Freeborn, and Vincent Nordhaus. I am also grateful to Gilles Gheerbrant for his strikingly beautiful cover design.

Special thanks also to a group who offered moral support, advice, and technical reviews of the material for both this book and the original work: Amir Atiya, Sébastien Bossu, Carl Chiarella, Elton Daal, Redouane El-Kamhi, Judith and James Farer, Jacqueline Gheerbrant, Emmanuel Gobet, Greg N. Gregoriou, Antoine Jacquier, Roy Horan, Dominique Legros, Pierre Leignadier, Alexey Medvedev, Sanjay K. Nawalkha, Razvan Pascalau, Jean Rouah, Olivier Scaillet, Martin Schmelzle, Giovanna Sestito, Nick Webber, and Estarose Wolfson. Finally, a special mention to Kevin Samborn at Sapient Global Markets for his help and support.

About This Book

This book is a condensed and readapted version of the original work entitled *The Heston Model and Its Extensions in Matlab and C#*, which was published by John Wiley & Sons in September 2013. It is geared for professionals who make extensive use of VBA in their professional lives. Much of the content in this book is taken directly from the original book, but with edits to condense the material and to present the VBA code with which the models are implemented. Readers of this book who seek theoretical details and mathematical derivations of the models may wish to consult the companion book.

This current work is light on theory but heavy on implementation. As such, it serves as a "VBA cookbook" for the models covered in the original book, rather than a reference guide for the theoretical aspects of the models. Indeed, the mathematical proofs and derivations of model results are omitted—these appear in the original book. Instead, the current book explains the VBA user-defined functions that implement the models; presents examples of how to run the functions; explains model results; and provides screen shots of the Excel files that accompany this book, all of which are available on the Wiley web site.

All the calculations for the implementation of the models covered in this book are done in VBA code that resides in Excel files. The code is used to create the user-defined VBA functions for the implementation. The Excel files serve as an interface between the model inputs and settings, and the VBA user-defined functions that process these inputs to produce model outputs such as prices, volatilities, and graphs. The VBA functions are arranged in separate modules that regroup functions with a common objective.

The VBA code and modules are available in the VBA editor, which can be accessed from Excel by pressing the <ALT> key, followed by <F11>. VBA code snippets are used throughout the book to illustrate how the user-defined VBA functions work. The snippets are for illustrative purposes only, and are therefore not complete—they contain only those portions of the functions that are vital to the calculations. Nonessential portions do not appear in the snippets. The VBA code itself appears as black-colored font in the snippets, comments appear as green-colored font, and text in quotations appears as red-colored font.

VBA Library for Complex Numbers

Most of the models covered in this book are heavily dependent on calculations that involve complex numbers. The VBA functions that are used to implement these models require a comprehensive VBA code library for defining complex numbers and for performing calculations on complex numbers. These include calculations not only between complex numbers themselves but also those between real numbers and complex numbers. The complex number library resides in a separate VBA module named ComplexLibrary, and this module forms part of every Excel file for which complex calculations are required.

The first part of the complex library contains elementary operations, such as the complex number type definition, the extraction of the real and imaginary part of a complex number, and the complex number conjugate.

```
' Structure of a complex number
Public Type cNum
    real As Double
    imag As Double
End Type
' Define a complex number
Function Complex(rPart, iPart) As cNum
    Complex.real = rPart
    Complex.imag = iPart
End Function
' Real part of a complex number
Function cReal(x As cNum) As Double
    cReal = x.real
End Function
' Imag part of a complex number
Function cImag(x As cNum) As Double
    cImag = x.imag
End Function
' Conjugate of a complex number
Function cConj(x As cNum) As cNum
    cConj.real = x.real
    cConj.imag = -x.imag
End Function
```

The second part contains functions for operations between complex numbers and between complex and real numbers. These include operations such as addition, subtraction, multiplication, and division, as well as multiplication of a complex number by a scalar.

```
' Addition of two complex numbers
Function cAdd(x As cNum, y As cNum) As cNum
    cAdd.real = x.real + y.real
    cAdd.imag = x.imag + y.imag
End Function
' Subtraction of two complex numbers
Function cSub(x As cNum, y As cNum) As cNum
    cSub.real = x.real - y.real
    cSub.imag = x.imag - y.imag
End Function
' Product of two complex numbers
Function cProd(x As cNum, y As cNum) As cNum
    cProd.real = (x.real * y.real) - (x.imag * y.imag)
    cProd.imag = (x.real * y.imag) + (x.imag * y.real)
End Function
' Product of a complex number by a real scalar
Function cProdScalar(x As cNum, a As Double) As cNum
    cProdScalar.real = a * x.real
    cProdScalar.imag = a * x.imag
End Function
' Division of a complex number by another complex number
Function cDiv(x As cNum, y As cNum) As cNum
    yc = cConj(y)
    cDiv.real = (x.real * yc.real - x.imag * yc.imag) ...
    cDiv.imag = (x.real * yc.imag + x.imag * yc.real) ...
End Function
```

The third part contains a function that finds the argument of a complex number. The argument is defined according to the quadrant of the complex plane (or which border point) in which the complex number resides. These quadrants, or regions, appear in Figure 0.0.

```
' Argument of a complex number
Function cArg(z As cNum) As Double
    pi = WorksheetFunction.pi()
    x = z.real
    y = z.imag
```

```
    ' Principal value of the argument of z in terms of its
    ' real and imaginary parts, arranged in a quadrant
    If x > 0 And y > 0 Then
        theta = Atn(y / x)          ' Quadrant I
    ElseIf x < 0 And y > 0 Then
        theta = pi + Atn(y / x)     ' Quadrant II
    ElseIf x < 0 And y < 0 Then
        theta = -pi + Atn(y / x)    ' Quadrant III
    ElseIf x > 0 And y < 0 Then
        theta = Atn(y / x)          ' Quadrant IV
    ElseIf x > 0 And y = 0 Then
        theta = 0                   ' Border of I and IV
    ElseIf x = 0 And y > 0 Then
        theta = pi / 2              ' Border of I and II
    ElseIf x < 0 And y = 0 Then
        theta = pi                  ' Border of II and III
    ElseIf x = 0 And y < 0 Then
        theta = -pi / 2             ' Border of III and IV
    ElseIf x = 0 And y = 0 Then
        Msg = "Error, argument of complex number not defined"
    End If
cArg = theta
End Function
```

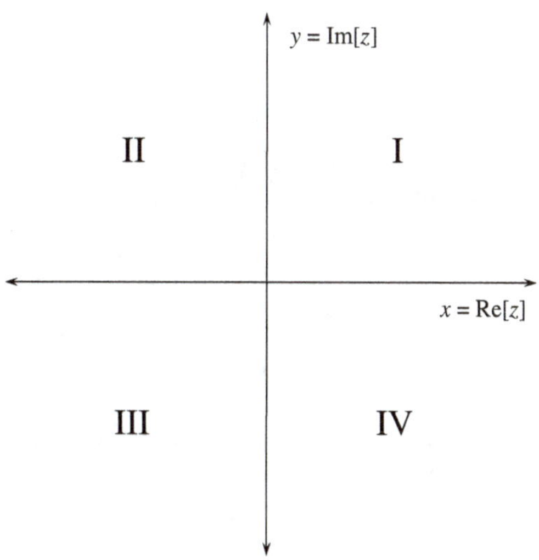

FIGURE 0.0 Quadrants of the Complex Plane

The last part of the library contains more advanced functions, such as that for the logarithm of a complex number or for its square root. Many of these functions rely on finding the argument of a complex number with the cArg function previously defined. Note that we avoid the use of exponentiation wherever possible and use multiplication instead. This is because exponentiation in VBA is computationally expensive.[1]

```
' Power of a complex number
Function cPow(z As cNum, N As Double) As cNum
    x = cReal(z)
    y = cImag(z)
    r = Sqr(x * x + y * y)
    If y = 0 Then
        cPow = Complex(x ^ N, 0)
    ElseIf x = 0 Then
        cPow = Complex(-y ^ N, 0)
    Else
    theta = cArg(z)
    cPow.real = r ^ N * Cos(theta * N)
    cPow.imag = r ^ N * Sin(theta * N)
    End If
End Function
' Exponent of a complex number
Function cExp(x As cNum) As cNum
    cExp.real = Exp(x.real) * Cos(x.imag)
    cExp.imag = Exp(x.real) * Sin(x.imag)
End Function
' Logarithm of a complex number
Function cLog(z As cNum) As cNum
    x = z.real
    y = z.imag
    T = cArg(z)
    ' Real and imaginary parts of Log(z)
    absx = Sqr(x * x + y * y)
    cLog.real = Log(absx)
    cLog.imag = T
End Function
' Complex number to the power of another complex number
Function cPowcNum(cNum1 As cNum, cNum2 As cNum) As cNum
    r = Sqr(cNum1.real * cNum1.real + cNum1.imag * cNum1.imag)
    y = cArg(cNum1)
    cPowcNum.real = r ^ cNum2.real * Exp(-cNum2.imag * y) ...
    cPowcNum.imag = r ^ cNum2.real * Exp(-cNum2.imag * y) ...
End Function
```

[1] We thank Nick Webber for pointing this out.

```
' Square root of a complex number
Function cSqr(z As cNum) As cNum
    x = z.real
    y = z.imag
    T = cArg(z)
    r = Sqr(x * x + y * y)
    cSqr.real = Sqr(r) * Cos(T / 2)
    cSqr.imag = Sqr(r) * Sin(T / 2)
End Function
```

Operations on complex numbers are presented in many textbooks on the subject, such as that by Rudin (1986).

CHAPTER 1

The Heston Model for European Options

Abstract

Here, we present the European call price under the Heston model. We first present the model and then illustrate that the call price in the Heston model can be expressed as the sum of two terms that each contains an in-the-money probability but obtained under a separate measure, a result demonstrated by Bakshi and Madan (2000). We then show how to incorporate a continuous dividend yield and how to compute the price of a European put, and demonstrate that the numerical integration can be speed up by consolidating the two numerical integrals into a single integral. Finally, we derive the Black-Scholes model as a special case of the Heston model.

CIR process, European call, characteristic function, dividend yield, put-call parity, Black-Scholes

In this chapter, we present the European call price under the Heston model. We first present the model and then illustrate that the call price in the Heston model can be expressed as the sum of two terms that each contains an in-the-money probability, but obtained under a separate measure, a result demonstrated by Bakshi and Madan (2000). We then show how to incorporate a continuous dividend yield and how to compute the price of a European put, and demonstrate that the numerical integration can be speeded up by consolidating the two numerical integrals into a single integral. Finally, we derive the Black-Scholes model as a special case of the Heston model.

MODEL DYNAMICS

The Heston model assumes that the underlying stock price, S_t, follows a Black-Scholes–type stochastic process, but with a stochastic variance, v_t, that follows a Cox, Ingersoll, and Ross (1985) process. Hence, the Heston model is represented by the bivariate system of stochastic differential equations (SDEs),

$$\begin{aligned} dS_t &= \mu S_t dt + \sqrt{v_t} S_t dW_{1,t} \\ dv_t &= \kappa(\theta - v_t)dt + \sigma\sqrt{v_t} dW_{2,t} \end{aligned}, \tag{1.1}$$

where $E^{\mathbb{P}}\left[dW_{1,t}dW_{2,t}\right] = \rho dt$. We will sometimes drop the time index and write $S = S_t$, $v = v_t$, $W_1 = W_{1,t}$ and $W_2 = W_{2,t}$ for notational convenience. The parameters of the model are

μ the drift of the process for the stock;

$\kappa > 0$ the mean reversion speed for the variance;

$\theta > 0$ the mean reversion level for the variance;

$\sigma > 0$ the volatility of the variance;

$v_0 > 0$ the initial (time zero) level of the variance;

$\rho \in [-1, 1]$ the correlation between the two Brownian motion W_1 and W_2; and

λ the volatility risk parameter (discussed below).

We will see in Chapter 2 that these parameters affect the distribution of the terminal stock price in a manner that is intuitive. Some authors refer to v_0 as an unobserved initial state variable rather than a parameter. Because volatility cannot be observed, only estimated, and because v_0 represents this state variable at time zero, this characterization is sensible. For the purposes of estimation, however, many authors treat v_0 as a parameter like any other. Parameter estimation is covered in Chapter 6.

The stock price and variance follow the processes in Equation (1.1) under the historical measure $\mathbb{P}$, also called the physical measure. For pricing purposes, however, we need the processes for (S_t, v_t) under the risk-neutral measure $\mathbb{Q}$. The risk-neutral process is

$$\begin{aligned} dS_t &= rS_t dt + \sqrt{v_t} S_t d\tilde{W}_{1,t} \\ dv_t &= \kappa^*(\theta^* - v_t)dt + \sigma\sqrt{v_t} d\tilde{W}_{2,t} \end{aligned}, \tag{1.2}$$

where $E^{\mathbb{Q}}\left[d\tilde{W}_{1,t}d\tilde{W}_{2,t}\right] = \rho dt$. The risk-neutral parameters of the variance process are where $\kappa^* = \kappa + \lambda$ and $\theta^* = \kappa\theta/(\kappa + \lambda)$.

Note that when $\lambda = 0$, we have $\kappa^* = \kappa$ and $\theta^* = \theta$ so that the parameters under the physical and risk-neutral measures are the same. Throughout this book, we set $\lambda = 0$, but this is not always needed. Indeed, λ is embedded in the risk-neutral parameters κ^* and θ^*. Hence, when we estimate the risk-neutral parameters to price options, we do not need to estimate λ. Estimation of λ is the subject of its own research, such as that by Bollerslev et al. (2011). For notational simplicity, throughout this book we will drop the asterisk on the parameters and the tilde on the Brownian motion when it is obvious that we are dealing with the risk-neutral measure.

For details on how the risk-neutral process is constructed, see Rouah (2013).

THE HESTON EUROPEAN CALL PRICE

In this section, we show that the call price in the Heston model can be expressed in a manner that resembles the call price in the Black-Scholes model, which we present in Equation (1.16). Authors sometimes refer to this characterization of the call price as "Black-Scholes–like" or "à la Black-Scholes." The time-t price of a European call on a non-dividend-paying stock with spot price S_t, when the strike is K and the time to maturity is $\tau = T - t$, is the discounted expected value of the payoff under the risk-neutral measure $\mathbb{Q}$

$$\begin{aligned} C(K) &= e^{-r\tau} E^{\mathbb{Q}}[(S_T - K)^+] \\ &= S_t P_1 - K e^{-r\tau} P_2. \end{aligned} \tag{1.3}$$

The last line of (1.3) is the "Black-Scholes–like" call price formula, with P_1 replacing $\Phi(d_1)$, and P_2 replacing $\Phi(d_2)$ in the Black-Scholes call price (1.16).

By introducing two measures, $\mathbb{Q}$ and $\mathbb{Q}^S$, the European call price of Equation (1.3) can be written

$$C(K) = S_t \mathbb{Q}^S(S_T > K) - K e^{-r\tau} \mathbb{Q}(S_T > K). \tag{1.4}$$

The measure $\mathbb{Q}$ uses the bond B_t as the numeraire, while the measure $\mathbb{Q}^S$ uses the stock price S_t. Bakshi and Madan (2000) present a derivation of the call price expressed as (1.4), but under a general setup. As shown in their paper, the change of measure that leads to (1.4) is valid for a wide range of models, including the Black-Scholes and Heston models. We will see later in this chapter that when S_T follows the lognormal distribution specified in the Black-Scholes model, then $\mathbb{Q}^S(S_T > K) = \Phi(d_1)$ and $\mathbb{Q}(S_T > K) = \Phi(d_2)$. Hence, the characteristic function approach to pricing options, pioneered by Heston (1993), applies to the Black-Scholes model also.

In the Heston model, it can be shown that P_1 and P_2 in (1.3) can be written

$$P_j = \Pr_j(\ln S_T > \ln K) = \frac{1}{2} + \frac{1}{\pi} \int_0^\infty \text{Re}\left[\frac{e^{-i\phi \ln K} f_j(\phi; x, v)}{i\phi}\right] d\phi, \tag{1.5}$$

where $i = \sqrt{-1}$ is the imaginary unit, $\Pr_1 = \mathbb{Q}^S$, $\Pr_2 = \mathbb{Q}$, and $f_j(\phi; x, v)$ are the characteristic functions for the logarithm of the terminal stock price $x_T = \ln S_T$. Heston (1993) postulates that these characteristic functions are of the log linear form,

$$f_j(\phi; x_t, v_t) = \exp\left(C_j(\tau, \phi) + D_j(\tau, \phi) v_t + i\phi x_t\right), \tag{1.6}$$

where C_j and D_j are constant coefficients and $\tau = T - t$ is the time to maturity.

The coefficients can be shown to be

$$D_j(\tau, \phi) = \frac{b_j - \rho\sigma i\phi + d_j}{\sigma^2}\left(\frac{1 - e^{d_j\tau}}{1 - g_j e^{d_j\tau}}\right) \tag{1.7}$$

and

$$C_j(\tau, \phi) = ri\phi\tau + \frac{a}{\sigma^2}\left[(b_j - \rho\sigma i\phi + d_j)\tau - 2\ln\left(\frac{1 - g_j e^{d_j\tau}}{1 - g_j}\right)\right], \tag{1.8}$$

where $a = \kappa\theta$,

$$\begin{aligned} d_j &= \sqrt{(\rho\sigma i\phi - b_j)^2 - \sigma^2(2u_j i\phi - \phi^2)}, \\ g_j &= \frac{b_j - \rho\sigma i\phi + d_j}{b_j - \rho\sigma i\phi - d_j}, \end{aligned}$$

and with $u_1 = \frac{1}{2}$, $u_2 = -\frac{1}{2}$, $b_1 = \kappa + \lambda - \rho\sigma$, and $b_2 = \kappa + \lambda$. See Rouah (2013) for a complete derivation of the coefficients (1.7) and (1.8).

We use two functions to implement the Heston call price in VBA using the trapezoidal rule, HestonProb and HestonPriceTrapz. The first function calculates the characteristic functions and returns the real part of the integrand. The functions allow to price calls or puts, and allow for a dividend yield, as explained in the following section. The following code snippet is taken from the Excel file Ch1Trapz.xls. To conserve space, parts of the functions have been omitted.

```
Function HestonProb(phi As Double, ...) As Double
' C = (r-q)*phi*tau*i + a/sigma^2*((b - rho*sigma*i*phi + d) ...
bigC = cAdd(Term3, term4)
' D = (b - rho*sigma*i*phi + d)/sigma^2 * ((1-exp(d*tau)) ...
bigD = cProd(Term5, Term6)
' The characteristic function.
' f = cExp(C + D*v0 + phi*x*i)
f = cExp(cAdd(cAdd(bigC, dv0), phixi))
' Return the real part of the integrand.
' HestonProb = real(Exp(-i * phi * Log(K)) * f / i / phi)
philogKi = cProd(Complex(-Log(K) * phi, 0), i)
E = cDiv(e2, cProd(i, Complex(phi, 0)))
HestonProb = cReal(E)
End Function
```

The second function calculates the price of a European call $C(K)$, or European put $P(K)$, by put-call parity in Equation (1.13). The function calls the HestonProb function at every point of the integration grid and uses the trapezoidal rule for integration when all the integration points have been calculated.

```
Function HestonPriceTrapz(PutCall As String, ...) As Double
' Integration increment and integration grid
dphi = (Uphi - Lphi) / (N - 1)
phi(1) = Lphi
For j = 2 To N
    phi(j) = phi(j - 1) + dphi
Next j
' Weights for trapezoidal rule
W(1) = 0.5 * dphi
W(N) = 0.5 * dphi
For j = 2 To N - 1
    W(j) = dphi
Next j
' Build the integrands for P1 and P2;
```

```
For j = 1 To N
    int1(j) = HestonProb(phi(j), ..., 1) * W(j)
    int2(j) = HestonProb(phi(j), ..., 2) * W(j)
Next j
' The integrals and the probabilities
I1 = Sum(int1)
I2 = Sum(int2)
P1 = 0.5 + 1 / pi * I1
P2 = 0.5 + 1 / pi * I2
' The call price and put price by put call parity
HestonC = S * Exp(-q * T) * P1 - K * Exp(-r * T) * P2
HestonP = HestonC - S * Exp(-q * T) + K * Exp(-r * T)
End Function
```

Pricing European calls and puts is straightforward. For example, the price of a six-month European put with strike $K = 100$ on a dividend-paying stock with spot price $S = 100$ and yield $q = 0.02$, when the risk-free rate is $r = 0.03$ and using the parameters $\kappa = 5$, $\sigma = 0.5$, $\rho = -0.8$, $\theta = v_0 = 0.05$, and $\lambda = 0$, along with the integration grid $\phi \in [1e^{-8}, 100]$ with 500 points is 5.7589. The price of the call with identical features is 6.2527. This is illustrated in Figure 1.1, which is a screen shot of the Excel file Ch1Trapz.xls.

If there is no dividend yield so that $q = 0$, then as expected, the put price decreases to 5.3789, and the call price increases to 6.8677.

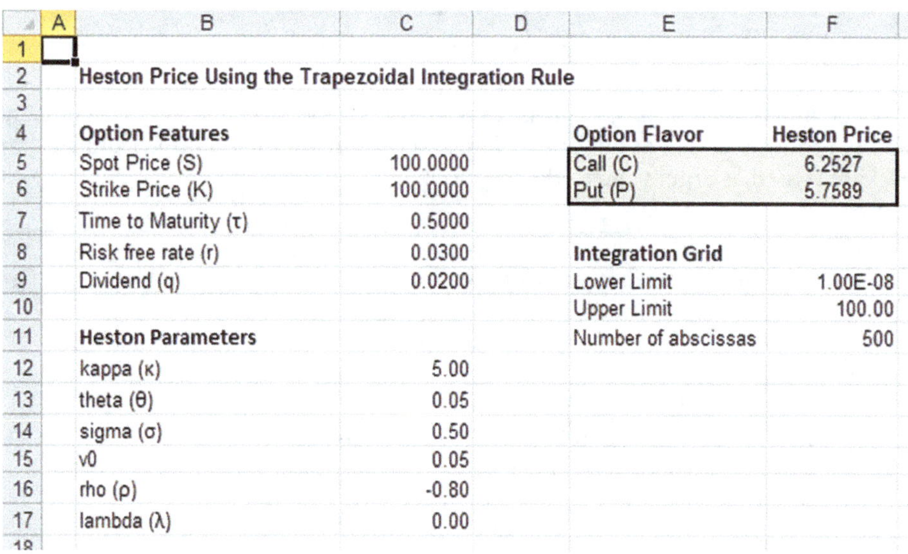

	A	B	C	D	E	F
1						
2		**Heston Price Using the Trapezoidal Integration Rule**				
3						
4		**Option Features**			**Option Flavor**	**Heston Price**
5		Spot Price (S)	100.0000		Call (C)	6.2527
6		Strike Price (K)	100.0000		Put (P)	5.7589
7		Time to Maturity (τ)	0.5000			
8		Risk free rate (r)	0.0300		**Integration Grid**	
9		Dividend (q)	0.0200		Lower Limit	1.00E-08
10					Upper Limit	100.00
11		**Heston Parameters**			Number of abscissas	500
12		kappa (κ)	5.00			
13		theta (θ)	0.05			
14		sigma (σ)	0.50			
15		v0	0.05			
16		rho (ρ)	-0.80			
17		lambda (λ)	0.00			

FIGURE 1.1 Heston Price Using the Trapezoidal Rule

The Excel files Ch1GLa.xls and Ch1GLe_GLo.xls implement the Heston price using Gauss-Laguerre integration, and Gauss-Legendre and Gauss-Lobatto integration, respectively, each using 32 integration points. These rules will be covered in Chapter 5. The pricing functions in these files are nearly identical to those for the trapezoidal rule, except that the integration points and weights are hard-coded outside the function. The functions also allow for the "Little Trap" formulation of the characteristic function of Albrecher et al. (2007), which we discuss in the following chapter.

The VBA function HestonProb from the Excel file Ch1GLa.xls illustrates this point.

```
Function HestonProb(...,trap as integer) As Double
If trap = 0 Then
    ' Original Heston formulation of the c.f.
    bigG = cDiv(Num2, Den2)
    bigC = cAdd(Term3, term4)
    bigD = cProd(Term5, Term6)
 ElseIf trap = 1 Then
    ' Little Trap formulation of the c.f.
    bigG = cDiv(Num2, Den2)
    bigC = cAdd(Term3, term4)
    bigD = cProd(Term5, Term6)
End If
' The characteristic function.
f = cExp(cAdd(cAdd(bigC, Dv0), phixi))
' Return the real part of the integrand.
HestonProb = cReal(E)
End Function
```

The function HestonPriceGaussLaguerre uses 32-point Gauss-Laguerre integration to produce the call or put price. Note that the integration points (x) and weights (W) are passed as arguments to the function.

```
Function HestonPriceGaussLaguerre(..., x, W)
' Build the integrands for P1 and P2;
For j = 1 To N
    phi = x(j)
    weight = W(j)
    int1(j) = HestonProb(phi, ...) * weight
    int2(j) = HestonProb(phi, ...) * weight
Next j
End Function
```

	A	B	C	D	E	F	G	H
1								
2		**Heston Price Using 32-Point Gauss-Laguerre Integration**						
3								
4		**Option Features**			**Option Flavor**	**Heston Price**		
5		Spot Price (S)	100.0000		Call (C)	6.2524		
6		Strike Price (K)	100.0000		Put (P)	5.7586		
7		Time to Maturity (τ)	0.5000					
8		Risk free rate (r)	0.0300		**Abscissas (x) and Weights (w)**			
9		Dividend (q)	0.0200		**32-point Gauss-Laguerre Numerical Integration**			
10					Number	Abscissas	Weights	
11					1	0.04449	0.11419	
12		**Heston Parameters**			2	0.23453	0.26607	
13		kappa (κ)	5.00		3	0.57688	0.41879	
14		theta (θ)	0.05		4	1.07245	0.57253	
15		sigma (σ)	0.50		5	1.72241	0.72765	
16		v0	0.05		6	2.52834	0.88454	
17		rho (ρ)	-0.80		7	3.49221	1.04362	
18		lambda (λ)	0.00		8	4.61646	1.20535	
19		Trap (0=Heston, 1=Albrecher)	1		9	5.90396	1.37022	
20					10	7.35813	1.53878	
21					11	8.98295	1.71162	
22					12	10.78300	1.88948	
23					13	12.76370	2.07298	
24					14	14.93136	2.26328	
25					15	17.29141	2.46221	
26					16	19.85856	2.66004	

FIGURE 1.2 Heston Price Using Gauss-Laguerre Integration

Figure 1.2 shows that the Heston prices obtained using 32-point Gauss-Laguerre integration are very close to those obtained with the trapezoidal rule in Figure 1.1.

Some applications require VBA code for the Heston characteristic function. The HestonProb function can be modified to return the characteristic function itself, instead of the integrand. In certain instances, the integrand for P_j,

$$\text{Re}\left[\frac{e^{-i\phi\ln K}f_j(\phi;x,v)}{i\phi}\right], \tag{1.9}$$

is well behaved in that it poses no difficulties in numerical integration. This corresponds to an integrand that does not oscillate much, that dampens quickly so that a large upper limit in the numerical integration is not required, and that does not contain portions that are excessively steep. In other instances, the integrand is not well behaved, and numerical integration loses precision. To illustrate, in the Excel file Ch1IntegrandPlot.xls, we plot the first integrand ($j = 1$) in Equation (1.9). This plot appears in Figure 1.3. The integrand has a discontinuity at $\phi = 0$, but this does not show up in the figure.

The plot indicates an integrand that has a fair amount of oscillation, especially at short maturities, and that is steep near the origin. In Chapter 2, we investigate other problems that can arise with the Heston integrand.

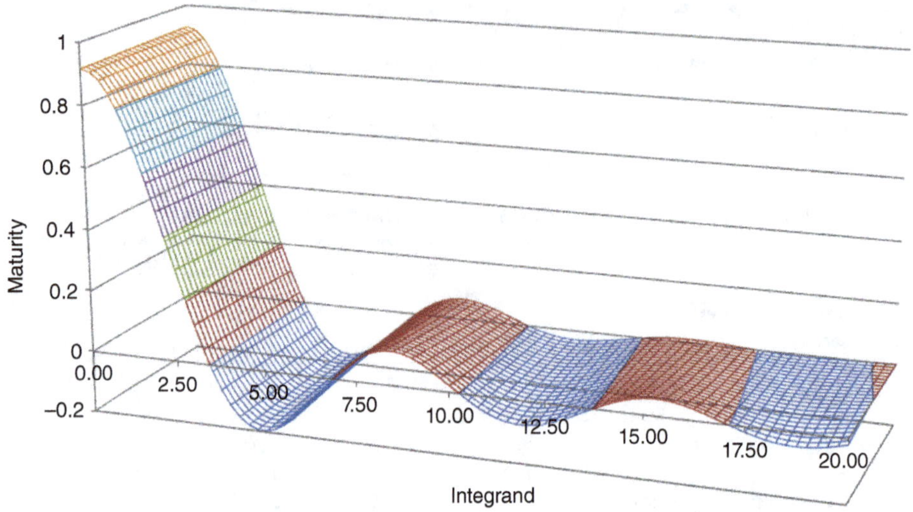

FIGURE 1.3 Heston Integrand and Maturity

DIVIDEND YIELD AND THE PUT PRICE

It is straightforward to include dividends into the model if it can be assumed that the dividend payment is a continuous yield, q. In that case, r is replaced by $r - q$ in Equation for the stock price process

$$dS_t = (r - q)S_t dt + \sqrt{v_t} S_t d\tilde{W}_{1,t}. \tag{1.10}$$

The solution for C_j becomes

$$C_j = (r - q)i\phi\tau + \frac{\kappa\theta}{\sigma^2}\left[(b_j - \rho\sigma i\phi + d_j)\tau - 2\ln\left(\frac{1 - g_j e^{d_j\tau}}{1 - g_j}\right)\right]. \tag{1.11}$$

To obtain the price $P(K)$ of a European put, first obtain the price $C(K)$ of a European call, using a slight modification of Equation (1.3) to include the term $e^{-q\tau}$ for the dividend yield, as explained by Whaley (2006),

$$C(K) = S_t e^{-q\tau} P_1 - K e^{-r\tau} P_2. \tag{1.12}$$

The put price is found by put-call parity

$$P(K) = C(K) + K e^{-r\tau} - S_t e^{-q\tau}. \tag{1.13}$$

CONSOLIDATING THE INTEGRALS

It is possible to regroup the integrals for the probabilities P_1 and P_2 into a single integral, which will speed up the numerical integration required in the call price calculation. Substituting the expressions for P_j into the call price in (1.12) and rearranging produces

$$\begin{aligned} C(K) = &\frac{1}{2}S_t e^{-q\tau} - \frac{1}{2}Ke^{-r\tau} \\ &+\frac{1}{\pi}\int_0^\infty \text{Re}\left[\frac{e^{-i\phi\ln K}}{i\phi}\left(S_t e^{-q\tau}f_1(\phi;x,v) - Ke^{-r\tau}f_2(\phi;x,v)\right)\right]d\phi. \end{aligned} \tag{1.14}$$

The advantage of this consolidation is that only a single numerical integration is required instead of two, so the computation time will be reduced by almost one-half. The put price can be obtained by using put-call parity, with the call price calculated using (1.14).

The integrand of the consolidated form is in the function HestonProbConsol in the Excel file Ch1ConsolCF.xls.

```
Function HestonProbConsol(phi As Double...) As Double
' Return the real part of the integrand.
expphilogK = cExp(cProd(cProd(im, Complex(phi, 0)) ...
HestonProbConsol = cReal(cProd(Term1, Term2))
End Function
```

This function is then fed into the HestonPriceConsol function, which calculates the call price in accordance with Equation (1.14). The function uses the trapezoidal rule for numerical integration.

```
Function HestonPriceConsol(PutCall As String...) As Double
' Build the consolidated integrand
For j = 1 To N
    inte(j) = HestonProbConsol(phi(j), ...) * W(j)
Next j
integral = Sum(inte)
' The call price and put price by put call parity
HestonC = 0.5 * S * Exp(-q * T) - 0.5 * K * Exp(-r * T) ...
HestonP = HestonC - S * Exp(-q * T) + K * Exp(-r * T)
' Output the option price
```

```
If PutCall = "C" Then
    HestonPriceConsol = HestonC
Else
    HestonPriceConsol = HestonP
End If
End Function
```

The consolidated form produces exactly the same prices for the call and the put, but with roughly one-half of the computation time.

BLACK-SCHOLES AS A SPECIAL CASE

With a little manipulation, it is straightforward to show that the Black-Scholes model is nested inside the Heston model. The Black-Scholes model assumes the following dynamics for the underlying price S_t under the risk-neutral measure $\mathbb{Q}$

$$dS_t = rS_t + \sigma_{BS} S_t d\tilde{W}_t. \tag{1.15}$$

It is shown in many textbooks, such as that by Hull (2011) or Chriss (1996), that (1.15) can be solved for the spot price S_t. The result is that, at time t, the natural logarithm of the stock price at expiry $\ln S_T$ is distributed as a normal random variable with mean $\ln S_t + (r - \frac{1}{2}\sigma_{BS}^2)\tau$ and variance $\sigma_{BS}^2\tau$, where $\tau = T - t$ is the time to expiry. Consequently, the Black-Scholes call price is given by

$$C_{BS}(K) = S_t \Phi(d_1) - Ke^{-r\tau}\Phi(d_2) \tag{1.16}$$

with

$$\begin{aligned} d_1 &= \frac{\ln(S_t/K) + (r + \sigma_{BS}^2/2)\tau}{\sigma_{BS}\sqrt{\tau}}, \\ d_2 &= \frac{\ln(S_t/K) + (r - \sigma_{BS}^2/2)\tau}{\sigma_{BS}\sqrt{\tau}} = d_1 - \sigma_{BS}\sqrt{\tau}, \end{aligned} \tag{1.17}$$

where $\Phi(x)$ is the standard normal cumulative distribution function. The volatility σ_{BS} is assumed to be constant.

If we set $\sigma = 0$, the volatility of variance parameter in the Heston model, then the Brownian component of the variance process in Equation (1.1) drops out. This will produce volatility that is time varying but deterministic. If we further set $\theta = v_0$, then this will produce volatility that is constant. Hence, setting $\sigma = 0$ and $\theta = v_0$ in the Heston model leads us to expect the same price as that produced by the Black-Scholes model, with $\sigma_{BS} = \sqrt{v_0}$ as the Black-Scholes implied volatility.

To implement the Black-Scholes model as a special case of the Heston model, we cannot simply substitute $\sigma = 0$ into the pricing functions, because that will lead to division by zero in the expressions for $C_j(\tau, \phi)$ and $D_j(\tau, \phi)$. Instead, we must use

$$D_j(\tau, \phi) = \frac{\left(u_j i\phi - \frac{1}{2}\phi^2\right)\left(1 - e^{-b_j\tau}\right)}{b_j} \tag{1.18}$$

and

$$C_j(\tau, \phi) = ri\phi\tau + \frac{a\left(u_j i\phi - \frac{1}{2}\phi^2\right)}{b_j}\left[\tau - \frac{\left(1 - e^{-b_j\tau}\right)}{b_j}\right]. \tag{1.19}$$

See Rouah (2013) for a detailed derivation.

The function HestonProbZeroSigma is used to implement the Black-Scholes model as a special case of the Heston model (when $\sigma = 0$). This function is in the Excel file Ch1BSHeston.xls. To conserve space, only the crucial portions of the function are presented.

```
Function HestonProbZeroSigma(phi As Double, ...) As Double
' D = (u*i*phi - phi^2/2)*(1-exp(-b*tau))/b;
bigD = cDiv(cProd(Term1, Term2), Term3)
'C = (r-q)*i*phi*tau + a*(u*i*phi-0.5*phi^2)/b ...
bigC = cAdd(Term1, Term2)
' The characteristic function.
' f = exp(C + D*theta + i*phi*x)
f = cExp(cAdd(cAdd(bigC, Dtheta), iphix))
' Return the real part of the integrand.
HestonProbZeroSigma = cReal(cDiv(Num1, Den1))
End Function
```

The function HestonPriceZeroSigma uses the trapezoidal rule to obtain the price when $\sigma = 0$. Again, only the relevant parts of the code are presented.

```
Function HestonPriceZeroSigma(...) As Double
' Integrands for probabilities P1 and P2
For j = 1 To N
    P1_int(j) = HestonProbZeroSigma(phi(j), ..., 1) * W(j)
    P2_int(j) = HestonProbZeroSigma(phi(j), ..., 2) * W(j)
Next j
End Function
```

With the settings $\tau = 0.5, S = K = 100, q = 0.02, r = 0.03, \kappa = 5, v_0 = \theta = 0.05$, and $\lambda = 0$, the Heston model and Black-Scholes model with $\sigma_{BS} = \sqrt{v_0}$ each return 6.4730 for the price of the call and 5.9792 for the price of the put.

CONCLUSION

The Heston model has become the most popular stochastic volatility model for pricing equity options. This is in part due to the fact that the call price in the model is available in closed form. Some authors refer to the call price as being in "semiclosed" form because of the numerical integration required to obtain P_1 and P_2. But the Black-Scholes model also requires numerical integration, to obtain $\Phi(d_1)$ and $\Phi(d_2)$. In this sense, the Heston model produces call prices that are no less closed than those produced by the Black-Scholes model. The difference is that programming languages often have built-in routines for calculating the standard normal cumulative distribution function, $\Phi(\cdot)$ (usually by employing a polynomial approximation), whereas the Heston probabilities are not built in and must be obtained using numerical integration. In the next chapter, we investigate some of the problems that can arise in numerical integration when the integrand

$$\text{Re}\left[\frac{e^{-i\phi \ln K} f_j(\phi; x, v)}{i\phi}\right]$$

is not well behaved. We encountered an example of such an integrand in Figure 1.3.

CHAPTER 2

Integration Issues, Parameter Effects, and Variance Modeling

Abstract

We investigate several issues around the Heston model. First, following Bakshi and Madan (2000), we show that the Heston call price can be expressed in terms of a single characteristic function. It is well known that the integrand for the call price can sometimes show high oscillation, can dampen very slowly along the integration axis, and can show discontinuities. All of these problems can introduce inaccuracies in numerical integration. The "Little Trap" formulation of Albrecher et al. (2007) provides an easy fix to many of these problems. Next, we examine the effects of the Heston parameters on implied volatilities extracted from option prices generated with the Heston model. Borrowing from Gatheral (2006), we examine how the fair strike of a variance swap can be derived under the model and present approximations to local volatility and implied volatility from the model. Finally, we examine moment explosions derived by Andersen and Piterbarg (2007) and bounds on implied volatility of Lee (2004b).

integrand, oscillation, discontinuity, Little Trap, Black-Scholes, parameter effects, implied volatility, local volatility, variance swap, variance modeling, moment explosion

In this chapter, we investigate several issues around the Heston model. First, following Bakshi and Madan (2000), we show that the Heston call price can be expressed in terms of a single characteristic function. It is well known that the integrand for the call price can sometimes show high oscillation, can dampen very slowly along the integration axis, and can show discontinuities. All of these problems can introduce inaccuracies in numerical integration. The "Little Trap" formulation of Albrecher et al. (2007) provides an easy fix to many of these problems. Next, we examine the effects of the Heston parameters on implied volatilities extracted from option prices generated with the Heston model. Borrowing from Gatheral (2006), we examine how the fair strike of a variance swap can be derived under the model and present approximations to local volatility and implied volatility from the model. Finally, we examine moment explosions derived by Andersen and Piterbarg (2007) and bounds on implied volatility of Lee (2004b).

REMARKS ON THE CHARACTERISTIC FUNCTIONS

In Chapter 1, we introduced the in-the-money probabilities P_1 and P_2:

$$P_j = \frac{1}{2} + \frac{1}{\pi}\int_0^\infty \text{Re}\left[\frac{e^{-i\phi \ln K} f_j(\phi; x, v)}{i\phi}\right] d\phi. \tag{2.1}$$

It makes sense that two characteristic functions, f_1 and f_2, be associated with the Heston model because P_1 and P_2 are obtained under different measures. However, it also seems that only a single characteristic function ought to exist because there is only one underlying stock price in the model. Indeed, some authors write the Heston probabilities P_1 and P_2 in terms of a single characteristic function, $f(\phi) = f(\phi; x, v)$, as

$$P_1 = \frac{1}{2} + \frac{1}{\pi}\int_0^\infty \text{Re}\left[\frac{e^{-i\phi \ln K} f(\phi - i)}{i\phi f(-i)}\right] d\phi \tag{2.2}$$

and

$$P_2 = \frac{1}{2} + \frac{1}{\pi}\int_0^\infty \text{Re}\left[\frac{e^{-i\phi \ln K} f(\phi)}{i\phi}\right] d\phi, \tag{2.3}$$

which suggests that $f_2(\phi) = f(\phi)$ and $f_1(\phi) = f(\phi - i)/f(-i)$. This is reconciled in Bakshi and Madan (2000), and a simplified but detailed version of their result appears in Rouah (2013). The conclusion is that the "true" characteristic function is actually f_2, since it is associated with the probability measure $\mathbb{Q}$ that makes $W_{1,t}$ and $W_{2,t}$ Brownian motions in the risk-neutral stochastic differential equations (SDEs) for S_t and v_t and for which the bond serves as numeraire.

The result is that the call price can be written in terms of the single characteristic function $f(\phi)$ for $x_T = \ln S_T$ as

$$C(K) = S_t P_1 - e^{-r(T-t)} K P_2,$$

where P_1 and P_2 are defined in (2.2) and (2.3).

This is a general setup that is valid for many models, not only the Heston model, as shown in Bakshi and Madan (2000). It is commonly referred to as the characteristic function approach for option pricing. For example, in the Black-Scholes model, x_T is normally distributed with mean $\ln(S_t) + (r - \sigma_{BS}^2/2)\tau$ and variance $\sigma_{BS}^2\tau$, and the corresponding characteristic function for x_T is

$$f(\phi) = \exp\left(i\phi\left[\ln S_t + \left(r - \frac{1}{2}\sigma_{BS}^2\right)\tau\right] - \frac{1}{2}\phi^2\sigma_{BS}^2\tau\right).$$

Substituting $f(\phi)$ into the expressions for P_1 and P_2 and evaluating the integrals numerically will produce the same call price as the closed-form solution for the Black-Scholes call price, up to approximation error.

It is straightforward to show that Heston prices generated using either one or two characteristic functions will be the same. This is illustrated in the Excel file Ch2TwoCF.xls. The VBA function HestonCF calculates the characteristic function and returns its real and imaginary parts separately.

```
Function HestonCF(phi As cNum, ...) as Variant
' G = (1 - g*exp(d*tau))/(1-g);
BigG = cDiv(Num2, Den2)
' C = (r-q)*phi*tau*i + a/sigma^2*((b ...
bigC = cAdd(Term3, term4)
' D = (b - rho*sigma*i*phi + d)/sigma^2 ...
bigD = cProd(Term5, Term6)
' The characteristic function.
' f = cExp(C + D*v0 + phi*x*i)
f = cExp(cAdd(cAdd(bigC, dv0), phixi))
' Output the real and imaginary parts of the CF separately
output(1, 1) = cReal(f)
output(2, 1) = cImag(f)
HestonCF = output
End Function
```

The VBA function HPriceTrapz2CF calculates the European option price using either one or two characteristic functions.

```
Function HPriceTrapz2CF(..., cf As Integer) As Double
For j = 1 To N
    ' The second characteristic function
    CF2 = HestonCF(phi(j), ..., 2)
    f2(j) = Complex(CF2(1, 1), CF2(2, 1))
    ' The first characteristic function
    If cf = 1 Then
        CF1 = HestonCF(phi(j), ..., 1)
        f1(j) = Complex(CF1(1, 1), CF1(2, 1))
    ElseIf cf = 2 Then
        ' f1(j) = HestonCF(phi-i)/(S*exp((r-q)*T));
        argument = cSub(phi(j), i)
        CF1 = HestonCF(argument, ..., 2)
        HestonCF1 = Complex(CF1(1, 1), CF1(2, 1))
        f1(j) = cDiv(HestonCF1, Complex(S * Exp((r - q) * T), 0))
    End If
    explogK = cExp(cProd(cProd(im, phi(j)), Complex(Log(K), 0)))
    ' The integrands
    int1(j) = W(j) * cReal(cDiv(Num1, Den))
    int2(j) = W(j) * cReal(cDiv(Num2, Den))
Next j
End Function
```

	A	B	C	D	E	F	G	H
1								
2		**Heston Price Using Two Formulations**				**Using**	**Using**	
3		**1. F2 and F1 separately**			**Strike**	**F1 and F2**	**F2 Only**	**Difference %**
4		**2. F2 and F1 expressed in terms of F1**			90	4.57491	4.57491	-7.38E-15
5					91	4.91750	4.91750	-6.86E-15
6		**Option Features**			92	5.27662	5.27662	-4.38E-15
7		Spot Price (S)	100.00		93	5.65244	5.65244	-3.77E-15
8		PutCall	P		94	6.04509	6.04509	-1.76E-15
9		Time to Maturity (τ)	0.25		95	6.45471	6.45471	-1.65E-15
10		Risk free rate (r)	0.03		96	6.88136	6.88136	-1.55E-15
11		Dividend (q)	0.02		97	7.32510	7.32510	-1.46E-15
12					98	7.78594	7.78594	-2.74E-15
13		**Heston Parameters**			99	8.26388	8.26388	-2.79E-15
14		kappa (κ)	0.20		100	8.75887	8.75887	-2.43E-15
15		theta (θ)	0.05		101	9.27084	9.27084	-2.30E-15
16		sigma (σ)	0.30		102	9.79969	9.79969	-1.27E-15
17		v0	0.22		103	10.34528	10.34528	-1.20E-15
18		rho (ρ)	-0.80		104	10.90747	10.90747	-2.12E-15
19		lambda (λ)	0.00		105	11.48606	11.48606	-1.55E-15
20					106	12.08085	12.08085	-1.47E-15
21		**Integration Grid**			107	12.69160	12.69160	-8.40E-16
22		Lower Limit	1.0000E-08		108	13.31807	13.31807	-1.20E-15
23		Upper Limit	100.00		109	13.95997	13.95997	-7.63E-16
24		Number of abscissas	100		110	14.61702	14.61702	-3.65E-16

FIGURE 2.1 Heston Price Using One or Two Characteristic Functions

The results of these functions appear in the screen shot of the Excel file Ch2TwoCF.xls in Figure 2.1.

PROBLEMS WITH THE INTEGRAND

Recall from Chapter 1 that the integrand from which the probabilities P_j are obtained is

$$F_j(\phi) = \text{Re}\left[\frac{e^{-i\phi \ln K} f_j(\phi; x, v)}{i\phi}\right] \tag{2.4}$$

for $\phi > 0$. In some instances, the integrand is well behaved and the integration poses no numerical problems. In other cases, however, the integrand is not well behaved, so numerical integration can be problematic.

The first problem is that the integrand is not defined at the point $\phi = 0$, even though the integration range is $[0, \infty)$. This implies that numerical integration must begin at a very small point close to zero. In order to avoid inaccuracies due to the removal of the origin, the integral must not be too steep there.

The second problem is that the integral may contain discontinuities. To illustrate, Figure 2.2 plots two integrands for f_1 in the range $\phi \in (0, 10]$. The first integrand has a maturity of $\tau = 3$ years and $\sigma = 0.75$, and the second has $\tau = 1$ year and $\sigma = 0.09$. Both integrands use $\kappa = 10, \theta = v_0 = 0.05, \rho = -0.9, r = 0$, along with spot $S_0 = 100$ and strike $K = 100$. The plot is taken from the Excel file Ch2Discontinuity.xls.

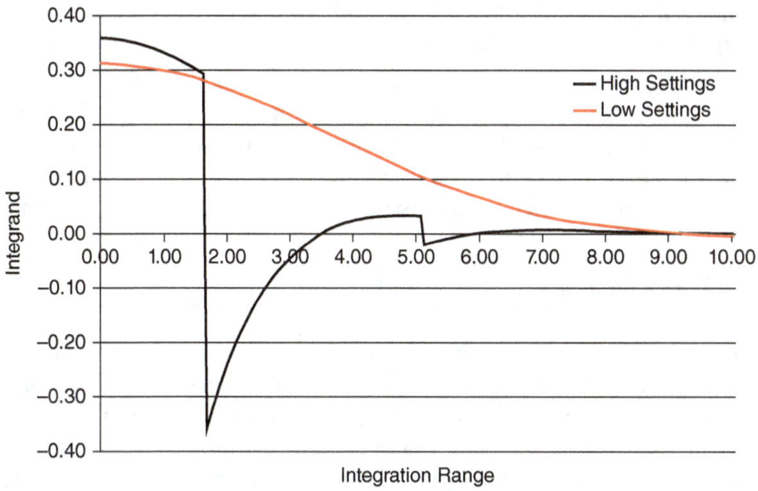

FIGURE 2.2 Discontinuities in the Heston Integrand

The first integrand (red line) is smooth and shows no particular numerical instability. The second integrand (black line), however, has discontinuities near the points $\phi = 1.7$ and $\phi = 5$, and it is steep near 1.7. In later sections, we present a simple modification of the integrand by Albrecher et al. (2007) that is effective at eliminating these discontinuities.

Finally, the third problem that can arise is that of an integrand that oscillates wildly. In Figure 2.3, the first integrand has a maturity of $\tau = 1/52$ years and uses $\sigma = 0.175$, $\theta = v_0 = 0.01$, and a spot $S_0 = 7$. The second has $\tau = 1$ year and uses $\sigma = 0.09$, $\theta = v_0 = 0.07$, and a spot $S_0 = 10$. Both use $\rho = -0.9$, $\kappa = 10$, $r = 0$, and a strike of $K = 10$. The plots are taken from the Excel file Ch2Oscillation.xls.

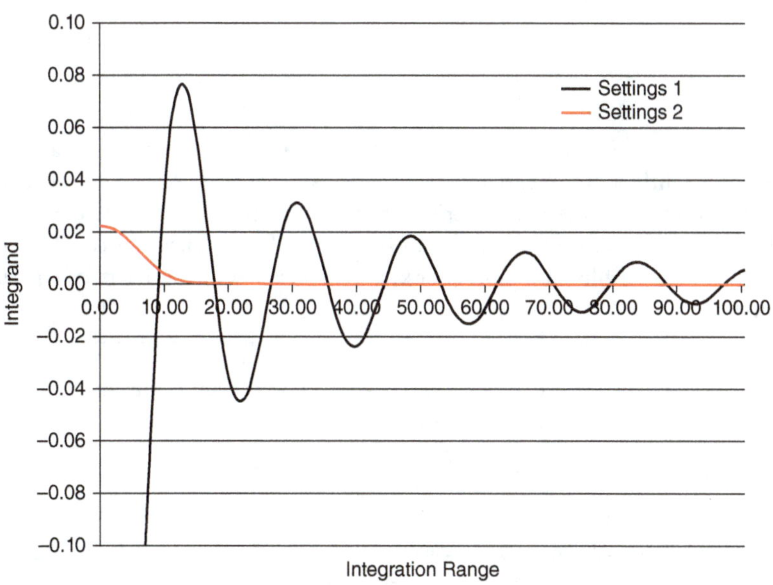

FIGURE 2.3 Oscillations in the Heston Integrand

The first integrand (black line) shows high oscillation, which is still not damped at $\phi = 100$. This implies that the numerical integral needs to extend much farther beyond $\phi = 100$ to converge. Moreover, the integrand is very steep near the origin, which requires a very fine grid for the numerical integral. The second integrand (red line) is well behaved and would pose no numerical difficulties: it does not oscillate, is not steep anywhere, and rapidly dampens to zero, starting at around $\phi = 10$. High oscillation of the integrand is usually associated with short-maturity options.

THE LITTLE HESTON TRAP

Albrecher et al. (2007) explain that the academic literature on the Heston model embodies two different formulations of the Heston characteristic function. The first is the original formulation of Heston (1993), while the second has a slightly different form. Albrecher et al. (2007) show that these two formulations are equivalent but that the second leads to a characteristic function that is much better behaved and, therefore, better suited for numerical integration.

The original formulation of the Heston characteristic function was presented in Chapter 1. To derive the second formulation, first note that the solution to D_j in Chapter 1 can be multiplied by $\exp(-d_j\tau)$ in the numerator and denominator, which leads to the equivalent form

$$D_j = \frac{b_j - \rho\sigma i\phi - d_j}{\sigma^2}\left(\frac{1 - e^{-d_j\tau}}{1 - c_j e^{-d_j\tau}}\right), \tag{2.5}$$

where

$$c_j = \frac{1}{g_j} = \frac{b_j - \rho\sigma i\phi - d_j}{b_j - \rho\sigma i\phi + d_j}. \tag{2.6}$$

This implies that C_j can be written in the equivalent form

$$C_j = ri\phi\tau + \frac{\kappa\theta}{\sigma^2}\left[(b_j - \rho\sigma i\phi - d_j)\tau - 2\ln\left(\frac{1 - c_j e^{-d_j\tau}}{1 - c_j}\right)\right]. \tag{2.7}$$

Implementing this formulation is very simple and involves only replacing C_j and D_j with the slightly different forms in Equations (2.7) and (2.5). The VBA function HestonProb computes the characteristic function using the original Heston (1993) formulation, and the Albrecher et al. (2007) "Little Trap" formulation. The function appears in the Excel file Ch2Albrecher.xls. To conserve space, parts of the function are omitted.

```
Function HestonProb(..., Trap As Integer) As Double
' Original Heston formulation of the c.f.
If Trap = 0 Then
    BigG = cDiv(Num2, Den2)
    bigC = cAdd(Term3, term4)
    bigD = cProd(Term5, Term6)
' Albrecher Little Trap formulation of the c.f.
```

```
ElseIf Trap = 1 Then
    BigG = cDiv(Num2, Den2)
    bigC = cAdd(Term3, term4)
    bigD = cProd(Term5, Term6)
End If
' The characteristic function.
' f = cExp(C + D*v0 + phi*x*i)
f = cExp(cAdd(cAdd(bigC, dv0), phixi))
' Return the real part of the integrand.
HestonProb = cReal(E)
End Function
```

Albrecher et al. (2007) explain that, although Heston's original formulation and their formulation are identical, their formulation causes fewer numerical problems in the implementation of the model. This is illustrated by plotting the integrand

$$\text{Re}\left[\frac{e^{-i\phi \ln K} f_j(\phi; x, v)}{i\phi}\right]$$

for the characteristic function f_1. The same parameter values as Albrecher et al. (2007) were used, namely, $\kappa = 1.5768$, $\sigma = 0.5751$, $\rho = -0.5711$, $\theta = 0.0398$, and $v_0 = 0.0175$. In addition, we use $S = K = 100$ and a maturity of $\tau = 5$ years. Figure 2.4 reproduces the figure for f_1 in their article. The integrand uses the integration range $\phi = (0, 10]$. The plot is taken from the Excel file Ch2Albrecher.xls.

The original Heston (1993) formulation (black line) shows a discontinuity at $\phi \approx 3.5$, which is corrected with the Albrecher et al. (2007) formulation in the red

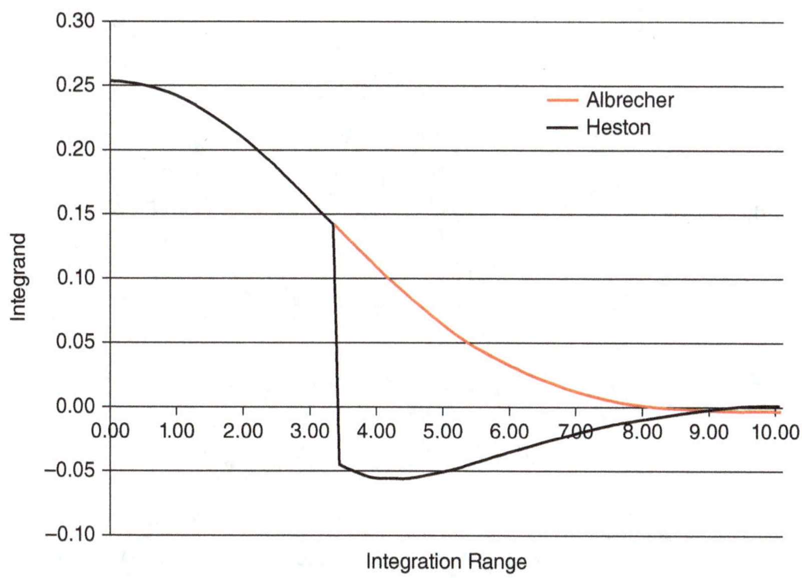

FIGURE 2.4 Integrand for P_1, Original and Little Trap Formulations

line. The results in the Ch2Albrecher.xls file show that the discontinuity leads to option prices that are not as accurate under the original Heston formulation.

Finally, the rotation algorithm of Kahl and Jäckel (2005) can be used to overcome the discontinuities brought on by the original Heston formulation. We do not cover the rotation algorithm in this book, but we refer interested readers to Kahl and Jäckel (2005), and also to the book by Zhu (2010) for alternate algorithms.

EFFECT OF THE HESTON PARAMETERS

Heston Terminal Spot Price

Under the Heston model, the distribution of the log stock price at maturity, $\ln S_T$, is able to exhibit skewness and excess kurtosis, depending on the parameter settings. In the following section, the effect of the correlation ρ and the volatility of variance σ on the distribution of $\ln S_T$ are investigated.

Effect of Correlation and Volatility of Variance

The correlation parameter ρ controls the skewness of the density of $\ln S_T$ and of the continuously compounded return $\ln(S_T/S_0)$ over $[0, T]$. When $\rho > 0$, the probability densities will be positively skewed, and when $\rho < 0$, the densities will be negatively skewed. The following figures use the parameter settings from Table 1 of Heston (1993) to demonstrate this. The parameter settings are $v_0 = 0.01$, $\kappa = 2$, $\theta = 0.01$, $\lambda = 0$, and $\sigma = 0.1$. The density of $\ln S_T$ can be recovered by inverting its characteristic function $f_2(\phi)$ and applying a numerical integration scheme. The densities in Figure 2.5 use $\rho = -0.5$, $\rho = 0$, and $\rho = 0.5$. The figure is similar to Figure 1 of Heston (1993) and clearly indicates the relationship between correlation and skewness. The plot is taken from the Excel file Ch2Correlation2.xls.

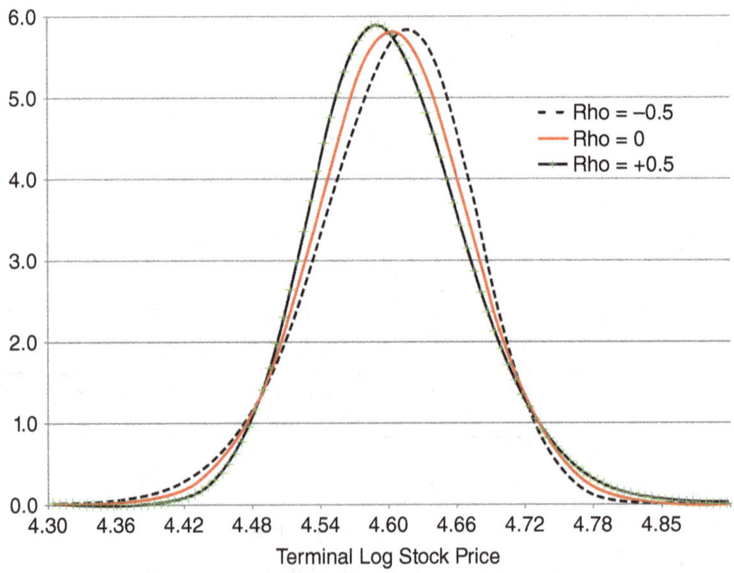

FIGURE 2.5 Effect of Correlation on Density

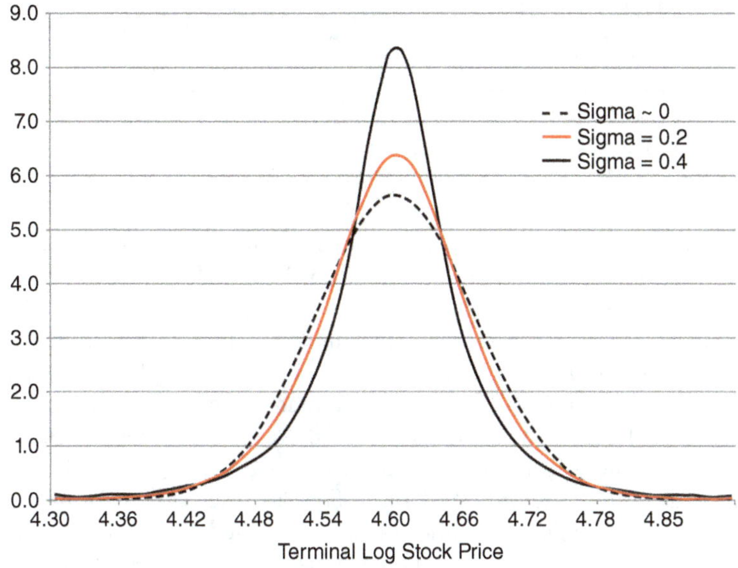

FIGURE 2.6 Effect of Volatility of Variance on Density

As explained by Heston (1993), positive correlation implies a rise in variance when the stock price rises. This has the effect of fattening the right tail of the distribution and thinning the left tail. When correlation is negative, the opposite happens. It will be shown in the next section that a negative correlation results in deep in-the-money calls being priced higher in the Heston model than in the Black-Scholes model.

The volatility of variance parameter σ controls the kurtosis. When σ is high, the variance process is highly dispersed, so we expect the distribution of returns to have higher kurtosis and fatter tails than when σ is small. This is illustrated in Figure 2.6 for $\sigma \approx 0$, $\sigma = 0.2$, and $\sigma = 0.4$. The figure is similar to Figure 3 of Heston (1993) and appears in the Excel file Ch2Sigma.xls.

Comparison with Black-Scholes Prices

The results illustrated in Figures 2.5 and 2.6 suggest that, because of the skew in returns produced by the Heston model, option prices generated by the Heston model should differ from those generated by the Black-Scholes model in a way that is sensible. In this section, we investigate the effect of the correlation parameter ρ and the volatility of variance parameter σ on call prices in this regard.

When $\rho > 0$, the skew in the distribution of $\ln S_T$ is positive, so more weight is assigned to the right tail of the distribution. Out-of-the-money (OTM) calls have a strike price that lies in the right tail. This implies that, when $\rho > 0$, deep OTM calls produced by the Heston model should be more expensive than those produced by the Black-Scholes model. In-the-money (ITM) calls have a strike price that lies in the left tail. Since less weight is assigned to the left tail, deep ITM calls from the Heston model should be less expensive than those produced by Black-Scholes. Similarly, when $\rho < 0$, the distribution of $\ln S_T$ is negatively skewed and the opposite happens: more weight is assigned to the left tail, and less in the right tail. This implies

TABLE 2.1 Price Comparisons Under Different Correlations

	$\rho > 0$	$\rho < 0$
OTM Calls	Heston > BS	Heston < BS
ITM Calls	Heston < BS	Heston > BS

that deep ITM calls from the Heston model should be more expensive than those produced by the Black-Scholes model, and deep OTM calls should be less expensive. Table 2.1 summarizes these observations.

Figure 2.7 reproduces the figure in Heston (1993). It plots the difference between call prices from both models (Heston price minus Black-Scholes price), as the spot price varies from \$70 to \$140. The figure is similar to Figure 2 of Heston (1993) and is taken from the Excel file Ch2Correlation.xls. We use the same parameter settings as the example earlier in this section, corresponding to those in Table 1 of Heston (1993). In order for the Heston and Black-Scholes price comparisons to be valid, however, the Black-Scholes volatilities must be matched to the Heston prices. This can be done by defining the Black-Scholes volatility σ_{BS} in terms of the standard deviation of the distribution of the returns $\ln(S_T/S_0)$. The moments of the returns can be obtained from the moments of $x_T = \ln S_T$, which are available by differentiation of the characteristic function $f_2(\phi)$

$$E[x_T^n] = i^{-n}\left[\frac{d^n}{d\phi^n}f_2(\phi)\right]_{\phi=0}. \tag{2.8}$$

The VBA function findHestonMoments, which appears in the Excel file Ch2MomentMatch.xls, approximates (2.8) using finite differences.

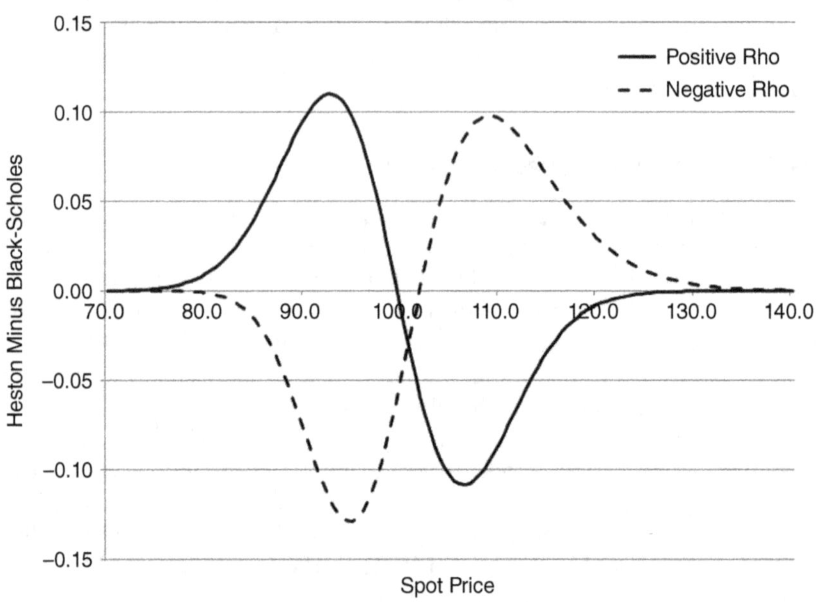

FIGURE 2.7 Effect of Correlation on Heston Prices Relative to Black-Scholes

```
Function findHestonMoments(...) As Variant
For j = 1 To 3
    rho = rhovec(j)
    cf = HestonCF(dphi...)
    dfp = Complex(cf(1, 1), cf(2, 1))
    cf = HestonCF(-dphi, ...)
    dfm = Complex(cf(1, 1), cf(2, 1))
    df = cDiv(cSub(dfp, dfm), cProd(two, Complex(dphi, 0)))
    ' First moment EX
    EX = cReal(cDiv(df, i))
    cf = HestonCF(2 * dphi, ...)
    dfpp = Complex(cf(1, 1), cf(2, 1))
    cf = HestonCF(-2 * dphi, ...)
    dfmm = Complex(cf(1, 1), cf(2, 1))
    dff1 = cDiv(cSub(dfpp, dfp), Complex(dphi, 0))
    dff2 = cDiv(cSub(dfm, dfmm), Complex(dphi, 0))
    dff = cDiv(cSub(dff1, dff2), cProd(three,
Complex(dphi, 0)))
    ' Second moment EX^2
    EX2 = -cReal(dff) - cImag(dff)
    ' Black-Scholes variance and volatility
    var = EX2 - EX * EX
    BSVol(j, 1) = Sqr(var)
Next j
findHestonMoments = BSVol
End Function
```

The results of the approximation suggest that, when $\rho = -0.5$, we use $\sigma_{BS} = \sqrt{2} \times 0.0710$ to generate the Black-Scholes prices, and when $\rho = +0.5$, we use $\sigma_{BS} = \sqrt{2} \times 0.0704$.

The left portion of Figure 2.7 corresponds to low stock prices and OTM calls, and the right portion to high stock prices and ITM calls. Clearly, when correlation is positive, Heston OTM calls are more expensive than Black-Scholes OTM calls, due to the thickness in the right tail of the distribution of $\ln S_T$ generated by the Heston model. When correlation is negative, the difference is positive in the ITM call region. Heston ITM calls are more expensive than Black-Scholes ITM calls, due to the thickness in the left tail of the distribution of $\ln S_T$ generated by the Heston model. Similar arguments can be made for negative differences.

The effect of increasing σ is to increase kurtosis. This makes sense, since a high volatility of variance will increase the range of terminal stock price values. This is illustrated in Figure 2.8, which compares the difference between the Heston and Black-Scholes call prices with $\rho = 0$, and when $\sigma = 0.1$ and $\sigma = 0.2$. It indicates that Heston prices are higher than Black-Scholes prices in ITM and OTM regions but lower in the at-the-money region. These two observations are consistent with thicker tails of the distribution of $\ln S_T$ generated by the Heston model. Not surprisingly, the

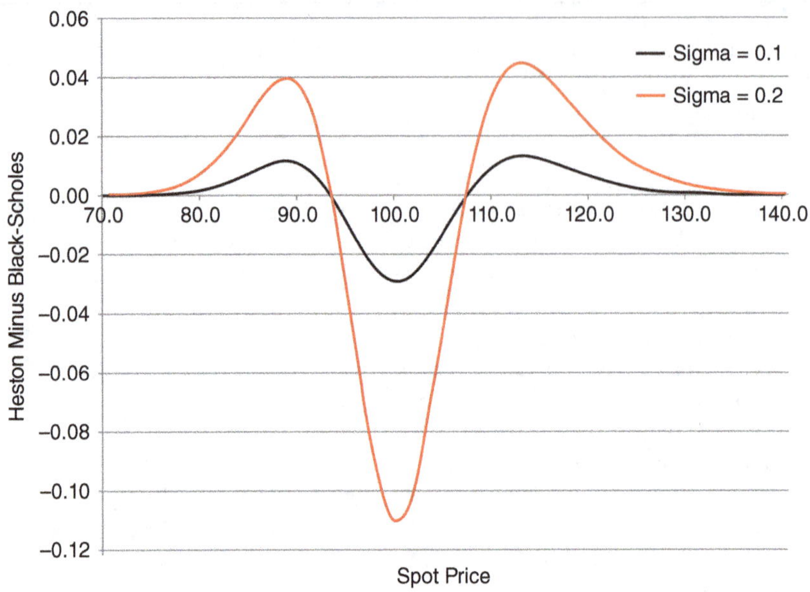

FIGURE 2.8 Effect of Volatility of Variance on Heston Prices Relative to Black-Scholes

difference is more pronounced when σ is higher. Figure 2.8 is similar to Figure 4 of Heston (1993). The plot is in the Excel file Ch2Sigma.xls.

Heston Implied Volatility

Another feature of the Heston model is that implied volatilities extracted from option prices generated by the model will show a smile or skew. The shape of the skew is driven by the values of the parameters. The correlation parameter ρ determines the direction of skew, with $\rho > 0$ corresponding to a positive slope, and $\rho < 0$ corresponding to a negative slope. This is illustrated in the first panel of Figure 2.9 by generating implied volatilities using $S = 100$, $r = 0.05$, $\tau = 0.25$, $\kappa = 2$, $\theta = 0.01$, $\lambda = 0$, and $v_0 = 0.01$ over the strike range 95 to 110. The plots appear in the Excel file Ch2IV.xls.

Equity options usually show a negative slope in their implied volatilities. Not surprisingly, when options data are used to estimate the parameters of the Heston model, the correlation will in most cases turn out to be negative.

Increasing values of the volatility of variance σ increases the curvature of the smile. This is illustrated in the second panel of Figure 2.9, which uses the same settings but with $\rho = 0$. Finally, the parameters κ, θ, and v_0 control the level of the smile, as illustrated in the remaining panels of Figure 2.9. The mean reversion speed κ also controls the curvature, to a certain extent, with higher values of κ flattening the implied volatility.

To generate the implied volatilities, we first create Heston prices using the VBA function HestonPriceTrapz over a range of strikes. We then apply the bisection algorithm to find the implied volatilities once the prices are generated. This is accomplished using the VBA function BisecBSIV.

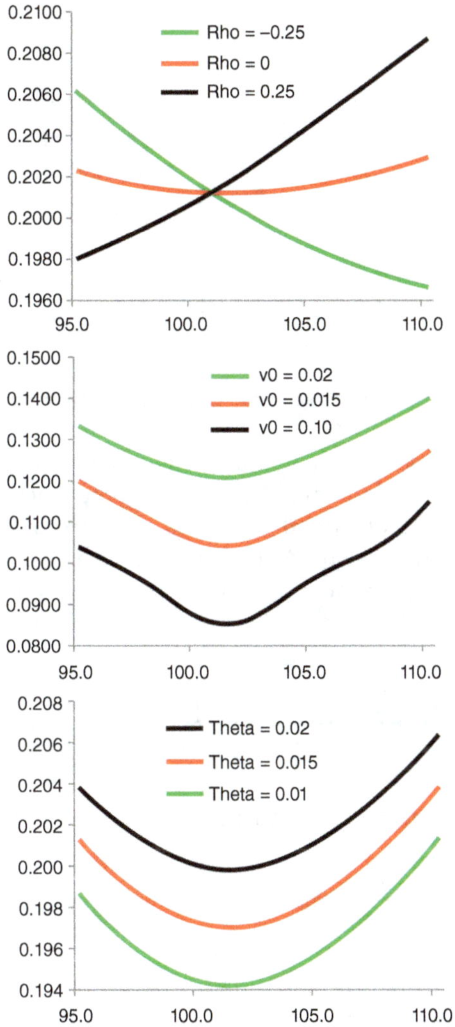

FIGURE 2.9 Effect of Heston Parameters on Implied Volatility

```
Function BisecBSIV(PutCall As String, ...)
lowCdif = MktPrice - BSPrice(..., a)
highCdif = MktPrice - BSPrice(..., b)
If lowCdif * highCdif > 0 Then
    BisecBSIV = -1
Else
    For x = 1 To MaxIter
        midP = (a + b) / 2
        midCdif = MktPrice - BSPrice(..., midP)
        If Abs(midCdif) < Tol Then
            Exit For
```

```
            Else
                If midCdif > 0 Then
                    a = midP
                Else
                    b = midP
                End If
            End If
        Next x
        BisecBSIV = midP
    End If
End Function
```

The first part of the function defines a function handle for calculating the price under the Black-Scholes model. The main part of the function calculates the Black-Scholes price at the midpoint of the two endpoints and compares the difference between this price and the market price. If the difference is greater than the user-specified tolerance, the function updates one of the endpoints with the midpoint and passes through the iteration again.

VARIANCE MODELING IN THE HESTON MODEL

Variance Swap

Recall from Chapter 1 that the volatility of the Heston model is driven by the CIR process

$$dv_t = \kappa(\theta - v_t)dt + \sigma\sqrt{v_t}dW_{2,t}.$$

As explained by Gatheral (2006), a variance swap requires an estimate of the future variance over the $(0, T)$ time period. Gatheral (2006) shows that in the Heston model the strike variance K^2_{var} for a variance swap is of the form

$$K^2_{\text{var}} = (v_0 - \theta)\left(\frac{1 - e^{-\kappa T}}{\kappa T}\right) + \theta. \tag{2.9}$$

This is the expression on page 138 of Gatheral (2006). See also Rouah (2013). It is easily implemented in VBA, with the function HestonVarSwap.

```
Function HestonVarSwap(...) As Double
' Heston fair variance and fair volatility
Hvar = (v0 - theta) * (1 - Exp(-kappa * T)) ...
Hvol = Sqr(Hvar) * 100
' Return the variance
HestonVarSwap = Hvar
End Function
```

The VBA function VarianceSwap implements the replication algorithm of Demeterfi et al. (1999). The function requires vectors of OTM calls and puts and their implied volatilities. The function is in the Excel file Ch2VarSwap.xls.

```
Function VarianceSwap(KCi As Variant, ...) As Double
' Do the calculations on calls
For j = 1 To N
    KCI2(j) = KCi(j)
    CallIV2(j) = CallVi(j)
Next j
For i = 1 To N - 1
    Temp(i) = (f(KCI2(i + 1), Sb, T) - f(KCI2(i), Sb, T)) ...
    If i = 1 Then
        CallWeight(1) = Temp(1)
    End If
    CallValue(i) = BSPrice("C", S, KCI2(i), ..., CallIV2(i))
    If i > 1 Then
        CallWeight(i) = Temp(i) - Temp(i - 1)
    End If
    CallContrib(i) = CallValue(i) * CallWeight(i)
Next i
Pi1 = Sum(CallContrib)
' Do the calculations on puts
For j = 1 To N
    KPI2(j) = KPi(N - j + 1)
    PutIV2(j) = PutVi(N - j + 1)
Next j
For i = 1 To N - 1
    Temp2(i) = (f(KPI2(i + 1), Sb, T) - f(KPI2(i), Sb, T)) ...
    If i = 1 Then
        PutWeight(1) = Temp2(1)
    End If
    PutValue(i) = BSPrice("P", S, KPI2(i), ..., PutIV2(i))
    If i > 1 Then
        PutWeight(i) = Temp2(i) - Temp2(i - 1)
    End If
    PutContrib(i) = PutValue(i) * PutWeight(i)
Next i
Pi2 = Sum(PutContrib)
' Total cost of the portfolio
Pi_CP = Pi1 + Pi2
' Estimate of fair variance
Kvar = 2 / T * (rf * T - (S / Sb * Exp(rf * T) - 1) ...
VarianceSwap = Kvar
End Function
```

We can refine the VarianceSwap function by increasing the number of calls and puts used in the calculations. This is done by interpolating the options and their implied volatilities in the VBA function VarianceSwapInterpolated.

```
Function VarianceSwapInterpolated(...) As Double
' Build a strike grid for the interpolated Put IV.
' Runs from K(1),...,K(ATM)
For j = 1 To Np
    KP(j) = K(j)
    PutIV(j) = PutsV(j)
Next j
' Build a strike grid for the interpolated Call IV.
' Runs from K(ATM),...,K(end)
For j = 1 To Nc
    KC(j) = K(Np + j - 1)
    CallIV(j) = CallsV(Np + j - 1)
Next j
' Interpolate both strike grids into KPi and KCi
dKP = (K(Np) - K(1)) / (Ni - 1)
dKC = (K(Nc) - K(1)) / (Ni - 1)
KPi(1) = KP(1)
KCi(1) = KC(1)
For j = 2 To Ni
    KPi(j) = KPi(j - 1) + dKP
    KCi(j) = KCi(j - 1) + dKC
Next j
' Interpolate the Put and Call implied vols
For j = 1 To Ni
    PutIVi(j) = LinearInterpolate(KP, PutIV, KPi(j))
    CallIVi(j) = LinearInterpolate(KC, CallIV, KCi(j))
Next j
VarianceSwapInterpolated = VarianceSwap(KCi, ...)
End Function
```

This requires linear interpolation with the LinearInterpolate function.

```
Function LinearInterpolate(x As Variant, y As Variant,
xi As Double)
' One dimensional linear interpolation
x1 = 0
x2 = 0
yi = 0
' Look for xi on the end points
```

```
If xi = x(1) Then
    yi = y(1)
ElseIf xi = x(N) Then
    yi = y(N)
Else
    ' Otherwise, interpolate
    For i = 2 To N
        If x(i - 1) <= xi And xi < x(i) Then
            x1 = i - 1
            x2 = i
            p = (xi - x(x1)) / (x(x2) - x(x1))
            yi = (1 - p) * y(x1) + p * y(x2)
        End If
    Next i
End If
LinearInterpolate = yi
End Function
```

We can use a strip of market prices for options with identical maturities to estimate the Heston parameters and obtain the fair strike variance from Equation (2.9). If the replication algorithm described in Demeterfi et al. (1999) and others is applied to the same set of options, we should obtain a fair strike that is identical, in principle at least. The level of agreement between both strikes will depend on how well the Heston model fits the options and on the interpolation and extrapolation methods used in the replication algorithm.[1]

To illustrate, we use a strip of options from the Dow Jones Industrial Average ETF (ticker DIA) with 15 days to maturity, and obtain the parameter estimates $\kappa = 3.000$, $\theta = 0.063$, $\sigma = 0.502$, $v_0 = 0.104$, and $\rho = -0.901$. Parameter estimation will be covered in Chapter 6. Using Equation (2.9), we obtain $K^2_{\text{var}} = 0.10197$; using the replication algorithm on the market option quotes, we obtain $K^2_{\text{var}} = 0.08298$. Finally, using the replication algorithm with interpolation produces $K^2_{\text{var}} = 0.08466$. These results are in the Excel file Ch2VarSwapDJIA.xls.

Dupire Local Volatility

Dupire's (1994) formula for local volatility is

$$\sigma_L(K,T) = \sqrt{\frac{\dfrac{\partial C}{\partial T}}{\dfrac{1}{2}K^2\dfrac{\partial^2 C}{\partial K^2}}}, \tag{2.10}$$

[1] We thank Jim Gatheral for pointing this out.

where $C = C(K)$ is the time-t call price with strike K and maturity T when the spot price is S_t.

Equation (2.10) stipulates that, given a set of option prices, the local volatility for a strike K and maturity T is obtained with first- and second-order derivatives of the call price. These derivatives can be obtained by finite differences, which we present in the next section. Finite differences, however, can be computationally extensive. In the Heston model, the derivatives required to evaluate (2.10) can be obtained analytically by straightforward differentiation.[2] Recall that the Heston call price is

$$C(K) = S_t P_1 - Ke^{-rT} P_2.$$

The derivative with respect to T is obtained using the product rule

$$\frac{\partial C}{\partial T} = S_t \frac{\partial P_1}{\partial T} - Ke^{-rT}\left(-rP_2 + \frac{\partial P_2}{\partial T}\right), \tag{2.11}$$

where

$$\frac{\partial P_j}{\partial T} = \frac{1}{\pi}\int_0^{\infty} \text{Re}\left[\frac{K^{-i\phi}\partial f_j/\partial T}{i\phi}\right] d\phi. \tag{2.12}$$

Differentiating the characteristic function $f_j = f_j(\phi)$ produces

$$\frac{\partial f_j}{\partial T} = \exp(C_j + D_j v_0 + i\phi x)\left(\frac{\partial C_j}{\partial T} + \frac{\partial D_j}{\partial T}v_0\right), \tag{2.13}$$

where $C_j = C_j(T, \phi)$ and $D_j = D_j(T, \phi)$. Differentiating C_j produces

$$\frac{\partial C_j}{\partial T} = ri\phi + \frac{\kappa\theta}{\sigma^2}\left[(b_j - \rho\sigma i\phi + d_j) + 2\left(\frac{g_j d_j e^{d_j T}}{1 - g_j e^{d_j T}}\right)\right], \tag{2.14}$$

while differentiating D_j produces

$$\frac{\partial D_j}{\partial T} = \left(\frac{b_j - \rho\sigma i\phi + d_j}{\sigma^2}\right)\left[\frac{d_j e^{d_j T}\left(g_j e^{d_j T} - 1\right) + \left(1 - e^{d_j T}\right) g_j d_j e^{d_j T}}{\left(1 - g_j e^{d_j T}\right)^2}\right]. \tag{2.15}$$

Hence, $\partial C/\partial T$ is found by substituting Equations (2.13), (2.14), and (2.15) into (2.12) and substituting the result into (2.11). Note that $\partial C/\partial T$ obtained in this way requires only one numerical integration for each P_j, while $\partial C/\partial T$ obtained by finite differences requires two numerical integrals for each P_j.

[2] See Chapter 11, The Heston Greeks, for more on these derivatives.

The second-order derivative $\partial^2 C/\partial K^2$ is

$$\frac{\partial^2 C}{\partial K^2} = S_t \frac{\partial^2 P_1}{\partial K^2} - e^{-rT}\left(2\frac{\partial P_2}{\partial K} + K\frac{\partial^2 P_2}{\partial K^2}\right). \tag{2.16}$$

The required derivatives are

$$\frac{\partial P_j}{\partial K} = -\frac{1}{\pi}\int_0^\infty \text{Re}\left[K^{-i\phi-1} f_j(\phi)\right] d\phi \tag{2.17}$$

and

$$\frac{\partial^2 P_j}{\partial K^2} = \frac{1}{\pi}\int_0^\infty \text{Re}\left[(i\phi+1)K^{-i\phi-2} f_j(\phi)\right] d\phi. \tag{2.18}$$

The bracketed expression on the right-hand side of (2.16) is therefore

$$2\frac{\partial P_2}{\partial K} + K\frac{\partial^2 P_2}{\partial K^2} = \frac{1}{\pi}\int_0^\infty \text{Re}\left[(i\phi-1)K^{-i\phi-1} f_2(\phi)\right] d\phi. \tag{2.19}$$

Note that $\partial^2 C/\partial K^2$ obtained in this way does not save computation time compared to finite differences, since two sets of numerical integrals are required under both methods.

If the "Little Trap" formulation of Albrecher et al. (2007) for C_j and D_j in Equations (2.7) and (2.5) is used, then

$$\frac{\partial C_j}{\partial T} = ri\phi + \frac{\kappa\theta}{\sigma^2}\left[(b_j - \rho\sigma i\phi - d_j) - 2\left(\frac{c_j d_j e^{-d_j T}}{1 - c_j e^{-d_j T}}\right)\right] \tag{2.20}$$

and

$$\frac{\partial D_j}{\partial T} = \left(\frac{b_j - \rho\sigma i\phi - d_j}{\sigma^2}\right)\left[\frac{d_j e^{-d_j T}\left(1 - c_j e^{-d_j T}\right) - \left(1 - e^{-d_j T}\right) c_j d_j e^{-d_j T}}{\left(1 - c_j e^{d_j T}\right)^2}\right]. \tag{2.21}$$

The other derivatives are the same, except that C_j and D_j in those derivatives take the "Little Trap" formulation.

The VBA function dPjdT implements the integrand that is used to obtain the derivatives $\partial P_j/\partial T$ in Equation (2.12) using $\partial f_j/\partial T$ from Equation (2.13). It allows for the original Heston (1993) formulation for C_j and D_j, and their derivatives, or for the "Little Trap" formulation in (2.7), (2.5), (2.20), and (2.21). To conserve space, parts of the function are omitted.

```
Function dPjdT(Pnum As Integer, ...) As Double
If trap = 1 Then
    ' Albrecher "Little Trap" formulation
    dDdT = cDiv(cProd(Term1, Term2), Term3)
    bigC = cAdd(Term1, Term2)
Else
    ' Original Heston formulation.
    dDdT = cDiv(cProd(Term1, Term2), Term3)
    bigC = cAdd(Term1, Term2)
End If
' dfdT = exp(C + D*v0 + i*phi*x) * (dCdT + dDdT*v0);
dfdT = cProd(Term1, Term2)
dPjdT = cReal(cDiv(cProd(t1, dfdT), iphi))
End Function
```

The function is then passed to the function dCdT for implementing the derivatives $\partial C/\partial T$ in Equation (2.11), using, in this case, Gauss-Laguerre weights and abscissas stored in the vectors x and w, respectively.

```
Function dCdT(params As Variant, ...) As Double
' Arrays for the integrands
For j = 1 To N
    int1(j) = W(j) * dPjdT(1, phi(j), ...)
    int2(j) = W(j) * dPjdT(2, phi(j), ...)
    int3(j) = W(j) * HestonProb(phi(j), ..., 0, 2, trap)
Next j
' The derivatives
dP1dT = (1 / pi) * Sum(int1)
dP2dT = (1 / pi) * Sum(int2)
P2 = (1 / 2) + (1 / pi) * Sum(int3)
dCdT = S * dP1dT - K * Exp(-r * T) * (-r * P2 + dP2dT)
End Function
```

The function d2P1dK2 implements the integrand that is used to obtain the derivative $\partial^2 P_1/\partial K^2$ (for P_1 only) in Equation (2.18).

```
Function d2P1dK2(phi As Double, ...) As Double
bigG = cDiv(Term1, Term2)
bigC = cAdd(Term1, Term2)
bigD = cDiv(cProd(Term1, Term2), Term3)
' The characteristic function
' f1 = exp(C + D*v0 + i*phi*x);
f1 = cExp(cAdd(cAdd(bigC, Dv0), iphix))
' Return the real part of the integrand.
d2P1dK2 = cReal(cProd(cProd(iphi1, Kiphi), f1))
End Function
```

The last function needed is that for $2\partial P_2/\partial K + K\partial^2 P_2/\partial K^2$ in Equation (2.19). This is the dP2dK2_2 function.

```
Function dP2dK2_2(phi As Double, ...) As Double
bigG = cDiv(Term1, Term2)
bigC = cAdd(Term1, Term2)
bigD = cDiv(cProd(Term1, Term2), Term3)
' The characteristic function
' f2 = exp(C + D*v0 + i*phi*x);
f2 = cExp(cAdd(cAdd(bigC, Dv0), iphix))
' Return the real part of the integrand.
dP2dK2_2 = cReal(cProd(cProd(iphi1, Kiphi), f2))
End Function
```

Finally, the function HestonLVAnalytic regroups these functions and obtains the analytic expression for local volatility $\sigma_L(K, T)$ in the Heston model, using Equation (2.10).

```
Function HestonLVAnalytic(S As Double, ...) As Double
' Integrands
For j = 1 To N
    phi = x(j)
    weight = W(j)
    int1(j) = weight * dPjdT(1, ...)
    int2(j) = weight * dPjdT(2, ...)
    int3(j) = weight * HestonProb(phi, ..., 0, 2, trap)
    int4(j) = weight * d2P1dK2(phi, ...)
    int5(j) = weight * dP2dK2_2(phi, ...)
```

```
Next j
dP1dT = (1 / pi) * Sum(int1)
dP2dT = (1 / pi) * Sum(int2)
P2 = (1 / 2) + (1 / pi) * Sum(int3)
' dC/dT : derivative of call with respect to T
dCdT = S * dP1dT - K * Exp(-r * T) * (-rf * P2 + dP2dT)
' d2C/dK2 : second derivative of call with respect to K^2
d2CdK2 = S * dP1dK2 - Exp(-rf * T) * TwodP2dK2
' Local Variance and local volatility
LocalVar = 2 * dCdT / (K ^ 2 * d2CdK2)
HestonLVAnalytic = Sqr(LocalVar)
End Function
```

All of the preceding VBA functions are in the Excel file Ch2LV_SPX_GLa.xls.

Instead of expressing the derivatives of Equation (2.10) analytically, we can approximate these derivatives using finite differences. This is the approach used to obtain local volatility in the next section.

Local Volatility with Finite Differences

The analytic expressions for the derivatives required of the Dupire (1994) local volatility formula require extensive coding, as illustrated in the previous section. From a coding point of view, it is simpler to approximate the derivatives using finite differences. Write $C(K) = C(K, T)$ to emphasize the dependence of the European call price on the maturity T. We use a small time increment dt and approximate the time derivative as the central difference

$$\frac{\partial C}{\partial T} \approx \frac{C(K, T + dt) - C(K, T - dt)}{2dt}. \tag{2.22}$$

Similarly, we can use a small strike increment dK and approximate the second-order strike derivative as the central difference

$$\frac{\partial^2 C}{\partial K^2} \approx \frac{C(K - dK, T) - 2C(K, T) + C(K + dK, T)}{(dK)^2}. \tag{2.23}$$

The function HestonLVFD obtains local volatility $\sigma_L(K, T)$ in the Heston model using the central difference approximation to the derivatives.

```
Function HestonLVFD(S As Double, ...) As Double
' dC/dT and dC2/dK2 by central finite difference
dCdT = (CT1 - CT_1) / (2 * dt)
dC2dK2 = (CK_1 - 2 * CK0 + CK1) / (dK) ^ 2
' Local variance
```

```
LocalVar = 2 * dCdT / (K ^ 2 * dC2dK2)
' Local volatility
HestonLVFD = Sqr(LocalVar)
End Function
```

The VBA code for $\sigma_L(K, T)$ in this section is indeed much simpler and more compact than the code in the previous section that uses analytic derivatives. The disadvantage is that, since finite differences require multiple calculations of the call price, the code that uses finite differences will run slower. Moreover, finite differences are only approximations to the derivatives, whereas the analytic expressions are exact.

Approximate Local Volatility

In his excellent book, *The Volatility Surface: A Practitioner's Guide*, Gatheral (2006) derives an approximation to local volatility in the Heston model that is valid when $\rho \approx \pm 1$. His approximation to local variance, u_T, is

$$u_T = \hat{v}'_T + \rho\sigma \frac{x_T}{\hat{w}_T} \int_0^T \hat{v}_t e^{-\kappa'(T-t)} dt \tag{2.24}$$

where

$$\hat{v}'_T = (v_0 - \theta')e^{-\kappa' T} + \theta',$$
$$\kappa' = \kappa - \rho\sigma/2 \text{ and } \theta' = \theta\kappa/\kappa'.$$

Equation (2.24) is Equation (3.15) of Gatheral (2006) and can be further integrated to produce

$$u_T = \hat{v}'_T + \rho\sigma \frac{x_T}{\hat{w}_T} e^{\kappa' T} \left[\frac{v_0 - \theta}{\kappa' - \kappa} (e^{(\kappa' - \kappa)T} - 1) + \frac{\theta}{\kappa'} (e^{\kappa' T} - 1) \right]. \tag{2.25}$$

See Gatheral (2006) or Rouah (2013) for details of the derivation.

The function HestonLVApprox implements Gatheral's (2006) approximation to local volatility $\sigma_L(K, T)$ in the Heston model, in accordance with (2.25).

```
Function HestonLVApprox(S As Double, ...) As Double
' Modified parameters kappa' and theta'
kappa_ = kappa - rho * sigma / 2
theta_ = theta * kappa / kappa_
' wT and vT'
xT = Log(K / S)
wT = (v0 - theta) * (1 - Exp(-kappa * T)) / kappa ...
vT = (v0 - theta_) * Exp(-kappa_ * T) + theta ...
' Integral
Integral = Exp(-kappa_ * T) * (f1 * E1 + f2 * E2)
```

```
' Local Variance and local volatility
uT = vT + rho * sigma * xT / wT * Integral
HestonLVApprox = Sqr(uT)
End Function
```

This function is in the Excel file Ch2LV_SPX_GLa.xls.

Numerical Illustration of Local Volatility

We illustrate local volatility in the Heston using a set of put options with 222 days to expiry, when the spot price is $S_t = 30.67$. The Heston parameters associated with this set of options were estimated as $\theta = 0.007$, $\kappa = 6.45 \times 10^{-6}$, $\sigma = 0.639$, $v_0 = 0.579$, and $\rho = -0.805$. We obtain exact local volatility $\sigma_L(K, T)$ in (2.10) using analytic derivatives and finite difference approximations and we also obtain Gatheral's (2006) approximate local volatility in (2.25), for $T = 222/365$ and for strikes running from $K = 15$ to $K = 65$. We have also added the implied volatility from Heston put prices generated with the parameter estimates. The results are illustrated in Figure 2.10.

Figure 2.10 illustrates the observation of Gatheral (2006) that the approximate form of local volatility (solid red line) tends to be less curved than the exact form. The figure also shows that the exact form using the analytic formulation (solid black line) and finite difference approximation (black circles) produce local volatilities that are nearly identical. Finally, the slope of local volatility is roughly 1.9 times that of implied volatility, on average, which is consistent with the rule of thumb of

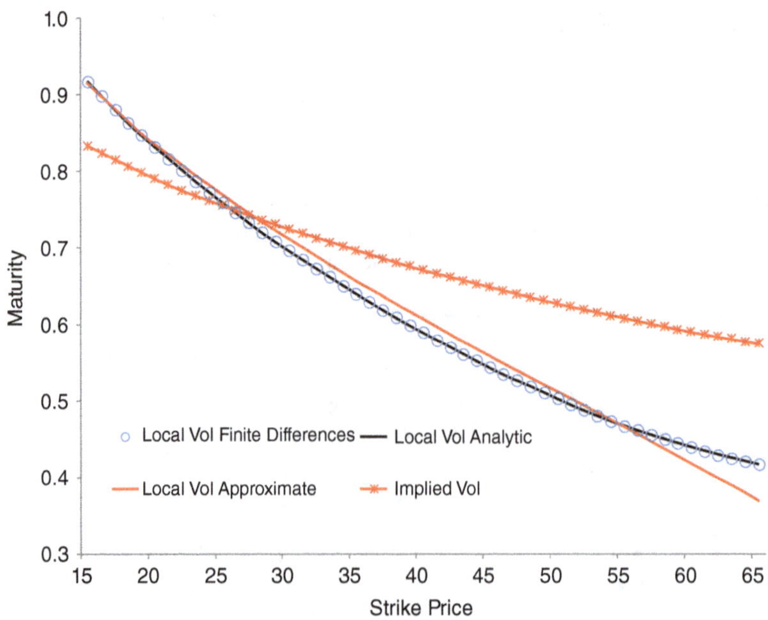

FIGURE 2.10 Heston Local Volatility and Implied Volatility

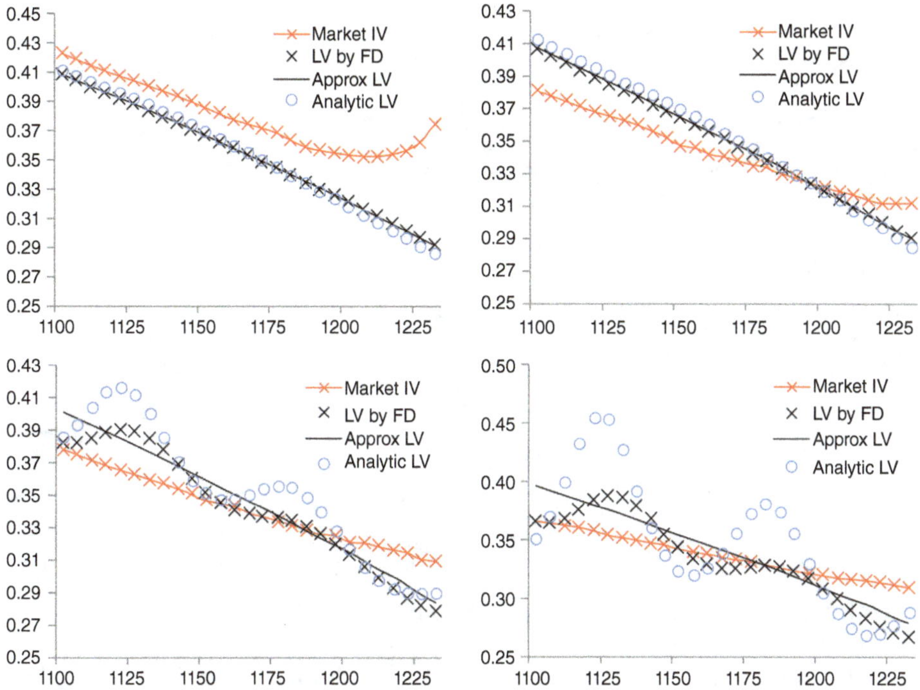

FIGURE 2.11 Market Implied Volatility and Heston Volatility, S&P 500 Index

Derman et al. (1995) that local volatility is roughly twice as steep as implied volatility. Figure 2.10 is in the Excel file Ch2Gatheral.xls.

We can also apply our three estimates of local volatility—analytic and finite differences in Equation (2.10), and approximate in (2.25)—to SPX options data. This appears in Figure 2.11 and is in the Excel file Ch2LV_SPX_GLa.xls.

As expected, and consistent with Figure 2.10, local volatility is generally steeper and more erratic than implied volatility. The approximation to local volatility preserves the larger slope, but does not preserve the erratic behavior. The analytic and finite difference local volatilities are very close, except for the maturity of 71 days, where the finite difference approximation breaks down slightly.

Implied Volatility

We noted earlier in this chapter that option prices obtained with the Heston model have an implied volatility smile that is built in, in the sense that implied volatilities extracted from those prices will exhibit an implied volatility smile. Moreover, the parameters ρ and σ have an effect on the skew and steepness of the smile.

In practice, implied volatilities extracted from Heston model prices will sometimes show a poor fit to market implied volatilities for short maturities. For longer maturities, however, the fit is better. We illustrate this by using put[3] options on the

[3] In practice, DIA puts are actually American style; using European-style index puts would be preferable here and lead to similar conclusions. (Editor's note)

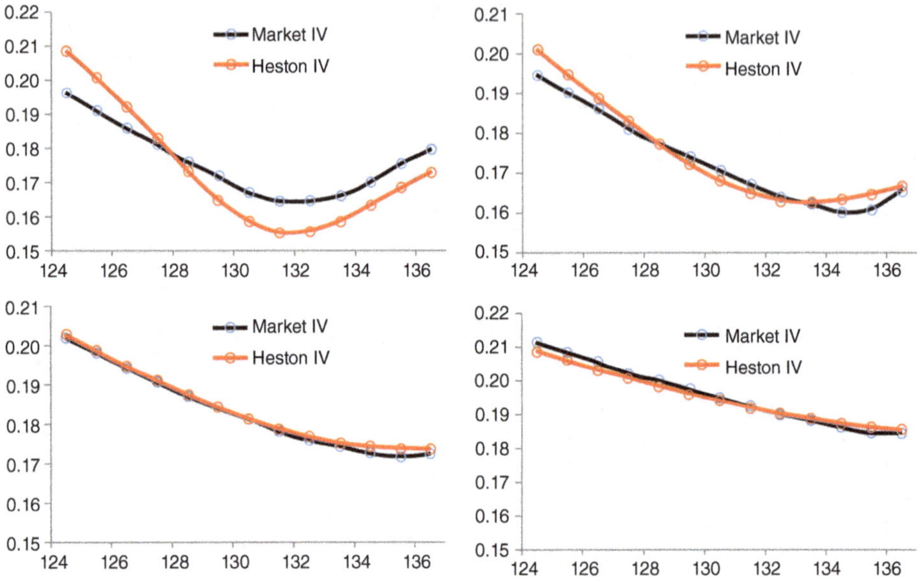

FIGURE 2.12 Market and Heston Implied Volatilities from Puts on DIA

Dow Jones Industrial Average ETF (ticker DIA) with four maturities (37, 72, 135, and 226 days). The closing price for DIA was \$129.14. We obtained the parameter estimates $\kappa = 8.8799$, $\theta = 0.0674$, $\sigma = 3.6706$, $v_0 = 0.0435$, and $\rho = -0.4171$. Parameter estimation methods for the Heston model are dealt with in Chapter 6. For simplicity, we set $r = q = 0$. Figure 2.12 presents market implied volatilities from the DIA, and implied volatilities obtained using the bisection algorithm on Heston prices generated with the earlier parameter estimates. The figure is in the Excel file Ch2IV_DJIA.xls.

Figure 2.12 clearly indicates that, for short maturity, the Heston implied volatilities fit to market implied volatilities is poor. For longer maturities, however, the Heston model provides a very good fit.

The bisection algorithm is used to obtain market and Heston implied volatilities. The VBA function BisecBSIV for this algorithm was presented earlier in this chapter. The algorithm finds the implied volatility by finding the root (also called zero) of the difference between the input market or Heston price and the Black-Scholes price. The advantage of using this algorithm is that a solution will always be found, provided that the function is continuous, and that the two initial endpoints of the interval are selected so that one value produces a negative difference, and the other produces a positive difference, indicating the presence of a root within the interval. Since Black-Scholes option prices are increasing functions of volatility, we can always use a very small value for the first initial endpoint (say 0.1 percent), and a very large value for the second endpoint (say 500 percent).

MOMENT EXPLOSIONS

Andersen and Piterbarg (2007) derive conditions under which the moments of the terminal stock price $E[S_T^{\omega}]$ explode (become infinite) after a finite amount of time. The results of their paper can be used to find values of $\omega > 1$, for which $E[S_T^{\omega}]$ remains finite for all $T > 0$, using their analytic expressions for the time to moment explosion $T^* = \sup\{t : E[S_t^{\omega}] < \infty\}$. The moment will be finite for $T < T^*$ but will explode to infinity for $T > T^*$. Define the quantities

$$k = \frac{\lambda_L^2}{2}\omega(\omega-1), \quad b = \frac{2k}{\sigma^2}, \quad a = \frac{2}{\sigma^2}(\rho\sigma\lambda_L\omega - \kappa), \quad D = a^2 - 4b. \tag{2.26}$$

The value of T^* arises from one of three possible cases:

Case 1. $D \geq 0$ and $a < 0$

$$T^* = \infty.$$

Case 2. $D \geq 0$ and $a > 0$

$$T^* = \frac{1}{\gamma\sigma^2}\ln\left(\frac{a/2+\gamma}{a/2-\gamma}\right), \text{where } \gamma = \frac{\sqrt{D}}{2}.$$

Case 3. $D < 0$

$$T^* = \begin{cases} \dfrac{2}{\beta\sigma^2}\arctan(2\beta/a) \text{ if } a \geq 0 \\ \dfrac{2}{\beta\sigma^2}(\pi + \arctan(2\beta/a)) \text{ if } a < 0 \end{cases}, \text{where } \beta = \frac{\sqrt{-D}}{2}.$$

In these equations, we can set $\lambda_L = 1$ (see, for example, Forde and Jacquier, 2009). Case 1 is the most desirable, since it implies that the time to moment explosion will never be reached.

The VBA function MomentExplode finds the time to moment explosion.

```
Function MomentExplode(w As Double, ...) As Double
' Andersen and Piterbarg moment explosion
k = lambda ^ 2 * w * (w - 1) / 2
b = 2 * k / sigma ^ 2
a = 2 * (rho * sigma * lambda * w - kappa) / sigma ^ 2
D = a ^ 2 - 4 * b
If D >= 0 And a < 0 Then      ' Infinite explosion time
    T = 1E+100
    MsgBox ("inf")
ElseIf D >= 0 And a > 0 Then ' Finite explosion time
    g = Sqr(D) / 2
    T = Log((a / 2 + g) / (a / 2 - g)) / g / sigma ^ 2
ElseIf D < 0 Then
    beta = Sqr(-D) / 2
    If a < 0 Then
        bigPi = Pi
```

```
        Else
            bigPi = 0
        End If
        T = 2 * (bigPi + Atn(2 * beta / a)) / beta / sigma ^ 2
    End If
    MomentExplode = T
    End Function
```

To illustrate, suppose that $\kappa = 0.1$ and $\sigma = 0.3$. If $\rho = -0.7$, the second moment ($\omega = 2$) will explode after $T^* = 5.14$ years; if $\rho = 0.7$, the second moment will never explode.

BOUNDS ON IMPLIED VOLATILITY SLOPE

One problem that arises in modeling the implied volatility surface is that extrapolation of the surface beyond observable strikes is often arbitrary. Lee (2004b) provides guidance on this issue, by deriving the slopes of the implied volatility at extreme strikes. These slopes were subsequently refined by Benaim and Friz (2008).

Define the log-moneyness to be $k = \ln(K/F)$, where $F = E[S_T]$ is the forward price, and let $\sigma(k, T)$ denote implied volatility at log-moneyness k and at maturity T. The extreme strike tail of the implied variance can be written as a linear function of $|k|$ for some value of the slope coefficient

$$\sigma^2(k,T) = \text{Coefficient} \times \frac{|k|}{T}. \tag{2.27}$$

The first moment formula is for implied variance for extreme strikes on the right-hand side of the tail, as $k \to \infty$. In this case, the tail slope is bounded above by 2, so that $\sigma^2(k, T) < 2|k|/T$. The actual value of the slope coefficient is found in the limit as

$$\beta_R = \limsup_{k\to\infty} \frac{\sigma^2(k,T)}{|k|/T}, \tag{2.28}$$

with $0 \le \beta_R \le 2$. Hence, as $k \to \infty$, we have that $\sigma^2(k, T) \to \beta_R|k|/T$. The result of Lee (2004b) is that β_R can be obtained as

$$\beta_R = 2 - 4\left(\sqrt{\tilde{p}^2 + \tilde{p}} - \tilde{p}\right), \tag{2.29}$$

where $\tilde{p} - 1$ is the largest finite moment of S_T, namely,

$$\tilde{p} = \sup\left\{p : E\left[S_T^{1+p}\right] < \infty\right\}. \tag{2.30}$$

The second moment formula is for implied variance for extreme strikes on the left-hand side of the tail, as $k \to -\infty$. The limiting value of the slope coefficient in this case is

$$\beta_L = \limsup_{k \to -\infty} \frac{\sigma^2(k,T)}{|k|/T}, \tag{2.31}$$

with $0 \le \beta_L \le 2$ given by

$$\beta_L = 2 - 4\left(\sqrt{\tilde{q}^2 + \tilde{q}} - \tilde{q}\right) \tag{2.32}$$

and with

$$\tilde{q} = \sup\left\{q : E\left[S_T^{-q}\right] < \infty\right\}. \tag{2.33}$$

Hence, β_R and β_L represent the slopes that must be respected when we extrapolate the implied volatility at large and small strikes, respectively.

The first step to finding these coefficients is to find the bounds on finite moments, $\tilde{p}$ and $\tilde{q}$. We can find these using the moment explosion formula of Andersen and Piterbarg (2007). We move away from $\omega > 1$ in increments and calculate T^* at each step, and stop when we encounter $T^* < \infty$.

This approach to finding the bounds on finite moments is implemented in the VBA function FindLeeBounds. The first part of the function uses the result of Andersen and Piterbarg (2007) to find the bounds on finite moments. To find the moment $\omega > 1$ at which $T^* < \infty$, we start with a wide grid $1 < \omega < 10$ and loop through the values to identify where $T^* < \infty$. We then reduce the size of the grid for ω and repeat. After several iterations, we have a fairly accurate estimate of the upper moment at which T^* starts to become finite. To find the lower moment, we use $-10 < \omega < 0$ and apply the same methodology.

```
Function FindLeeBounds(S As Double, ...) As Variant
' Upper moment bound
For y = 1 To HiLimit
    W(y) = y
Next y
For K = 1 To 15
    While (T = 1E+100)
        T = MomentExplode(W(j), ...)
    Wend
    For y = 2 To Nw
        W(y) = W(y - 1) + E
    Next y
Next K
UpperAP = W(j)
' Lower moment bound
For j = 1 To Abs(LoLimit) + 1
    W(j) = LoLimit + j - 1
```

```
Next j
For K = 1 To 15
    While (T < 1E+100)
        T = MomentExplode(W(j), ...)
    Wend
    For y = 2 To Nw
        W(y) = W(y - 1) + E
    Next y
Next K
LowerAP = W(j)
p = UpperAP - 1
q = -LowerAP
' Moment formula part 1 - - Limit of right tail slope
bR = 2 - 4 * (Sqr(p ^ 2 + p) - p)
' Moment formula part 2 - - Limit of the left tail slope
bL = 2 - 4 * (Sqr(q ^ 2 + q) - q)
End Function
```

To illustrate, we use the parameter estimates from put options on the Dow Jones Industrial Average ETF with maturity 37 days. The spot price is \$129.14. The parameter estimates are $\kappa = 4.52$, $\sigma = 2.11$, $\rho = -0.27$. The upper moment bound is 3.6842, so $\tilde{p} = 2.6842$. The lower moment bound is -1.3376, so $\tilde{q} = 1.3376$. We substitute the values of $\tilde{p}$ and $\tilde{q}$ into Equations (2.29) and (2.32) to obtain the limiting slope coefficients $\beta_L = 0.2773$ and $\beta_R = 0.1580$.

We can use these limiting slope coefficients to find the slope of the implied volatility at extreme strikes for the set of 37-day maturity puts on the Dow Jones Industrial Average ETF that were used to generate them. This is illustrated in Figure 2.13.

The range of observed strikes is [124, 136] in increments of \$1.00, and the spot is $S_t = 129.14$, so the range of observed log-moneyness is $[-0.0406, 0.0518]$. We fit Heston prices to the expanded range of strikes [120, 140], corresponding to the range of log-moneyness $[-0.0734, 0.0807]$, and extract implied volatilities from those prices. Finally, we expand the log-moneyness range to $[-0.1534, 0.1407]$ and use β_L and β_R to obtain the slopes at the extreme values of log-moneyness. Note that the slopes of the implied volatility at the extreme strikes in Figure 2.13 are not β_L and β_R, since these are the slopes for variance.

The VBA function FindLeeBounds, and the plot in Figure 2.13, are in the Excel file Ch2LeeSlopes.xls.

CONCLUSION

In this chapter, we showed that the Heston call price can be expressed in terms of a single characteristic function and that the Heston model fits into the framework described by Bakshi and Madan (2000). Next, we presented the "Little Trap" formulation of Albrecher et al. (2007) that can remedy some of the problems with the

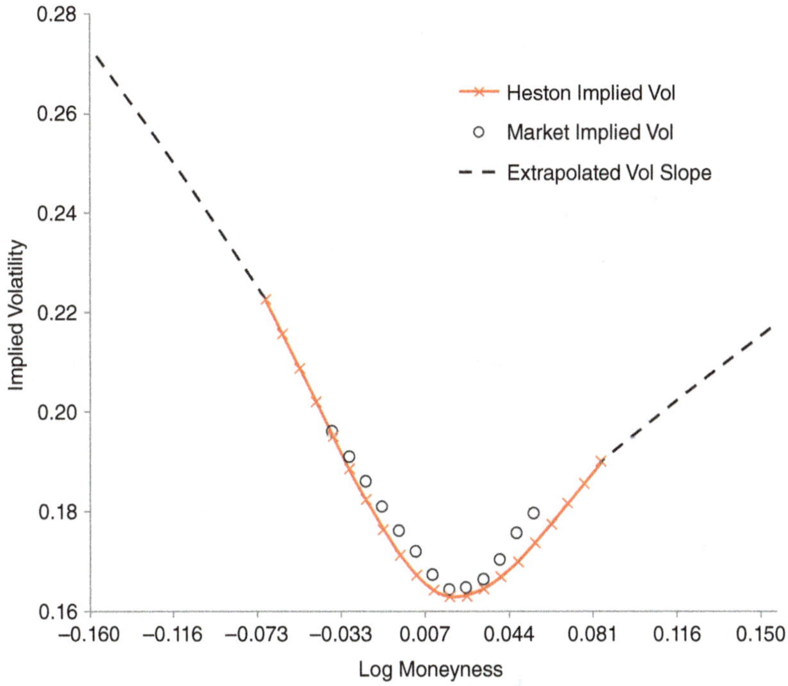

FIGURE 2.13 Implied Volatility at Extreme Strikes, DJIA Puts

numerical integration that arise when the integrand is discontinuous. We then examined the effect of the Heston parameters on the implied volatilities, and showed that varying these parameters can induce substantial changes in the pattern of implied volatility smiles and skews. We also presented Gatheral's (2006) fair strike of a variance swap under the Heston model, his approximation to local and implied volatility in the model, and formulas for analytical local volatility and finite difference approximations to local volatility. Finally, we showed how the moment explosion times of Andersen and Piterbarg (2007) can be used to find the bounds on implied volatility due to Lee (2004b) and illustrated the value of these bounds on extreme strikes in an implied volatility smile.

The formulas for the Heston call price have so far involved inversion of the characteristic function to obtain the probabilities P_1 and P_2. In the next chapter, we present a popular method to obtain the call price due to Carr and Madan (1999) that uses the Fourier transform of the call price itself. We also present an alternate derivation of the Heston call price due to Gatheral (2006) that makes use of Fourier transforms of P_1 and P_2. Finally, we present a call price formula due to Attari (2004) that makes use of a single integral that decays very quickly and therefore requires a short integration domain.

CHAPTER 3

Derivations Using the Fourier Transform

Abstract

Here, we present several pricing methods based on the Fourier transform. We follow the derivations described by Gatheral (2006) and Attari (2004). Next, we present the Carr and Madan (1999) representation of the Heston call price, a method in which the Fourier transform plays a key role. We also discuss the optimal choice of the damping factor that is required of their method.

Fourier transform, Gatheral derivation, Attari representation, Carr-Madan representation, OTM options, Gil-Pelaez inversion, optimal damping

The Heston model laid the foundation for the popularity of Fourier transforms in mathematical finance. Fourier transforms have now earned their place as crucial tools in pricing models for equity derivatives. This owes to the fact that, in most cases, the terminal price density has no analytic structure. The characteristic function, however, is often readily available for many models, including the Heston model. The Heston model is a perfect illustration of why Fourier transforms are useful. Indeed, if the characteristic function is available for the price process, then the Fourier transform can be used to extract the probabilities from the characteristic function and obtain the call price using the Black-Scholes–style representation.

The application of Fourier transforms to option pricing is not limited to obtaining probabilities, as is done in Heston's (1993) original derivation. As explained by Wu (2008), the literature approaches Fourier transforms in option pricing in two broad ways. The first approach considers option prices to be analogous to cumulative distribution functions. This is the approach adopted by Heston (1993), Carr and Madan (1999), Bakshi and Madan (2000), and others. The second approach considers option prices to be analogous to probability density functions. This is the approach of Lewis (2000, 2001).

Here, we present several pricing methods based on the Fourier transform. We follow the derivations described by Gatheral (2006) and Attari (2004). Next, we present the Carr and Madan (1999) representation of the Heston call price, a method in which the Fourier transform plays a key role. We also discuss the optimal choice of the damping factor that is required of their method.

DERIVATION OF GATHERAL (2006)

Gatheral (2006) derives the Albrecher et al. (2007) formulation of the Heston (1993) characteristic function by working with the log-moneyness of the forward price, $x_t = \ln(F_{t,T}/K)$, where K is the strike price of the option and $F_{t,T} = S_t e^{\mu(T-t)}$ is the forward price of the stock. His derivation is slightly different than that of Heston (1993) since Gatheral works with the Fourier transforms of the in-the-money probabilities P_1 and P_2 directly.

Consider the Fourier transform $\hat{P}_j$ of the probabilities $P_j = P_j(x, v, \tau)$:

$$\hat{P}_j(k, v, \tau) = \int_{-\infty}^{\infty} e^{-ikx} P_j(x, v, \tau)dx.$$

Gatheral's (2006) ansatz is that the $\hat{P}_j$ are of the form

$$\hat{P}_j(k, v, \tau) = \exp[C_j(k, \tau)\theta + D_j(k, \tau)v]\hat{P}_j(k, v, 0). \tag{3.1}$$

The solution for D_j is

$$D_j = r_-^j \left(\frac{1 - e^{-d_j\tau}}{1 - c_j e^{-d_j\tau}} \right), \tag{3.2}$$

where $c_j = r_-^j / r_+^j$, and

$$r_\pm^j = \frac{\beta_j \pm \sqrt{\beta_j^2 - 4\alpha_j\gamma}}{2\alpha_j} = \frac{b_j - \rho\sigma ik \pm d_j}{\sigma^2},$$

$$d_j = \sqrt{(\rho\sigma ik - b_j)^2 - \sigma^2(2u_j ik - k^2)}.$$

Note that c_j is identical to that in the "Little Trap" formulation of Albrecher et al. (2007), which we encountered in Chapter 2, but with ϕ replaced by k. The solution for C_j is, remembering that the interest rate $r = 0$ in this derivation,

$$\begin{aligned} C_j &= \frac{\kappa}{\sigma^2} \left[(b_j - \rho\sigma i\phi - d_j)\tau - 2\ln\left(\frac{1 - c_j e^{-d_j\tau}}{1 - c_j} \right) \right] \\ &= \kappa \left[r_-^j \tau - \frac{2}{\sigma^2} \ln\left(\frac{1 - c_j e^{-d_j\tau}}{1 - c_j} \right) \right] \end{aligned} \tag{3.3}$$

since θ cancels out. The expressions for D_j and C_j in (3.2) and (3.3) are Equation (2.12) in Gatheral (2006). The resulting characteristic function for the Heston model in Equation (2.15) of Gatheral (2006) is identical to the "Little Trap" formulation of Albrecher et al. (2007), but with $r = 0$. For details of this derivation, see Gatheral (2006) or Rouah (2013).

ATTARI (2004) REPRESENTATION

Attari (2004) presents an alternate formula for the Heston call price. The formula is similar to that proposed earlier by Lewis (2001), which we present in the next chapter. Attari (2004) writes the terminal stock price as $S_T = S_t e^{r\tau + x(t,T)}$, where $x = x(t, T)$ now denotes the stochastic component of the stock price process.

Attari's (2004) formula for the call price is

$$C(K) = S_t - \frac{1}{2}Ke^{-r\tau} - \frac{Ke^{-r\tau}}{\pi}\int_0^\infty A(u)du, \tag{3.4}$$

$$A(u) = \frac{\left(R_2(u) + \frac{I_2(u)}{u}\right)\cos(u\ell) + \left(I_2(u) - \frac{R_2(u)}{u}\right)\sin(u\ell)}{1+u^2}, \tag{3.5}$$

where $\ell = \ln(Ke^{-r\tau}/S_t)$ and $R_2(u)$, $I_2(u)$ are the real and imaginary parts of the characteristic function of $\mathbf{1}_{x>\ell}$.

For a detailed derivation of the call price formula, see Attari (2004) or Rouah (2013).

The main advantage of Attari's representation is that a single numerical integration only is required to produce the call price. Moreover, the u^2 term in the denominator of $A(u)$ causes the integrand to dampen quickly, so that truncation of the upper limit in the integral for the purposes of numerical integration causes less loss of precision. This is illustrated in Figure 3.1 using $S = 30$, $K = 20$, $r = 0.01$, $q = 0$, a maturity of one month, along with the parameter values $\kappa = 1.4$, $\theta = v_0 = 0.05$, $\sigma = 0.3$, and

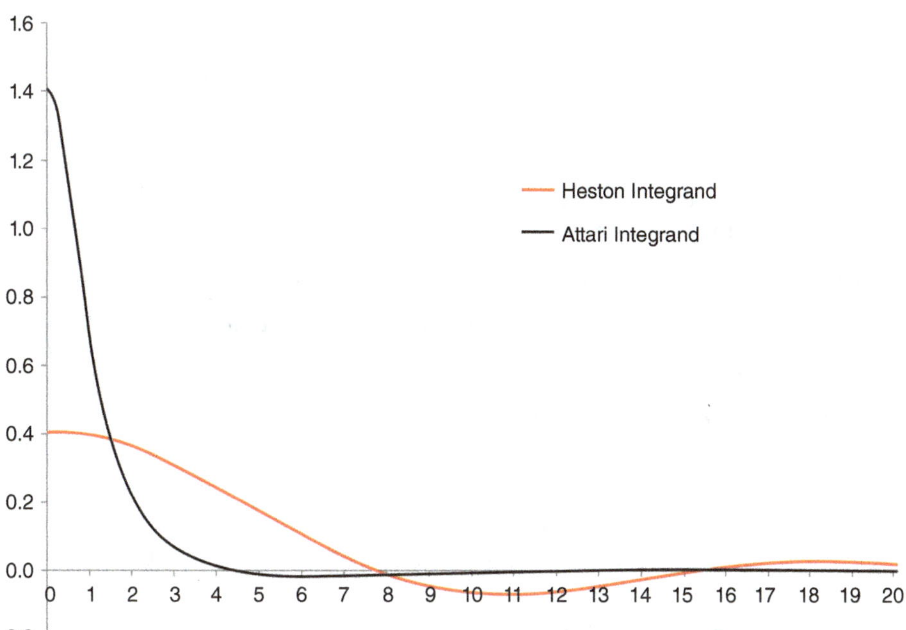

FIGURE 3.1 Attari (2004) and Heston (1993) Integrands

$\rho = -0.8$. The figure shows that the Attari integrand decays much faster than the Heston integrand but that it is much steeper at the origin. Consequently, there exists the potential for problems in numerical integration in that region.

The VBA function AttariProb implements the integrand in Equation (3.5). It is based on the same function used to implement the Heston characteristic function $f_2(\phi)$ and is therefore not presented in its entirety.

```
Function AttariProb(phi As Double, ...) As Double
' Returns the integrand for the Attari integrand
If trap = 0 Then
    ' Original Heston formulation of the c.f.
    bigG = cDiv(Num2, Den2)
    bigC = cAdd(Term3, term4)
    bigD = cProd(Term5, Term6)
ElseIf trap = 1 Then
    ' Little Trap formulation of the c.f.
    bigG = cDiv(Num2, Den2)
    bigC = cAdd(Term3, term4)
    bigD = cProd(Term5, Term6)
End If
' The characteristic function for Attari.
f = cExp(cAdd(bigC, cSub(Dv, iphirtau)))
' The "L" function
Dim L As Double
L = Log(Exp(-r * tau) * K / S)
' The Attari (2004) integrand
AttariProb = ((cReal(f) + cImag(f) / phi) * Cos(L * phi) ...
End Function
```

The function AttariPriceGaussLaguerre returns the call price in Equation (3.4) or the put price by put-call parity.

```
Function AttariPriceGaussLaguerre(PutCall As String, ...) As Double
' The integrands
For j = 1 To N
    weight = w(j)
    phi = x(j)
    int1(j) = weight * AttariProb(phi, ...)
Next j
' The call price
AttariC = S * Exp(-q * T) - K * Exp(-r * T) ...
' The put price by put-call parity
AttariP = AttariC - S * Exp(-q * T) + K * Exp(-r * T)
End Function
```

To illustrate pricing with the Attari (2004) method, we use the same settings as those in Figure 3.1, along with 32-point Gauss-Laguerre integration. The Heston price is 10.0152, and the Attari price is 10.0167, which is very close.

The VBA code for the Attari price functions is in the Excel file Ch3Attari.xls.

CARR AND MADAN (1999) REPRESENTATION

Carr and Madan (1999) present a derivation of the call price based on the Fourier transform. It offers advantages in terms of reduced computation time and an integrand that decays faster than the integrand of the original Heston (1993) formulation. The Carr and Madan (1999) call price is

$$C(k) = \frac{e^{-\alpha k}}{\pi} \int_0^\infty \text{Re}[e^{-ivk}\hat{c}(v)]dv, \tag{3.6}$$

where

$$\hat{c}(v) = \frac{e^{-r\tau}\varphi(v-(\alpha+1)i)}{\alpha^2+\alpha-v^2+iv(2\alpha+1)} \tag{3.7}$$

and where $\varphi(u)$ is the characteristic function of $x = \ln S_T$, which we have denoted $f_2(\phi)$ in previous chapters. The quantity α is a damping factor, which we discuss later in this chapter. See Carr and Madan (1999) or Rouah (2013) for details of the derivation leading to the call price (3.6).

Lord and Kahl (2007) point out at least three advantages to the representation of the call price in (3.6). First, only a single numerical integration is required, instead of two. Second, the denominator in the integrand in (3.7) is a quadratic function of the integration variable, v, and thus decays faster than the integrands in the original Heston formulation, in which the denominators are linear functions of the integration variable. This implies that truncation of the integration domain from $(0, \infty)$ to some finite range $(0, M)$, where $M < \infty$, is less problematic. Finally, there is computational accuracy to be gained from the representation, provided that the damping factor α is appropriately chosen. We address this issue in a later section of this chapter.

The VBA function CarrMadanIntegrand returns the Carr and Madan (1999) integrand. It calls the function HestonCF, which returns the Heston characteristic function.

```
Function CarrMadanIntegrand(u As Double, ...) As Double
' First numerator is product of two exponentials
Numerator1 = cProd(exp1, exp2)
' Second denominator is the Heston cf
charfun = HestonCF(ualphai, params, tau, K, S, r, q, Trap)
Numerator2 = Complex(charfun(1, 1), charfun(2, 1))
' The Denominator
' (alpha^2 + alpha - u^2 + (2*alpha+1)*i*u);
Denominator = cAdd(cSub(cAdd(calpha2, calpha), cu2), ...)
bigI = cDiv(cProd(Numerator1, Numerator2), Denominator)
CarrMadanIntegrand = cReal(bigI)
End Function
```

The function HestonCallGaussLaguerre implements the call price using either the original Heston form, or the Carr-Madan form.

```
Function HestonCallGaussLaguerre(...) As Double
' Heston formulation of the integrand
If Integrand = "Heston" Then
    For j = 1 To N
        phi = x(j)
        weight = w(j)
        int1(j) = weight * HestonIntegrand(phi, ..., 1)
        int2(j) = weight * HestonIntegrand(phi, ..., 2)
    Next j
    P1 = 0.5 + 1 / pi * Sum(int1)
    P2 = 0.5 + 1 / pi * Sum(int2)
    ' The Call price
    CallPrice = S * exp(-q * T) * P1 - K ...
' Carr-Madan formulation of the integrand
ElseIf Integrand = "CarrMadan" Then
    For j = 1 To N
        phi = x(j)
        weight = w(j)
        int1(j) = weight * CarrMadanIntegrand(phi, ...)
    Next j
    ' The Call Price
    CallPrice = exp(-alpha * Log(K)) ...
End If
End Function
```

These functions are in the Excel file Ch2CMCalls.xls. The file also contains the following example, using the settings $S = K = 100$, $r = 0.10$, $q = 0.07$, and a maturity of six months, with $\kappa = 2$, $\theta = v_0 = 0.06$, $\sigma = 0.1$, $\rho = -0.7$, and the damping factor $\alpha = 1.75$. A screen shot appears in Figure 3.2.

VBA returns the call prices as 7.3461 for both the Heston and Carr-Madan representations. Note that to implement the Carr-Madan price on the stock paying continuous dividend yield, q, we have replaced the spot price S by $Se^{-q\tau}$ before passing the price to the function.

Bounds on the Damping Factor and Optimal Value

Carr and Madan (1999) suggest using $\alpha = \alpha_{\max}/4$ where $\alpha_{\max}$ is the maximum value for α such that $E(S_T^{\alpha+1}) < \infty$, which can sometimes be determined analytically. They illustrate this choice for the Variance Gamma model, for which they chose $\alpha = 1.5$ (see also Carr, Madan, and Chang, 1998). Other studies, such as those by Raible (2000), Schoutens et al. (2004), and Borak et al. (2011) have used ad-hoc choices ranging from $\alpha = 0.75$ to $\alpha = 25$.

While ad-hoc values of the damping factor α can serve as a general guide, it is more useful to have a range of admissible values for α. To this end, Lee (2004a) shows how minimum and maximum values for α can be obtained. Denote by

	A	B	C	D	E	F	G
1							
2		**Comparison of call prices using the Heston and Carr-Madan formulations**					
3							
4		**Option Features**			**Method**	**Call Price**	
5		Spot Price (S)	100.0000		Heston	7.346092101	
6		Strike Price (K)	100.0000		Carr Madan	7.346075582	
7		Time to Maturity (τ)	0.5000				
8		Risk free rate (r)	0.1000				
9		Dividend (q)	0.0700				
10		PutCall (C or P)	C				
11							
12		**Heston Parameters**			**Abscissas (x) and Weights (w)**		
13		kappa (κ)	2.0000		**For 32-point Gauss-Laguerre Integration**		
14		theta (θ)	0.0600		**Number**	**Abcissas**	**Weights**
15		sigma (σ)	0.1000		1	0.04449	0.11419
16		v0	0.0600		2	0.23453	0.26607
17		rho (ρ)	-0.7000		3	0.57688	0.41879
18		lambda (λ)	0.0000		4	1.07245	0.57253
19		Trap (0=Heston, 1=Albrecher)	1		5	1.72241	0.72765
20					6	2.52834	0.88454
21		Carr Madan Damping Factor (α)	1.7500		7	3.49221	1.04362
22					8	4.61646	1.20535
23		Dividend-Discounted Spot	96.5605		9	5.90396	1.37022

FIGURE 3.2 Heston (1993) and Carr and Madan (1999) Call Price

$A_X = (a_-, a_+)$ the interval of allowable values for $\alpha + 1$, where $a_- < 0$ and $a_+ > 1$, so that α can be selected from anywhere from the interval of allowable values defined by $(a_- - 1, a_+ - 1) = (\alpha_{\min}, \alpha_{\max})$. When $\kappa - \rho\sigma > 0$, we can define a_- to be the largest solution in $(-\infty, y_-)$ and a_+ to be the smallest solution in (y_+, ∞), where

$$y_\pm = \frac{\sigma - 2\kappa\rho \pm \sqrt{\sigma^2 - 4\kappa\rho\sigma + 4\kappa^2}}{2\sigma(1-\rho^2)}. \tag{3.8}$$

See Lee (2004a) or Rouah (2013) for details of the derivation.

For example, using the settings in Lord and Kahl (2007), namely, $S = 1$, $r = 0$, $K = 1.2$, $\rho = -0.7$, $v_0 = \theta = 0.1$, $\kappa = \sigma = 1$, and $\tau = 1$ produces $(y_-, y_+) = (-0.3851, 5.0910)$. Next, we find $A_X = (-2.2292, 10.0840)$. This range is sensible, since the lower limit of A_X should be less than $y_- = -0.3851$, while the upper limit of A_X should be greater than $y_+ = 5.0910$. The range of admissible values for α is therefore $(\alpha_{\min}, \alpha_{\max}) = (-3.2292, 9.0840)$. We return to this example in detail later in this chapter.

Optimal Damping Factor

While $(\alpha_{\min}, \alpha_{\max})$ forms a region of admissible values for the damping factor α, it does not indicate which value of α in the region is optimal, in the sense that an optimal value produces an integrand in Equation (3.6) that oscillates as little as possible. Recall that the Carr and Madan (1999) representation is

$$C(k) = \frac{e^{-\alpha k}}{\pi} \int_0^\infty \psi(v, \alpha) dv,$$

where the integrand is

$$\psi(v,\alpha) = \text{Re}[e^{-ivk}\hat{c}(v)] = \text{Re}\left[\frac{e^{-ivk}e^{-r\tau}\varphi(v-(\alpha+1)i)}{\alpha^2+\alpha-v^2+iv(2\alpha+1)}\right]. \tag{3.9}$$

Lord and Kahl (2007) argue that the optimal α^* is that which reduces the total variation of the integrand $\psi(v,\alpha)$ over the integration domain $[0,\infty)$. Under the assumption that $\psi(v,\alpha)$ is monotone in v on $[0,\infty)$, they show that the optimal α is given by

$$\alpha^* = \underset{\alpha_{\min}\leq\alpha\leq\alpha_{\max}}{\arg\min}\left[-\alpha k + \frac{1}{2}\ln\left(\psi(v,\alpha)^2\right)\right], \tag{3.10}$$

which they define as the function $\Psi(\alpha,k)$. Using the settings from the example in the previous section and running the optimization in Equation (3.10) produces $\alpha^* = 7.4781$. Note that this optimal value is within the range of admissible values $(\alpha_{\min},\alpha_{\max}) = (-3.2292, 9.0840)$ obtained in the previous section.

Numerical Implementation and Illustration

We continue to illustrate the bounds on α and the optimal α^* using the settings for the previous example, namely $S=1$, $r=0$, $K=1.2$, $\rho=-0.7$, $v_0=\theta=0.1$, $\kappa=\sigma=1$, and $\tau=1$. The following functions are in the Excel file Ch3LKAlpha.xls.

We saw earlier that this example produces $(y_-,y_+) = (-0.3851, 5.0910)$. This is accomplished with the FindY function.

```
Function FindY(sigma As Double, ...) As Variant
' Ymin and Ymax
ymax = (sigma - 2 * kappa * rho + Sqr(sigma ^ 2 ...
ymin = (sigma - 2 * kappa * rho - Sqr(sigma ^ 2 ...
If Num = 1 Then
    FindY = ymin
Else
    FindY = ymax
End If
End Function
```

Next, we use the NewtonLee function to find $A_X = (-2.2292, 10.0840)$.

```
Function NewtonLee(x0 As Double, ...) As Double
Do
    f = RogerLeeGexpD(x, kappa, rho, sigma, tau)
    df = (RogerLeeGexpD(x + dx) - RogerLeeGexpD(x - dx)) ...
    newx = x - f / df
    x = newx
    NumIter = NumIter + 1
```

```
Loop Until (NumIter >= MaxIters Or f < tol)
NewtonLee = x
End Function
```

The function RogerLeeGExpD defines an objective function that is required in the NewtonLee function.

```
Function RogerLeeGexpD(x As Double, ...) As Double
' Function to find g*exp(d) for Roger Lee bounds
E = cReal(gexpdtau)
' y = (E - 1)^2;
RogerLeeGexpD = (E - 1) ^ 2
End Function
```

Based on $A_X = (-2.2292, 10.0840)$, the range of admissible values for α is $(\alpha_{\min}, \alpha_{\max}) = (-3.2292, 9.0840)$. Finally, α^*, the optimal damping factor, is found using the Bisection function.

```
Function Bisection(a As Double, ...) As Double
' Bisection method for optimal alpha
Do While (NumIters < MaxIters Or (b - a) / 2 > tol)
    c = (a + b) / 2
    fc = dLordKahlFindAlpha(c, ...)
    fa = dLordKahlFindAlpha(a, ...)
    fb = dLordKahlFindAlpha(b, ...)
    If fc * fa > 0 Then
        a = c
    Else
        b = c
    End If
Loop
Bisection = c
End Function
```

This function returns $\alpha^* = 7.4781$ as the optimal damping factor. This example is illustrated in Figure 3.3, which is a screen shot of the Excel file Ch3LKAlpha.xls.

In Figure 3.4, we plot the optimal alpha function $\Psi(\alpha, k)$ and its derivative, and identify visually the local minima of $\Psi(\alpha, k)$.

The function $\Psi(\alpha, k)$ illustrated in Figure 3.4 has several local minima, as indicated by the dots. Lord and Kahl (2007) explain that since $\Psi(\alpha, k)$ explodes to infinity when $\alpha = -1$ or 0, which is reflected in Figure 3.4, $\Psi(\alpha, k)$ will have local minima in the intervals $(\alpha_{\min}, 0)$, $(-1, 0)$, and $(0, \alpha_{\max})$. Since our range of admissible values is $\alpha \in (-3.2292, 9.0840)$, we select $\alpha^* = 7.4781$. To ascertain whether this choice of

	A	B	C	D	E	F	G
1							
2		**Lord and Kahl Optimal Alpha for Carr-Madan**					
3					**Ymin and Ymax**		
4		**Option Features**			Ymin	-0.3851	
5		Spot (S)	1.00		Ymax	5.0910	
6		Strike (K)	1.20				
7		Maturity (τ)	1.00000				**Starting**
8		Risk Free Rate (r)	0.00000		**Range for Ax (y-, y+)**		**Values**
9		Dividend Yield (q)	0.00000		Yneg	-2.2292	-1.3851
10		Trap (0=Heston, 1=Albrecher)	1		Ypos	10.0840	10.0910
11		PutCall (C=Call, P=Put)	C				
12					**AlphaMin, AlphaMax**		
13		**Heston Parameters from S&P500 Estimation**			AlphaMin	-3.2292	
14		kappa (κ)	1.0000		AlphaMax	9.0840	
15		theta (θ)	0.1000				
16		sigma (σ)	1.0000		**Optimal Alpha**	**Starting Values**	
17		v0	0.1000		-2.9633	-3.0000	-2.0000
18		rho (ρ)	-0.7000		-0.3000	-0.4000	-0.3000
19		lambda	0.0000		7.4781	7.0000	8.0000
20							
21		**Integration Grid**					
22		Lower Limit	1.00E-15				
23		Upper Limit	200.00				
24		Number of abscissas	2000				
25							
26		**Settings for Bisection Method**					
27		Maximum iterations	1000				
28		Tolerance	1.00E-04				

FIGURE 3.3 Roger Lee Bounds and Optimal Damping Factor

α^* actually leads to a well-behaved integrand, in Figure 3.5 we plot the integrand in Equation (3.9) for three values of the damping factor, $\alpha = 3.25$, $\alpha = 9.25$, and the optimal value $\alpha^* = 7.4781$.

The graph indicates that the integrand with the optimal value of $\alpha^* = 7.4781$ behaves better than the other integrands, which have nonoptimal values of α, in the sense that the integrand with optimal alpha oscillates less, is flatter at the origin, and converges to zero at least as quickly as the others.

Lee (2004b) also suggests selecting the damping factor with a minimization procedure. In his approach, α is chosen by simultaneously minimizing two errors that occur when the integral in Equation (3.9) is evaluated numerically: truncation error, which arises because the upper limit of the numeric integral is finite, and sampling error, which arises because the integrand is only evaluated at the grid points of any numerical integration scheme. Readers are referred to his paper for details.

The Representation for Puts

We can always use put-call parity to find the value of the put, or we can apply a damping factor to the put price and find a representation for the put itself. Using results from Schmelzle (2010) and Carr and Madan (1999), the put price $P(k)$ is

$$P(k) = \frac{e^{-\alpha k}}{\pi} \int_0^\infty \text{Re}\left[e^{-ivk}\hat{p}(v)\right] dv, \tag{3.11}$$

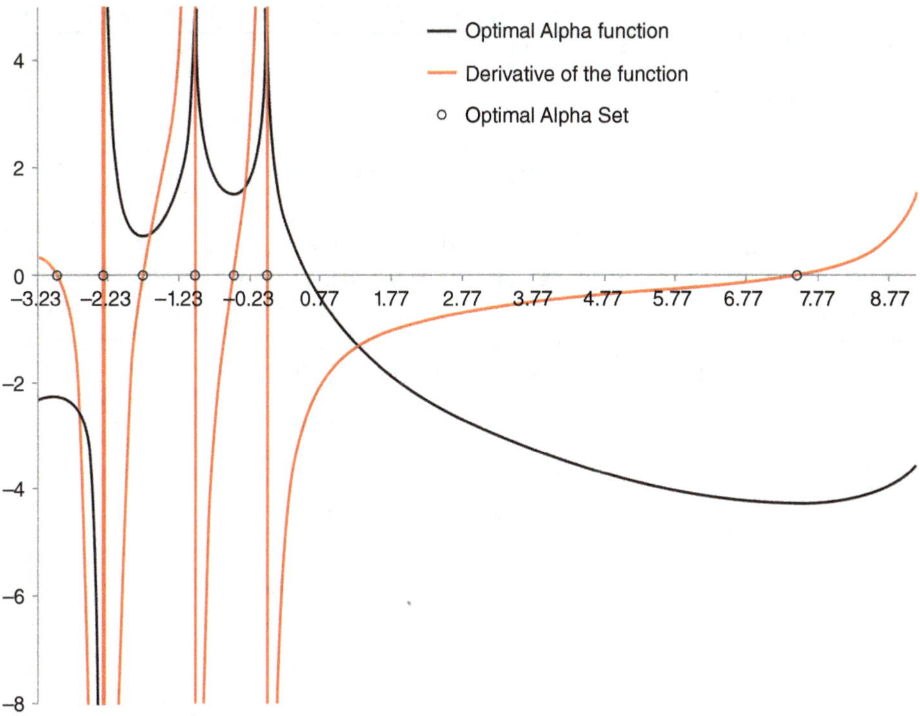

FIGURE 3.4 Lord and Kahl Optimal Alpha Function

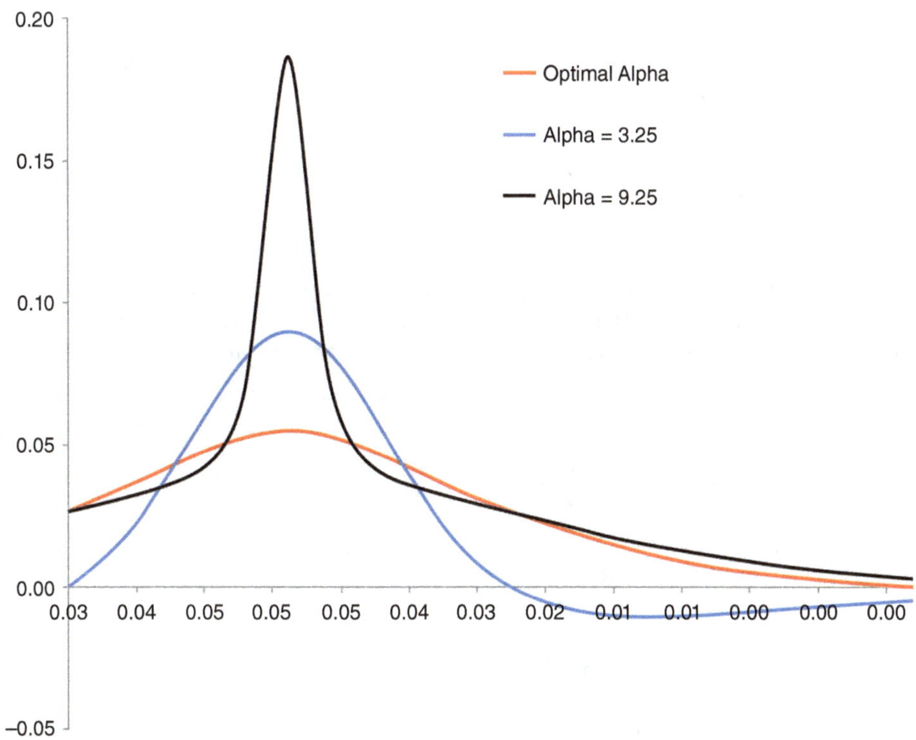

FIGURE 3.5 Carr-Madan Integrands

where the integrand is

$$\hat{p}(v) = \frac{e^{-r\tau}\varphi(v + (\alpha - 1)i)}{\alpha^2 - \alpha - v^2 + iv(1 - 2\alpha)}, \tag{3.12}$$

provided that the damping factor is such that $-\alpha + 1 < 0$, i.e., $\alpha > 1$. For details of the derivation, see Carr and Madan (1999), Schmelzle (2010), or Rouah (2013).

To implement the Carr and Madan (1999) representation for puts in VBA, we modify the CarrMadanIntegrand function presented earlier in this chapter to include a subroutine for puts. This function also can handle calls.

```
Function CarrMadanIntegrand(u As Double, ...) As Double
' The second num and the den depend on the option flavor
If PutCall = "C" Then
    ' Second numerator is the Heston cf
    Numerator2 = Complex(charfun(1, 1), charfun(2, 1))
    ' The Denominator (alpha^2 + alpha - u^2 ...
    Denominator = cAdd(cSub(cAdd(...), cu2), ...)
ElseIf PutCall = "P" Then
    ' Second numerator is the Heston cf
    Numerator2 = Complex(charfun(1, 1), charfun(2, 1))
    ' The Denominator (alpha^2 - alpha - u^2 ...
    Denominator = cAdd(cSub(cSub(...), cu2), ...)
End If
bigI = cDiv(cProd(Numerator1, Numerator2), Denominator)
CarrMadanIntegrand = cReal(bigI)
End Function
```

We also use a more general function for the Heston price, which can return the price of either a call or a put, using the Heston or Carr-Madan representation. In the VBA function HestonPriceGaussLaguerre, we use Gauss-Laguerre integration. The function uses put-call parity to return the put price under the Heston representation but uses Equation (3.11) to return the put price under the Carr and Madan (1999) representation.

```
Function HestonPriceGaussLaguerre(...) As Double
If Integrand = "Heston" Then
    For j = 1 To N
        intH1(j) = weight * HestonIntegrand(phi, ..., 1)
        intH2(j) = weight * HestonIntegrand(phi, ..., 2)
    Next j
    HestonPriceGaussLaguerre = ...
ElseIf Integrand = "CarrMadan" Then
    For j = 1 To N
        intCM(j) = weight * CarrMadanIntegrand(phi, ...)
```

```
        Next j
        HestonPriceGaussLaguerre = ...
    End If
    End Function
```

Using the same settings as the example presented earlier in this chapter, we obtain the put price as 5.9085 with the Heston form, and 5.9083 with the Carr-Madan form. The results are in the Excel file Ch3CMCallsPuts.xls.

The Representation for OTM Options

Carr and Madan (1999) emphasize the fact that, for very short maturities, the integrand in Equation (3.6) can be highly oscillatory and therefore difficult to integrate. This was illustrated with figures in Chapters 1 and 2. Carr and Madan (1999) define $z(k)$ to be the time-t price of the out-of-the-money (OTM) option with strike $K = e^k$: a call if $k > \ln(S_0)$ and a put if $k < \ln(S_0)$. For convenience, they assume that $S_t = 1$, but their argument can be easily generalized to other values of S_t, as shown in the following section. The price $z(k)$ of an OTM option with strike $K = e^k$ is shown to be

$$z(k) = \frac{1}{\pi}\int_0^{\infty} \text{Re}[e^{-ivk}\hat{z}(v)]dv, \tag{3.13}$$

where

$$\hat{z}(v) = e^{-r\tau}\left(\frac{1}{iv+1} - \frac{e^{r\tau}}{iv} + \frac{\varphi(v-i)}{v^2 - iv}\right), \tag{3.14}$$

and $\varphi(v) = E^{Q}(e^{ivx})$ with $x = \ln(S_T)$ is the Heston characteristic function.

Carr and Madan (1999) point out that the integrand $\hat{z}(v)$ can become highly oscillatory for short maturities and when $k \approx 0$. Instead of basing their derivation on $z(k)$, Carr and Madan suggest basing it on $y(k) = z(k)\sinh(\alpha k)$, which makes use of the dampening factor α, through the hyperbolic sin function $\sinh(x) = \frac{1}{2}(e^x - e^{-x})$. The OTM option price $z(k)$ is then

$$z(k) = \frac{1}{2\pi\sin(\alpha k)}\int_0^{\infty} \text{Re}[e^{-ivk}\hat{y}(v)]dv, \tag{3.15}$$

where

$$\hat{y}(v) = \frac{\hat{z}(v - i\alpha) - \hat{z}(v + i\alpha)}{2}. \tag{3.16}$$

For details of the derivation, see Carr and Madan (1999) or Rouah (2013).

The damped and regular integrands $\hat{y}(v)$ and $\hat{z}(v)$ are each illustrated in Figure 3.6, which reproduces the figure in Carr and Madan (1999). We use the settings $S_t = 1$, $K = 0.96$, maturities running from 1 to 4 weeks, $r = 0.03$, $\kappa = 2$, $\theta = 0.25$,

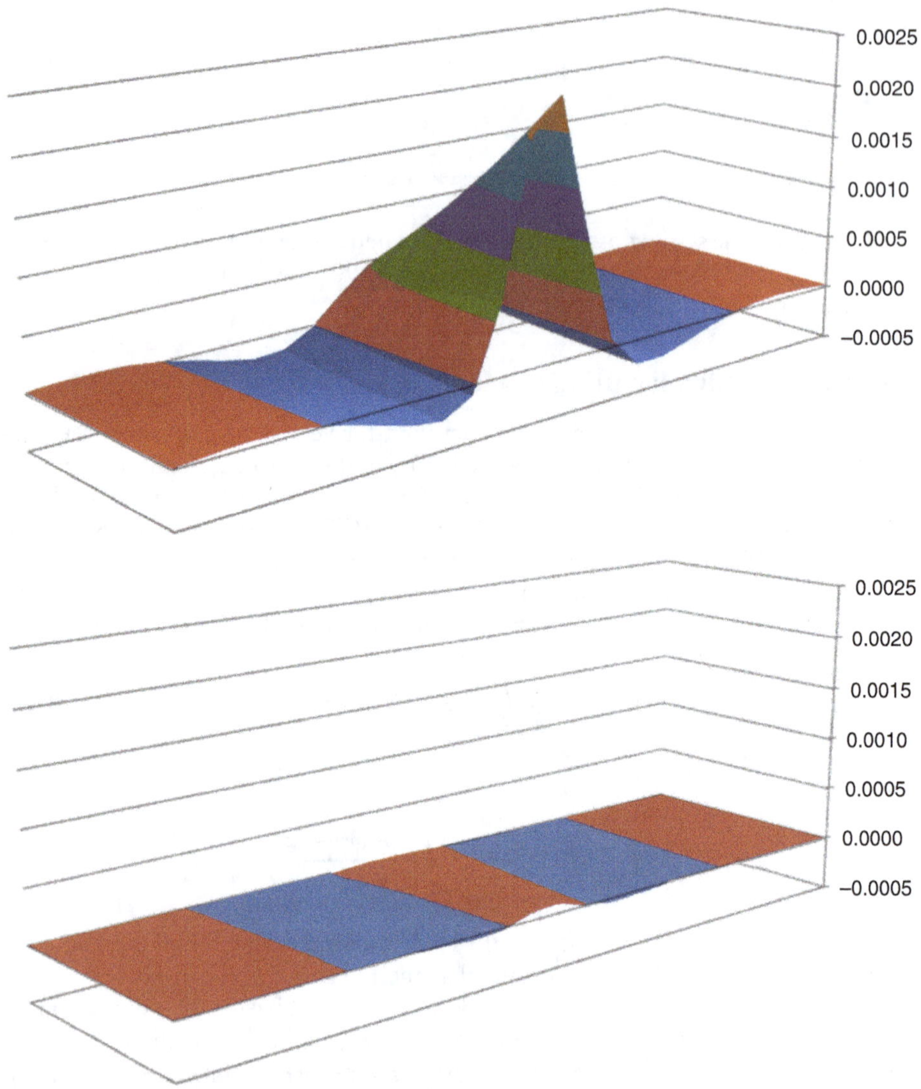

FIGURE 3.6 Carr-Madan Integrands for OTM Options

$\sigma = 0.3$, $v_0 = 0.05$ and $\rho = -0.8$, and $\alpha = 1.1$. The undamped integrand $\hat{z}(v)$ uses Equation (3.14), while the damped integrand uses Equation (3.17) defined in the next section.

The undamped integrand is in the top panel of Figure 3.6, and the damped integrand in the bottom panel. Clearly, adding a damping factor leads to an integrand that is much less oscillatory and on which it is much easier to apply a numerical integration scheme.

The undamped and damped prices of OTM options in Equations (3.13) and (3.15), respectively, are designed for $S_t = 1$ only. It is desirable to obtain these formulas for any value of $S_t > 0$. This is the subject of the following section.

Generalization of the OTM Representation

It is straightforward to generalize the OTM representation for any value of $S_t > 0$ because that involves only changing the limits in the required integrals. The required integrand is Equation (3.17) and represents a generalization of the integrand (3.14):

$$\hat{z}(v) = e^{-r\tau}\left(\frac{S_t^{iv+1}}{iv+1} - \frac{e^{r\tau}S_t^{iv+1}}{iv} - \frac{\varphi(v-i)}{v^2 - iv}\right). \tag{3.17}$$

To obtain the undamped version of the OTM option price $z(k)$ for general S_t, we substitute the integrand (3.17) into the pricing equation (3.13) and apply a numerical integration technique. To obtain the damped version, we substitute the integrand (3.17) into Equation (3.15) and integrate.

The following VBA function implements the undamped OTM Carr and Madan (1999) integrand in Equation (3.17).

```
Function CarrMadanIntegrandOTM(...) As Double
' The Heston characteristic function
charfun = HestonCF(u_i, params, ...)
' The first two numerators
Numerator1 = cExp(cProd(Complex(-Log(K), 0), ui))
Numerator2 = cExp(Complex(-r * tau, 0))
' The third numerator
Numerator3 = cSub(cSub(SpowDiv, exprS), t2)
' The integrand
bigI = cProd(cProd(Numerator1, Numerator2), ...)
' Return the real part
CarrMadanIntegrandOTM = cReal(bigI)
End Function
```

The next function implements the damped OTM in Equation (3.16).

```
Function CarrMadanDampedIntegrandOTM(...) As Double
charfun = HestonCF(u_i, params, ...)
' z2 = exp(-r*T)*(S^(i*u+1)/(1+i*u) ...
z2 = cProd(exprtaum, cSub(cSub(SpowDiv, exprS), t2))
' Calculate the Fourier transform
' y = exp(-i*u*log(K)) * (z1 - z2)/2;
y = cProd(explogK, z1z2)
' Return the real part only
CarrMadanDampedIntegrandOTM = cReal(y)
End Function
```

These functions are passed to the pricing function HestonPriceLaguerre, which in this version accepts the OTM integrand. As usual, only the most relevant portion of the function is presented here.

```
Function HestonPriceGaussLaguerre(...) As Double
If integrand = "Heston" Then For j = 1 To N
        intH1(j) = weight * HestonIntegrand(phi, ..., 1)
        intH2(j) = weight * HestonIntegrand(phi, ..., 2)
    Next j
    ' The Call price
    CallPrice = S * exp(-q * T) * P1 - K * exp(-r * T) ...
ElseIf integrand = "CarrMadan" Then
    For j = 1 To N
        intCM(j) = weight * CarrMadanIntegrandOTM(phi, ...)
    Next j
    ' The Option Price
    HestonPriceGaussLaguerre = Sum(intCM) / pi
ElseIf integrand = "CarrMadanDamped" Then
    For j = 1 To N
        intCMD(j) = weight * CarrMadanDampedIntegrandOTM(...)
    Next j
    ' The Option Price
    HestonPriceGaussLaguerre = 1 / Sinh(alpha * Log(K)) ...
End If
End Function
```

We illustrate the pricing of OTM options using a spot price of $S_t = 1$ and maturity $\tau = 1$ year, and using $r = 0.03$, $\kappa = 2$, $\theta = 0.25$, $\sigma = 0.3$, $v_0 = 0.05$, $\rho = -0.8$, and $\alpha = 1.1$. The strike prices are $K = 0.95$ for the puts and $K = 1.05$ for the calls. For a

Carr-Madan Prices of OTM Calls and Puts

Option Features	
Time to Maturity (τ)	1.0000
Risk free rate (r)	0.0300
Dividend (q)	0.0000
Heston and Carr-Madan Parameters	
kappa (κ)	2.0000
theta (θ)	0.2500
sigma (σ)	0.3000
v0	0.0500
rho (ρ)	-0.8000
lambda (λ)	0.0000
Trap (0=Heston, 1=Albrecher)	1
Sihn damping factor (α)	1.1000

Spot Price = 1

Method	**OTM put K = 0.95**	**OTM call K = 1.05**
Heston	0.1170	0.1485
Carr-Madan	0.1182	0.1470
CM OTM Damped	0.1105	0.1569

Spot Price = 25

Method	**OTM put K = 20**	**OTM call K = 30**
Heston OTM Put	1.4944	2.3819
CM OTM Put	1.5022	2.4009

FIGURE 3.7 OTM Pricing Using the Heston and Carr-Madan Methods

general spot price S_t, we use the same parameter and option settings except that we set $S_t = 25$ and change the strike prices to $K = 20$ and $K = 30$. This is accomplished with the following code. The results are in Figure 3.7. All integration is done using 32-point Gauss-Laguerre integration.

The VBA functions covered in this section, and the preceding example, are in the Excel file Ch3OTMCalls.xls.

CONCLUSION

In this chapter, we have presented the characteristic function of Gatheral (2006), and we have presented the Attari (2004) version of the Heston call price. We have also presented several formulations of the call price due to Carr-Madan (1999), along with optimal choices for, and bounds on, the damping factor. In Chapter 5, we present the fast Fourier transform (FFT) of Carr and Madan (1999), and the fractional FFT of Chourdakis (2005), both of which allow for a very fast calculation of a large set of option prices.

Fourier methods have been applied to option pricing by other authors. Among these, for example, are the cosine method of Fang and Oosterlee (2008), the convolution method of Lord et al. (2008), and the methods of Lewis (2000, 2001). The Lewis methods are the subject of the next chapter.

CHAPTER 4

The Fundamental Transform for Pricing Options

Abstract

In his excellent book, *Option Valuation Under Stochastic Volatility: With Mathematica Code*, Alan Lewis (2000) offers a powerful valuation approach that is applicable to a wide range of European options. We explain Lewis's fundamental transform approach for option valuation, and we also present his subsequent paper (Lewis, 2001) that uses Parseval's identity to obtain option prices. In that paper, simple variations in the contours of integrations give rise to different forms of the call price encountered in the literature. Finally, we present Lewis's (2000) volatility of volatility series expansion, an approximation that allows the Heston price of European options to be calculated very quickly and without the need for numerical integration.

fundamental transform, Fourier transform, generalized transform, payoff transform, Parseval's identity, contour variations, series expansion

In his excellent book, *Option Valuation Under Stochastic Volatility: With Mathematica Code*, Alan Lewis (2000) offers a powerful valuation approach that is applicable to a wide range of European options. His method requires that the fundamental transform, a generalization of the characteristic function that allows complex arguments, be available. It also requires the Fourier transform of the option payoff. Since payoff transforms are available for a wide set of options, however, Lewis's approach is readily applicable to path-independent European options of various sorts. The advantage of this approach over other approaches that use Fourier transforms is that, once the fundamental transform of a given model is obtained, it can be used repeatedly to price European options for which the payoff transform is known. This greatly simplifies pricing, since payoff transforms are much easier to obtain than the Fourier transform of the option price itself.

We explain Lewis's fundamental transform approach for option valuation, and we also present his subsequent paper (Lewis, 2001) that uses Parseval's identity to obtain option prices. In that paper, simple variations in the contours of integrations give rise to different forms of the call price encountered in the literature. Finally, we present Lewis's (2000) volatility of volatility series expansion, an approximation that allows the Heston price of European options to be calculated very quickly and without the need for numerical integration.

THE PAYOFF TRANSFORM

In the following sections, we present the fundamental transform approach of Lewis (2000) for pricing options. In his approach, the Fourier transform of the option value is not required, only the Fourier transform of the option payoff. This simplification allows for the pricing of a variety of options under a general setting. The approach, however, does require the fundamental transform. The Lewis (2000) recipe for pricing options thus requires two Fourier transforms:

- The payoff transform for a given option, which is model independent and does not depend on the fundamental transform.
- The fundamental transform for a given model, which is model dependent and analogous to the characteristic function.

The first element required for Lewis's (2000) fundamental transform approach to option valuation is the generalized Fourier transform $\hat{f}(k,t)$ of the derivative value $f(x,t)$ at time t,

$$\hat{f}(k,t) = \int_{-\infty}^{\infty} e^{ikx} f(x,t)dx, \tag{4.1}$$

where $x = \ln S_t$ since we are at time t. Equation (4.1) is identical to the Fourier transform, except that the argument k is allowed to be complex, so that $k = k_r + ik_i$, where k_r and k_i are real numbers. The generalized Fourier transform at expiry, $\hat{f}(x,T)$, is called the payoff transform.

For example, the payoff transform of a European call option is

$$\hat{f}(k,T) = -\frac{K^{ik+1}}{k^2 - ik}, \tag{4.2}$$

where the last equality holds provided that $k_i > 1$. In Equation (4.2), we now denote $t = T$ and $x = \ln S_T$, since we are at maturity. Payoff transforms for other options are in Table 2.2.1 of Lewis (2000).

To illustrate, in Figure 4.1, we reproduce Figure 4 of Schmelzle (2010) and plot the real portion payoff for the put, over the integration range $-1 < k_i < 0$ and $-4 < k_r < 0$. This figure is in the Excel file Ch4PutPayoff.xls.

Since $\hat{f}(k,t)$ in Equation (4.1) is the generalized Fourier transform, its inverse transform is

$$f(x,t) = \frac{1}{2\pi} \int_{ik_i-\infty}^{ik_i+\infty} e^{-ikx} \hat{f}(k,t)dk. \tag{4.3}$$

The generalized Fourier transform is slightly different from the regular Fourier transform, which assumes that k is real only. The generalized Fourier transform is obtained by integrating Equation (4.3) along the strip of regularity. For most derivative payoffs, this strip of regularity is defined as $\alpha < k_i < \beta$, as in Table 2.2.1 of Lewis

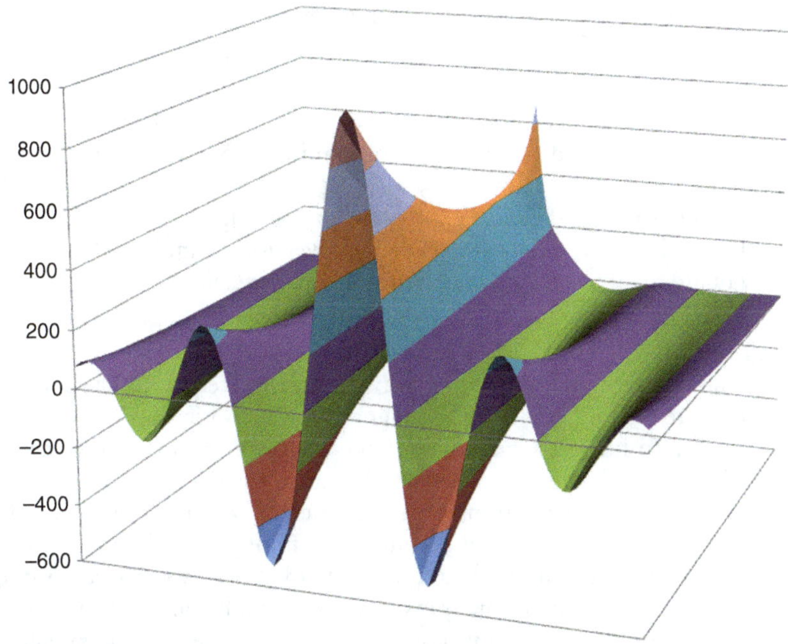

FIGURE 4.1 Real Part of the Put Payoff Transform

(2000). For the payoff of the European call, the strip is $k_i > 1$, and for the put it is $k_i < 0$.

The Fundamental Transform and the Option Price

The second element required for Lewis's (2000) fundamental transform approach is the fundamental transform itself. Lewis (2000) derives the fundamental transform for a general class of stochastic volatility models, but we restrict his derivation to the Heston model.

A solution $\hat{H}(k, v, \tau)$ to the partial differential equation (PDE) in Equation (4.4) that satisfies the initial condition $\hat{H}(k, v, 0) = 1$ is called a fundamental transform,

$$\frac{\partial \hat{H}}{\partial \tau} = \frac{1}{2}\sigma^2 v \frac{\partial^2 \hat{H}}{\partial v^2} + \left[\kappa(\theta - v) - \lambda v - ik\rho\sigma v\right] \frac{\partial \hat{H}}{\partial v} - vc(k)\hat{H}(k, v, \tau), \tag{4.4}$$

where $c(k) = \frac{1}{2}(k^2 - ik)$. Equation (4.4) is Equation (2.2.7) of Lewis (2000), but for the Heston model, Lewis explains that only the special case of a payoff of 1, namely, $\hat{H}(k, v, 0) = 1$, needs to be considered. All other payoffs can be handled by multiplying $\hat{H}(k, v, 0)$ by the appropriate payoff transform. The fundamental transform is called regular if it is regular in k within the strip $\alpha < k_i < \beta$, where $k_i = \text{Im}[k]$, the imaginary part of k. For details of the derivation as it applies to the Heston model, see Rouah (2013).

Once the fundamental transform has been found by solving Equation (4.4), Lewis's (2000) recipe to calculate option prices is straightforward. All that is required is that the payoff transform be known, such as that for the European call in (4.2), for example. The recipe is as follows:

- Multiply the fundamental transform $\hat{H}(k, v, \tau)$ by the payoff transform $\hat{f}(k, T)$. The payoff transform depends on the option under consideration, but the fundamental transform does not.
- Multiply the result by the term $\exp([-r - ik(r - q)]\tau)$.
- Pass the resulting expression through the inversion formula in Equation (4.3) and evaluate the integral, taking care to respect the strip of regularity.

Recall that, in the Carr and Madan (1999) approach, which was covered in Chapter 3, the Fourier transform of the derivative price is required. The consequence is that a separate Fourier transform is required for each type of option for which we need a price. To further aggravate matters, Fourier transforms of prices can be complicated. The advantage of the Lewis (2000) recipe is that once the fundamental transform is obtained, only the transform of the derivative payoffs is required. Since the fundamental transform is model dependent, but not payoff dependent, the same fundamental transform can be applied to value many different European options; all that is required is that their payoff transforms be available analytically. Moreover, since payoffs are specified in options contracts and therefore known explicitly, their Fourier transforms are much easier to obtain than the Fourier transforms of the option prices themselves.

In the next sections, we illustrate the Lewis recipe for a European call. First, we present the fundamental transform for the Heston model.

The Fundamental Transform for the Heston Model

From Equation (4.4), the PDE for $\hat{H}(k, v, \tau)$ using $\lambda = 0$ is

$$\frac{\partial \hat{H}}{\partial \tau} = \frac{1}{2}\sigma^2 v \frac{\partial^2 \hat{H}}{\partial v^2} + \left[\kappa(\theta - v) - ik\rho\sigma v\right] \frac{\partial \hat{H}}{\partial v} - c(k)v\hat{H}(k, v, \tau). \tag{4.5}$$

The fundamental transform for the Heston model is the solution to the PDE (4.5)

$$\hat{H}(k, v, \tau) = \exp\left(C(t) + D(t)v\right), \tag{4.6}$$

where

$$D(t) = \frac{\tilde{\kappa} + d}{2}\left(\frac{1 - e^{dt}}{1 - ge^{dt}}\right), \tag{4.7}$$

$$C(t) = \tilde{\kappa}\tilde{\theta}\left[\frac{\tilde{\kappa} + d}{2}t - \ln\left(\frac{1 - ge^{dt}}{1 - g}\right)\right], \tag{4.8}$$

$$\tilde{\kappa} = \frac{2(\kappa + ik\rho\sigma)}{\sigma^2}, \; \tilde{\theta} = \frac{\kappa\theta}{\kappa + ik\rho\sigma}, \; g = -K = (\tilde{\kappa} + d)/(\tilde{\kappa} - d),$$

and with $d = \sqrt{\tilde{\kappa} + 4\tilde{c}}$ and $\tilde{c}(k) = (k^2 - ik)/\sigma^2$. The initial condition at $t = 0$ implies that we set $v = v_0$, the parameter for the initial variance, in (4.6). See Lewis (2000) or Rouah (2013) for a detailed derivation.

The fundamental transform in (4.6) is identical to the characteristic function derived in Chapter 1, with the notation $C(t)$ and $D(t)$ denoting $C(\tau, \phi)$ and $D(\tau, \phi)$. Lewis (2000, Section 2.4) describes the conditions under which $\hat{H}(k, v, \tau)$ is an analytic characteristic function.

The fundamental transform in (4.6) is identical to the Heston characteristic function derived in Chapter 1, with the notation $C(t)$ and $D(t)$ denoting $C(\tau, \phi)$ and $D(\tau, \phi)$. Lewis (2000, Section 2.4) describes the conditions under which $\hat{H}(k, v, \tau)$ is an analytic characteristic function.

The Call Price Using the Fundamental Transform

Recall that the Lewis recipe requires a payoff transform for the option being priced. To apply the Lewis recipe to the European call price, we use the payoff transform obtained in Equation (4.2). Following the recipe, the integral for the call price $C_1(K)$ is

$$C_1(K) = \frac{1}{2\pi} \int_{ik_i-\infty}^{ik_i+\infty} e^{-ikx} \times e^{[-r-ik(r-q)]\tau} \times \hat{H}(k, v, \tau) \times \left(\frac{-K^{ik+1}}{k^2 - ik} \right) dk, \tag{4.9}$$

where $x = \ln S_t$. Defining $X = \ln(S_t/K) + (r-q)\tau$, the call price can be written in the form of Equation (2.2.8) in Lewis (2000), namely,

$$C_1(K) = -\frac{Ke^{-r\tau}}{2\pi} \int_{ik_i-\infty}^{ik_i+\infty} e^{-ikX} \frac{1}{k^2 - ik} \hat{H}(k, v, \tau) dk, \tag{4.10}$$

where the integral is defined for $1 < k_i < \beta$.

Lewis (2000) also finds an alternative solution to the call price in (4.10), based on put-call parity and a covered call. Applying the Lewis (2000) recipe to the covered call and using put-call parity, the second solution is

$$C_2(K) = S_t e^{-q\tau} - \frac{Ke^{-r\tau}}{2\pi} \int_{ik_i-\infty}^{ik_i+\infty} e^{-ikX} \frac{1}{k^2 - ik} \hat{H}(k, v, \tau) dk, \tag{4.11}$$

where $\max(0, \alpha) < k_i < \min(1, \beta)$. The value $C_2(K)$ is identical to $C_1(K)$ in (4.10) except for the presence of the term $S_t e^{-q\tau}$ and a different strip. Equation (4.11) is Equation (2.2.10) in Lewis (2000).

The integral for the call price $C_1(K)$ in (4.10) or for $C_2(K)$ in (4.11) can be simplified by noting that the integrand is also even in its real part, and odd in its imaginary part. Hence, the expressions for the call price can be written

$$C_1(K) = -\frac{Ke^{-r\tau}}{\pi} \int_0^{\infty} \text{Re} \left[e^{-ikX} \frac{1}{k^2 - ik} \hat{H}(k, v, \tau) \right] dk, \tag{4.12}$$

where $1 < k_i < \beta$, and

$$C_2(K) = S_t e^{-q\tau} - \frac{Ke^{-r\tau}}{\pi} \int_0^\infty \text{Re}\left[e^{-ikX} \frac{1}{k^2 - ik} \hat{H}(k, v, \tau) \right] dk, \tag{4.13}$$

where $\max(0, \alpha) < k_i < \min(1, \beta)$ and where $X = \ln(S_t/K) + (r - q)\tau$. The integrals in Equations (4.12) and (4.13) are identical, except that the expression for $C_2(K)$ includes the term $S_t e^{-q\tau}$, while that for $C_1(K)$ does not. Hence, it seems unintuitive that both would produce the same call value. Remember, however, that the integration strips are different. Indeed, in $C_2(K)$, we can take $k_i = 1/2$, but in $C_1(K)$ we must take $k_i > 1$. This difference means that the integrals will have different values; the net effect is that $C_1(K) = C_2(K)$.

When a numerical integration scheme is applied to the integrals in Equations (4.12) and (4.13), their upper limits are often truncated and replaced by a large number. Lewis uses the range $(0, k_{\max})$ where $k_{\max} = \max(1000, 10/\sqrt{v_0 \tau})$. We return to this issue in Chapter 5.

The VBA function LewisIntegrand implements the fundamental transform $\hat{H}(k, v, \tau)$ from Equation (4.6).

```
Function LewisIntegrand(k As cNum, ...) As Double
' Define the updated "tilde" parameters
kappa_ = cProd(Complex(2 / sigma ^ 2, 0), t1)
theta_ = cDiv(cProd(kappa_, Complex(theta, 0)), ...)
c = cDiv(cSub(k2, ik), Complex(sigma ^ 2, 0))
T = tau * sigma ^ 2 / 2
' Compute the required quantities
d = cSqr(cAdd(cPow(kappa_, 2), cProd(c, Complex(4, 0))))
alpha = cProd(cSub(d, kappa_), Complex(0.5, 0))
beta = cProd(cAdd(kappa_, d), Complex(-0.5, 0))
g = cDiv(beta, alpha)
' The functions B(t) and A(t)
bigD = cDiv(cProd(Num1, Num2), Den)
bigC = cProd(Term1, cSub(Term2, Term3))
' The fundamental transform, H(k,S,t)
bigH = cExp(cAdd(bigC, Dv0))
' Return the real part of the integrand.
LewisIntegrand = cReal(cDiv(cProd(expXik, bigH), Den))
End Function
```

This function is then passed to the function HestonLewisCallPrice, which calculates either $C_1(K)$ from (4.12) or $C_2(K)$ from (4.13). The function can use either the trapezoidal integration rule, or Gauss-Laguerre integration.

```
Function HestonLewisCallPrice(S As Double, ...) As Double
' Lewis Parameters
kmax = Floor(Max(1000, ...)
bigX = Log(S / Strike) + (r - q) * tau
If IntRule = 1 Then         ' Trapezoidal rule
    For j = 1 To Nphi
        u = cAdd(Complex(phi(j), 0), cProd(i, Complex(ki, 0)))
        inte(j) = wt(j) * LewisIntegrand(u, ...)
    Next j
    Integral = Sum(inte)
Else                        ' Gauss-Laguerre rule
    For j = 1 To Nx
        u = cAdd(Complex(phivar, 0), cProd(i, Complex(ki, 0)))
        inte(j) = weight * LewisIntegrand(u, ...)
    Next j
    Integral = Sum(inte)
End If
If form = 2 Then
    ' C2(S,K,t) Equation (2.10) page 41 of Lewis (2000)
    HestonLewisCallPrice = S * Exp(-q * tau) - (1 / pi) ...
Else
    ' C1(S,K,t) Equation (2.8) page 40 of Lewis (2000)
    HestonLewisCallPrice = -(1 / pi) * Strike ...
End If
End Function
```

We illustrate with call prices obtained using Lewis's (2000) recipe, using $S_t = K = 100$, $r = 0.05$, $q = 0.01$, and a maturity of 3 months, along with parameter values $\kappa = 2$, $\theta = v_0 = 0.05$, $\sigma = 0.1$, and $\rho = -0.9$. For the trapezoidal rule, we choose an upper limit of integration of 100 and 10,000 integration points. Gauss-Laguerre integration uses 32 points. The results are in Table 4.1 and indicate high agreement between the call prices $C_1(K)$ and $C_2(K)$ in Equations (4.12) and (4.13) respectively, and those of the original Heston (1993) formulation, regardless of the integration rule chosen.

The results in Table 4.1 and the VBA functions presented in this section are in the Excel file Ch4LewisFT.xls.

TABLE 4.1 Comparison of Call Prices

Call Price Formula	Integration Rule	Call Price
Original Heston Formulation	Gauss-Laguerre	4.9391
$C_1(K)$ in (4.12)	Trapezoidal	4.9323
$C_1(K)$ in (4.12)	Gauss-Laguerre	4.9346
$C_2(K)$ in (4.13)	Trapezoidal	4.9323
$C_2(K)$ in (4.13)	Gauss-Laguerre	4.9276

OPTION PRICES USING PARSEVAL'S IDENTITY

In a follow-up paper to his book, Lewis (2001) makes use of Parseval's identity to obtain option prices that are valid under any Lévy price process for which the characteristic function is known, including the Heston model. In this section, we describe and implement his approach. First, we present Parseval's identity for Fourier transforms.

Parseval's Identity and the Option Price

Parseval's identity for two functions f and g is

$$\int_{-\infty}^{\infty} f(x)\overline{g(x)}dx = \frac{1}{2\pi}\int_{-\infty}^{\infty} \hat{f}(k)\overline{\hat{g}(k)}dk,$$

where $\overline{g(x)}$ is the complex conjugate of $g(x)$. We can also write

$$\int_{-\infty}^{\infty} f(x)g(x)dx = \frac{1}{2\pi}\int_{-\infty}^{\infty} \hat{f}(k)\hat{g}(-k)dk. \tag{4.14}$$

The fact that $\hat{g}(-k)$ rather than $\hat{g}(k)$ appears in the integral on the right-hand side of (4.14) is a consequence of the convolution theorem for Fourier transforms. See, for example, Section 7.2.5 of Beerends et al. (2003).

If we need the generalized Fourier transform, which allows complex values for k so that $k = k_r + ik_i$, Parseval's identity in Equation (4.14) becomes

$$\int_{-\infty}^{\infty} f(x)g(x)dx = \frac{1}{2\pi}\int_{ik_i-\infty}^{ik_i+\infty} \hat{f}(k)\hat{g}(-k)dk. \tag{4.15}$$

Writing $x_t = \ln S_t$, the time-t value $f(x_t, t)$ of a derivative with payoff $w(x_T)$ can be written as

$$f(x_t, t) = \frac{e^{-r\tau}}{2\pi}\int_{-\infty}^{\infty} \hat{w}(k)\hat{q}(-k)dk,$$

where the last equality follows from Equation (4.14). Since $\hat{q}(k)$ is the Fourier transform of the density for $\ln S_T$, it is also the characteristic function, $\varphi(k)$. Hence, the derivative value can be expressed in terms of the characteristic function and the Fourier transform of the payoff. When k is a complex number, the option value, using Parseval's identity in Equation (4.15), is,

$$f(x_t, t) = \frac{e^{-r\tau}}{2\pi}\int_{ik_i-\infty}^{ik_i+\infty} \hat{w}(k)\hat{q}(-k)dk = \frac{e^{-r\tau}}{2\pi}\int_{ik_i-\infty}^{ik_i+\infty} \hat{w}(k)\varphi(-k)dk. \tag{4.16}$$

Parseval's Identity for the Heston Model

Lewis (2001) derives an option pricing formula under a general setup for the stock price. Suppose that the stock price S_T at time T evolves from S_0 at time $t = 0$ as

$$S_T = S_0 e^{(r-q)T+X_T}, \tag{4.17}$$

where T is the exercise time of the option, r is the risk-free rate, q is the dividend yield, and X_T is a Lévy process for which $E[e^{X_T}] = 1$. Under certain regularity conditions, the option price $U(S_0)$ at time $t = 0$ is

$$U(S_0) = \frac{e^{-rT}}{2\pi} \int_{ik_i-\infty}^{ik_i+\infty} e^{-ikY}\varphi(-k)\hat{w}(k)dk, \tag{4.18}$$

where $Y = \ln S_0 + (r-q)T$, $\hat{w}(k)$ is the Fourier transform of the payoff $w(x_T)$, and $\varphi(k)$ is the characteristic function of the Lévy process X_T evaluated at the complex number $k = k_r + ik_i$.

The valuation formula (4.18) is Equation (3.5) in Lewis (2001) and the main result of that paper. Lewis (2000) explains that it is applicable to a wide range of models, including the Variance Gamma model, the Heston model, and many others. All that is needed is the characteristic function and its strip of regularity. For details of the derivation leading to (4.18), see Lewis (2001) or Rouah (2013).

For the call option, the integral in Equation (4.18) is defined in the region $S_U^{Call} = -k : 1 < k_i < \beta$" corresponding to the intersection of the blue- and gray-shaded areas, as illustrated in Figure 4.2.

Lewis (2001) provides an alternate derivation using the complex form of Parseval's identity in (4.15). By an application of Parseval's identity we have

$$U(S_0) = \frac{e^{-rT}}{2\pi} \int_{ik_i-\infty}^{ik_i+\infty} e^{-ikY}\varphi(-k)\hat{w}(k)dk. \tag{4.19}$$

Substituting for payoff transforms $\hat{w}(x)$ produces valuation formulas corresponding to those payoffs. The call option has payoff transform $\hat{w}(x)$ given in Equation (4.2). Hence, the call price $C(S_0)$ is found by substituting for $\hat{w}(x)$ into (4.19)

$$C(S_0) = -\frac{Ke^{-rT}}{2\pi} \int_{ik_i-\infty}^{ik_i+\infty} e^{-ikW}\varphi(-k)\frac{1}{k^2 - ik}dk \tag{4.20}$$

for $1 < k_i < \beta$ and where $W = \ln(S_0/K) + (r-q)T$, which we denoted by X earlier in this chapter. Equation (4.20) is Equation (3.9) of Lewis (2001). Recall that the condition $k_i > 1$ must hold in order for the call option payoff transform to be defined (where $k_i = \text{Im}[k]$). Note the identical forms of the call price in Equation (4.20) and the call price $C_1(K)$ in (4.12), which shows that

$$\hat{H}(k, v, \tau) = \varphi(-k).$$

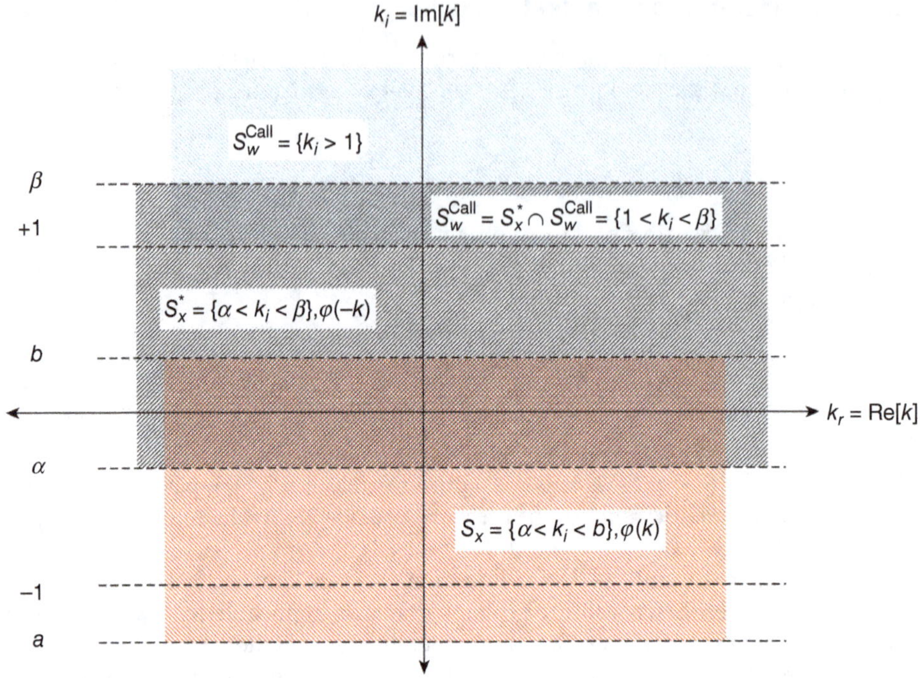

FIGURE 4.2 Integration Strip for the Call Option

Contour Variations and the Call Price

The residue of a complex-valued function $f(k)$ at a simple pole c is defined as

$$\text{Res}(c) = \lim_{k \to c} f(k)(k - c).$$

The residue theorem stipulates that a complex integral evaluated along a contour is equal to $2\pi i$ times the sum of the residues at all poles contained within the contour. This greatly simplifies the evaluation of a complex integral, since we only need to know the value of the residues at the poles.

To integrate Equation (4.20), we can select a contour composed of a horizontal line just above $k_i = 1$ but below β, and a semicircle above. Since there are no poles in this region, we do not apply the residue theorem and the call price $C(S_0)$ is obtained by direct integration. This is illustrated by the blue semicircle A in Figure 4.3. The poles are indicated by solid dots. The pole $k = 0$ lies at the origin, and the pole $k = i$ lies at the point $(k_r, k_i) = (0, 1)$.

Lewis (2001) shows how variations on the call price arise by modifying the contour. If we move the integration contour in Equation (4.20) down to another value $v_2 \in (0, 1)$, say, instead of at $\beta > 1$, then we include the pole at $k_i = 1$ in the integration contour, as illustrated by the red semicircle B in Figure 4.3. By the residue theorem, $C(S_0)$ will be equal to the integral evaluated along this new integration

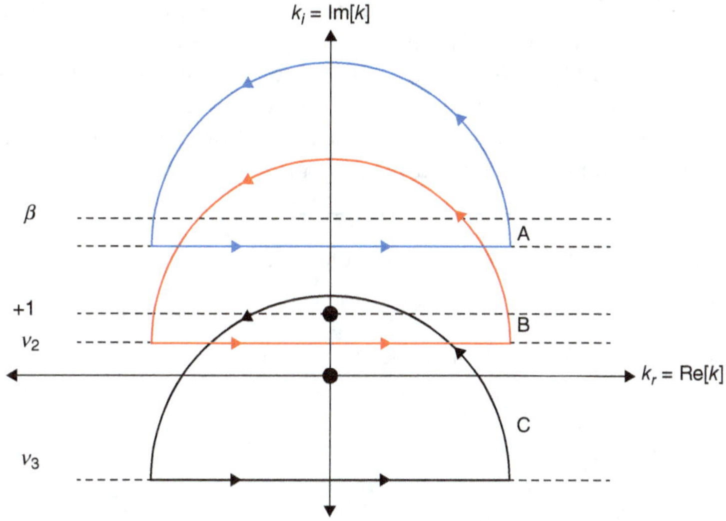

FIGURE 4.3 Contours of Integration

contour, minus $2\pi i$ times the residue at i, which has been excluded. Hence, Equation (4.20) becomes

$$C(S_0) = S_0 e^{-qT} - \frac{Ke^{-rT}}{2\pi} \int_{iv_2-\infty}^{iv_2+\infty} e^{-ikW} \varphi(-k) \frac{1}{k^2 - ik} dk \tag{4.21}$$

for $v_2 \in (0, 1)$. The second line of (4.21) is Equation (3.10) of Lewis (2001).

Finally, Lewis (2001) shows that if the integration contour is moved to $v_3 \in (\alpha, 0)$, with $\alpha < 0$, then both poles are included, as shown by the black semicircle C in Figure 4.3. Applying the residue theorem again, $C(S_0)$ will be equal to the integral along this new contour, minus $2\pi i$ times the sum of both residues. Denoting the value of the put by $P(S_0)$, Equation (4.20) becomes

$$C(S_0) = P(S_0) - 2\pi i \left(\frac{S_0 e^{-qT} i}{2\pi} - \frac{Ke^{-rT} i}{2\pi} \right) = P(S_0) + S_0 e^{-qT} - Ke^{-rT},$$

which is the price of the call by put-call parity.

If we choose $v_2 = \frac{1}{2}$ in Equation (4.20), then we are integrating along the line $k_i = \frac{1}{2}$ in between the two poles in Figure 4.3. Writing $k = u + \frac{1}{2}i$ so that $k^2 - ik = u^2 + \frac{1}{4}$, we can express (4.21) as

$$C(S_0) = S_0 e^{-qT} - \frac{\sqrt{KS_0} e^{-(r+q)T/2}}{\pi} \int_0^\infty \text{Re}\left[e^{iuW} \varphi\left(u - \tfrac{1}{2}i\right) \frac{1}{u^2 + \frac{1}{4}} \right] du. \tag{4.22}$$

Equation (4.22) is Equation (3.11) of Lewis (2001). See Itkin (2010) for a similar derivation, under the Variance Gamma model. An expression similar to (4.22) was derived by Lipton (2002) for foreign exchange options. For details of the derivations of the results of this section, see Lewis (2001) or Rouah (2013).

The following VBA functions implement the call price in Equation (4.22). The function LewisIntegrand311 calculates the integrand in (4.22).

```
Function LewisIntegrand311(u As cNum, ...) As Double
If trap = 1 Then
    ' "Little Heston Trap" formulation
    bigD = cProd(cDiv(Num1, Den1), Term1)
    bigG = cDiv(Num1, Den1)
    bigC = cAdd(Term1, Term2)
ElseIf trap = 0 Then
    ' Original Heston formulation.
    bigG = cDiv(Num1, Den1)
    bigC = cAdd(Term1, Term2)
    bigD = cProd(cDiv(Num1, Den1), Term1)
End If
' The Heston characteristic function f2 for ln S(T)
CFlnST = cExp(cAdd(cAdd(bigC, Dv0), iux))
' The cf for the Levy process XT
CFXT = cProd(expiuY, CFlnST)
' The integrand in Equation (3.11) of Lewis (2001)
u = cAdd(u, cProd(i, Complex(0.5, 0)))
expiuW = cExp(cProd(ui, Complex(w, 0)))
LewisIntegrand311 = cReal(cDiv(cProd(expiuW, CFXT), u214))
End Function
```

The function LewisPrice311 calculates the call price using the integration weights w and the abscissas x passed to the function. It is similar to the function HestonLewis-CallPrice defined earlier in this chapter, except that it passes the integration points $u_j = x_j - i/2$ to the integrand.

```
Function LewisPrice311(S As Double, ...) As Double
' Compute the integral.  Integration variable is complex.
For j = 1 To N
    u = cSub(Complex(x(j), 0), cProd(i, Complex(0.5, 0)))
    inte(j) = w(j) * LewisIntegrand311(u, ...)
Next j
Integral = Sum(inte)
' Equation (3.11) in Lewis (2011)
LewisPrice311 = S * Exp(-q * T) - (1 / pi) * Sqr(K * S)  ...
End Function
```

	A	B	C	D	E	F	G	H
1								
2		**Lewis (2001) and Heston (1993) Call Prices**			**Strike**	**Lewis Price**	**Heston Price**	**%Error**
3					95	7.9791	7.9835	0.0550
4		**Option Features**			96	7.3041	7.3085	0.0604
5		Spot Price (S)	100.0000		97	6.6611	6.6656	0.0669
6		Time to Maturity (τ)	0.2500		98	6.0514	6.0559	0.0746
7		Risk free rate (r)	0.0500		99	5.4756	5.4802	0.0837
8		Dividend (q)	0.0100		100	4.9344	4.9391	0.0945
9		PutCall (C or P)	C		101	4.4280	4.4327	0.1072
10		Trap (0=Heston,1=Albrecher)	1		102	3.9564	3.9613	0.1220
11					103	3.5195	3.5244	0.1392
12		**Heston Parameters**			104	3.1166	3.1216	0.1592
13		kappa (κ)	2.0000		105	2.7470	2.7521	0.1823
14		theta (θ)	0.0500					
15		sigma (σ)	0.1000					
16		v0	0.0500					
17		rho (ρ)	-0.9000					
18		lambda (λ)	0.0000					

FIGURE 4.4 Comparison of Call Prices

To illustrate, we use the same settings as those used to generate Table 4.1 to generate call prices using (4.22) for strikes ranging from $K = 95$ to $K = 105$. We use 32-point Gauss-Laguerre integration to obtain the call prices using the original Heston (1993) formulation and Equation (3.11) of Lewis (2001). The results in Figure 4.4 indicate high agreement between both sets of prices.

The screen shot in Figure 4.4 and the VBA functions presented in this section are in the Excel file Ch4Lewis311.xls.

VOLATILITY OF VOLATILITY SERIES EXPANSION

Lewis (2000) derives a volatility of volatility series expansion for the call price and for the implied volatility that are valid under a general class of stochastic volatility models. In this section, we present this expansion for the Heston model only. Obtaining the Heston call price using this method is very fast, because numerical integration is not required. The name is derived from the fact that both the series expansions are in terms of powers of the volatility of variance parameter, σ. The first series is based on an expansion about the Black-Scholes price evaluated at the average variance $\bar{v}$,

$$C_{BS}(S_0, \bar{v}, T) = S_0 e^{-qT}\Phi(d_1) - Ke^{-rT}\Phi(d_2), \tag{4.23}$$

where

$$d_1 = \frac{\log(S_0/K) + \left(r - q + \frac{\bar{v}}{2}\right)T}{\sqrt{\bar{v}T}},$$

and with $d_2 = d_1 - \sqrt{\bar{v}T}$. The quantity $\bar{v}$ denotes the average expected variance over $(0, T)$ of the CIR process that we first encountered in Chapter 2,

$$\bar{v} = (v_0 - \theta)\left(\frac{1 - e^{-\kappa T}}{\kappa T}\right) + \theta. \tag{4.24}$$

The average expected variance $\bar{v}$ is also the fair strike of a variance swap in the Heston model, as seen in Chapter 2. The first series expansion call price uses the derivative of the Black-Scholes call price with respect to the variance v, again evaluated at $\bar{v}$,

$$C_v(S_0, \bar{v}, T) = \left.\frac{\partial C_{BS}}{\partial v}\right|_{v=\bar{v}} = \sqrt{\frac{T}{8\pi\bar{v}}} S_0 e^{-qT} \exp\left(-\tfrac{1}{2}d_1^2\right). \tag{4.25}$$

Both expansions make use of the integrals J_1, J_3, and J_4, which in the Heston model take the following form, using $\varphi = \frac{1}{2}$ in Equations (3.3.7), (3.3.8), and (3.3.9) on page 86 of Lewis (2000).

$$J_1(v, T) = \frac{\rho}{\kappa}\left[\theta T + \left(1 - e^{-\kappa T}\right)\left(\frac{v}{\kappa} - \frac{2\theta}{\kappa}\right) - e^{-\kappa T}(v - \theta)T\right] \tag{4.26}$$

$$\begin{aligned} J_3(v, T) &= \frac{\theta}{2\kappa^2}\left[T + \frac{1}{2\kappa}\left(1 - e^{-2\kappa T}\right) - \frac{2}{\kappa}\left(1 - e^{-\kappa T}\right)\right] \\ &\quad + \frac{(v - \theta)}{2\kappa^2}\left[\frac{1}{\kappa}\left(1 - e^{-2\kappa T}\right) - 2Te^{-\kappa T}\right] \end{aligned} \tag{4.27}$$

$$\begin{aligned} J_4(v, T) &= \frac{\rho^2\theta}{\kappa^3}\left[T\left(1 + e^{-\kappa T}\right) - \frac{2}{\kappa}\left(1 - e^{-\kappa T}\right)\right] \\ &\quad - \frac{\rho^2}{2\kappa^2}T^2 e^{-\kappa T}(v - \theta) + \frac{\rho^2(v - \theta)}{\kappa^3}\left[\frac{1}{\kappa}\left(1 - e^{-\kappa T}\right) - Te^{-\kappa T}\right]. \end{aligned} \tag{4.28}$$

Finally, the following ratios of Black-Scholes derivatives are needed:

$$\begin{aligned} R^{1,2} &= \left[\frac{1}{2} - W\right], R^{1,2} = \left[W^2 - W - \frac{4 - Z}{Z}\right], R^{2,0} = T\left[\frac{W^2}{2} - \frac{1}{2Z} - \frac{1}{8}\right], \\ R^{2,2} &= T\left[\frac{W^4}{2} - \frac{W^3}{2} - \frac{3X^2}{Z^3} + \frac{X(12 + Z)}{8Z^3} + \frac{48 - Z^2}{32Z^2}\right]. \end{aligned} \tag{4.29}$$

Lewis (2000) defines $W = X/Z$, $X = \log(S_0/K) + (r - q)T$ as in the previous sections of this chapter, and $Z = \bar{v}T$. The first series expansion produces Heston call prices directly, while the second series produces an implied volatility that is then fed into the Black-Scholes model to produce the Heston call price. The first expansion (Series I) produces the call price $C_I(S_0, v_0, T)$ directly:

$$
\begin{aligned}
C_I(S_0, v_0, T) \approx\ & C_{BS}(S_0, \bar{v}, T) + \sigma\frac{J_1}{T}R^{1,1}C_v(S_0, \bar{v}, T) \\
& + \sigma^2 C_v(S_0, \bar{v}, T)\left[\frac{J_2}{T} + \frac{J_3 R^{2,0}}{T^2} + \frac{J_4 R^{1,2}}{T} + \frac{(J_1)^2 R^{2,2}}{2T^2}\right].
\end{aligned}
\tag{4.30}
$$

The second expansion (Series II) produces the implied volatility

$$
\begin{aligned}
v_{imp} \approx\ & \bar{v} + \sigma\frac{J_1}{T}R^{1,1} \\
& + \sigma^2\left[\frac{J_2}{T} + \frac{J_3 R^{2,0}}{T^2} + \frac{J_4 R^{1,2}}{T} + \frac{(J_1)^2}{2T^2}\left(R^{2,2} - \left(R^{1,1}\right)^2 R^{2,0}\right)\right],
\end{aligned}
\tag{4.31}
$$

which is then fed into the Black-Scholes call formula in (4.23) to produce $C_{II}(S_0, v_0, T)$, the Heston call price under Series II. In other words, we use (4.23) to obtain the call price, but we replace $\bar{v}$ with v_{imp}^2 from (4.31):

$$
C_{II}(S_0, v_0, T) = C_{BS}(S_0, v_{imp}^2, T). \tag{4.32}
$$

Finally, in the expressions for the call price in Equations (4.30) and (4.32) the integrals J_1, J_3, and J_4 are all evaluated at the initial variance v_0, so that v is replaced by Heston parameter v_0 everywhere in (4.26), (4.27), and (4.28). For details of the derivations leading to pricing equations in this section, see Lewis (2000) or Rouah (2013).

The formulas presented in this section are easy to implement in VBA. The functions $J_1(v, T)$ through $J_4(v, T)$ in Equations (4.26) through (4.28) reside in the function J.

```
Function J(rho As Double, ...) As Double
If Number = 1 Then
    J = (theta * T + (1 - Exp(-K * T)) * (v0 / K ...
    J = J * rho / K
ElseIf Number = 3 Then
    J = theta * T + theta / 2 / K * (1 - Exp(-2 ...
    J = J / 2 / K ^ 2
ElseIf Number = 4 Then
    J = theta / K * (T * (1 + Exp(-K * T)) - 2 ...
    J = J * rho ^ 2 / K
End If
End Function
```

The functions $R^{p,q}$ in Equation (4.29) are also implemented in a single VBA function, R.

```
Function R(p As Double, ...) As Double
If p = 2 And q = 0 Then
    R = T * (0.5 * (x / z) ^ 2 - 0.5 / z - 1 / 8)
ElseIf p = 1 And q = 1 Then
    R = -x / z + 0.5
ElseIf p = 1 And q = 2 Then
    R = (x / z) ^ 2 - x / z - 0.25 / z * (4 - z)
ElseIf p = 2 And q = 2 Then
    R = T * (0.5 * (x / z) ^ 4 - 0.5 * (x / z) ^ 3 ...
End If
End Function
```

The function SeriesICall returns the Series I call price in Equation (4.30). It uses functions for the Black-Scholes price in (4.23) and its variance derivative in (4.25).

```
Function SeriesICall(S As Double, ...) As Double
' The "J" integrals
J1 = J(..., 1)
J3 = J(..., 3)
J4 = J(..., 4)
' Time average of the deterministic volatility
v = theta + (v0 - theta) * (1 - Exp(-kappa * T)) ...
' X and Z required for the ratios of B-S derivatives
x = Log(S * Exp((rf - q) * T) / K)
z = v * T
' The ratios of Black Scholes derivatives
R20 = R(2, 0, ...)
R11 = R(1, 1, ...)
R12 = R(1, 2, ...)
R22 = R(2, 2, ...)
' Black Scholes call price evaluated at v
c = BSC(S, K, rf, q, v, T)
' Black Scholes vega evaluated at v
cv = BSV(S, K, rf, q, v, T)
' Series I volatility of volatility expansion for the i.v.
SeriesICall = c + sigma / T * J1 * R11 * cv + sigma ^ 2 ...
End Function
```

The function SeriesIICall returns the implied volatility in Equation (4.31) or the Series II call price in (4.32).

```
Function SeriesIICall(S As Double, ...) As Double
' The "J" integrals
J1 = J( ..., 1)
J3 = J( ..., 3)
J4 = J( ..., 4)
' Time average of the deterministic volatility
v = theta + (v0 - theta) * (1 - Exp(-kappa * T)) ...
' X and Z required for the ratios of B-S derivatives
x = Log(S * Exp((rf - q) * T) / K)
z = v * T
' The ratios of Black Scholes derivatives
R20 = R(2, 0, ...)
R11 = R(1, 1, ...)
R12 = R(1, 2, ...)
R22 = R(2, 2, ...)
' Series II volatility of volatility expansion for the i.v.
iv = v + sigma / T * J1 * R11 + sigma ^ 2 ...
' Series II call price
Price = BSC(S, K, rf, q, iv, T)
' Return the volatility
ivx = Sqr(iv)
' Output the call price or the volatility
If OutputType = 1 Then
    SeriesIICall = Price
Else
    SeriesIICall = ivx
End If
End Function
```

To illustrate, we calculate the prices of out-of-the money calls with 3 months to maturity, using $S_0 = 100$, $K = 105$, $r = 0.05$, $q = 0.01$. For the Heston parameters, we use $\kappa = 10$, $\theta = 0.07$, $v_0 = 0.06$, $\sigma = 0.9$, and $\rho = 0.9$. The average expected variance $\bar{v}$ from Equation (4.24) is $\bar{v} = 0.06633$, which when used in (4.23), produces $C_{BS}(S_0, \bar{v}, T) = 3.4843$ for the Black-Scholes price. The complete results are in Figure 4.5, which is a screen shot of the Excel file Ch4Expansion.xls.

The functions presented earlier in this section also reside in the Excel file Ch4Expansion.xls.

With the parameter values used in Table 3.3.1 of Lewis (2000), namely, $\rho = -0.5$, $v_0 = 0.0225$, $\kappa = 4$, $\theta = 0.09/4$, $\sigma = 0.1$, as well as $T = 0.25$ and $S = K = 100$, we obtain from (4.24) the average variance $\bar{v} = 0.0225$. The Excel file Ch4LewisTable reproduces the entries in Table 3.3.1 on page 81 of Lewis (2000), and Figure 3.3.1 on

	A	B	C	D	E	F
1						
2		**Lewis (2001) Volatility of Volatility Expansion**				
3		**for the Heston Call Price**			**Method**	**Price**
4					Black Scholes	3.4843
5		**Option Features**			Exact	3.6508
6		Spot Price (S)	100.0000		Series I	3.6522
7		Strike Price (K)	105.0000		Series II	3.6611
8		Time to Maturity (τ)	0.2500			
9		Risk free rate (r)	0.0500		**Volatilities and Variances**	
10		Dividend (q)	0.0100		Deterministic Volatility	0.25754
11		PutCall (C or P)	C		Series II Implied Volatility	0.26667
12		Trap (0=Heston, 1=Albrecher)	1		Series II Implied Variance	0.07111
13						
14		**Heston Parameters**			**Trapezoidal Rule Integration Grid**	
15		kappa (κ)	10.0000		Lower Limit	1.00E-10
16		theta (θ)	0.0700		Upper Limit	300.00
17		sigma (σ)	0.9000		Number of abscissas	500
18		v0	0.0600			
19		rho (ρ)	0.9000		**Time Average of the**	
20		lambda (λ)	0.0000		**Deterministic Variance**	0.0663

FIGURE 4.5 Call Prices Using the Volatility Expansion

page 80. His figure is reproduced in Figure 4.6, along with the additional maturity of 18 months.

As indicated in Lewis (2000), for the 3-month maturity, the Series II expansion implied volatility (green line with crosses) is more accurate than the Series I expansion implied volatility (red line with crosses), since it is closer to the implied volatility extracted from the exact price (solid black line). For the 18-month maturity, however, both series are accurate.

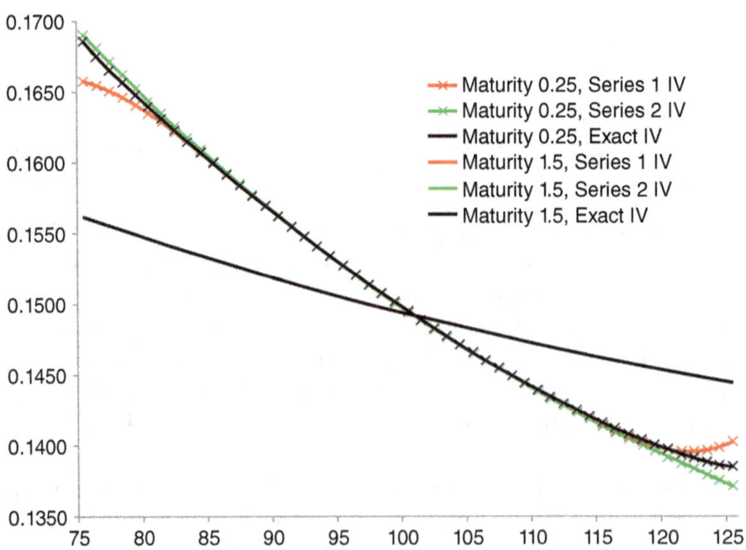

FIGURE 4.6 Reproduction of Figure 3.3.1. of Lewis (2000)

CONCLUSION

In this chapter, we have presented several powerful and novel approaches developed by Alan Lewis (2000, 2001) for pricing options under stochastic volatility. The fundamental transform is extremely convenient because once the fundamental transform for a given stochastic volatility model is obtained, European option prices under the model are readily obtained via their payoff transform. Moreover, in Lewis (2000), the fundamental transform is available for a wide range of models, and not restricted to the Heston model. We also examine the approach of Lewis (2001) for pricing options using Parseval's identity. Finally, we present the volatility of volatility series expansion of Lewis (2000), which approximates the Heston (1993) call price with a sum of analytic terms. The chief advantage of this expansion is that numerical integration is not required, so option prices can be calculated very quickly.

Most models encountered in this book, however, do require numerical integration. This poses challenges along several fronts, among which the integration domain $[0, \infty)$ must often be reduced to a more manageable domain and possible extreme oscillations in the integrand. A desirable numerical integration scheme is one that both overcomes these difficulties and requires little computational time. This is the subject of the next chapter.

CHAPTER 5

Numerical Integration Schemes

Abstract

In this chapter, we present Newton-Cotes formulas and Gaussian quadrature, and we also show how they can be used to approximate double integrals. The probabilities P_j in the Heston (1993) model require the integration domain $(0, \infty)$ so that $a = 0$ and $b = \infty$ are required as the limits of the integral in the equation. When we use Newton-Cotes formulas, however, we must truncate the upper limit. Here we show how this can be done sensibly using multidomain integration described by Zhu (2010). Alternatively, Kahl and Jäckel (2005) transform the domain of integration to $[0, 1]$, which eliminates the need for truncation altogether. Finally, in the last two sections, we present the fast Fourier transform (FFT) pioneered by Carr and Madan (1999) and the fractional FFT of Chourdakis (2005), a refinement to the FFT that is more flexible than its predecessor. Both of these methods are very fast because they are able to produce a set of option prices along a grid of strikes in a single calculation.

integration domain, numerical integration, midpoint rule, trapezoidal rule, Simpson's rule, Simpson's three-eighths rule, double integral, Newton-Cotes, Gaussian quadrature, Gauss-Laguerre, Gauss-Legendre, Gauss-Lobatto, integration limits, multidomain integration, Kahl-Jäckel transformation, fast Fourier transform, fractional fast Fourier transform

The calculation of the call price in the Heston model often requires the evaluation of an integral. This is true for most of the formulations of the call price we have encountered: Heston (1993), Lewis (2000, 2001), Carr and Madan (1999), and Attari (2004). Integration usually involves finding the antiderivative of the integrand, and applying the Fundamental Theorem of Calculus, according to which the value of the integral can be expressed in terms of the antiderivative evaluated at the endpoints of the integration domain. Unfortunately, in the Heston model, the antiderivative of the integrals for the probabilities cannot be found and the integrals must be approximated numerically.

Quadratures approximate an integral on $[a, b]$ as the sum of functional values evaluated at discrete points along the integration domain, and multiplied by a weight:

$$\int_a^b f(x)dx \approx \sum_{j=1}^{N} w_j f(x_j). \tag{5.1}$$

The points $(x_1, \ldots, x_N)$ are called nodes, points, or abscissas, and the points $(w_1, \ldots, w_N)$ are called weights or coefficients. In this chapter, we present two general classes of quadrature: Newton-Cotes formulas and Gaussian quadrature. Newton-Cotes formulas are easy to implement, but they assume equally spaced abscissas. This means that many abscissas are required in order for the approximation in Equation (5.1) to be accurate, especially if there are regions in the integration range where the function is steep or highly oscillatory. The consequence is that the computing time required to evaluate the sum in (5.1) can be dramatically increased. Gaussian quadrature requires far fewer abscissas, sometimes as little as 10, but they are more difficult to understand, and the abscissas and weights are not easy to obtain. Once these are obtained, however, they can be stored and used when needed. In this chapter, we present Newton-Cotes formulas and Gaussian quadrature, and we also show how they can be used to approximate double integrals.

The probabilities P_j in the Heston (1993) model require the integration domain $(0, \infty)$ so that $a = 0$ and $b = \infty$ are required as the limits of the integral in (5.1). When we use Newton-Cotes formulas, however, we must truncate the upper limit. This chapter shows how this can be done sensibly using multidomain integration described by Zhu (2010). Alternatively, Kahl and Jäckel (2005) transform the domain of integration to $[0, 1]$, which eliminates the need for truncation altogether. Finally, in the last two sections of this chapter, we present the fast Fourier transform (FFT) pioneered by Carr and Madan (1999) and the fractional FFT of Chourdakis (2005), a refinement to the FFT that is more flexible than its predecessor. Both of these methods are very fast because they are able to produce a set of option prices along a grid of strikes in a single calculation.

THE INTEGRAND IN NUMERICAL INTEGRATION

The literature on numerical integration method is rich and extensive, and there are many excellent textbooks on the subject, such as those by Burden and Faires (2010) and Cohen (2011).

In (5.1), the abscissas are denoted as x_j, but in the formulas for the integrals of the Heston model, the integration variable is denoted as ϕ, so the abscissas should be denoted as ϕ_j. The form of the integrand depends on which formula we are using to obtain the Heston call price. If we are using the original Heston (1993) formulation, the integrand in (5.1) for P_j is

$$f(\phi_j) = \text{Re}\left[\frac{e^{-i\phi_j \ln K} f_k(\phi_j; x, v)}{i\phi_j}\right] \quad \text{for } k = 1, 2. \tag{5.2}$$

If we are using the fundamental transform of Lewis (2000) covered in Chapter 4, the integrand is

$$f(\phi_j) = \text{Re}\left[e^{-i\phi_j X} \frac{1}{\phi_j^2 - i\phi_j} \hat{H}(\phi_j, v, \tau)\right]. \tag{5.3}$$

Finally, if we apply the Carr and Madan (1999) formulation covered in Chapter 3, the integrand in (5.1) becomes

$$f(\phi_j) = \text{Re}\left[e^{-i\phi_j \ln K}\psi(\phi_j)\right], \tag{5.4}$$

where

$$\psi(\phi_j) = \frac{e^{-rT} f_2(\phi_j - (\alpha+1)i; x, v)}{\alpha^2 + \alpha - \phi_j^2 + i(2\alpha+1)\phi_j}$$

and where f_2 is the characteristic function of the Heston model.

NEWTON-COTES FORMULAS

Newton-Cotes are the simplest integration rules, but also the ones that require the most computing power. Closed Newton-Cotes formulas partition the domain of integration $[a, b]$ into equally spaced subintervals using the abscissas $x_1, x_2, \ldots, x_N$. The definition of the abscissas depends on the formula being used. We consider four types of Newton-Cotes formulas: the midpoint rule, the trapezoidal rule, Simpson's rule, and Simpson's three-eighths rule. We consider the closed version of these rules only, so called because the endpoints a and b are used as abscissas.

In the Heston model, we usually require an integral evaluated over the integration domain $(0, \infty)$. This means that, when we apply Newton-Cotes formulas, we must select the domain as $[\phi_{\min}, \phi_{\max}]$, where $\phi_{\min}$ is a small number and $\phi_{\max}$ is a large number. We saw in Chapter 1 that the Heston integrand can sometimes be highly oscillatory. Hence, when we select $\phi_{\max}$, we must ensure that it is large enough so that the integrand is sufficiently damped to not cause a loss of accuracy in the approximation (5.1). Since the Heston integrand is not defined at $\phi = 0$, instead we use $\phi_{\min}$ as the lower limit of the integration domain.

One exception to the requirement of the integration domain $(0, \infty)$ is due to Kahl and Jäckel (2005). They transform the domain $(0, \infty)$ to the closed interval $[0, 1]$. Hence, in their approach, we need not worry about choosing $\phi_{\min}$ or $\phi_{\max}$. We will see in this chapter that their transformation is particularly well suited to Gauss-Lobatto quadrature, rather than Newton-Cotes formulas.

Midpoint Rule

This is the simplest of the Newton-Cotes formulas we present. It approximates the integral in Equation (5.1) as the sum of rectangles, each with equal width $x_{j+1} - x_j$, and with height given by the integrand $f(x)$ evaluated at the midpoint of the interval (x_j, x_{j+1}). Define the abscissas $x_j = a + (j-1)h$ for $j = 1, \ldots, N$, where $h = (b-a)/(N-1)$ so that $x_1 = a$ and $x_N = b$. The midpoint approximation to (5.1) involves $N - 1$ terms:

$$\int_a^b f(x)dx \approx h \sum_{j=1}^{N-1} f\left(\frac{x_j + x_{j+1}}{2}\right).$$

The midpoint rule formula thus uses the weights $w_j = h$ for $j = 1, \ldots, N-1$ and $w_N = 0$. The following code implements the midpoint rule in VBA. It is taken from the VBA function HestonPriceNewtonCotes.

```
' Increment and weights
h = (b - a) / (N - 1)
phi(1) = a
For j = 2 To N
    phi(j) = phi(j - 1) + h
Next j
' Integrand
For j = 1 To N - 1
    mid = (phi(j) + phi(j + 1)) / 2
    int1(j) = wt(j) * HestonProb(mid, ..., 1, trap)
    int2(j) = wt(j) * HestonProb(mid, ..., 2, trap)
Next j
```

Trapezoidal Rule

This rule is only slightly more complicated as it approximates the integral in Equation (5.1) as the sum of trapezoids, each with equal width $x_{j+1} - x_j$, but with height defined by the value of $f(x)$ at each of the endpoints. The trapezoidal rule approximation to (5.1) is

$$\int_a^b f(x)dx \approx \frac{h}{2}f(x_1) + h\sum_{j=2}^{N-1} f(x_j) + \frac{h}{2}f(x_N).$$

The VBA code for implementing the trapezoidal rule is straightforward also. It appears in the VBA function HestonPriceNewtonCotes.

```
' Increment and weights
wt(1) = h / 2
wt(N) = h / 2
For j = 2 To N - 1
   wt(j) = h
Next j
' Integrand
For j = 1 To N
    int1(j) = wt(j) * HestonProb(phi(j), ..., 1, trap)
    int2(j) = wt(j) * HestonProb(phi(j), ..., 2, trap)
Next j
```

These functions are in the Excel file Ch5NewtonCotes.xls.

Trapezoidal Rule for Double Integrals

In Chapter 8, we will encounter the model of Chiarella and Ziogas (2006), which requires a routine for the numerical evaluation of a double integral. One of the simplest methods for double integration is the composite trapezoidal rule described by Burden and Faires (2010). Suppose we wish to evaluate a double integral on the domain $[a, b] \times [c, d]$. The composite trapezoidal rule approximates the integral as

$$\int_a^b \left(\int_c^d f(x, y)dy \right) dx \approx \frac{(b-a)(d-c)}{16}$$
$$\times \left[f(a, c) + f(a, d) + f(b, c) + f(b, d) \right.$$
$$+ 2\left(f\left(\tfrac{a+b}{2}, c\right) + f\left(\tfrac{a+b}{2}, d\right) + f\left(a, \tfrac{c+d}{2}\right) + f\left(b, \tfrac{c+d}{2}\right) \right)$$
$$\left. + \, 4f\left(\tfrac{a+b}{2}, \tfrac{c+d}{2}\right) \right]. \tag{5.5}$$

The VBA function DoubleTrapz implements the composite trapezoidal rule, in accordance with Equation (5.5).

```
Function DoubleTrapz(f As String, ...) As Double
' Create X and Y vectors
dx = (zx - zlo) / (N - 1)
dy = (zy - zlo) / (N - 1)
X(1) = zlo
y(1) = zlo
For i = 2 To N
    X(i) = X(i - 1) + dx
    y(i) = y(i - 1) + dy
Next i
' Double integrand
For j = 2 To N
    a = y(j - 1)
    b = y(j)
    For i = 2 To N
        c = X(i - 1)
        d = X(i)
        term1 = Run(f, a, c) + Run(f, a, d) + Run(f, b, c) + ...
        term2 = Run(f, (a + b) / 2, c) + Run(f, (a + b) / 2, d) + ...
        term3 = Run(f, (a + b) / 2, (c + d) / 2)
        Sum = Sum + (b - a) * (d - c) / 16 * (term1 + 2 * term2 + ...
    Next i
Next j
DoubleTrapz = Sum
End Function
```

To illustrate, the DoubleTrapz function returns the value 0.18075 for the value of the standard normal bivariate distribution function at the point $(x, y) = (-0.515, 0.243)$, which is very close to the true value. These results, along with the DoubleTrapz function, are in the Excel file Ch5DoubleIntegration.xls.

Simpson's Rule

Simpson's rule is more complicated than either the midpoint rule or the trapezoidal rule, since it uses quadratic polynomials in the approximation (5.1), rather than straight lines. As such, however, it is much more accurate. Simpson's rule uses the same abscissas as the midpoint and trapezoidal rules, but defines the weights as $w_1 = w_N = h/3$, along with $w_j = 4h/3$ when j is even, and $w_j = 2h/3$ when j is odd. Hence, we can represent the approximation (5.1) as

$$\int_a^b f(x)dx \approx \frac{h}{3}f(x_1) + \frac{4h}{3}\sum_{j=1}^{N/2-1} f(x_{2j}) + \frac{2h}{3}\sum_{j=1}^{N/2} f(x_{2j-1}) + \frac{h}{3}f(x_N).$$

Implementing Simpson's rule in VBA is no more complicated than implementing the midpoint or trapezoidal rule. We only need to be careful of the alternating nature of the weights that depend on whether j is even or odd. The following code, taken from the VBA function HestonPriceNewtonCotes, is used to implement this rule.

```
' Increment and weights
wt(1) = h / 3
wt(N) = h / 3
For j = 2 To N - 1
    wt(j) = (3 + (-1) ^ j) * h / 3
Next j
' Integrand
For j = 1 To N
    int1(j) = wt(j) * HestonProb(phi(j), ..., 1, trap)
    int2(j) = wt(j) * HestonProb(phi(j), ..., 2, trap)
Next j
```

Simpson's Three-Eighths Rule

Simpson's three-eighths rule is a refinement to Simpson's rule. It uses cubic polynomials in the approximation (5.1), rather than quadratic polynomials. To implement Simpson's three-eighths rule, it is more convenient to start the abscissas at x_0 and define them as $x_j = a + ih$ for $i = 0, \ldots, N$ where N is a number divisible by three and with $h = (b - a)/N$. The weights w_j for Simpson's three-eighths rule depend on whether j is divisible by three:

$$w_j = \begin{cases} 3h/8 & \text{if } j = 0 \text{ or } j = N \\ 6h/8 & \text{if } j = 3, 6, 9, \cdots \\ 9h/8 & \text{otherwise.} \end{cases}$$

For example, with $N = 12$, the weights are

j	0	1	2	3	4	5	6	7	8	9	10	11	12
w_j	$\frac{3h}{8}$	$\frac{9h}{8}$	$\frac{9h}{8}$	$\frac{6h}{8}$	$\frac{9h}{8}$	$\frac{9h}{8}$	$\frac{6h}{8}$	$\frac{9h}{8}$	$\frac{9h}{8}$	$\frac{6h}{8}$	$\frac{9h}{8}$	$\frac{9h}{8}$	$\frac{3h}{8}$.

Simpson's three-eighths rule is, therefore,

$$\int_a^b f(x)dx \approx \frac{3h}{8}f(x_0) + \frac{6h}{8}\sum_{j=3,6,9,\cdots}^{N-3} f(x_j) + \frac{9h}{8}\sum_{j\neq 3,6,9,\cdots}^{N-1} f(x_j) + \frac{3h}{8}f(x_N).$$

The following snippet of code implements Simpson's three-eighths rule. It is taken from the VBA function HestonPriceNewtonCotes.

```
' Ensure that N-1 is divisible by 3
N = N - N Mod 3 + 1
' Build the new grid
h = (b - a) / (N - 1)
phi(1) = a
For j = 2 To N
    phi(j) = phi(j - 1) + h
Next j
' The weights
wt(1) = 3 / 8 * h
wt(N) = 3 / 8 * h
For j = 2 To N
    If (j - 1) Mod 3 = 0 Then
        wt(j) = 6 / 8 * h
        Else
            wt(j) = 9 / 8 * h
        End If
Next j
' Integrand
For j = 1 To N
    int1(j) = wt(j) * HestonProb(phi(j), ..., 1, trap)
    int2(j) = wt(j) * HestonProb(phi(j), ..., 2, trap)
Next j
End If
```

Heston Price Comparisons of Newton-Cotes Formulas

Option Features	
Spot Price (S)	100.0000
Time to Maturity (τ)	0.2500
Risk free rate (r)	0.0300
Dividend (q)	0.0200
Heston Parameters	
kappa (κ)	0.2000
theta (θ)	0.2500
sigma (σ)	0.3000
v0	0.0200
rho (ρ)	-0.8000
lambda (λ)	0.0000
Trap (0=Heston, 1=Albrecher)	1
Settings for Newton-Cotes	
Lower Integration Limit	1.00E-06
Upper Integration Limit	250
Number of points (abscissas)	1000
Method	
1 = Mid-point Rule	
2 = Trapezoidal Rule	
3 = Simpson's Rule	
4 = Simpson's 3/8 Rule	

Call Prices Using 1000 Integration Points

	Method			
Strike	Mid-Point	Trapezoidal	Simpson's	Simpson's 3/8
80	20.1655	20.1655	20.1655	20.1655
90	10.7276	10.7276	10.7276	10.7276
100	3.2039	3.2039	3.2039	3.2039
110	0.1685	0.1685	0.1685	0.1685
120	0.0007	0.0007	0.0007	0.0007

Put Prices Using 1000 Integration Points

	Method			
Strike	Mid-Point	Trapezoidal	Simpson's	Simpson's 3/8
80	0.0665	0.0665	0.0665	0.0665
90	0.5539	0.5539	0.5539	0.5539
100	2.9555	2.9555	2.9555	2.9555
110	9.8453	9.8453	9.8453	9.8453
120	19.6028	19.6028	19.6028	19.6028

FIGURE 5.1 Heston Prices Using Newton-Cotes Rules

To implement this rule in VBA, we need to ensure that $N - 1$ is divisible by three. The first part of the code ensures that this holds.

Figure 5.1 provides examples of the Newton-Cotes rules for pricing Heston calls and puts. The figure is taken from the Excel file Ch5NewtonCotes.xls.

GAUSSIAN QUADRATURE

In Newton-Cotes formulas, the abscissas are fixed and usually spaced equally. Gaussian quadrature uses unequally spaced abscissas and weights that can easily be computed in VBA. Gaussian quadrature requires far fewer abscissas than the Newton-Cotes formulas. Moreover, since the abscissas are specified for us in advance, we need not worry about selecting the upper and lower limits ϕ_{min} and ϕ_{max} for the integration range $(0, \infty)$.

Gaussian quadrature approximates the integral over the range $[a, b]$ by the weighted sum of the integrand evaluated at the abscissas, as in Equation (5.1), reproduced here for convenience:

$$\int_a^b f(x)dx \approx \sum_{k=1}^{N} w_k f(x_k).$$

Similar to Newton-Cotes formulas, Gaussian quadrature requires a set of abscissas $(x_1, \ldots, x_N)$ along with a set of weights $(w_1, \ldots, w_N)$. The values of the abscissas and weights depends on the choice of quadrature and on the choice of N. For our purposes, the choice of method depends largely on the integration range for which the quadrature is designed. Quadrature is described in many textbooks on the subject, such as that by Cohen (2011), Stroud and Secrest (1966), or on the Wolfram website (www.mathworld.wolfram.com). In the following sections, we describe Gauss-Laguerre, Gauss-Legendre, and Gauss-Lobatto quadrature, and present algorithms for finding the weights and abscissas of each method.

Gauss-Laguerre Quadrature

Gauss-Laguerre quadrature is especially relevant for the purposes of evaluating the integral for the Heston model because it is designed for integrals over the integration domain $(0, \infty)$. Suppose we wish to apply Gauss-Laguerre quadrature with N points. The abscissas $(x_1, \ldots, x_N)$ are the roots of the Laguerre polynomial $L_N(x)$ of order N defined as

$$L_N(x) = \sum_{k=0}^{N} \frac{(-1)^k}{k!} \binom{N}{k} x^k, \tag{5.6}$$

where $\binom{N}{k}$ is the binomial coefficient. There are N roots in all. The weights as $(w_1, \ldots, w_N)$ are obtained with the derivative of $L_N(x)$

$$w_j = \frac{(n!)^2 e^{x_j}}{x_j \left[L'_N(x_j)\right]^2} \text{ for } j = 1, \ldots, N.$$

Note that the Laguerre polynomial in Equation (5.6) has $N + 1$ terms, but its derivative has N terms, which is the correct number of terms required for the approximation (5.1).

It is straightforward to use VBA to calculate the abscissas and weights for any N. First, the CreateGLaCoefficients function generates the coefficients of the Laguerre polynomial in (5.6).

```
Function CreateGLaCoefficients(n As Double) As Variant
For k = 0 To n
    La(k + 1) = (-1) ^ k / Factorial(k) * nchoosek(n, k)
Next k
' Flip the vector to get the coefficients in correct order
' L = C(1)* x^N + C(2)* x^(N-1) + ... C(N-1)*x^2 + C(N)*x + C(N+1)
For k = 0 To n
    L(k + 1) = La(n + 1 - k)
Next k
' Return the coefficients C(1), C(2), ..., C(N), C(N+1) of the
polynomial
CreateGLaCoefficients = L
End Function
```

Next, the CreateGLaPolynomial function uses the coefficients to construct the Laguerre polynomial.

```
Function CreateGLaPolynomial(n As Double, x As Double) As Variant
' Create the coefficients C(1), C(2), ... , C(N), C(N+1) of the
polynomial
' L = C(1)* x^N + C(2)* x^(N-1) + ... C(N-1)*x^2 + C(N)*x + C(N+1)
c = CreateGLaCoefficients(n)
' Return the value of the Gauss-Laguerre polynomial, evaluated at x
sum = 0
For j = 1 To n + 1
    sum = sum + c(j) * x ^ (n + 1 - j)
Next j
CreateGLaPolynomial = sum
End Function
```

Finally, the GenerateGaussLaguerre function returns the abscissas and weights required for Gauss-Laguerre integration.

```
Function GenerateGaussLaguerre(n As Double,...) As Variant
' Apply the bisection algorithm if a root appears in (Ld(j-1),
Ld(j)),
For j = 2 To nx
    a = CreateGLaPolynomial(n, x(j - 1))
    b = CreateGLaPolynomial(n, x(j))
    If Sgn(a) <> Sgn(b) Then
        ' Bisection algorithm.  Roots are the abscissas
        roots(count) = Bisection(n, x(j - 1), x(j), Tol, MaxIter)
    End If
Next j
' Find the weights
For j = 1 To n
    ' The coefficients of the derivative of the Laguerre polynomial
    For k = 1 To n
        dL(k, j) = (-1) ^ k / Factorial(k - 1) ...
    Next k
    ' The weight w(j) = 1/x(j)/sum(dL(:,j))^2;
    For k = 1 To n
        SumdL = SumdL + dL(k, j)
    Next k
    w(j) = 1 / roots(j) / SumdL ^ 2
    ' The total weight w(j)exp(x(j))
    w(j) = w(j) * Exp(roots(j))
Next j
For j = 1 To n
    output(j, 1) = roots(j)        ' Abscissas
    output(j, 2) = w(j)            ' Weights
Next j
GenerateGaussLaguerre = output
End Function
```

The VBA functions presented in this section are in the Excel file Ch5GLa.xls.

To numerically evaluate the Heston integrals for P_1 and P_2 using Gauss-Laguerre integration, we first generate abscissas and weights, evaluate the integrand at each abscissa, apply the weight, and then take the sum. This is implemented as part of the VBA function HestonPriceGaussLaguerre, which we have covered in previous sections.

```
Function HestonPriceGaussLaguerre(PutCall As String, ...) As Double
' Integrands
For j = 1 To N
    phi = x(j)
    weight = W(j)
    int1(j) = HestonProb(phi,.., 1, trap) * weight
    int2(j) = HestonProb(phi,.., 2, trap) * weight
Next j
I1 = Sum(int1)
I2 = Sum(int2)
End Function
```

It is straightforward to plot the Laguerre polynomial and obtain a visual confirmation of its roots. For example, suppose that $N = 5$ so that the Laguerre polynomial in Equation (5.6) is

$$L_5(x) = 1 - 5x + 5x^2 - \frac{5}{3}x^3 + \frac{5}{24}x^4 - \frac{1}{120}x^5. \tag{5.7}$$

This polynomial is plotted in Figure 5.2. The plot is in the Excel file Ch5PlotGLa(5).xls.

The figure indicates the location of the five roots of $L_5(x)$ with circles.

Gauss-Legendre Quadrature

Gauss-Legendre quadrature is designed for integrals over the integration domain $[-1, +1]$, but this can be modified to accept any finite domain $[a, b]$ through the transformation

$$\int_a^b f(x)dx = \frac{b-a}{2}\int_{-1}^{1} f\left(\frac{b-a}{2}x + \frac{a+b}{2}\right)dx. \tag{5.8}$$

Since the endpoints a and b are not included in the abscissas, to implement Gauss-Legendre quadrature for the Heston model we can select $a = 0$. We must,

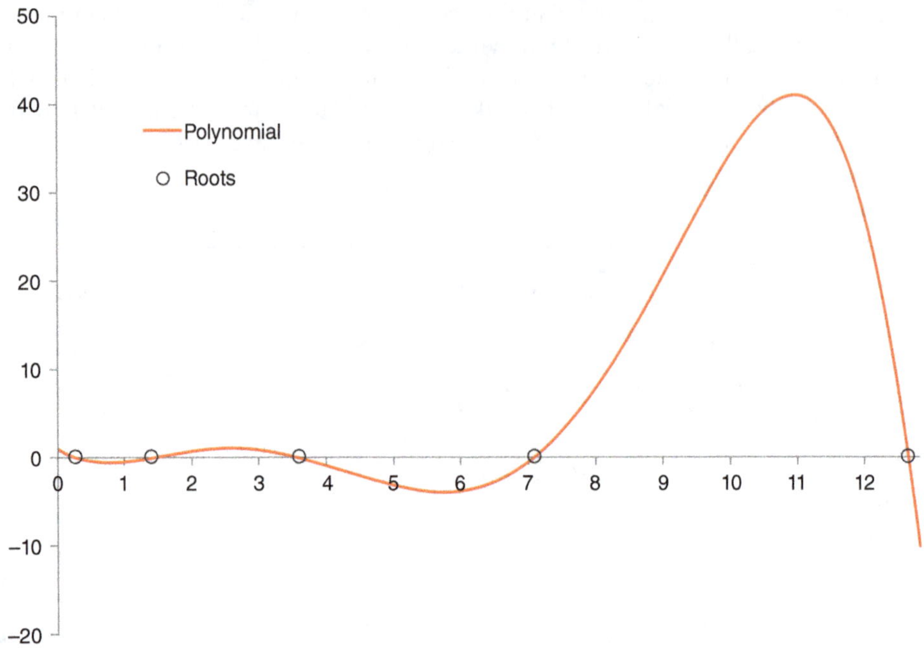

FIGURE 5.2 Laguerre Polynomial of Fifth Order

however, still set $b = \phi_{\max}$, a large number. In Gauss-Legendre quadrature with N points, the abscissas $(x_1, \ldots, x_N)$ are the roots of the Legendre polynomial $P_N(x)$, defined as

$$P_N(x) = \frac{1}{2^N} \sum_{k=0}^{\lfloor N/2 \rfloor} (-1)^k \frac{(2N-2k)!}{k!(N-k)!(N-2k)!} x^{N-2k}, \tag{5.9}$$

where $\lfloor\ \rfloor$ is the floor function. The weights $(w_1, \ldots, w_N)$ are obtained with the derivative of $P_N(x)$ evaluated at the abscissas:

$$w_j = \frac{2}{\left(1 - x_j^2\right)\left[P'_N(x_j)\right]^2} \text{ for } j = 1, \ldots, N.$$

The Legendre polynomials $P_N(x)$ are defined in such a way that some of the coefficients are zero. Indeed, when N is even, $P_N(x)$ contains only even powers of x, and when N is odd, $P_N(x)$ contains only odd powers. Hence, when we calculate Legendre polynomials in VBA, we must ensure that we include these zero values when we create the Gauss-Legendre polynomial. This is illustrated with the VBA function CreateGLeCoefficients.

```
Function CreateGLeCoefficients(n As Double) As Variant
m = Floor(n / 2, 1)
For k = 0 To m
    Le(k + 1) = (1 / 2 ^ n) * (-1) ^ k * Factorial(2 * n - 2 * k) ...
Next k
' Fill in blank powers of Le
For k = 1 To n + 1
    If k Mod 2 = 0 Then
        P(k) = 0
    Else
        P(k) = Le((k + 1) / 2)
    End If
Next k
' Return the coefficients C(1), C(2), ..., C(N), C(N+1) of the
polynomial
CreateGLeCoefficients = P
End Function
```

To numerically evaluate the Heston integrals for P_1 and P_2 using Gauss-Legendre integration, we proceed in the same way as we did earlier for Gauss-Laguerre integration. We first generate abscissas and weights, evaluate the integrand at each abscissa, apply the weight, and then take the sum. We must ensure, however, that the transformation in (5.8) is correctly applied. This is implemented as part of the function HestonPriceGaussLegendre encountered in Chapter 1.

```
Function HestonPriceGaussLegendre(PutCall As String, ...) As Double
' Integrands
For j = 1 To N
    phi = (a + b) / 2 + (b - a) / 2 * x(j)
    weight = w(j)
    int1(j) = HestonProb(phi, ..., 1, trap) * weight
    int2(j) = HestonProb(phi, ..., 2, trap) * weight
Next j
' Integrals
I1 = Sum(int1)
I2 = Sum(int2)
End Function
```

The difference with Gauss-Laguerre integration is that we need to specify the upper and lower limits a and b of the integrand. Since the endpoints are not part of the abscissas, we can specify $a = 0$, and for b we can select a large number, such as $b = 100$. The functions presented in this section are in the Excel file Ch5GLe.xls.

Gauss-Lobatto Quadrature

Gauss-Lobatto quadrature is also designed for integrals over the integration range $[-1, +1]$ and can be modified to accept any finite range $[a, b]$ through the transformation (5.8). The quadrature can be easily constructed from Legendre polynomials. The advantage of Gauss-Lobatto quadrature over Gauss-Laguerre and Gauss-Legendre quadrature is that the endpoints of the interval, a and b, are included in the set of abscissas, so that $x_1 = a$ and $x_N = b$. The remaining $N - 2$ abscissas $(x_2, \ldots, x_{N-1})$ are the roots of $P'_{N-1}(x)$, the derivative of the Legendre polynomial, but of order $N - 1$. The weights $(w_2, \ldots, w_{N-1})$ are given as in terms of the Legendre polynomials $P_{N-1}(x)$ from (5.9):

$$w_j = \frac{2}{N(N-1)\left[P_{N-1}(x_j)\right]^2} \text{ for } j = 2, \ldots, N-1.$$

The weights at the endpoints are

$$w_1 = \frac{2}{N(N-1)}$$

and

$$w_N = w_1.$$

The VBA function GenerateGaussLobatto generates the abscissas and weights for a given number of points. The function depends on the VBA functions CreateGLoCoefficients and CreateGLoPolynomial, but these are not presented here. These functions are all in the Excel file Ch5GLo.xls.

```
Function GenerateGaussLobatto(n As Double, ...) As Variant
' Apply the bisection algorithm if a root appears in (Ld(j-1),
Ld(j)),
For j = 2 To nx
    A = CreateGLoPolynomial(n, x(j - 1), 2)
    B = CreateGLoPolynomial(n, x(j), 2)
    If Sgn(A) <> Sgn(B) Then
        ' Bisection algorithm.  Roots are the abscissas
        roots(count) = Bisection(n, x(j - 1), x(j), Tol, MaxIter)
    End If
Next j
' Rework the roots so that even n get non-zero roots, odd n get
one zero root
' Additionally, augment the roots with -1 and +1 at the endpoints
If n Mod 2 = 0 Then
    ' Even n, remove middle roots, which is zero
    For j = 1 To nroots
```

```
        If j <> (nroots + 1) / 2 Then
            newroots.Add roots(j)
        End If
    Next j
Else
    ' Odd n, add the middle root which is zero
    For j = 1 To nroots
        newroots.Add roots(j)
    Next j
End If
' Find the weights
P = CreateGLoCoefficients(n, 1)
For j = 2 To n - 1
    For k = 1 To n
        Poly(k) = P(k) * newroots2(j, 1) ^ (n - k)
    Next k
    w(j) = 2 / n / (n - 1) / Sum(Poly) ^ 2
Next j
End Function
```

To implement Gauss-Lobatto quadrature for the Heston call or put price, we can use the HestonPriceGaussLegendre function described earlier. We simply pass the Gauss-Lobatto weights and abscissas to the function, instead of the Gauss-Legendre weights and abscissas. Since the endpoints a and b form part of the abscissas, however, we cannot specify $a = 0$ but must select a small number instead.

Gaussian Quadrature for Double Integrals

The generalization of Gaussian quadrature to double integrals is straightforward. We illustrate using the Gauss-Legendre quadrature, since it can be used for integrals over a general domain of integration, using the transformation (5.8). Burden and Faires (2010) show that Gauss-Legendre approximation to the double integral over the domain $[a, b] \times [c, d]$ is

$$\int_a^b \left(\int_c^d f(x, y) dy \right) dx \approx \sum_{j=1}^{N_2} \sum_{i=1}^{N_1} h_1 k_1 w_{i,1} w_{j,2} \cdot f(h_1 x_{i,1} + h_2, k_1 x_{j,2} + k_2). \quad (5.10)$$

The approximation uses two sets of Gauss-Legendre abscissas and weights, of sizes N_1 and N_2. In (5.10), $w_{i,1}$ and $w_{j,2}$ are the weights, $x_{i,1}$ and $x_{j,2}$ are the abscissas, and $h_1 = (b - a)/2$, $h_2 = (b + a)/2$, $k_1 = (d - c)/2$, and $k_2 = (d + c)/2$. The approximation (5.10) is implemented with the DoubleGaussLegendre function.

```
Function DoubleGaussLegendre(f As String, ...) As Double
N1 = Count(x1)
N2 = Count(x2)
' Increments
h1 = (b - a) / 2
h2 = (b + a) / 2
k1 = (d - c) / 2
k2 = (d + c) / 2
' Integrand
For i = 1 To N1
    For j = 1 To N2
        Sum = Sum + h1 * k1 * w1(i) * w2(j) _
            * Run(f, h1 * x1(i) + h2, k1 * x2(j) + k2)
    Next j
Next i
DoubleGaussLegendre = Sum
End Function
```

This function is in the Excel file Ch5DoubleIntegration.xls. Continuing with the earlier example that illustrated the composite trapezoidal rule via the VBA function DoubleTrapz, the DoubleGaussLegendre returns the value 0.18075 for the standard normal bivariate distribution function evaluated at the point $(x, y) = (-0.515, 0.243)$. Again, this is very close to the true value.

INTEGRATION LIMITS, MULTIDOMAIN INTEGRATION, AND KAHL AND JÄCKEL TRANSFORMATION

When we implement Gauss-Laguerre integration, the abscissas are provided to us, so we need not worry about choosing the lower and upper limits of integration. When we implement the Newton-Cotes formulas and Gauss-Legendre or Gauss-Lobatto quadrature, however, we need to provide the limits. The lower limit required in Equation (5.1) is $a = 0$, but if we use the original Heston formulation of the integrand in (5.2), then we cannot use zero since the integrand is undefined there. We therefore must use a small number $\phi_{\min}$ for a. The upper limit required in (5.1) is $b = \infty$, so we must truncate the integration domain and choose a large number, $b = \phi_{\max}$, for the upper limit. How large a number is required depends on how fast the integrand, which typically oscillates, decays to zero. In general, both the oscillation and the speed of decay vary inversely with maturity, so that short maturities oscillate substantially and require a large number for the upper limit. This is illustrated in Figure 5.3 for typical values of Heston parameters and option settings.

In general, it is not wise to use ad-hoc choices for the upper integration limit but, rather, use a choice that takes into consideration the speed of decay of the integrand, as illustrated in Figure 5.3. For example, in his Mathematica code, Lewis (2000) uses $\phi_{\max} = \max[1000, 10/\sqrt{v_0\tau}]$.

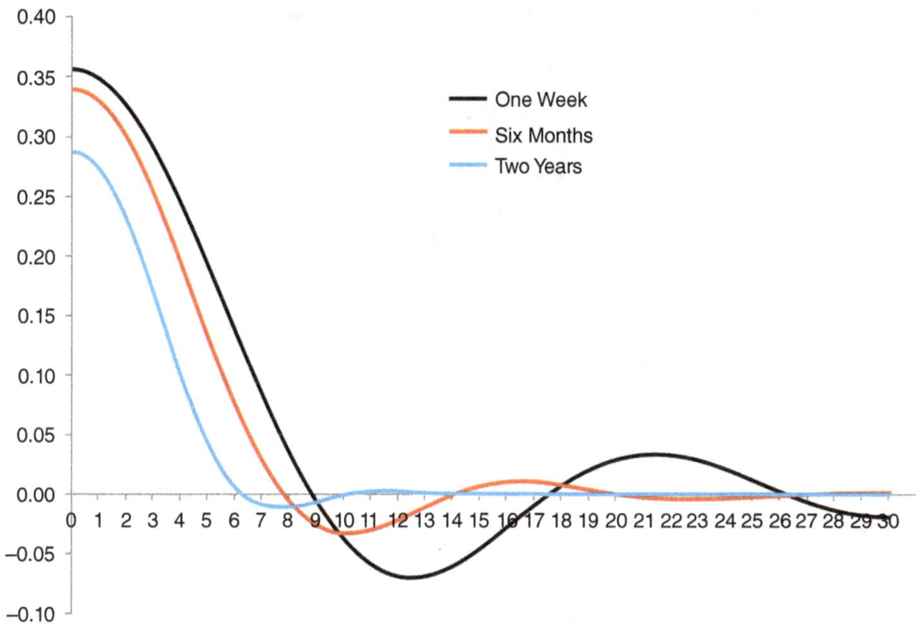

FIGURE 5.3 Integrand Decay and Maturity

We can also use the multidomain integration approach described by Zhu (2010) to select the upper integration limit. In this method, the domain of integration is separated into subdomains $(a_0, a_1]$, $(a_1, a_2]$, $(a_2, a_3]$ and so on, where $a_0 = 0$ and $a_0 < a_1 < a_2 < a_3 < \cdots$. The integral for the probability P_j is constructed by aggregating the integrals over each subdomain, as

$$\sum_{k\geq 0} \int_{a_k}^{a_{k+1}} \text{Re}\left[\frac{e^{-i\phi \ln K} f_j(\phi; x, v)}{i\phi}\right] d\phi.$$

The summation stops when the subdomain integrals cease to contribute to the sum. In other words, when we observe

$$\left| \int_{a_M}^{a_{M+1}} \text{Re}\left[\frac{e^{-i\phi \ln K} f_j(\phi; x, v)}{i\phi}\right] d\phi \right| < \varepsilon, \tag{5.11}$$

for some integer M, where ε is a tolerance level. The integration domain is thus $(0, a_M]$ so that $\phi_{\max} = a_M$. Zhu (2010) explains that this method has the advantage of assigning the upper limit optimally, with the ability to adapt to different strikes, maturities, and parameter values. Moreover, the method will automatically assign a wider domain to shorter maturity options, for which the integrand tends to oscillate, and a narrower domain to longer maturity options, for which the integrand is better behaved. The method is thus able to reduce computation time by avoiding domains that are needlessly wide. It also increases accuracy by assigning a wide domain to those integrals that require it.

Gauss-Legendre or Gauss-Lobatto quadrature is particularly well suited for this method, since both can accommodate integrals on any domain, by using the transformation (5.8). Hence, to apply the multidomain integration method of Zhu (2010), we can generate abscissas and weights once, and use these to obtain the integrals on the subdomains, applying the transformation each time. We stop when the condition (5.11) is satisfied. The VBA function HestonPriceGaussLegendreMD implements the multidomain integration method.

```
Function HestonPriceGaussLegendreMD(PutCall As String, ...) As
Variant
' Build the integration Domain = (0,a1], (a1,a2], (a2,a3]
dA = (hiA - loA) / (NA - 1)
Domain(1) = loA
For j = 2 To NA
    Domain(j) = Domain(j - 1) + dA
Next j
' Perfom the subdomain integrations
NX = Count(GLeX)
For i = 2 To NA
    For j = 1 To NX
        ' The Gauss-Laguerre abscissa and weight
        abscissa = GLeX(j)
        weight = GLeW(j)
        ' Lower and upper limits of the subdomain
        a = Domain(i - 1)
        b = Domain(i)
        x = (a + b) / 2 + (b - a) / 2 * abscissa
        ' The integrands
        int1(i, j) = weight * HestonProb(x, ..., 1) * (b - a) / 2
        int2(i, j) = weight * HestonProb(x, ..., 2) * (b - a) / 2
    Next j
    For u = 1 To NX
        sum1(i) = sum1(i) + int1(i, u)
        sum2(i) = sum2(i) + int2(i, u)
    Next u
    ' Stopping criterion
    If Abs(sum1(i)) < tol And Abs(sum2(i)) < tol Then
        Exit For
    End If
Next i
End Function
```

The function accepts as input a set of points defining the subdomains. It outputs the call price or the put price by put-call parity. It also outputs the resulting domain of

	A	B	C	D	E	F	G	H
1								
2		**Heston Price Using 32-Point Gauss-Legendre with Multi-Domain Integration**						
3								
4		**Option Features**			**Method**	**Price**	**Upper Limit**	**# Points**
5		Spot Price (S)	100.0000		Mutli-Domain Integration	4.8719	67.24	448
6		Strike Price (K)	100.0000		32-Point Gauss-Laguerre	4.8722	111.75	32
7		Time to Maturity (τ)	0.2500		Trapezoidal with 1500 Points	4.8719	150	1500
8		Risk free rate (r)	0.0500					
9		Dividend (q)	0.0100		**Domain of Integration and Tolerance**			
10		PutCall ("C" or "P")	C		Tolerance	1.00E-06		
11					Lower limit of domain	1.00E-10		
12		**Heston Parameters**			Upper limit of domain	150		
13		kappa (κ)	2.0000		Number of points in domain	30		
14		theta (θ)	0.0500					
15		sigma (σ)	0.3000		**Settings for the Trapezoidal Rule**			
16		v0	0.0500		Lower Limit	1.00E-10		
17		rho (ρ)	0.4500		Upper Limit	150		
18		lambda (λ)	0.0000		Number of Points	1500		
19		Trap (0=Heston, 1=Albrecher)	1					

FIGURE 5.4 Multidomain Integration

integration and the number of points used. Figure 5.4 provides a screen shot example of multidomain integration.

The price using multidomain integration with a tolerance level of $\varepsilon = 10^{-6}$ and a maturity of three months is 4.8719, which is identical to the price obtained with the trapezoidal rule with 5,000 points and an integration range of $(0, 150]$. With this tolerance level, the multidomain algorithm returns $\phi_{\max} = 67.24$, so the integration range is substantially narrower and the computation time is decreased. If we reduce the maturity to one month, the price drops to 2.7222, which again is identical to the trapezoidal rule price. The algorithm now returns $\phi_{\max} = 82.76$, however, so the domain of integration is substantially wider than that for the three-month maturity and the computation time is increased. The examples and functions presented in this section are all in the Excel file Ch5MD.xls.

Another approach to finding an adequate domain of integration is to transform the domain $\phi \in [0, \infty)$ to a more manageable interval $x \in [0, 1]$, as suggested by Kahl and Jäckel (2005). Their form of the call price is

$$C(K) = e^{-r\tau} \int_0^1 y(x)dx, \tag{5.12}$$

where

$$y(x) = \frac{1}{2}(F - K) + \frac{Ff_1\left(-\ln x/C_\infty\right) - Kf_2\left(-\ln x/C_\infty\right)}{x\pi C_\infty}, \tag{5.13}$$

where $F = e^{(r-q)\tau}$, $C_\infty = \sqrt{1-\rho^2}(v_0 + \kappa\theta\tau)\Big/\sigma^2$and where τ is the time to maturity. In the form of (5.13) the integral $y(x)$ is not defined at the endpoints $x = 0$ and $x = 1$, which implies that the integration can only be done over the range $(0, 1)$. However,

Kahl and Jäckel (2005) derive the limits of the integrand analytically. The expressions for $\lim_{u\to 0} f_j(u)$ are given in their Equations (44) and (50). Hence,

$$\lim_{u\to 0} f_1(u) = \ln(F/K) + \text{Im}\left[C'(-i)\right] + \text{Im}\left[D'(-i)\right] v_0, \tag{5.14}$$

and

$$\lim_{u\to 0} f_2(u) = \ln(F/K) + \text{Im}\left[C'(0)\right] + \text{Im}\left[D'(0)\right] v_0. \tag{5.15}$$

In this last expression, we have

$$\text{Im}\left[C'(0)\right] = -\frac{e^{-\kappa\tau}\theta\kappa + \theta\kappa(\kappa\tau - 1)}{2\kappa^2}, \quad \text{Im}\left[D'(0)\right] = \frac{e^{-\kappa\tau/2} - 1}{2\kappa}.$$

In Equation (5.14), when $\kappa - \rho\sigma \neq 0$, we have

$$\begin{aligned}
\text{Im}\left[C'(-i)\right] &= \frac{e^{(\rho\sigma-\kappa)\tau}\theta\kappa + \theta\kappa\left((\kappa - \rho\sigma)\tau - 1\right)}{2(\kappa - \rho\sigma)^2} \\
\text{Im}\left[D'(-i)\right] &= \frac{1 - e^{-(\kappa-\rho\sigma)\tau}}{2(\kappa - \rho\sigma)},
\end{aligned}$$

but when $\kappa - \rho\sigma = 0$, these simplify to

$$\text{Im}\left[C'(-i)\right] = \frac{\kappa\theta\tau^2}{4}, \quad \text{Im}\left[D'(-i)\right] = \frac{\tau}{2}.$$

Kahl and Jäckel (2005) recommend the use of Gauss-Lobatto quadrature for the integral in (5.12). This is sensible because this quadrature includes in the abscissas, the endpoints of the integration domain $[-1, +1]$. When the transformation (5.8) is applied, the result is that the endpoints of the transformed domain $[0, 1]$ required of the Kahl and Jäckel method are included in the abscissas.

The VBA function HestonPriceKahlJackel implements the call price in (5.12) and returns the call price, or the put price by put-call parity.

```
Function HestonPriceKahlJackel(PutCall As String, ...) As Double
Cinf = Sqr(1 - rho ^ 2) / sigma * (v0 + kappa * theta * T)
' Required quantities for f1
If (kappa - rho * sigma) <> 0 Then
    ImC1 = (Exp((rho * sigma - kappa) * T) ...
    ImD1 = (1 - Exp((rho * sigma - kappa) * T)) ...
Else
    ImC1 = kappa * theta * T ^ 2 / 4
    ImD1 = T / 2
End If
```

```
' Required quantities for f2
ImC2 = -(Exp(-kappa * T) * theta * kappa ...
ImD2 = -(1 - Exp(-kappa * T / 2)) / 2 / kappa
' The integrands
For u = 1 To N
    ' Transformation of the abscissa from [-1,1] to [0,1]
    xint = 0.5 * x(u) + 0.5
    If xint = 0 Then
        ' Integrand at left abscissa 0
        y(u) = 0.5 * (F - K)
    ElseIf xint = 1 Then
        ' Integrand at right abscissa 1
        f1 = Log(F / K) + ImC1 + ImD1 * v0
        f2 = Log(F / K) + ImC2 + ImD2 * v0
        y(u) = 0.5 * (F - K) + (F * f1 - K * f1) ...
    Else
        ' Integrand at remaining abscissas
        f1 = HestonProb(-Log(xint) / Cinf, ..., 1)
        f2 = HestonProb(-Log(xint) / Cinf, ..., 2)
        y(u) = 0.5 * (F - K) + (F * f1 - K * f2) ...
    End If
    ' Multiply by the weights
    weight = w(u)
    z(u) = weight * y(u)
Next u
' The call price
KJCall = Exp(-rf * T) * (1 / 2) * Sum(z)
End Function
```

To illustrate, we use the following settings: $S = 10$, $K = 7$, $r = 0.06$, $q = 0.04$, a maturity of one month, and the parameters $\kappa = 1$, $\theta = 0.06$, $\sigma = 0.5$, $v_0 = 0.06$, and $\rho = -0.8$. Gauss-Laguerre and Gauss-Lobatto integration using the Heston formulation and 32 abscissas produce a call price of 3.0024 and 3.0017, respectively. The same Gauss-Lobatto weights, along with the Kahl and Jäckel (2005) formulation produce a price of 2.9992.

Kahl and Jäckel's integrand is plotted in Figure 5.5 along with the values of the integrand at the 32 Gauss-Lobatto abscissas. The integral is highly oscillatory, but since it dampens quickly, the oscillation causes a negligible loss of precision only.

The VBA functions presented in this section, the illustrative example, and the plot in Figure 5.5 are all in the Excel file Ch5KJ.xls.

ILLUSTRATION OF NUMERICAL INTEGRATION

The VBA function HestonPriceNewtonCotes contains all the code necessary to implement the four Newton-Cotes formulas in this chapter.

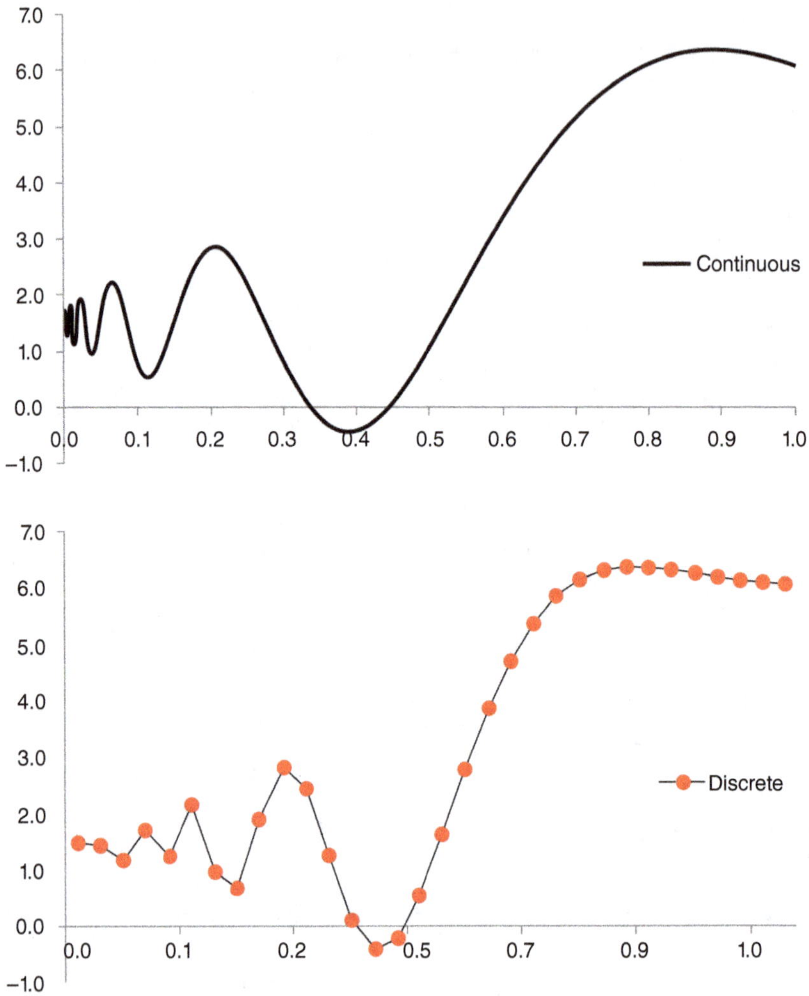

FIGURE 5.5 The Kahl and Jäckel (2005) Integrand

```
Function HestonPriceNewtonCotes(method As Integer, ...) As Double
If method = 1 Then
    ' Mid-Point rule
    For j = 1 To N - 1
        wt(j) = h
    Next j
    For j = 1 To N - 1
        mid = (phi(j) + phi(j + 1)) / 2
        int1(j) = wt(j) * HestonProb(mid, ..., 1)
        int2(j) = wt(j) * HestonProb(mid, ..., 2)
    Next j
ElseIf method = 3 Then
    ' Simpson's Rule
```

```
    For j = 1 To N
        int1(j) = wt(j) * HestonProb(phi(j), ..., 1)
        int2(j) = wt(j) * HestonProb(phi(j), ..., 2)
    Next j
    ...
End If
' The integrals and the probabilities
I1 = Sum(int1)
I2 = Sum(int2)
P1 = 0.5 + 1 / pi * I1
P2 = 0.5 + 1 / pi * I2
' The call price and put price
HestonC = S * Exp(-q * T) * P1 - K * Exp(-r * T) * P2
HestonP = HestonC - S * Exp(-q * T) + K * Exp(-r * T)
End Function
```

The functions HestonPriceGaussLaguerre and HestonPriceGaussLegendre are used for Gaussian quadrature. These are similar to those presented earlier and are not presented here.

In the following example, we calculate the price of one-month European calls and puts when the spot is $S = 100$ and with $r = 0.03$ and $q = 0.07$. We use common parameter settings. We use 100 abscissas for the Newton-Cotes formulas, but only 5 abscissas for the Gaussian quadrature. The prices for strikes ranging from $K = 98$ to $K = 102$ are in Table 5.1 for the calls and in Table 5.2 for the puts.

The results indicate that the four Newton-Cotes formulas produce prices that are fairly accurate. The Gauss-Legendre and Gauss-Lobatto quadratures are also accurate, especially in light of the fact that they use five abscissas only. The Gauss-Laguerre quadrature is the least accurate of all the methods. This example is in the Excel file Ch5AllRules.xls. See Rouah (2013) for details of the Newton-Cotes formulas and Gaussian quadrature as they apply to the Heston model.

TABLE 5.1 Comparison of Quadrature on Call Prices

Method	$K = 98$	$K = 99$	$K = 100$	$K = 101$	$K = 102$
True Price	2.70	1.99	1.37	0.83	0.43
100-pt. Midpoint	2.70	1.99	1.37	0.83	0.43
100-pt. Trapezoidal	2.70	1.99	1.37	0.83	0.43
100-pt. Simpsons	2.70	1.99	1.37	0.83	0.43
100-pt. Simpsons 3/8	2.70	1.99	1.37	0.83	0.43
5-pt. Gauss Laguerre	1.80	1.16	0.61	0.16	−0.21
5-pt. Gauss Legendre	2.71	2.04	1.41	0.83	0.38
5-pt. Gauss Lobatto	2.80	1.92	1.24	0.65	0.19

TABLE 5.2 Comparison of Quadrature on Put Prices

Method	$K = 98$	$K = 99$	$K = 100$	$K = 101$	$K = 102$
True Price	0.87	1.16	1.54	2.00	2.59
100-pt. Midpoint	0.87	1.16	1.54	2.00	2.59
100-pt. Trapezoidal	0.87	1.16	1.54	2.00	2.59
100-pt. Simpsons	0.87	1.16	1.54	2.00	2.59
100-pt. Simpsons 3/8	0.87	1.16	1.54	2.00	2.59
5-pt. Gauss Laguerre	−0.03	0.32	0.78	1.32	1.96
5-pt. Gauss Legendre	0.88	1.21	1.58	2.00	2.54
5-pt. Gauss Lobatto	0.97	1.09	1.40	1.81	2.35

FAST FOURIER TRANSFORM

The fast Fourier transform (FFT) was applied by Carr and Madan (1999) to speed up the computation of option prices. Recall from Chapter 3 that the Fourier-based Carr and Madan (1999) price of the call at the log strike $k = \ln K$ is

$$C(k) = \frac{e^{-\alpha k}}{\pi} \int_0^\infty \text{Re}\left[e^{-ivk}\psi(v)\right] dv,$$

where

$$\psi(v) = \frac{e^{-r\tau} f_2(v - (\alpha + 1)i)}{\alpha^2 + \alpha - v^2 + iv(2\alpha + 1)},$$

and where f_2 is the Heston characteristic function, which we have sometimes denoted as φ in Chapter 3. To implement the FFT on the call price, we first create the integration grid $\{v_j\}_{j=1}^N$ and the log-strike grid $\{k_u\}_{u=1}^N$. These are, respectively,

$$v_j = (j - 1)\eta \text{ for } j = 1, \dots, N, \tag{5.16}$$

$$k_u = -b + (u - 1)\lambda + \ln S_t \text{ for } u = 1, \dots, N, \tag{5.17}$$

where η and λ are the grid increments, $b = N\lambda/2$, and S_t is the spot price of the underlying stock. We define the points x_j for $j = 1, \dots, N$ as

$$x_j = e^{i(b - \ln S_t)v_j}\psi(v_j)w_j. \tag{5.18}$$

In (5.18), $\psi(v_j)$ is the function ψ evaluated at the grid point v_j:

$$\psi(v_j) = \frac{e^{-r\tau} f_2(v_j - (\alpha + 1)i)}{\alpha^2 + \alpha - v_j^2 + iv_j(2\alpha + 1)},$$

where $f_2(v_j - (\alpha+1)i)$ is the Heston characteristic function evaluated at $v_j - (\alpha+1)i$. Define $\hat{x}_u = C(k_u)$, the call price evaluated at the log-strike point k_u. Each call price $\hat{x}_u$ can be obtained from the set $\{x_j\}_{j=1}^N$ via the FFT as the sum

$$\hat{x}_u = \frac{\eta e^{-\alpha k_u}}{\pi} \sum_{j=1}^{N} \text{Re}\left[e^{-i\frac{2\pi}{N}(j-1)(u-1)} x_j\right] \text{ for } u = 1, \dots, N. \tag{5.19}$$

Call prices are obtained from (5.19) directly. Hence, $C(k_u) = \hat{x}_u$ is the price of the call struck at $\exp(k_u)$.

The structure of the grids imply the following constraint on the increments:

$$\lambda\eta = \frac{2\pi}{N}.$$

This is an important limitation of the FFT, since it entails a trade-off between the grid sizes. For a fixed N, choosing a fine grid for the integration range will produce a coarse grid for the log strikes range, and vice versa. The only way to increase the granularity of both grids is to increase N, and consequently, the computation time. This issue is rectified with the fractional FFT that we will encounter in the next section. See Carr and Madan (1999) or Rouah (2013) for a detailed derivation of the FFT call prices in (5.19).

The fast Fourier transform for the Heston call price is implemented using the VBA function HestonCallFFT. The function calls the HestonCF function, which constructs the Heston characteristic function $f_2(\phi; x, v)$.

```
Function HestonCallFFT(N As Integer,..) As Variant
' Grid for the integration: v = eta.*[0:N-1]';
For j = 0 To N - 1
    v(j + 1) = j * eta
Next j
' Grid for the log-strikes: k = -b + lambdainc.*[0:N-1]' + s0;
For j = 0 To N - 1
    k(j + 1) = -b + lambdainc * j + s0
Next j
' Create the strikes and identify ATM
For j = 1 To N
    bigK(j) = Exp(k(j))
Next j
' Implement the FFT
For u = 1 To N
    For j = 1 To N
        psi(j) = Complex(charfun(1, 1), charfun(2, 1))
        phi(j) = cDiv(Num, Den)
        x(j) = cProd(t1, t2)
        e(j) = cReal(cProd(t1, x(j)))
    Next j
    CallFFT(u) = eta * Exp(-alpha * k(u)) / pi ...
Next u
End Function
```

To illustrate, suppose that the spot price is $S_t = 50$ and that the Heston parameters are $\kappa = 0.2$, $v_0 = \theta = 0.05$, $\sigma = 0.3$, and $\rho = -0.7$. Suppose that the maturity is six months, the risk-free rate is $r = 0.03$, and the dividend yield is $q = 0.05$. Using $N = 2^8 = 256$ and a damping parameter of $\alpha = 1.5$, we obtain the call prices in Figure 5.5 along with the exact price obtained using 32-point Gauss-Laguerre integration.

Even with as few as 256 points, the FFT produces prices that are accurate, regardless of whether Simpson's rule or the trapezoidal rule is used. In this example, the integration increment is $\eta = 0.39$ and the log-strike increment is $\lambda = 6.28$. The screen shot in Figure 5.5 and the functions presented in this section are taken from the Excel file Ch5FFT.xls.

FRACTIONAL FAST FOURIER TRANSFORM

The fractional fast Fourier transform (FRFT) was applied to option pricing by Chourdakis (2005). The FRFT is a refinement of the FFT that relaxes the restrictive constraint $\lambda\eta = 2\pi/N$ on the grid size parameters, so that the term $1/N$ in the exponent of the FFT (5.19) is replaced with a general term β. The relationship between the grid size parameters λ and η becomes $\lambda\eta = 2\pi\beta$. We can therefore choose the grid size parameters freely and then set $\beta = \lambda\eta/(2\pi)$. The FFT arises as the special case $\beta = 1/N$.

To implement the FRFT on a set of points $x_1, \ldots, x_N$, first define the vectors $\mathbf{y}$ and $\mathbf{z}$, each of dimension $2N$:

$$\begin{aligned}\mathbf{y} &= \left(\left\{e^{-i\pi(j-1)^2\beta_j}x_j\right\}_{j=1}^{N}, \quad \{0\}_{j=1}^{N}\right)\\ \mathbf{z} &= \left(\left\{e^{i\pi(j-1)^2\beta_j}\right\}_{j=1}^{N}, \quad \left\{e^{i\pi(N-j+1)^2\beta}\right\}_{j=1}^{N}\right)\end{aligned}, \tag{5.20}$$

where the points x_j for $j = 1, \ldots, N$ are defined exactly as in Equation (5.18):

$$x_j = e^{i(b-\ln S_t)v_j}\psi(v_j)w_j.$$

Next, take the FFT of $\mathbf{y}$ and $\mathbf{z}$ to obtain the vectors $\hat{\mathbf{y}} = D(\mathbf{y})$ and $\hat{\mathbf{z}} = D(\mathbf{z})$, and take their product element by element, which produces the vector $\hat{\mathbf{h}}$ of dimension $2N$ defined as

$$\hat{\mathbf{h}} = \hat{\mathbf{y}} \odot \hat{\mathbf{z}} = \left\{y_j z_j\right\}_{j=1}^{2N}.$$

Now take the inverse FFT of $\hat{\mathbf{h}}$ to produce the vector $\mathbf{h} = D^{-1}(\hat{\mathbf{h}})$ of dimension $2N$. Finally, multiply element by element, the resulting vector, with the vector $\mathbf{e}$ of dimension $2N$ defined as

$$\mathbf{e} = \left(\left\{e^{-i\pi(j-1)^2\beta}\right\}_{j=1}^{N}, \quad \{0\}_{j=1}^{N}\right).$$

Hence, we can write the fractional FFT in compact form as

$$\hat{\mathbf{x}} = \mathbf{e} \odot D^{-1}(D(\mathbf{y}) \odot D(\mathbf{z})). \tag{5.21}$$

The first N elements of $\hat{\mathbf{x}}$ are retained and the remaining N elements are discarded, as these are zeros. Note that similar to the FFT, the FRFT takes the N-vector $\mathbf{x}$ and maps it to the N-vector $\hat{\mathbf{x}}$. The FRFT, however, uses the intermediate $2N$-vectors $\mathbf{y}$ and $\mathbf{z}$, and requires that two FFTs be computed in the intermediate steps. Nevertheless, the increase in computational time required by the two intermediate FFTs is usually offset by the increase in accuracy due to being able to choose the integration and strike grids independently and as arbitrarily small as we wish. For details of the derivation of the FRFT as it applies to the Heston model, see Chourdakis (2005) or Rouah (2013).

To implement the FRFT, we choose an arbitrary number of points, N, an integration increment, η, and a log-strike increment, λ. We then set $\beta = \lambda\eta/(2\pi)$ and proceed as described in this section. For the points x_j that appear in the vector $\mathbf{z}$ in Equation (5.20), we use $x_j = \exp[i(b - \ln S_t)v_j]\psi(v_j)w_j$, exactly the same points as in (5.18) for the FFT. Finally, the integration grid $\{v_j\}_{j=1}^N$ and log-strike grid $\{k_u\}_{u=1}^N$ are built exactly as in (5.16) and (5.17) respectively, with $b = N\lambda/2$, as before.

We do not have built-in functions in VBA for the FFT or the inverse FFT, so these must be created. The function FFT implements the fast Fourier transform.

```
Function FFT(xReal As Variant, xImag As Variant) As Variant
For k = 1 To N
    coeff = Complex(0, 0)
    For j = 1 To N
        t1 = Complex(-2 * pi * (j - 1) * (k - 1) / N, 0)
        t2 = cExp(cProd(i, t1))
        t3 = cProd(t2, x(j))
        coeff = cAdd(t3, coeff)
    Next j
    xhat(k) = coeff
    output(k, 1) = cReal(xhat(k))
    output(k, 2) = cImag(xhat(k))
Next k
' Output the FFT xhat separately, real and imaginary parts
FFT = output
End Function
```

The VBA function IFFT implements the inverse FFT.

```
Function IFFT(xhatReal As Variant, xhatImag As Variant) As Variant
For k = 1 To N
    coeff = Complex(0, 0)
    For j = 1 To N
        t1 = Complex(2 * pi * (j - 1) * (k - 1) / N, 0)
        t2 = cExp(cProd(i, t1))
        t3 = cProd(t2, xhat(j))
        coeff = cAdd(t3, coeff)
    Next j
    x(k) = cDiv(coeff, Complex(N, 0))
    output(k, 1) = cReal(x(k))
    output(k, 2) = cImag(x(k))
Next k
' Output the FFT xhat separately, real and imaginary parts
IFFT = output
End Function
```

The VBA function FRFT implements the fractional FFT.

```
Function FRFT(xReal As Variant, ...) As Variant
' Construct the y and z vectors, positions 1 to N
For j = 1 To N
    piJJbeta = Complex(pi * (j - 1) * (j - 1) * beta, 0)
    piJJbetam = Complex(-pi * (j - 1) * (j - 1) * beta, 0)
    z(j) = cExp(cProd(piJJbeta, i))
    y(j) = cProd(cExp(cProd(piJJbetam, i)), x(j))
Next j
' Construct the y and z vectors, positions N+1 to 2N
For j = N + 1 To 2 * N
    y(j) = Complex(0, 0)
    M = Complex(2 * N - j + 1, 0)
    piMMbeta = cProd(cProd(M, M), Complex(pi * beta, 0))
    z(j) = cExp(cProd(piMMbeta, i))
Next j
' Run the FFT on y and z
DDy = FFT(yReal, yImag)
DDz = FFT(zReal, zImag)
' Create the h vector
For j = 1 To 2 * N
    h(j) = cProd(Dy(j), Dz(j))
Next j
' Create the ih vector using IFFT and recombine
ihh = IFFT(hReal, hImag)
```

```
For j = 1 To 2 * N
    ih(j) = Complex(ihh(j, 1), ihh(j, 2))
Next j
' Create the e vector
For j = 1 To N
    piJJbetam = Complex(-pi * (j - 1) * (j - 1) * beta, 0)
    e(j) = cExp(cProd(piJJbetam, i))
Next j
' Output the FFT xhat separately, real and imaginary parts
FRFT = output
End Function
```

Finally, the function HestonCallFRFT implements the FRFT and returns the strikes and call prices.

```
Function HestonCallFRFT(N As Integer, ...) As Variant
' Implement the FRFT Part 1
For j = 1 To N
    charfun = HestonCF(increment, ...)
    psi(j) = Complex(charfun(1, 1), charfun(2, 1))
    phi(j) = cDiv(Num, Den)
    x(j) = cProd(t1, t2)
    xReal(j) = cReal(x(j))
    xImag(j) = cImag(x(j))
Next j
' Implement the FRFT Part 2
For j = 1 To N
    y(j) = Complex(FRFTvec(j, 1), FRFTvec(j, 2))
Next j
' Implement the FRFT Part 3
For u = 1 To N
    ' Calls = eta * Exp(-alpha * k(u)) * y(u) / pi
    Calls = cProd(y(u), Complex(temp1, 0))
    CallFRFT(u) = cReal(Calls)
Next u
' Output the strikes and the FRFT call price
HestonCallFRFT = output
End Function
```

To illustrate, we use the same settings at those used to produce the FFT prices in Figure 5.5, but using $\lambda = \eta = 0.01$ for the grid increments and increasing the integration points to $N = 2^{10}$. The results are presented in Figure 5.6, along with the errors

	A	B	C	D	E	F	G	H	I	J	K
1											
2		**Heston Price Using the Fast Fourier Transform**			**Trapezoidal Rule**			**Simpson's Rule**			
3					**Strike**	**Price**		**Strike**	**Price**		**Exact Price**
4		**Option Features**			41.4102	8.6381		41.4102	8.6380		8.6378
5		Spot Price (S)	50.0000		44.0956	6.4761		44.0956	6.4760		6.4765
6		Time to Maturity (τ)	0.5000		46.9551	4.4454		46.9551	4.4453		4.4453
7		Risk free rate (r)	0.0300		50.0000	2.6782		50.0000	2.6781		2.6778
8		Dividend (q)	0.0500		53.2424	1.3267		53.2424	1.3266		1.3269
9		Little Trap (0=Heston, 1=Albrecher)	1		56.6950	0.5018		56.6950	0.5017		0.5020
10					60.3716	0.1424		60.3716	0.1423		0.1421
11		**Heston Parameters**									
12		kappa (κ)	0.2000		**Errors**						
13		theta (θ)	0.0500		**Trapezoidal**	**Simpson's**					
14		sigma (σ)	0.3000		-0.004%	-0.003%					
15		v0	0.0500		0.007%	0.009%					
16		rho (ρ)	-0.7000		-0.001%	0.001%					
17		lambda (λ)	0.0000		-0.012%	-0.008%					
18		Trap (0=Heston, 1=Albrecher)	0		0.015%	0.022%					
19					0.042%	0.061%					
20		**FFT Settings**			-0.194%	-0.128%					
21		Number of points	256								
22		Dampening factor	1.5								
23		Upper Limit of integration	100								
24		Integration(T=Trapezoidal, S=Simpson's)	T								

FIGURE 5.6 Call Prices Using the Fast Fourier Transform

relative to the exact prices, which are obtained using 32-point Gauss-Laguerre integration.

The FRFTprices are less accurate than the FFT prices in Figure 5.5. One advantage of using the FRFT is that we are able to choose the log-strike grid size and obtain call prices in increments of roughly \$0.50 in Figure 5.6. Compare that to the call prices in Table 5.1, which are in increments that are much coarser, roughly \$3.00.

Another advantage of the FRFT is that we can restrict the range of strikes on which the algorithm is applied. Suppose we want the range of strikes to begin at K'. Selecting the log-strike increment λ as

$$\lambda = \frac{2}{N} \log \left(S_t / K' \right) \tag{5.22}$$

will guarantee that the first log strike will be $k_1 = \log K'$ and that the last strike will be approximately $k_N \approx S_t^2 / K'$. Hence, by selecting K' close to S_t we can make λ as small as we wish, and obtain a very narrow discretization range for the strike price. We then select an arbitrary value for the integration grid size η. This is illustrated in Figure 5.7, where we have used $K' = 20$ (recall that $S_t = 50$). The FRFT constructs the strike grid in increments of approximately \$0.04 in near-the-money region. Note that cell C28 for λ contains the Excel formula 2/N*LOG(Spot/20) to reflect Equation (5.22), rather than being hard coded as 0.01, as is the case in Figure 5.6. The value for λ based on (5.22) is approximately 0.00078.

We could also apply Equation (5.22) to construct a narrow strike range for the FFT itself, but since we are constrained in the relationship between λ and η, this would result in a large value for η, and consequently a very coarse integration grid, as seen in Figure 5.8.

The VBA functions, examples, and screen shots in this section are all in the Excel file Ch5FRFT.xls.

	B	C	E	F	H	I	K
1							
2	**Heston Price Using the Fractional FFT**		**Trapezoidal Rule**		**Simpson's Rule**		
3			**Strike**	**Price**	**Strike**	**Price**	**Exact Price**
4	**Option Features**		48.5223	3.4438	48.5223	3.4439	3.4792
5	Spot Price (S)	50.0000	49.0099	3.1949	49.0099	3.1949	3.2025
6	Time to Maturity (τ)	0.5000	49.5025	2.9556	49.5025	2.9557	2.9352
7	Risk free rate (r)	0.0300	50.0000	2.7261	50.0000	2.7263	2.6778
8	Dividend (q)	0.0500	50.5025	2.5066	50.5025	2.5068	2.4311
9	Little Trap (0=Heston, 1=Albrecher)	1	51.0101	2.2971	51.0101	2.2973	2.1956
10			51.5227	2.0976	51.5227	2.0978	1.9719
11	**Heston Parameters**						
12	kappa (κ)	0.2000	**Errors**				
13	theta (θ)	0.0500	**Trapezoidal**	**Simpson's**			
14	sigma (σ)	0.3000	1.0%	1.0%			
15	v0	0.0500	0.2%	0.2%			
16	rho (ρ)	-0.7000	-0.7%	-0.7%			
17	lambda (λ)	0.0000	-1.8%	-1.8%			
18	Trap (0=Heston, 1=Albrecher)	0	-3.1%	-3.1%			
19			-4.6%	-4.6%			
20	**FRFT Settings**		-6.4%	-6.4%			
21	Number of points	1024					
22	Dampening factor	1.5					
23	Upper Limit of integration	100					
24	Integration(T=Trapezoidal, S=Simpson's)	T					
25							
26	**Integration Increments**						
27	For the integration η (eta)	1.00E-02					
28	For the strikes λ (lambda)	1.00E-02					

FIGURE 5.7 Call Prices Using the Fractional Fast Fourier Transform

	B	C	E	F	H	I	K
1							
2	**Heston Price Using the Fractional FFT**		**Trapezoidal Rule**		**Simpson's Rule**		
3			**Strike**	**Price**	**Strike**	**Price**	**Exact Price**
4	**Option Features**		49.8836	2.7787	49.8836	2.7789	2.7369
5	Spot Price (S)	50.0000	49.9223	2.7611	49.9223	2.7613	2.7172
6	Time to Maturity (τ)	0.5000	49.9612	2.7436	49.9612	2.7437	2.6975
7	Risk free rate (r)	0.0300	50.0000	2.7261	50.0000	2.7263	2.6778
8	Dividend (q)	0.0500	50.0389	2.7087	50.0389	2.7088	2.6583
9	Little Trap (0=Heston, 1=Albrecher)	1	50.0778	2.6914	50.0778	2.6915	2.6388
10			50.1167	2.6741	50.1167	2.6742	2.6193
11	**Heston Parameters**						
12	kappa (κ)	0.2000	**Errors**				
13	theta (θ)	0.0500	**Trapezoidal**	**Simpson's**			
14	sigma (σ)	0.3000	-1.5%	-1.5%			
15	v0	0.0500	-1.6%	-1.6%			
16	rho (ρ)	-0.7000	-1.7%	-1.7%			
17	lambda (λ)	0.0000	-1.8%	-1.8%			
18	Trap (0=Heston, 1=Albrecher)	0	-1.9%	-1.9%			
19			-2.0%	-2.0%			
20	**FRFT Settings**		-2.1%	-2.1%			
21	Number of points	1024					
22	Dampening factor	1.5					
23	Upper Limit of integration	100					
24	Integration(T=Trapezoidal, S=Simpson's)	T					
25							
26	**Integration Increments**						
27	For the integration η (eta)	1.00E-02					
28	For the strikes λ (lambda)	0.000777227					

FIGURE 5.8 Call Prices Using the FRFT, Narrow Strike Range

CONCLUSION

In this chapter, we have presented a variety of numerical integration methods, all of which work reasonably well. Newton-Cotes formulas are easy to understand and implement, but require more abscissas and therefore more computing time, than Gaussian quadrature. Among these methods, Gauss-Laguerre quadrature is well suited to the Heston model. Gauss-Lobatto quadrature, however, works very well for the Kahl and Jäckel (2005) transformation of the integration domain. We also showed that it is straightforward to adapt Newton-Cotes formulas and Gaussian quadrature for the approximation of double integrals. Finally, we presented the fast Fourier transform (FFT) and the fractional fast Fourier transform (FRFT). Both of these methods work very well for the Heston model, and produce a large set of option prices very quickly. In Chapter 11, we will show that the FFT and FRFT can be applied to calculate Greeks also.

All of the methods to produce option prices in the Heston model that we have encountered require a set of parameter values. Up till now, we have assumed these values to be given. In reality, parameters must be estimated from market data. In the next chapter, we explain how this is done.

CHAPTER 6

Parameter Estimation

Abstract

All of the pricing methodologies we have covered have assumed the Heston model parameters to be given. In this chapter, we describe how to estimate these parameters. We first present the most common estimation method, the loss function approach, which minimizes the difference between quoted and model option price. Alternatively, implied volatilities can be used instead of prices. Next, we summarize the Nelder and Mead (1965) minimization algorithm and we show how to code it in VBA. Then we describe the method of Gauthier and Rivaille (2009) to select starting values and the Strike-Vector Computation of Kilin (2007), which constructs the loss function in a way that greatly speeds up the estimation. We then present the Differential Evolution algorithm, which has been shown by Vollrath and Wendland (2009) to be effective in the Heston model. Next we introduce a method by Atiya and Wall (2009) to obtain maximum likelihood estimates of the Heston model parameters. Finally, we show how the risk-neutral density and total volatility can be used to determine whether the implied volatility surface is arbitrage-free. Throughout this chapter, the Heston parameters are represented as the vector $\Theta = (\kappa, \theta, \sigma, v_0, \rho)$, and their corresponding estimates as $\hat{\Theta}$.

loss function, objective function, Nelder-Mead algorithm, starting value, Smart Parameter, Strike-Vector Computation, state variable, Differential Evolution, maximum likelihood estimation, risk-neutral density, arbitrage free

All of the pricing methodologies we have covered have assumed the Heston model parameters to be given. In this chapter, we describe how to estimate these parameters. We first present the most common estimation method, the loss function approach, which minimizes the difference between quoted and model option price. Alternatively, implied volatilities can be used instead of prices. Next, we summarize the Nelder and Mead (1965) minimization algorithm, and we show how to code it in VBA. Then we describe the method of Gauthier and Rivaille (2009) to select starting values and the Strike-Vector Computation of Kilin (2007), which constructs the loss function in a way that greatly speeds up the estimation. We then present the Differential Evolution algorithm, which has been shown by Vollrath and Wendland (2009) to be effective in the Heston model. Next, we introduce a method by Atiya and Wall (2009) to obtain maximum likelihood estimates of the Heston model parameters. Finally, we show how the risk-neutral density and total volatility can be used to determine whether the implied volatility surface is arbitrage free. Throughout this chapter, the Heston parameters are represented as the vector $\Theta = (\kappa, \theta, \sigma, v_0, \rho)$, and their corresponding estimates as $\hat{\Theta}$.

ESTIMATION USING LOSS FUNCTIONS

The most popular way to estimate the parameters of the Heston model is with loss functions. This method uses the error between quoted market prices and model prices, or between market and model implied volatilities. The parameter estimates, $\hat{\Theta}$, are those values that minimize the value of the loss function, so that the model prices or implied volatilities are as close as possible to their market counterparts. A constrained minimization algorithm must be used to ensure that the constraints on the parameters

$$\kappa > 0, \theta > 0, \sigma > 0, v_0 > 0, \rho \in [-1, +1] \tag{6.1}$$

are respected. Since loss functions use market option prices (or implied volatility derived from those prices) as inputs, they produce estimates of the risk-neutral parameters of the Heston model.

Suppose we have a set of N_T maturities, τ_i $(t = 1, \ldots, N_T)$, and a set of N_K strikes, K_k $(k = 1, \ldots, N_K)$. For each maturity-strike combination (τ_t, K_k), we have a market price $C(\tau_t, K_k) = C_{tk}$ and a corresponding model price $C(\tau_t, K_k; \Theta) = C^{\Theta}_{tk}$ generated by the Heston model. Attached to each option is an optional weight w_{tk}. There are many possible ways to define a loss function, but they usually fall into one of the two categories: those based on prices, and those based on implied volatilities.

The first category of loss functions are those that minimize the error between quoted and model prices. The error is usually defined as the squared difference between the quoted and model prices, or the absolute value of the difference; relative errors can also be used. For example, parameter estimates obtained using the mean error sum of squares (MSE) loss function are obtained by minimizing

$$\frac{1}{N}\sum_{t,k} w_{tk}\left(C_{tk} - C^{\Theta}_{tk}\right)^2 \tag{6.2}$$

with respect to Θ, where N is the number of quotes. The relative mean error sum of squares (RMSE) parameter estimates are obtained with the loss function

$$\frac{1}{N}\sum_{t,k} w_{tk}\frac{\left(C_{tk} - C^{\Theta}_{tk}\right)^2}{C_{tk}}. \tag{6.3}$$

Alternatively, we can define the error in terms of the absolute value, so that $|C_{tk} - C^{\Theta}_{tk}|$ can set up a loss function as in Equations (6.2) and (6.3).

One well-known disadvantage of the MSE loss function is that short maturity, deep out-of-the money options, with very little value contribute little to the sum in (6.2). Hence, the optimization will tend to fit long maturity, in-the-money options well, at the detriment of the other options. One remedy is to use in-the-money options only, so that in (6.2), call options are used for strikes less than the spot price, and put options are used for strikes greater than the spot price. The other remedy is to use the RMSE loss function in (6.3). The problem with RMSE, however, is that the opposite effect occurs. Indeed, because of the presence of C_{tk} in the denominator, options with low market value will over-contribute to the sum in (6.3). The over- and undercontribution, however, can be mitigated by assigning weights w_{tk} to the individual terms in the objective function, although the choice of the weights is usually subjective.

The second category of loss functions are those that minimize the error between quoted and model implied volatilities. Again, the error is usually defined as the squared difference, absolute difference, or relative difference, between quoted and model implied volatilities. This category of loss function is sensible, since options are often quoted in terms of implied volatility, and since the fit of the model is often assessed by comparing quoted and model implied volatilities. Hence, for example, the implied volatility mean error sum of squares (IVMSE) parameter estimates are based on the loss function

$$\frac{1}{N}\sum_{t,k} w_{tk}\left(IV_{tk} - IV_{tk}^{\Theta}\right)^2, \tag{6.4}$$

where $IV_{tk} = IV(\tau_t, K_k)$ and $IV_{tk}^{\Theta} = IV(\tau_t, K_k; \Theta)$ are the quoted and model implied volatilities, respectively. The relative and absolute versions can also be used.

The main disadvantage of Equation (6.4) is that it is numerically intensive. Indeed, at each iteration of the optimization, we must first obtain every Heston price C_{tk}^{Θ}, and then apply a root-finding algorithm such as the bisection algorithm to extract the implied volatility IV_{tk}^{Θ} from C_{tk}^{Θ} so that the quantity $(IV_{tk} - IV_{tk}^{\Theta})^2$ can be constructed. One remedy is to use the approximate implied volatility from Lewis's (2000) Series II expansion described in Chapter 4, and use that instead of IV_{tk}^{Θ}. This allows us to bypass the bisection algorithm entirely. Another remedy is to use the loss function described in Christoffersen et al. (2009), which serves as an approximation to the IVMSE in (6.4). It uses the reciprocal of the squared Black-Scholes vega as the weight in (6.2). The parameter estimates from their method are, therefore, based on the loss function

$$\frac{1}{N}\sum_{t,k} \frac{\left(C_{tk} - C_{tk}^{\Theta}\right)^2}{\text{BSVega}_{tk}^2}, \tag{6.5}$$

where BSVega_{tk} is the Black-Scholes sensitivity of the option price with respect to the market implied volatility IV_{tk}, evaluated at the maturity τ_t and the strike K_k

$$\text{BSVega}_{tk} = S\exp(-q\tau_t)n(d_{tk})\sqrt{\tau_t},$$

with

$$d_{tk} = \frac{\log(S/K_k) + (r - q - IV_{tk}^2/2)\tau_t}{IV_{tk}\sqrt{\tau_t}}$$

and where $n(x) = \exp(-x^2/2)/\sqrt{2\pi}$ is the standard normal density. The chief advantage of loss functions based on the approximations of Lewis (2000) or Christoffersen et al. (2009) is that a considerable amount of computation time is saved, albeit at the expense of a loss in precision in the parameter estimates.

Estimation of the Heston model parameters by loss functions has been used by Bakshi et al. (1997); Bams et al. (2009); Christoffersen and Jacobs (2004); Mikhailov and Nögel (2003); and many others. There is no consensus as to which loss function is the best one, but Christoffersen and Jacobs (2004) point out that the same loss function should be used for parameter estimation and for evaluating model fit.

The VBA function HestonObjFun implements the loss functions covered in this section. The function can be modified to include additional loss functions.

```
Function HestonObjFun(params As Variant, ...) As Variant
For i = 1 To NK
    Strike = K(i)
    For j = 1 To NT
        Mat = T(j)
        MarketPrice = MktPrice(i, j)
        ' Heston Call price with Gauss Laguerre int.
        ModelPrice = HestonPriceGaussLaguerre(PutCall, ...)
        ' Select the objective function
        If ObjFun = 1 Then           ' MSE
            Errors(i, j) = (MarketPrice - ModelPrice) ^ 2
        ElseIf ObjFun = 2 Then       ' RMSE
            Errors(i, j) = (MarketPrice - ModelPrice) ^ 2 / ...
        ElseIf ObjFun = 3 Then       ' IVMSE
            ModelIV = BisecBSIV(PutCall, ...)
            Errors(i, j) = (ModelIV - MktIV(i, j)) ^ 2
        ElseIf ObjFun = 4 Then       ' IVRMSE Christoffersen et al.
            ImpVol = MktIV(i, j)
            d = (Log(S / Strike) + (rf - q + ImpVol ^ 2 / 2) ...
            Vega = S * Norm_S_Dist(d, 0) * Sqr(Mat)
            Errors(i, j) = (ModelPrice - MarketPrice) ^ 2 / ...
        End If
    Next j
Next i
If kappa <= 0 Or theta <= 0 Or sigma <= 0 Or ... Then
    ' Penalty for non-admissible parameter values
    HestonObjFun = 1E+100
Else
    ' Otherwise, return the mean of the errors
    HestonObjFun = Sum(Errors) / (NT * NK)
End If
End Function
```

To obtain the parameter estimates, we pass the HestonObjFun function to the VBA function NelderMead. The Nelder-Mead algorithm is designed for

TABLE 6.1 Results of Parameter Estimation with Various Objective Functions

Loss Function	IVMSE	$\hat{\kappa}$	$\hat{\theta}$	$\hat{\sigma}$	$\hat{v}_0$	$\hat{\rho}$	Est Time
MSE (6.2)	1.17×10^{-5}	1.1533	0.1124	0.8573	0.0341	−0.7740	48.8
RMSE (6.3)	9.05×10^{-6}	2.8452	0.0757	1.1343	0.0357	−0.7810	74.6
IVMSE (6.4)	2.05×10^{-3}	5.5401	0.0515	0.5855	0.0651	−0.5293	18.2
CHJ (2009) (6.5)	5.41×10^{-6}	2.5760	0.0808	1.1106	0.0336	−0.7701	66.0

unconstrained optimization, so we add a penalty to ensure that the parameter constraints in (6.1) are respected. The Nelder-Mead algorithm and the VBA code to implement the algorithm are described in the next section.

To illustrate, we estimate the Heston parameters using call options collected on April 13, 2012, on the Standard & Poor's (S&P) 500 index for four maturities: 45, 98, 261, and 348 days, and seven strikes, running from 120 to 150 in increments of 5. We use 32-point Gauss-Laguerre integration to obtain the model price C^{Θ}_{tk} (by setting Method=1 in the function HestonObjFunction), and we compare the parameter estimates from the MSE loss function (6.2), the RMSE loss function (6.3), the IVMSE loss function (6.4), and the Christoffersen, Heston, and Jacobs (CHJ) (2009) loss function (6.5). We also report the IVMSE between the model and the quoted implied volatilities and the estimation time in seconds. We use 250 iterations in the Nelder-Mead algorithm. The results are shown in Table 6.1.

The parameter estimates vary, and in this example CHJ (2009) estimates seem to provide the best fit to the implied volatilities, slightly better than the RMSE estimates. As is usually the case, ρ is negative. The plots of quoted implied volatilities and implied volatilities generated from Heston prices that use RMSE parameter estimates are presented in Figure 6.1. These indicate that the fit of implied volatilities is slightly better for longer-term options than for shorter-term ones.

The excellent fit of the Heston model to the implied volatilities of the S&P 500 index, especially for the short maturities, is exceptional. As noted by Gatheral (2006) and others, in most cases the fit to short maturities will be poor. The Excel file Ch6DIA.xls, which produces parameter estimates using options on the Dow Jones Industrial Average index (ticker DIA), contains a graph similar to that in Figure 6.1, but that is more realistic.

The parameter estimates in Table 6.1 were obtained using the risk-free rate and dividend yield implied from the prices of the puts and calls. See Shimko (1993) for details. The VBA functions presented in this section and the examples that are used in Table 6.1 are in the Excel file Ch6SPX.xls.

Finally, we can incorporate the fast Fourier transform (FFT) or the fractional fast Fourier transform (FRFT) in the objective function. The VBA objective functions HestonObjFunFFT and HestonObjFunFRFT construct the loss functions described in the first section of this chapter, but using the FFT and FRFT to obtain model prices. The functions return parameter estimates that are in line with those obtained with the regular objective function, but the estimation time is very long. These functions are not presented here, but they are in the Excel files Ch6FFT.xls and Ch6FRFT.xls, respectively.

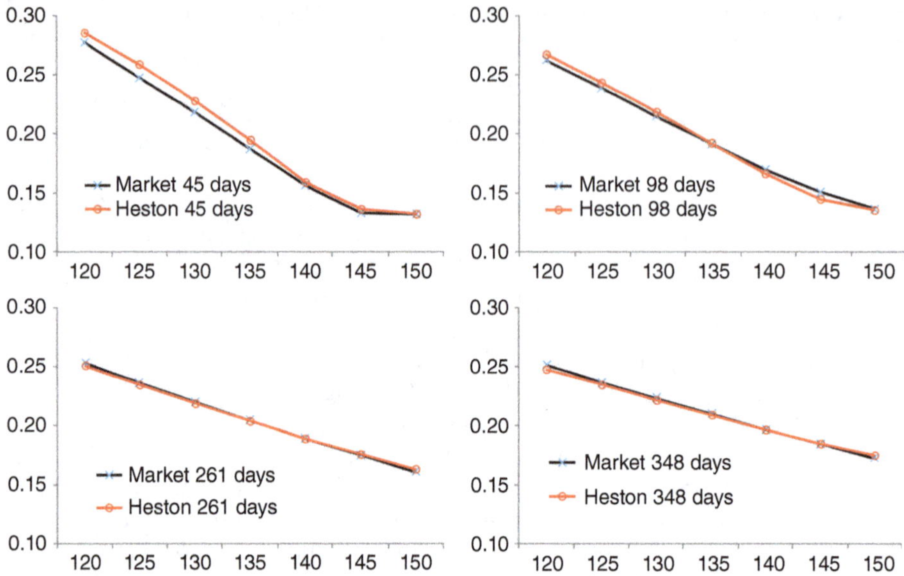

FIGURE 6.1 S&P 500 Market and Heston Implied Volatilities with RMSE Parameter Estimates.

The Nelder-Mead Algorithm in VBA

The Nelder-Mead algorithm is designed to find the global minimum of an objective function $f(\mathbf{x}) : \mathbb{R}^n \rightarrow \mathbb{R}$. The algorithm requires a set of $n+1$ starting values, each of which is a vector of dimension n. At each iteration, the algorithm replaces the vector that produces the worst value of f (namely, the largest value) with a vector that produces a smaller value of f. The Nelder-Mead algorithm is explained in Nelder and Mead (1965) and in many other sources, such as Dréo et al. (2009), for example. The algorithm consists of the following steps:

Step 0. Initialization. Define the $n+1$ vertices $\mathbf{x}_0, \mathbf{x}_1, \ldots, \mathbf{x}_n$ in terms of ranked values of the objective function

$$f(\mathbf{x}_0) \leq f(\mathbf{x}_1) \leq \cdots \leq f(\mathbf{x}_{n-1}) \leq f(\mathbf{x}_n).$$

Hence, $\mathbf{x}_0$ is the best point, since it has the lowest value of the objective function, and $\mathbf{x}_n$ is the worst point. Calculate the mean $\bar{\mathbf{x}} = (\mathbf{x}_0 + \mathbf{x}_1 + \cdots + \mathbf{x}_{n-1})/n$. Note that $\bar{\mathbf{x}}$ excludes the worst point $\mathbf{x}_n$.

Step 1. Reflection rule. Calculate the reflection point $\mathbf{x}_r$ as

$$\mathbf{x}_r = \bar{\mathbf{x}} + \rho(\bar{\mathbf{x}} - \mathbf{x}_n).$$

If $f(\mathbf{x}_1) \leq f(\mathbf{x}_r) \leq f(\mathbf{x}_n)$, then replace $\mathbf{x}_n$ with the reflection point $\mathbf{x}_r$ and proceed to the next iteration in Step 0. Otherwise, continue to Step 2.

Step 2. Expansion rule. If $f(\mathbf{x}_r) \leq f(\mathbf{x}_0)$, calculate the expansion point

$$\mathbf{x}_e = \bar{\mathbf{x}} + \chi(\mathbf{x}_r - \bar{\mathbf{x}}).$$

If $f(\mathbf{x}_e) \leq f(\mathbf{x}_r)$, then replace $\mathbf{x}_n$ with the expansion point $\mathbf{x}_e$ and proceed to the next iteration in Step 0. If $f(\mathbf{x}_e) > f(\mathbf{x}_r)$, then replace $\mathbf{x}_n$ with the reflection point $\mathbf{x}_r$ and proceed to the next iteration.

If $f(\mathbf{x}_r) > f(\mathbf{x}_0)$, then continue to Step 3.

Step 3. Outside contraction rule. Calculate the outside contraction point

$$\mathbf{x}_{oc} = \bar{\mathbf{x}} + \gamma(\mathbf{x}_r - \bar{\mathbf{x}}).$$

If $f(\mathbf{x}_{n-1}) \leq f(\mathbf{x}_r) < f(\mathbf{x}_n)$ and $f(\mathbf{x}_{oc}) < f(\mathbf{x}_n)$, then replace $\mathbf{x}_n$ with $\mathbf{x}_{oc}$ and proceed to the next iteration in Step 0. Otherwise, continue to Step 4.

Step 4. Inside contraction rule. Calculate the inside contraction point

$$\mathbf{x}_{ic} = \bar{\mathbf{x}} + \gamma(\mathbf{x}_n - \bar{\mathbf{x}}).$$

If $f(\mathbf{x}_n) \leq f(\mathbf{x}_r)$ and $f(\mathbf{x}_{ic}) < f(\mathbf{x}_{n+1})$, then replace $\mathbf{x}_n$ with $\mathbf{x}_{ic}$ and proceed to the next iteration in Step 0. Otherwise, continue to Step 5.

Step 5. Shrinkage. Replace $\mathbf{x}_i$ with $\mathbf{x}_i + \sigma(\mathbf{x}_0 - \mathbf{x}_i)$ for $i = 1, \ldots, n$. Note that the best point $\mathbf{x}_0$ does not undergo shrinkage.

Standard values for the coefficients in the steps described earlier are $\rho =$ 1 for reflection, $\chi = 2$ for expansion, $\gamma = 1/2$ for contraction, and $\sigma = 1/2$ for shrinkage.

The Nelder-Mead algorithm stops when the number of iterations reaches a specified value, or when the absolute difference between the best and worst function values, $|f(\mathbf{x}_0) - f(\mathbf{x}_n)|$, reaches a specified tolerance level.

The algorithm is implemented in VBA with the NelderMead function. The following snippet of code contains Steps 1 through 5 described earlier. The reflection, expansion, and inside and outside contraction points are calculated earlier in the function and are not presented here.

```
Function NelderMead(fname As String, ...) As Variant
For iter = 1 To MaxIters
    ' Reflection point
    For i = 1 To N
        xr(i) = xbar(i) + rho * (xbar(i) - xn1(i))
    Next i
    fr = Run(fname, xr, ...)
    If ((fr >= f1) And (fr < fn)) Then
        newpoint = xr
        newf = fr
    ElseIf (fr < f1) Then
        ' Expansion point
        For i = 1 To N
            xe(i) = xbar(i) + xi * (xr(i) - xbar(i))
        Next i
        fe = Run(fname, xe, ...)
```

```
        If (fe < fr) Then
            newpoint = xe
            newf = fe
        End If
    ElseIf (fr >= fn) Then
        If ((fr >= fn) And (fr < fn1)) Then
            ' Outside contraction
            For i = 1 To N
                xoc(i) = xbar(i) + gam * (xr(i) - xbar(i))
            Next i
        foc = Run(fname, xoc, ...)
        If (foc <= fr) Then
            newpoint = xoc
            newf = foc
        End If
    Else
        ' Inside contraction
        For i = 1 To N
            xic(i) = xbar(i) - gam * (xbar(i) - xn1(i))
        Next i
        fic = Run(fname, xic, ...)
        If (fic < fn1) Then
            newpoint = xic
            newf = fic
        End If
    End If
    If (shrink = 1) Then
        For scnt = 2 To N + 1
            For i = 1 To N
                ' Shrinkage step
                resmat(scnt, i + 1) = x1(i) + sigma ...
                passParams(i) = resmat(scnt, i + 1)
            Next i
            resmat(scnt, 1) = Run(fname, ...)
        Next scnt
    End If
End Function
```

The VBA function BubSortRows is used to sort rows of matrices in the Nelder-Mead function, but this function is not presented here. All of the necessary functions for the implementation of the Nelder-Mead algorithm are in the Excel files Ch6SPX.xls and Ch6DIA.xls.

Starting Values

The VBA function NelderMead described in previous sections requires a set of starting values for the parameters. As with any optimization, it is important that these

TABLE 6.2 Parameter Estimates from the Literature

Source	$\hat{\kappa}$	$\hat{\theta}$	$\hat{\sigma}$	$\hat{v}_0$	$\hat{\rho}$	Data, Date
GS (2012)[a]	0.3369	0.0551	0.1927	0.0746	−1.000	S&P 500, 09/2008
Forde et al. (2010)	1.7609	0.0494	0.4086	0.0464	−0.5195	Eurostoxx 50, 02/2006
Gatheral (2006)	1.3253	0.0354	0.3877	0.0174	−0.7165	S&P 500, 09/2005
CHJ (2009)[b]	1.6048	0.0464	0.3796	n/a	−0.7670	S&P 500, 2004
SST (2004)[c]	0.6067	0.0707	0.2928	0.0654	−0.7571	Eurostoxx 50, 10/2003
BCC (1997)[d]	1.15	0.04	0.39	0.0348	−0.64	S&P 500, 1988–1991

[a]Guillaume and Schoutens (2012).
[b]Christoffersen et al. (2009).
[c]Schoutens et al. (2004).
[d]Bakshi et al. (1997).
n/a = not applicable.

starting values lie not too far away from the true values. We can look to estimates from the empirical literature, such as those in Table 6.2, for clues on appropriate starting values.

We must also apply good judgment when selecting starting values. For example, volatility and price are usually negatively correlated, so we may specify for the starting value for the correlation to lie in $(-1, 0)$. Aït-Sahalia and Kimmel (2007) use 30-day at-the-money implied volatility as a proxy for instantaneous unobserved volatility, so we can use that value as a starting estimate for v_0.

To find starting values of ρ and σ, we can use the "Smart Parameter" method of Gauthier and Rivaille (2009), which is described in the remainder of this section. In VBA the simplest way to implement their method is to find the values of (ρ, σ) that minimize the objective function:

$$\begin{aligned} f(\rho, \sigma) = {} & \left(A(K_1) + B(K_1)\sigma^2 + C(K_1)\rho\sigma + D(K_1)\rho^2\sigma^2 - P(K_1)\right)^2 \\ & + \left(A(K_2) + B(K_2)\sigma^2 + C(K_2)\rho\sigma + D(K_2)\rho^2\sigma^2 - P(K_2)\right)^2, \end{aligned} \tag{6.6}$$

where $P(K_1)$ is a quoted put with strike K_1 and $P(K_2)$ is a quoted put with strike K_2, each with the same maturity. The other quantities in (6.6) are

$$\begin{aligned} & A = P_{BS}(x, \hat{w}_\tau), B = (r_0 v_0 + \theta r_1)\frac{\partial^2 P_{BS}}{\partial y^2}, C = (v_0 p_0 + \theta p_1)\frac{\partial^2 P_{BS}}{\partial x \partial y}, \\ & D = \left[(v_0 q_0 + \theta q_1)\frac{\partial^3 P_{BS}}{\partial x^2 \partial y} + \frac{1}{2}(r_0 p_0 + \theta p_1)\frac{\partial^4 P_{BS}}{\partial x^2 \partial y^2}\right]. \end{aligned} \tag{6.7}$$

In Equation (6.7) the derivatives of the Black-Scholes put $P_{BS}(x, \hat{w}_\tau)$ are expressed in terms of the log-stock price $x = \ln S_t$ and the total integrated variance $\hat{w}_\tau = (v_0 - \theta)(1 - e^{-\kappa\tau})/\kappa + \theta$ we encountered in Chapter 2. Formulas for these derivatives are presented in Chapter 9. Finally, the coefficients in (6.7), namely, m_0, m_1, p_0, p_1, q_0, q_1, r_0 and r_1 can be found in Gauthier and Rivaille (2009) or in Benhamou et al. (2010).

The objective function (6.6) is implemented with the VBA function GauthierObjFun.

```
Function GauthierObjFun(params As Variant, ...) As Double
If sigma > 0 And Abs(rho) < 1 Then
    GauthierObjFun = (A1 + B1 * sigma ^ 2 ... - Put1) ^ 2 _
                   + (A2 + B2 * sigma ^ 2 ... - Put2) ^ 2
Else
    ' Penalty for inadmissible parameter values
    GauthierObjFun = 1E+100
End If
End Function
```

The VBA function GauthierCoefficients returns the coefficients in (6.7).

```
Function GauthierCoefficients(kappa As Double, ...) As Variant
' Parameter values
p0 = Exp(-kT) * (Exp(kT) - kT - 1) / kappa ^ 2
p1 = Exp(-kT) * (Exp(kT) * (kT - 2) + kT + 2) / kappa ^ 2
q0 = Exp(-kT) * (2 * Exp(kT) - kT * (kT + 2) - 2) / 2 ...
q1 = Exp(-kT) * (2 * Exp(kT) * (kT - 3) + kT * (kT + 4) + 6) ...
r0 = Exp(-2 * kT) * (2 * Exp(2 * kT) - 4 * Exp(kT) * kT - 2) ...
r1 = Exp(-2 * kT) * (Exp(2 * kT) * (2 * kT - 5) + 4 * Exp(kT) ...
' Generate the Black-Scholes derivatives
output = BlackScholesDerivatives(kappa, theta, v0, ...)
P11 = output(1)
P21 = output(2)
P02 = output(3)
P22 = output(4)
' Black Scholes Put Price
g = y ^ (-1 / 2) * (-x + Log(K) - (rf - q) * T) - (1 / 2) ...
f = y ^ (-1 / 2) * (-x + Log(K) - (rf - q) * T) + (1 / 2) ...
BSPut = K * Exp(-rf * T) * normcdf(f) - S * Exp(-q * T) ...
' Return the coefficients
A = BSPut
B = (v0 * r0 + theta * r1) * P02
C = (v0 * p0 + theta * p1) * P11
D = (v0 * q0 + theta * q1) * P21 + 0.5 * (v0 * p0 + theta * p1) ^ 2 ...
end
```

The VBA function BlackScholesDerivatives returns the derivatives required in (6.7).

```
Function BlackScholesDerivatives(kappa As Double, ...) As Variant
' Black Scholes Put Price
g = y ^ (-1 / 2) * (-x + Log(K) - (rf - q) * T) ...
f = y ^ (-1 / 2) * (-x + Log(K) - (rf - q) * T) ...
BSPut = K * Exp(-rf * T) * normcdf(f) - S * Exp(-q * T) ...
' Normal pdf, phi(f) and phi(g)
phif = Exp(-f ^ 2 / 2) / Sqr(2 * pi)
phig = Exp(-g ^ 2 / 2) / Sqr(2 * pi)
' Derivatives of f and g
fx = -y ^ (-1 / 2)
fy = -1 / 2 / y * g
gx = fx
gy = -1 / 2 / y * f
' Derivatives of the cdf PHI(f)
PHIfxy = (1 / 2) * y ^ (-3 / 2) * phif * (1 - f * g)
PHIfx2y = (1 / 2) * y ^ (-2) * phif * (2 * f + g ...)
' Derivatives of cdf PHI(g)
PHIgx = -phig * y ^ (-1 / 2)
PHIgy = -(1 / 2) * f * phig / y
' Derivatives of Black-Scholes Put
dPdxdy = K * Exp(-rf * T) * PHIfxy - Exp(-q * T) ...
dPdx2dy = K * Exp(-rf * T) * PHIfx2y - Exp(-q * T) ...
End Function
```

Finally, the function GetGauthierValues returns the starting values for ρ and σ.

```
Function GetGauthierValues(kappa As Double, ...) As Variant
' Find the Gauthier coefficients for each strike
Coeff1 = GauthierCoefficients(K1, ...)
Coeff2 = GauthierCoefficients(K2, ...)
' Return rho and sigma
output(1, 1) = RhoFinal
output(2, 1) = SigmaFinal
GetGauthierValues = output
End Function
```

The screen shot in Figure 6.2 illustrates the method of Gauthier and Rivaille (2009). The starting values are $\sigma = 3.5791$ and $\rho = -0.3469$.

The VBA functions described in this section, and the screen shot in Figure 6.2, are in the Excel file Ch6StartValues.xls.

	A	B	C	D	E	F	G	H	I	J	K	L	M
1													
2		"Smart Parameter" Starting Values of Gauthier and Rivaille											
3						Set 1	Set 2			Market Implied Volatilities of Puts			
4		Option Features			Gauthier Coefficients	10.0199	21.6164			Maturities			
5		Spot Price (S)	137.14			-0.1908	-0.1799		Strikes	0.2685	0.7151	0.9534	1.7644
6		Risk free rate (r)	0			-0.1929	1.0824		120	1.620	4.965	6.620	11.300
7		Dividend (q)	0			-0.1395	-0.2682		125	2.325	6.140	7.970	12.980
8		Flavor (P or C)	P						130	3.345	7.600	9.550	14.890
9					Parameter Estimates				135	4.840	9.380	11.395	16.985
10		Heston Parameters			Sigma (σ)	3.5791			140	7.010	11.615	13.625	19.185
11		kappa (κ)	10		Rho (ρ)	-0.3469			145	10.055	14.305	16.320	21.550
12		theta (θ)	0.1		Objective Function	2.02E-16			150	14.085	17.555	19.380	24.435
13		v0	0.01		Number of Iterations	89							
14													
15		Settings for the Smart Parameters			Starting Values								
16		First strike number	3		sigma	0.50							
17		Second strike number	7		rho	-0.25							
18		Maturity number	2										
19					Settings for Nelder-Mead								
20		Settings for the Smart Parameters			Tolerance	1.00E-15							
21		First strike value	130		Maximum # iterations	100							
22		Second strike value	150		Shock for starting values	5%							
23		First put price	7.600										
24		Second put price	17.555										
25		Maturity value	0.7151										

FIGURE 6.2 Starting Values for Rho and Sigma

SPEEDING UP THE ESTIMATION

One drawback of loss function estimation is that it can be very time consuming, especially if many maturities and strikes are used. Kilin (2007) suggests a very simple trick for speeding up the optimization routines required for loss function estimation. Recall that the integrand for the in-the-money probabilities P_j $(j = 1, 2)$ is

$$\text{Re}\left[\frac{e^{-i\phi \ln K} f_j(\phi)}{i\phi}\right]. \tag{6.8}$$

Kilin (2007) notes that the characteristic function $f_j(\phi)$ does not depend on the strike K, but it does depend on the maturity τ. This implies that, in the optimization, the values of $f_1(\phi)$ and $f_2(\phi)$ can be calculated once for each maturity, cached, and used repeatedly for the different strikes. This is important because the term $f_j(\phi)$ is by far the one that requires the most computation time in the integrand, as it contains a number of complex operations, including logarithms, exponents, and square roots. Zhu (2010) refers to Kilin's trick as Strike-Vector Computation, and Schmelzle (2010) calls it the caching technique. Kilin (2007) points out that, in order for this to work, the outer loop of the optimization must be for the maturities and the inner loop for the strikes. When coupled with a pricing formula that requires a single integrand, such as those by Attari (2004) or Lewis (2001), the caching technique leads to an estimation time that is considerably reduced.

The VBA function HestonObjFunSVC implements the method of Kilin (2007) using Gauss-Laguerre integration. The function allows for the original Heston (1993) or Attari (2004) formulation of the characteristic function. If the IVMSE loss function is selected, the function calls the VBA function BisecBSV for finding implied volatilities with the bisection method. The outer loop is for maturities and the inner loop is for strikes. At the beginning of each strike loop, we calculate the value of the characteristic functions f_1 and f_2 at the Gauss-Laguerre abscissas ϕ_j. We then retain these values, form the integrand at each of the strikes, and calculate the call prices or the put prices using put-call parity.

```
Function HestonObjFunSVC(params As Variant, ...) As Variant
For tt = 1 To NT
    For j = 1 To NX
        ' Store the characteristic function at each time step
        f2(j) = Complex(CharFun(1, 1), CharFun(2, 1))
        f1(j) = cDiv(Complex(CharFun(1, 1), CharFun(2, 1)), ...)
    Next j
    For kk = 1 To NK
        For j = 1 To NX
            ' The integrals
            I1 = cDiv(cProd(expiphi, f1(j)), iphi)
            I2 = cDiv(cProd(expiphi, f2(j)), iphi)
            int1(j) = wt * cReal(I1)
            int2(j) = wt * cReal(I2)
        Next j
        ' The call price, and put price by put-call parity
        P1 = 0.5 + 1 / pi * Sum(int1)
        P2 = 0.5 + 1 / pi * Sum(int2)
        CallPrice = S * Exp(-q * Mat) * P1 - Strike * ...
        If PutCall = "C" Then
            ModelPrice = CallPrice
        Else
            ModelPrice = CallPrice - S * Exp(-q * Mat) + ...
        End If
        ' Select the objective function
        If ObjFun = 1 Then          ' MSE
            Errors(kk, tt) = (MarketPrice - ModelPrice) ^ 2
        ElseIf ObjFun = 2 Then      ' RMSE
            Errors(kk, tt) = (MarketPrice - ModelPrice) ...
        ElseIf ObjFun = 3 Then      ' IVMSE
            ModelIV = BisecBSIV(PutCall, ...)
            Errors(kk, tt) = (ModelIV - MarketIV) ^ 2
        ElseIf ObjFun = 4 Then      ' IVRMSE Christoffersen et al.
            d = (Log(S / Strike) + (rf - q + ImpVol ^ 2 / 2) ...
            Vega = S * Norm_S_Dist(d, 0) ...
            Errors(kk, tt) = (ModelPrice - MarketPrice) ...
        End If
    Next kk
Next tt
```

To illustrate, we obtain RMSE parameter estimates on the S&P 500 call options, used to generate Figure 6.1, but using the SVC objective function. The results are in Figure 6.3.

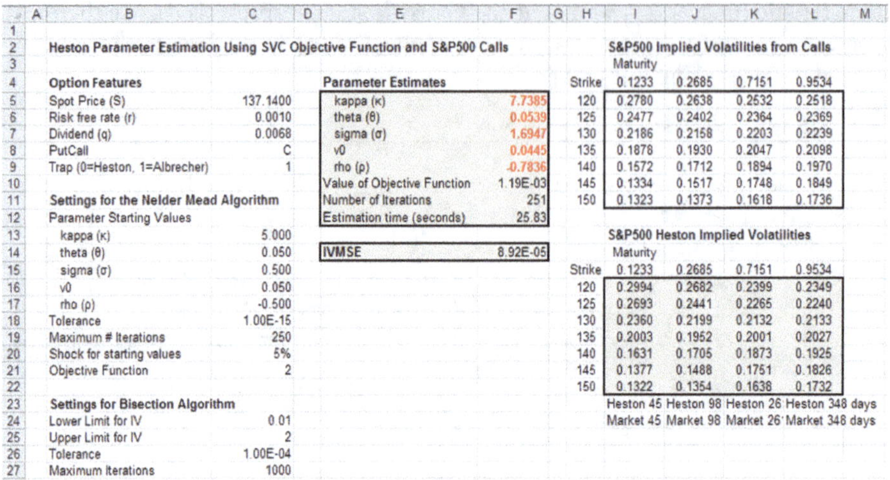

Heston Parameter Estimation Using SVC Objective Function and S&P500 Calls

Option Features	
Spot Price (S)	137.1400
Risk free rate (r)	0.0010
Dividend (q)	0.0068
PutCall	C
Trap (0=Heston, 1=Albrecher)	1

Settings for the Nelder Mead Algorithm	
Parameter Starting Values	
kappa (κ)	5.000
theta (θ)	0.050
sigma (σ)	0.500
v0	0.050
rho (ρ)	-0.500
Tolerance	1.00E-15
Maximum # Iterations	250
Shock for starting values	5%
Objective Function	2

Settings for Bisection Algorithm	
Lower Limit for IV	0.01
Upper Limit for IV	2
Tolerance	1.00E-04
Maximum Iterations	1000

Parameter Estimates	
kappa (κ)	7.7385
theta (θ)	0.0539
sigma (σ)	1.6947
v0	0.0445
rho (ρ)	-0.7836
Value of Objective Function	1.19E-03
Number of Iterations	251
Estimation time (seconds)	25.83
IVMSE	8.92E-05

S&P500 Implied Volatilities from Calls

Strike	Maturity 0.1233	0.2685	0.7151	0.9534
120	0.2780	0.2638	0.2532	0.2518
125	0.2477	0.2402	0.2364	0.2369
130	0.2186	0.2158	0.2203	0.2239
135	0.1878	0.1930	0.2047	0.2098
140	0.1572	0.1712	0.1894	0.1970
145	0.1334	0.1517	0.1748	0.1849
150	0.1323	0.1373	0.1618	0.1736

S&P500 Heston Implied Volatilities

Strike	Maturity 0.1233	0.2685	0.7151	0.9534
120	0.2994	0.2682	0.2399	0.2349
125	0.2693	0.2441	0.2265	0.2240
130	0.2360	0.2199	0.2132	0.2133
135	0.2003	0.1952	0.2001	0.2027
140	0.1631	0.1705	0.1873	0.1925
145	0.1377	0.1488	0.1751	0.1826
150	0.1322	0.1354	0.1638	0.1732
	Heston 45	Heston 98	Heston 26	Heston 348 days
	Market 45	Market 98	Market 26	Market 348 days

FIGURE 6.3 RMSE Parameter Estimates Using the SVC Objective Function

The parameter estimates and IVMSE are similar to those obtained using the ordinary objective function, but the estimation time is reduced by roughly two-thirds. The VBA code and screen shot in Figure 6.3 are in the Excel file Ch6SVC.xls.

One recent trend to improve the speed of estimation is to reduce the set of parameters to estimate. We will see in Chapter 11, for example, that the sensitivity of the Heston option price to changes in κ is low. Hence, we can fix κ at an arbitrary, but reasonable, value. In their version of the Heston model with time-dependent parameters, which we cover in Chapter 9, Benhamou et al. (2010) allow the parameters to be piecewise constant, but restrict κ to a single value. Aït-Sahalia and Kimmel (2007) use short-term (30-day) at-the-money (ATM) implied volatility to proxy instantaneous volatility. Janek et al. (2010) and Zhu (2010) calibrate v_0 to the ATM implied volatility in the FX market, and suggest setting κ large enough so that Feller's condition $2\kappa\theta > \sigma^2$ is satisfied. This leaves only the parameters set (θ, σ, ρ) to estimate. Guillaume and Schoutens (2012) calibrate v_0 and θ to the VIX, and estimate (κ, σ, ρ) only.

Modifying VBA functions for parameter estimation in which one or more of the parameters is fixed is straightforward. In the first argument to the objective function, we pass only those parameters to be optimized, and we pass the fixed parameters as additional arguments to the function.

DIFFERENTIAL EVOLUTION

The Differential Evolution (DE) algorithm of Storn and Price (1997) has been applied to option pricing by Nykvist (2009) and Gilli and Schumann (2011). Vollrath and Wendland (2009) have applied the algorithm to the Heston model and have found the algorithm effective in identifying the global minimum in the parameter space, albeit at the expense of high computation time. The algorithm updates a randomly chosen population of parameter values by creating a new candidate member from each existing member in the population. Each existing member is compared to its candidate, and the candidate replaces the member in the population if the candidate's objective function is smaller than the member's. A new population is thus created, and the process is repeated over successive iterations, or generations. In the final generation, the member with the smallest value of the objective function is chosen as the solution.

The DE algorithm can thus be implemented in the following steps:

Step 1. Initial selection of the population. Form a matrix of size $5 \times N_P$ of randomly chosen parameter values, where N_P is the number of population members. The matrix must be constructed so that each row respects the constraints on the parameters. Lower and upper bounds can be chosen so that the random values for the parameters are reasonable, for example, $0 < \kappa < 20$, $0 < \theta, v_0, \sigma < 2$, and $-1 < \rho < 0$. In order for Step 2 to work, we must have $N_P \geq 4$. This implies we have the population

$$\underset{(5\times N_P)}{\mathbf{P}} = \begin{pmatrix} \mathbf{x}_1 & \mathbf{x}_2 & \cdots & \mathbf{x}_{N_P} \end{pmatrix}, \tag{6.9}$$

where each member of $\mathbf{P}$ is a vector of parameters, namely $\mathbf{x}_i = (\kappa_i, \theta_i, \sigma_i, v_{0i}, \rho_i)^T$.

Step 2. Mutation of the population members. For each member $\mathbf{x}_i$ of the population ($i = 1, \ldots, N_P$), randomly select three other members $\mathbf{x}_{r1}$, $\mathbf{x}_{r2}$, and $\mathbf{x}_{r3}$ distinct from each other and from $\mathbf{x}_i$ as well. This implies that we must select the indices r_1, r_2, and r_3 so that $i \neq r_1 \neq r_2 \neq r_3$. For each member, form a donor member defined by

$$\mathbf{y}_i = \mathbf{x}_{r1} + F(\mathbf{x}_{r2} - \mathbf{x}_{r3}t), \tag{6.10}$$

where $F \in [0, 2]$ is a constant mutation factor. The elements of the donor member $\mathbf{y}_i$ are used to construct a candidate member that may or may not replace $\mathbf{x}_i$, based on the results of Steps 3 and 4.

Step 3. Recombination of the donor members. The candidate member $\mathbf{u}_i$ is constructed element-by-element from the elements y_{ij} of the donor and the elements of the member x_{ij} ($j = 1, \ldots, 5$) according to the following rule. For each element j, we generate a uniform random number U_{ij} and we form the candidate element as

$$u_{ij} = \begin{cases} y_{ij} & \text{if } U_{ij} \leq CR \text{ or } j = R \\ x_{ij} & \text{otherwise} \end{cases}, \tag{6.11}$$

where R is a randomly chosen integer from 1 to 5 and where CR is a probability called the crossover ratio.

Step 4. Selection of the candidate. The member $\mathbf{x}_i$ and its candidate $\mathbf{u}_i$ are each fed into the objective function $f(\mathbf{x})$. If the candidate's value is lower than that of the member, the candidate replaces $\mathbf{x}_i$ as the ith member of the population $\mathbf{P}$ in (6.9). The rule is therefore

$$\mathbf{P} = \begin{cases} (\mathbf{x}_1 & \cdots & \mathbf{u}_i & \cdots & \mathbf{x}_{N_P}) & \text{if } f(\mathbf{u}_i) < f(\mathbf{x}_i) \\ (\mathbf{x}_1 & \cdots & \mathbf{x}_i & \cdots & \mathbf{x}_{N_P}) & \text{otherwise.} \end{cases}, \tag{6.12}$$

When all the members have received the treatment, the population is updated and the next generation starts again at Step 2. The algorithm is thus run over all N_G generations, or iterations. The parameter estimate is chosen as the member with the lowest value of $f(\mathbf{x})$ from the population of the final generation.

The DE algorithm is implemented using the HestonDE function. The first part of the function creates the population of members and generates random uniform numbers outside the loop. In the mutation and recombination steps, the function verifies that the candidate (Pnew) falls within the range of acceptable parameter values. If not, a new candidate is created. The population is updated with the candidate, if applicable. At the last generation, the member with the lowest value of the Heston objective function is returned as the parameter estimate.

```
Function HestonDE(NG As Integer, NP As Integer, ...) As Variant
' Step1.  Generate the population matrix of random params
For j = 1 To NP
    For i = 1 To 5
        P(i, j) = StartValues(i) * (1 + random)
    Next i
Next j
' Generate the random numbers outside the loop
For X = 1 To 5
    For Y = 1 To NP
        For Z = 1 To NG
            bigU(X, Y, Z) = Rnd()
        Next Z
    Next Y
Next X
' Loop through the generations
For k = 1 To NG
    ' Loop through the population
    For i = 1 To NP
        ' Select the i-th member of the population
        For w = 1 To 5
            P0(w) = P(w, i)
        Next w
        Do While Condition < 5
            ' Random indices for 3 other distinct members
            II = RandPerm(NP)
            JJ = findI(II, i)
            ' The 3 distinct members of the population
            For w = 1 To 5
                Pr1(w) = P(w, r(1))
                Pr2(w) = P(w, r(2))
                Pr3(w) = P(w, r(3))
            Next w
            bigR = RandPerm(5)
            ' Steps 2 and 3.  Mutation and recombination
            Pnew(j) = Pr1(j) + F * (Pr2(j) - Pr3(j))
```

```
        Loop
        ' Step 4.  Selection
        f0 = HestonObjFun(P0, ...)
        fnew = HestonObjFun(Pnew, ...)
        ' Verify if candidate should replace i-th member
        If fnew < f0 Then
            For w = 1 To 5
                P(w, i) = Pnew(w)
            Next w
        End If
    Next i
Next k
End Function
```

The HestonDE function makes use of several intermediate functions. The RandPerm function returns a vector of random permutations of integers.

```
Function RandPerm(N As Integer) As Variant
' Vector of random permutation of integers
For j = 1 To N
    X(j, 1) = Rnd()
    X(j, 2) = j
Next j
Y = BubSortRows(X)
For j = 1 To N
    Z(j) = Y(j, 2)
Next j
RandPerm = Z
End Function
```

The findI VBA function removes an element from a vector.

```
Function findI(X As Variant, exclude As Integer) As Variant
' Removes an element from a vector
For j = 1 To N
    If X(j) <> exclude Then
        ReDim Preserve Y(Count)
        Y(Count) = X(j)
        Count = Count + 1
    End If
Next j
findI = Y
End Function
```

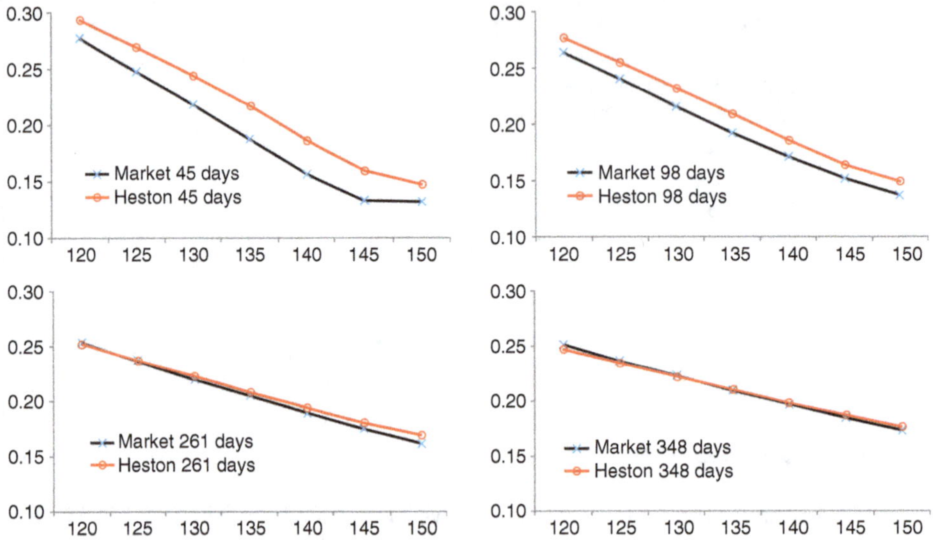

FIGURE 6.4 Market and DE Implied Volatilities

The DE algorithm is particularly useful when we have very poor starting values. This is because, even with poor values, the algorithm will converge to the global optimum, albeit at the expense of many iterations. To illustrate we run the HestonDE function on the S&P 500 data used to create Table 6.1, and using the MSE loss function. Following Vollrath and Wendland (2009), we set the number of population parameters equal to 15 times the number of parameters so that $N_P = 75$, the crossover ratio to $CR = 0.5$, and the mutation factor to $F = 0.8$. We use $N_G = 50$ generations. The market implied volatilities, and those from Heston prices obtained using the DE parameter estimates, are shown in Figure 6.4.

Even with arbitrary starting values and a small number of generations, the DE algorithm produces fitted implied volatilities that are reasonably close to their market counterparts.

All of the VBA functions and examples presented in this section are in the Excel file Ch6DE.xls.

MAXIMUM LIKELIHOOD ESTIMATION

When there exists a set of liquid and reliable market quotes of option prices or implied volatilities, then estimation through loss functions is feasible. If there are no such quotes, however, then alternate methods must be used. Atiya and Wall (2009) show how to obtain the maximum likelihood estimates of the physical parameters of the Heston model using a time series of historical stock prices. Recall that under the risk-neutral measure, the log-stock price $x_t = \ln S_t$ and variance v_t follow the bivariate stochastic differential equation

$$\begin{aligned} dx_t &= \left(r - q - \frac{1}{2}v_t\right)dt + \sqrt{v_t}dW_{1,t} \\ dv_t &= \kappa(\theta - v_t)dt + \sigma\sqrt{v_t}dW_{2,t}, \end{aligned} \tag{6.13}$$

with $E^Q[dW_{1,t}dW_{2,t}] = \rho dt$. The transition probability density for the joint log-stock price/variance process from time t to $t+1$ is bivariate normal. Suppose that we have a time series of log-stock prices $x_1, x_2, \ldots, x_N$ observed at equal time increments dt. The likelihood for the unobserved variances can be approximated from the likelihood of stock prices. The likelihood at time $t+1$, given a value v_t at time t, is

$$L_{t+1}(v_{t+1}) \propto d_t(ab_t)^{-1/4}e^{-2\sqrt{ab_t}}L_t\left(\sqrt{\frac{b_t}{a}}\right). \tag{6.14}$$

The log-likelihood is therefore

$$\ell_{t+1}(v_{t+1}) \propto \ln d_t - \frac{1}{4}\ln(ab_t) - 2\sqrt{ab_t} + \ell_t\left(\sqrt{\frac{b_t}{a}}\right). \tag{6.15}$$

These expressions use the following quantities, defined as Equations (14) through (16) in Atiya and Wall (2009):

$$a = \frac{(\kappa')^2 + \rho\sigma\kappa' dt + \sigma^2(dt)^2/4}{2\sigma^2(1-\rho^2)dt}, \tag{6.16}$$

$$b_t = \frac{(v_{t+1} - \alpha dt)^2 - 2\rho\sigma(v_{t+1} - \alpha dt)(\Delta x_{t+1} - \mu dt) + \sigma^2(\Delta x_{t+1} - \mu dt)^2}{2\sigma^2(1-\rho^2)dt}, \tag{6.17}$$

$$d_t = \frac{1}{D}\exp\left(\frac{(2\kappa' + \rho\sigma dt)(v_{t+1} - \alpha dt) - (2\rho\sigma\kappa' + \sigma^2 dt)(\Delta x_{t+1} - \mu dt)}{2\sigma^2(1-\rho^2)dt}\right), \tag{6.18}$$

with $\mu = r - q$ the drift, $\Delta x_{t+1} = x_{t+1} - x_t$ the increment between log-stock prices, $\kappa' = 1 - \kappa dt$, $\alpha = \kappa\theta$, $D = 2\pi\sigma\sqrt{1-\rho^2}dt$, and dt is the time increment between t and $t+1$. If the observations are daily, for example, then $dt = 1/252$.

The likelihood in (6.14) depends also on v_{t+1}, through the terms b_t and d_t. Atiya and Wall (2009) write

$$v_{t+1} = \sqrt{B^2 - C} - B, \tag{6.19}$$

where

$$B = -\alpha dt - \rho\sigma(\Delta x_{t+1} - \mu dt),$$
$$C = (\alpha dt)^2 + 2\rho\sigma\alpha dt(\Delta x_{t+1} - \mu dt) + \sigma^2(\Delta x_{t+1} - \mu dt)^2 - 2v_t^2 a\sigma^2(1-\rho^2)dt.$$

Hence, to evaluate the likelihood in Equation (6.14) or the log-likelihood in (6.15), we start with initial values $L_0(v_0)$ or $\ell_0(v_0)$. To evaluate $L_{t+1}(v_{t+1})$ or $\ell_{t+1}(v_{t+1})$ given $L_t(v_t)$ or $\ell_t(v_t)$, we first obtain v_{t+1} from (6.19). We then apply Equation (6.14) or (6.15). We continue until time T, at which time we have $L_T(v_T)$ or $\ell_T(v_T)$, to which we apply an optimization routine to find the maximum. The initial value suggested by Atiya and Wall (2009) is $L_0(v_0) = e^{-v_0}$, where v_0 is the initial variance parameter from the Heston model.

The VBA function LikelihoodAW returns the negative of the likelihood or log-likelihood. This is because the Nelder-Mead algorithm we apply to optimize the likelihood or log-likelihood is designed for minimization.

```
Function LikelihoodAW(params As Variant, ...) As Double
' Construction the likelihood for time t = 1 through t = T
For T = 1 To N - 1
    ' Stock price increment
    dx = x(T + 1) - x(T)
    ' Equations (31) and (32)
    B = -alpha * dt - rho * sigma * (dx - mu * dt)
    C = alpha ^ 2 * dt ^ 2 + 2 * rho * sigma * alpha * dt ...
    ' Equation (30) to update the variance
    If (B ^ 2 - C) > 0 Then
        v(T + 1) = Sqr(B ^ 2 - C) - B
    Else
        ' If v(t+1) is imaginary use approximation in Eq. (33)
        bt = ((v(T) - alpha * dt) ^ 2 - 2 * rho * sigma ...
        If bt / a > 0 Then
            ' Equation (33)
            v(T + 1) = Sqr(bt / a)
        Else
            ' If v(t+1) still negative, take previous value
            v(T + 1) = v(T)
        End If
    End If
    ' Equation (15) and (16)
    bt = ((v(T + 1) - alpha * dt) ^ 2 - 2 * rho * sigma ...
    x1 = ((2 * betap + rho * sigma * dt) * (v(T + 1) ...) ...
    x2 = -2 * Sqr(a * bt)
    ' Combined exponent for Equation (34)
    E = Exp(x1 + x2) / D
    If method = 1 Then
        ' Equation (34) for the likelihood L(t+1)
        L(T + 1) = (a * bt) ^ (-1 / 4) * E * L(T)
    ElseIf method = 2 Then
        ' Alternatively, use log-likelihood, log of Eq. (34)
        L(T + 1) = -1 / 4 * Log(a * bt) + x1 + x2 - Log(D) ...
    End If
Next T
' Negative likelihood is the last term.
If kappa <= eps Or theta <= eps Or sigma <= eps Or v0 <= eps
...
    ' Penalty for inadmissible parameter values
    LikelihoodAW = 1E+100
Else
    LikelihoodAW = -L(N)
End If
End Function
```

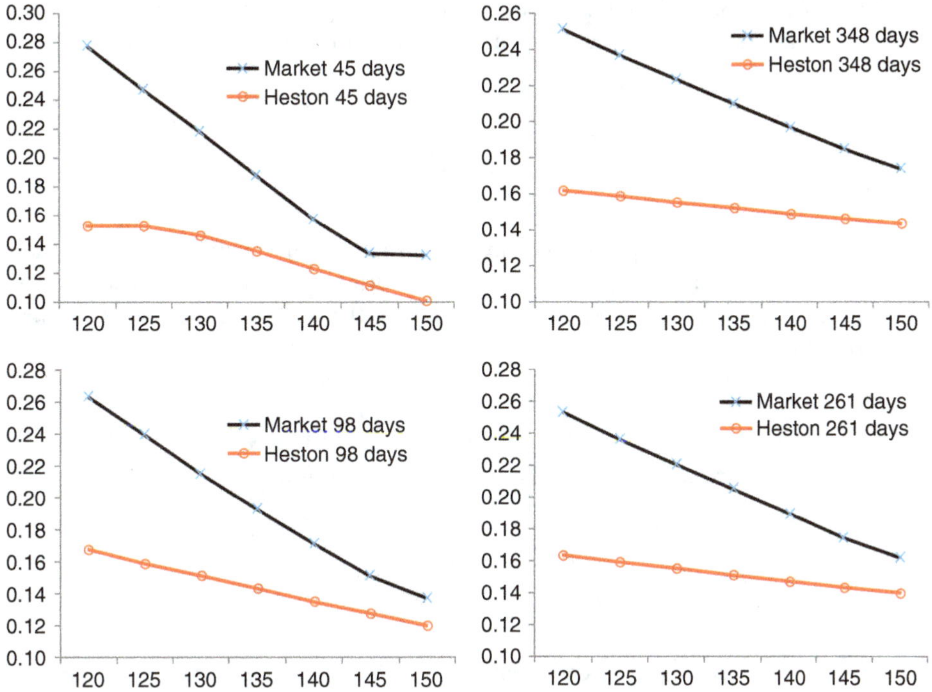

FIGURE 6.5 Market and Heston Implied Volatilities Using MLEs

The LikelihoodAW function is then passed to the NelderMead function, which finds the minimum of the negative likelihood or log-likelihood, and returns the corresponding parameter estimates.

To illustrate, we continue with the example for the S&P 500 index. Recall that the example involved SPY option quotes on April 13, 2012, with maturities of 45, 98, 261, and 348 days and seven strikes, running from 120 to 150 in increments of 5. We obtain MLEs of the parameters using 45 days of log-stock prices. We then use these estimates to obtain Heston implied volatilities, and we plot these alongside the market implied volatilities. The plots are shown in Figure 6.5.

Finally, the results in Figure 6.5 are for illustrative purposes only. Indeed, if a set of market option prices is available, then parameter estimation can be done using loss functions and the maximum likelihood estimation (MLE) method of Atiya and Wall (2009) is not needed. The VBA code presented in this section and the plot in Figure 6.3 are from the Excel file Ch6AW.xls.

RISK-NEUTRAL DENSITY AND ARBITRAGE-FREE VOLATILITY SURFACE

When faced with parameter estimates, $\hat{\Theta}$, the question arises whether the volatility surface generated from the parameter estimates is able to produce prices that are arbitrage free. Arbitrage can be present along one or both dimensions of the volatility surface: strikes and maturities.

The absence of arbitrage across strikes for a single maturity can be identified using the risk-neutral density (RND) of Breeden and Litzenberger (1978)

$$e^{-r\tau} f_{S_T}(S) = \left. \frac{\partial^2 C(K)}{\partial K^2} \right|_{K=S}, \tag{6.20}$$

where $C(K)$ is the price of a call struck at K generated from the implied volatility, and $f_{S_T}(S)$ is the RND. One convenient way to check for the absence of arbitrage across strikes is to obtain $f_{S_T}(S)$ across a wide domain, and ensure that the following three properties hold:

Non-negativity property. The RND must be such that $f_{S_T}(S) \geq 0$ for all $S \geq 0$.

Integrability property. The RND must integrate to unity

$$\int_0^\infty f_{S_T}(S)dS = 1.$$

Martingale property. The RND must be able to recover the market prices of calls.

$$\int_0^\infty \max(S - K, 0) f_{S_T}(S)dS = e^{r\tau} C(K, \tau),$$

where $C(K, \tau)$ is the market price of a call struck at K with maturity $\tau = T - t$. See Brunner and Hafner (2003) and Carr (2004). The first two properties verify that the RND is a density function. The third property is sometimes expressed with $K =$ 0, in which case the left-hand side becomes $E^{\mathbb{Q}}[S_T] = S_t e^{r(T-t)} = F_{t,T}$, where $F_{t,T}$ is the forward price. Hence, the third property is sometimes verified in terms of the ability of the RND to recover forward prices rather than call prices, and as such, it is sometimes called the forward property.

To implement the no-arbitrage check across strikes for a single maturity we use the parameter estimates $\hat{\Theta}$ to generate a set of Heston (1993) call prices at a finely spaced grid of strikes. We then use central finite differences to approximate the second derivative in Equation (6.20), generate the RND, and verify that the three earlier properties hold. Jondeau et al. (2006) caution that the RND estimated with finite differences can be inaccurate and unstable, since even small pricing errors are amplified when finite differences are applied twice. To ensure that the prices are accurate, it is preferable to use an integration method that uses many abscissas, such as the Gauss-Legendre multidomain integration rule described by Zhu (2010), which was covered in Chapter 5.

The VBA function ExtractRND applies central differences to find the RND (6.20). It accepts as inputs a vector of finely spaced strikes and call prices, and returns the same vector of strikes but with four endpoints removed and the value of the RND at each strike.

```
Function ExtractRND(K, CallPrice) As Variant
' First derivatives of calls w.r.t. strike K.
For i = 2 To NK - 1
    dK = K(i + 1) - K(i - 1)
    dC = CallPrice(i + 1) - CallPrice(i - 1)
    dCdK(i - 1) = dC / dK
Next i
NC = Count(dCdK)
' Calculate the RND using central f.d.
For i = 2 To NC - 1
    dK = K(i + 1) - K(i - 1)
    dC2 = dCdK(i + 1) - dCdK(i - 1)
    RNDensity(i - 1) = dC2 / dK
Next i
' Retain the relevant strikes
For i = 1 To NK - 4
    K2(i) = K(i + 2)
Next i
' Output the results into a matrix
For i = 1 To NK - 4
    output(i, 1) = K2(i)
    output(i, 2) = RNDensity(i)
Next i
ExtractRND = output
End Function
```

We use S&P 500 index parameter estimates from Table 6.1 to illustrate risk neutral density estimation in the Heston (1993) model. The call prices are obtained using multidomain integration using a domain of $A = (0, 500)$ divided into 50 subdomains along with a strike increment of $dK = 0.5$. The estimated risk-neutral densities are shown in Figure 6.6.

The RNDs behave as expected. In particular, the RNDs for the longer maturities are more spread out than those for the short maturities, reflecting increasing market uncertainty about future prices with increasing maturity. Note also the negative skew in each density, induced by the negative correlation used to generate them.

Once RND is generated, we need to verify each of the three properties described earlier. We use the VBA function Trapezoidal to verify whether the area under each RND is unity.

```
Function Trapezoidal(x, y) As Double
N = Count(x)
' Calculate the numerical integral
```

```
For j = 1 To N - 1
    Integrand(j) = (x(j + 1) - x(j)) * (y(j + 1) ...
Next j
Trapezoidal = Sum(Integrand)
End Function
```

We use the RecoverCalls VBA function to verify that each RND can recover the call prices from which it is constructed.

```
Function RecoverCalls(ST, RND, ...) As Double
N = Count(ST)
' Trapezoidal weights
w(1) = dK / 2
w(N) = dK / 2
For i = 2 To N - 1
    w(i) = dK
Next i
Sum = 0
' Calculate the call price
```

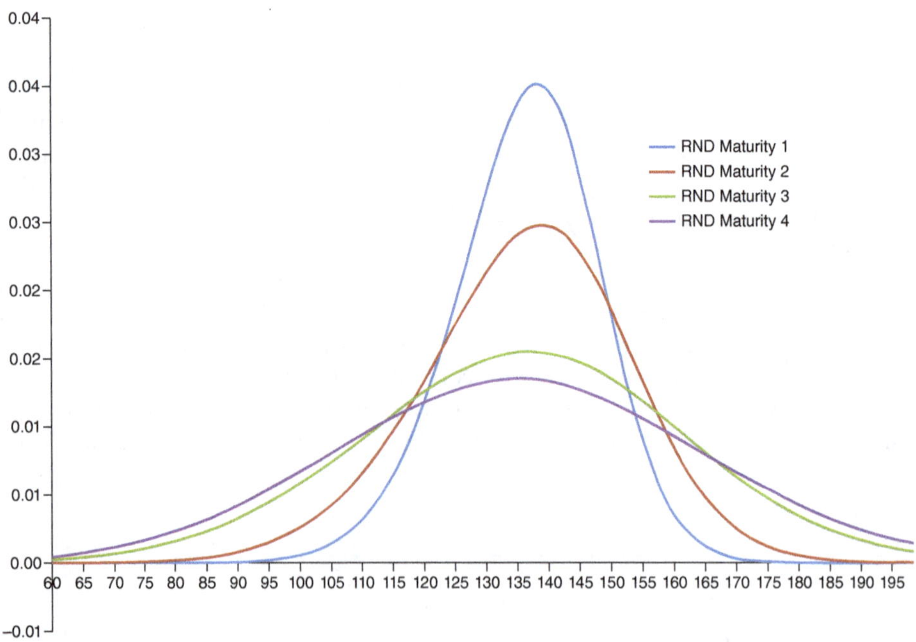

FIGURE 6.6 Risk-Neutral Densities for the S&P Index

```
For i = 1 To N
    payoff = Max(ST(i) - Strike, 0)
    prod = payoff * RND(i) * w(i)
    Sum = Sum + prod
Next i
RecoverCalls = Sum * Exp(-Rate * Mat)
End Function
```

Finally, we use the Excel function CountIf() to count the number of negative RND values. The assessments on the three properties are shown in Figure 6.7.

The area under the short-maturity RNDs is approximately one, but that for the long-maturity RNDs are smaller, owing to the fact that the chosen domain of strikes we selected is too narrow. All RNDs except the first, show no negative values. Finally, the ability of each RND to recover call prices is mixed; only those for shorter maturities are able to recover prices reasonably well, especially for in-the-money strikes. Increasing the strike range, and decreasing the strike increment, would help each RND satisfy the three required properties. The VBA functions and figures presented in this section are in the Excel file Ch6RND.xls.

The RND is a convenient tool for verifying the absence of arbitrage across strikes, but since it is designed for a single maturity, it cannot verify the absence of arbitrage across maturities. As explained by Carr and Madan (2005), ensuring the absence of calendar arbitrage usually involves verifying that calendar spreads have a non-negative price. For a given maturity $\tau = T - t$, Kahalé (2004) and Fengler (2009) show that a test of calendar arbitrage can be formulated in terms of the total implied variance $v^2(K, \tau) = IV^2(K, \tau) \times \tau$, where $IV(K, \tau)$ is the implied volatility corresponding to strike K and maturity τ. The test stipulates that there is no calendar arbitrage if $v^2(K, \tau)$ is a strictly increasing function of τ.

Continuing with the S&P 500 example and the implied volatility root mean squared error (IVRMSE) parameter estimates from Table 6.1, Figure 6.8 plots the

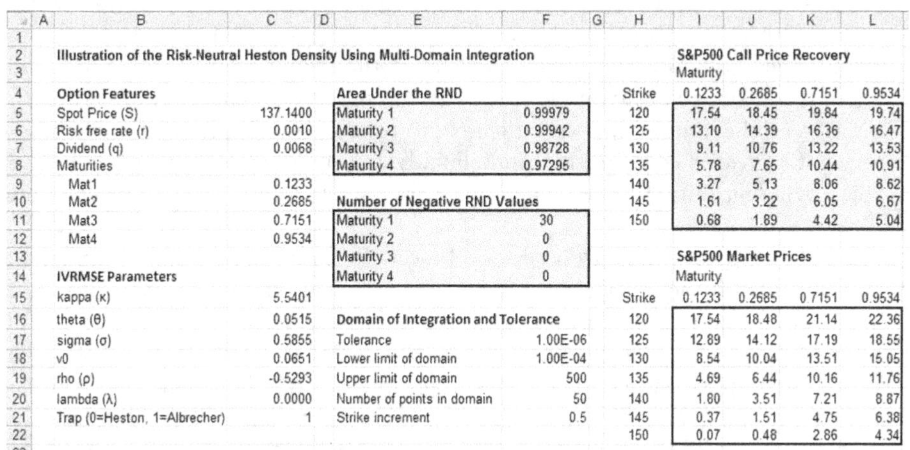
Illustration of the Risk-Neutral Heston Density Using Multi-Domain Integration

Option Features	
Spot Price (S)	137.1400
Risk free rate (r)	0.0010
Dividend (q)	0.0068
Maturities	
Mat1	0.1233
Mat2	0.2685
Mat3	0.7151
Mat4	0.9534

IVRMSE Parameters	
kappa (κ)	5.5401
theta (θ)	0.0515
sigma (σ)	0.5855
v0	0.0651
rho (ρ)	-0.5293
lambda (λ)	0.0000
Trap (0=Heston, 1=Albrecher)	1

Area Under the RND	
Maturity 1	0.99979
Maturity 2	0.99942
Maturity 3	0.98728
Maturity 4	0.97295

Number of Negative RND Values	
Maturity 1	30
Maturity 2	0
Maturity 3	0
Maturity 4	0

Domain of Integration and Tolerance	
Tolerance	1.00E-06
Lower limit of domain	1.00E-04
Upper limit of domain	500
Number of points in domain	50
Strike increment	0.5

S&P500 Call Price Recovery

	Maturity			
Strike	0.1233	0.2685	0.7151	0.9534
120	17.54	18.45	19.84	19.74
125	13.10	14.39	16.36	16.47
130	9.11	10.76	13.22	13.53
135	5.78	7.65	10.44	10.91
140	3.27	5.13	8.06	8.62
145	1.61	3.22	6.05	6.67
150	0.68	1.89	4.42	5.04

S&P500 Market Prices

	Maturity			
Strike	0.1233	0.2685	0.7151	0.9534
120	17.54	18.48	21.14	22.36
125	12.89	14.12	17.19	18.55
130	8.54	10.04	13.51	15.05
135	4.69	6.44	10.16	11.76
140	1.80	3.51	7.21	8.87
145	0.37	1.51	4.75	6.38
150	0.07	0.48	2.86	4.34

FIGURE 6.7 Three Properties of the RNDs

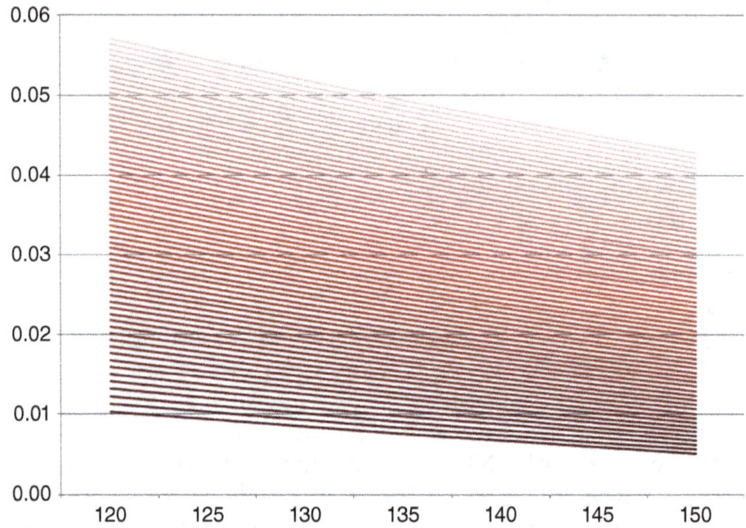

FIGURE 6.8 Total Variance for the S&P 500 Data

total variance for maturities ranging from 45 to 360 days, in 5-day increments. The lines lighten as the maturity increases, with the darkest lines corresponding to the shortest maturities. The figure clearly shows increasing monotonic total variance with increasing maturity, indicating the absence of calendar arbitrage in the volatility surface generated with the IVRMSE parameters.

CONCLUSION

In this chapter, we have presented methods to estimate the parameters of the Heston model. Estimation by loss functions is the most popular method to estimate risk-neutral parameters of the Heston model, but it requires a set of market quotes of implied volatilities or prices. The maximum likelihood estimation proposed by Atiya and Wall (2009) is relatively straightforward to implement but is designed for the Heston model only. This is contrary to other methods that are applicable to a wide range of stochastic volatility models, such as that of Aït-Sahalia and Kimmel (2007). The differential evolution algorithm is able to produce precise estimates, but at the expense of increased computation time. Finally, the risk-neutral density can be used to verify whether option prices generated from a set of estimated parameters admit arbitrage.

A number of researchers have developed alternate methods to estimate the parameters of diffusions such as those specified by the Heston model. The literature is rich and varied and includes methods for univariate processes, as in Aït-Sahalia (2002), as well as for multivariate processes, as in Singleton (2001). The methods encompass estimation by maximum likelihood (Aït-Sahalia and Kimmel, 2007), estimation by the method of moments (Chernov and Ghysels, 2000), Bayesian estimation (Jones, 2003), and particle filtering (Christoffersen et al., 2007; Johannes et al., 2009). In some studies, returns data are employed exclusively, as in Pan (2002), and sometimes a combination of returns data and option prices is employed, as in Eraker (2004). In this chapter, however, we bypass these methods altogether and focus mostly on estimation with loss functions.

All of the pricing methods covered in this book so far have used the closed-form approach to obtain the value of the call in the Heston model. Another popular method of option valuation is through simulation of the stock price and volatility processes of the model. One advantage of this approach is that these simulated quantities can be used in the algorithm of Longstaff and Schwartz (2001) to obtain the prices of American options. In response, a number of researchers have adapted existing simulation schemes to the Heston model and have created new schemes designed exclusively for the model. We deal with some of these schemes in the next chapter.

CHAPTER 7

Simulation in the Heston Model

Abstract

Monte Carlo simulation in the context of the Heston model refers to a set of techniques to generate artificial time series of the stock price and variance over time, from which option prices can be derived. There are several choices available in this regard. The first choice is to apply a standard method such as the Euler, Milstein, or implicit Milstein scheme, as described by Gatheral (2006) and Kahl and Jäckel (2006), for example. The advantage of these schemes is that they are easy to understand, and their convergence properties are well known. The other choice is to use a method that is better suited, or that is specifically designed for the model. These methods include the IJK scheme of Kahl and Jäckel (2006), the quadratic-exponential scheme of Andersen (2008), the transformed volatility scheme of Zhu (2010) or the moment-matching scheme of Andersen and Brotherton-Ratcliffe (2005). These schemes are designed to have faster convergence to the true option price, and in some cases to avoid the negative variances that can sometimes be generated from standard methods. These and other schemes are reviewed by Van Haastrecht and Pelsser (2010).

simulation, Euler, Milstein, transformed volatility, full truncation, reflection, implicit Milstein, balanced implicit Milstein, IJK, path-wise adapted linearization, quadratic-exponential, martingale correction, moment matching

All the methods we have encountered so far for pricing options under the Heston model have been analytic, in the sense that the option price is expressed in closed form and involves one or more complex integrals that must be evaluated numerically. This is one standard approach for many option-pricing methodologies. Another approach is to use simulation, which we describe in this chapter.

Monte Carlo simulation in the context of the Heston model refers to a set of techniques to generate artificial time series of the stock price and variance over time, from which option prices can be derived. There are several choices available in this regard. The first choice is to apply a standard method such as the Euler, Milstein, or implicit Milstein scheme, as described by Gatheral (2006) and Kahl and Jäckel (2006), for example. The advantage of these schemes is that they are easy to understand, and their convergence properties are well known. The other choice is to use a method that is better suited, or that is specifically designed for the model. These methods include the IJK scheme of Kahl and Jäckel (2006), the quadratic-exponential scheme of Andersen (2008), the transformed volatility scheme of Zhu (2010), or the moment-matching scheme of Andersen and Brotherton-Ratcliffe (2005). These schemes are designed to have faster convergence to the true option price, and in some cases to avoid the negative variances that can sometimes be generated from standard methods. These and other schemes are reviewed by Van Haastrecht and Pelsser (2010).

GENERAL SETUP

Recall that the stock price and its variance are driven by the following bivariate system of stochastic differential equations (SDEs):

$$
\begin{aligned}
dS_t &= (r-q)S_t dt + \sqrt{v_t} S_t dW_{1,t} \\
dv_t &= \kappa(\theta - v_t)dt + \sigma\sqrt{v_t} dW_{2,t},
\end{aligned}
\tag{7.1}
$$

where $E[dW_{1,t}dW_{2,t}] = \rho dt$. The processes in Equation (7.1) are specified in continuous time. Simulation, however, is done at discrete time steps. Consequently, the first step in a simulation scheme is usually to approximate a continuous-time process with a discrete time process, a task known as discretization. The stock price and its volatility can each be written in the general form

$$
dX_t = \mu(X_t, t)dt + \sigma(X_t, t)dW_t, \tag{7.2}
$$

where W_t is Brownian motion. We simulate X_t over the time interval $[0, \tau]$, which we assume to be divided into N points as $0 = t_1 < t_2 < \cdots < t_N = \tau$, where the time increments are equally spaced with width $dt = t_i - t_{i-1}$ for $i = 2, \cdots, N$. All the results derived with equally spaced increments are easily generalized to unequal spacing, however. Integrating dX_t from t to $t + dt$ produces

$$
X_{t+dt} = X_t + \int_t^{t+dt} \mu(X_u, u)du + \int_t^{t+dt} \sigma(X_u, u)dW_u. \tag{7.3}
$$

Equation (7.3) is the starting point for discretization. The idea is that at time t the value of X_t is known, and we wish to obtain the next value X_{t+dt} at time $t + dt$.

To obtain the price of a European option using simulation in the Heston model, we first simulate the bivariate process (S_t, v_t) and generate N paths from $t = 0$ to $t = \tau$. We then retain the last stock price from each stock price path and obtain the payoff of the European option at expiry, take the average over all stock price paths and discount back to time zero. Hence, for example, the call and put price $C(K)$ and $P(K)$ are

$$
\begin{aligned}
C(K) &= e^{-r\tau}\frac{1}{N}\sum_{i=1}^{N}\max\left(0, S_T^{(i)} - K\right) \\
P(K) &= e^{-r\tau}\frac{1}{N}\sum_{i=1}^{N}\max\left(0, K - S_T^{(i)}\right),
\end{aligned}
\tag{7.4}
$$

where $S_T^{(i)}$ is the terminal stock price generated by the ith stock price path, $i = 1, \cdots, N$. This requires that we have estimates of the parameters κ, θ, σ, v_0, and ρ.

There are two issues that arise when simulating the bivariate process (S_t, v_t). The first is the slow speed of convergence. The second, more serious issue, is that since v_t follows a CIR process, many simulation schemes, including the Euler and Milstein schemes, will generate negative values for v_t, even if the Feller condition $2\kappa\theta > \sigma^2$ is met. This is because the Feller condition is valid for continuous time processes, but simulation is done in discrete time and serves as an approximation to continuous time processes.

The simplest way to deal with negative variances is to override them as they arise. There are at least two ways to do this:

- In the *full truncation scheme*, a negative value for v_t is floored at zero. Hence, v_t is replaced by $v_t^+ = \max(0, v_t)$ everywhere in the discretization.
- In the *reflection scheme*, a negative value for v_t is reflected with $-v_t$. Hence, v_t is replaced by $|v_t|$ everywhere in the discretization.

The disadvantage of the full truncation scheme is that it creates zero variances, which is unrealistic because stock prices never exhibit zero variance. The disadvantage of the reflection scheme is that it reflects a large negative variance to a large positive variance. Hence, it transforms realizations of low volatility into high volatility.

Another way to deal with negative simulated values of v_t is to devise simulation schemes for v_t that do not produce negative values in the first place. Much of the research on simulating the CIR variance process in the Heston model is devoted to this approach. Yet another way is to simulate $\ln v_t$ or $\sqrt{v_t}$, and then exponentiate or square the result. For the stock price, we can simulate S_t itself, but we will see in this chapter that a better approach is to simulate the log price $x_t = \ln S_t$ instead, and then exponentiate.

All of the simulation schemes for the Heston model contain the same basic steps. First, two independent standard normal random variables are generated, and then made dependent by applying Cholesky decomposition. These are multiplied by $\sqrt{dt}$ to make them proxy Brownian motion increments. Second, we obtain the updated value v_{t+dt}. Third, we obtain the updated value S_{t+dt} (or x_{t+dt}).

Step 0. Initialize S_0 to the spot price (or x_0 to the log spot price), and initialize v_0 to the current variance parameter.

Step 1. Generate two independent random variables Z_1 and Z_2, and define $Z_V = Z_1$ and $Z_S = \rho Z_V + \sqrt{1-\rho^2} Z_2$. Proxy the Brownian motion by $dW_{1,t} = \sqrt{dt} Z_S$ and $dW_{2,t} = \sqrt{dt} Z_V$.

Step 2. Obtain the updated value v_{t+dt}.

Step 3. Given v_{t+dt}, obtain the updated value S_{t+dt} (or x_{t+dt}) and return to Step 1.

Note that Z_V and Z_S are constructed so that $E[Z_V] = E[Z_S] = 0$, and so that $E[Z_V Z_S] = \rho E[Z_1^2] + \sqrt{1-\rho^2} E[Z_1 Z_2] = \rho$, as required.

In this chapter, we describe some common discretization schemes for (S_t, v_t). We assume that the time grid is discretized as $0 = t_1 < t_2 < \cdots < t_M = T$, where the time increments are equally spaced with width dt.

EULER SCHEME

The simplest way to discretize the process in Equation (7.3) is to use Euler discretization. This is equivalent to approximating the integrals using the left-point rule. Hence, Euler discretization of Equation (7.3) is

$$X_{t+dt} = X_t + \mu(X_t, t)dt + \sigma(X_t, t)\sqrt{dt}Z, \tag{7.5}$$

where Z is a standard normal variable. Euler discretization of the SDE for the variance v_t is

$$v_{t+dt} = v_t + \kappa(\theta - v_t)dt + \sigma\sqrt{v_t}\sqrt{dt}Z_V. \tag{7.6}$$

As mentioned earlier, when we apply Euler discretization to the variance, we must also apply the full truncation scheme or the reflection scheme to override any negative values that are generated in the simulation.

There are two common approaches to simulating the stock price. We can either simulate S_t directly, or we can simulate $\ln S_t$ and then exponentiate. Euler discretization of the stock price is

$$S_{t+dt} = S_t + (r - q)S_t dt + \sqrt{v_t}S_t\sqrt{dt}Z_S. \tag{7.7}$$

To simulate the log-stock price, we apply Itō's Lemma to the first equation in Equation (7.1), and then apply Euler discretization to the process for $\ln S_{t+dt}$. We thus obtain

$$\ln S_{t+dt} = \ln S_t + \left(r - q - \frac{1}{2}v_t\right) dt + \sqrt{v_t}\sqrt{dt}Z_S. \tag{7.8}$$

Euler discretization of S_t is obtained by exponentiation of Equation (7.8):

$$S_{t+dt} = S_t \exp\left(\left(r - q - \frac{1}{2}v_t\right) dt + \sqrt{v_t}\sqrt{dt}Z_S\right). \tag{7.9}$$

Again, to avoid negative variances we must apply the full truncation or reflection scheme by replacing v_t everywhere with v_t^+ or with $|v_t|$.

To implement Euler simulation we start with initial values S_0 (or $x_0 = \ln S_0$) for the stock price (or log-stock price) and v_0 for the variance. Given the values (S_t, v_t), we obtain the updated value v_{t+dt} from Equation (7.6), and we obtain S_{t+dt} from either (7.7) or (7.9).

MILSTEIN SCHEME

This scheme is described in Glasserman (2003) and in Kloeden and Platen (1992) for general processes, and in Kahl and Jäckel (2006) for stochastic volatility models. For the Heston model, the coefficients in Equation (7.2) depend on X_t only, and do not depend on t directly. Hence, for simplicity, we can assume that the stock price and variance are driven by the SDE:

$$dX_t = \mu(X_t)dt + \sigma(X_t)dW_t = \mu_t dt + \sigma_t dW_t.$$

The idea behind the Milstein scheme is that the accuracy of the discretization can be increased by expanding the coefficients $\mu_t = \mu(X_t)$ and $\sigma_t = \sigma(X_t)$ via Itō's lemma. This is sensible since the coefficients are also functions of X_t. Indeed, we can apply Itō's Lemma to the functions μ_t and σ_t as we would for any differentiable function of X_t. After some manipulation, we obtain the general form of Milstein discretization as

$$X_{t+dt} = X_t + \mu_t dt + \sigma_t \sqrt{dt}Z + \frac{1}{2}\sigma_t' \sigma_t dt(Z^2 - 1). \tag{7.10}$$

Hence, Milstein discretization of dX_t in Equation (7.10) is identical to Euler discretization in (7.5), except for the extra term $\frac{1}{2}\sigma_t'\sigma_t dt(Z^2 - 1)$ that appears in (7.10). This extra term improves the accuracy of Milstein discretization over Euler discretization. See Rouah (2013) for a detailed derivation of (7.10).

Recall that the Heston model is specified by the bivariate process given in Equation (7.1). In the processes for S_t and v_t, the drift and volatility coefficients do not depend on t directly. Thus, Milstein discretization Equation (7.10) can be applied to both processes and also to the process for $\ln S_t$.

First, the coefficients of the variance process are $\mu(v_t) = \kappa(\theta - v_t)$ and $\sigma(v_t) = \sigma\sqrt{v_t}$ so an application of Equation (7.10) to v_t produces

$$v_{t+dt} = v_t + \kappa(\theta - v_t)dt + \sigma\sqrt{v_t}\sqrt{dt}Z_V + \frac{1}{4}\sigma^2 dt\left(Z_V^2 - 1\right), \tag{7.11}$$

which can be written as

$$v_{t+dt} = \left(\sqrt{v_t} + \frac{1}{2}\sigma\sqrt{dt}Z_V\right)^2 + \kappa(\theta - v_t)dt - \frac{1}{4}\sigma^2 dt. \tag{7.12}$$

This last equation is also Equation (2.18) of Gatheral (2006). Milstein discretization of the variance process produces far fewer negative values for the variance than Euler discretization. Nevertheless, the full truncation scheme or the reflection scheme must be applied to (7.10) and (7.12) as well.

Second, the coefficients of the stock price process are $\mu(S_t) = (r - q)S_t$ and $\sigma(S_t) = \sqrt{v_t}S_t$, so Equation (7.10) becomes

$$S_{t+dt} = S_t + (r - q)S_t dt + \sqrt{v_t}\sqrt{dt}S_t Z_S + \frac{1}{2}v_t S_t dt\left(Z_S^2 - 1\right). \tag{7.13}$$

We can also discretize the log-stock process. An application of Itō's Lemma shows that the coefficients for $\ln S_t$ are $\mu(S_t) = (r - q - v_t/2)$ and $\sigma(S_t) = \sqrt{v_t}$ so that $\mu_t' = \sigma_t' = 0$. Since v_t is known at time t, we can treat it as a constant in the coefficients. An application of Equation (7.10) produces

$$\ln S_{t+dt} = \ln S_t + \left(r - q - \frac{1}{2}v_t\right) dt + \sqrt{v_t}\sqrt{dt}Z_S, \tag{7.14}$$

which is identical to Euler discretization in (7.8). Hence, Milstein discretization of $\ln S_t$ in the Heston model does not produce a more accurate approximation than Euler discretization. The stock price is obtained by exponentiation of (7.14). Again, it is necessary to apply the full truncation or reflections schemes to (7.13) and (7.14).

To implement Milstein simulation, we start with initial values S_0 (or $x_0 = \ln S_0$) for the stock price and v_0 for the variance. Given the simulated values (S_t, v_t), we obtain v_{t+dt} from Equation (7.12), and we obtain S_{t+dt} from either (7.13) or by exponentiating (7.14).

Simulation schemes can serve as a powerful illustrator of how the Heston model parameters affect the behavior of the stock price and the volatility. In Chapter 2, for example, we saw that the parameter ρ drives the correlation between the processes driving the stock price and the variance. The following figures each contain a single daily simulated stock price path and variance path over one trading year (250 days), starting with initial values $(S_0, v_0) = (100, 0.05)$ and using typical values of the parameters. Figure 7.1 uses $\rho = -0.9$ and clearly illustrates the negative relationship between price and variance. Indeed, increases in variance are associated with a decreasing stock price, while the opposite is true for decreases in variance.

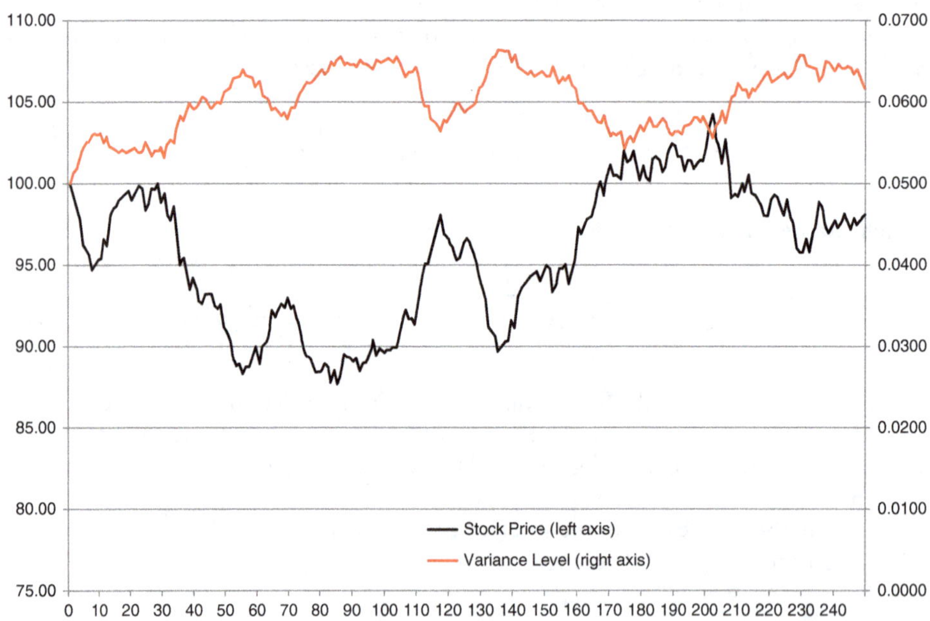

FIGURE 7.1 Stock Price and Variance under Negative Correlation

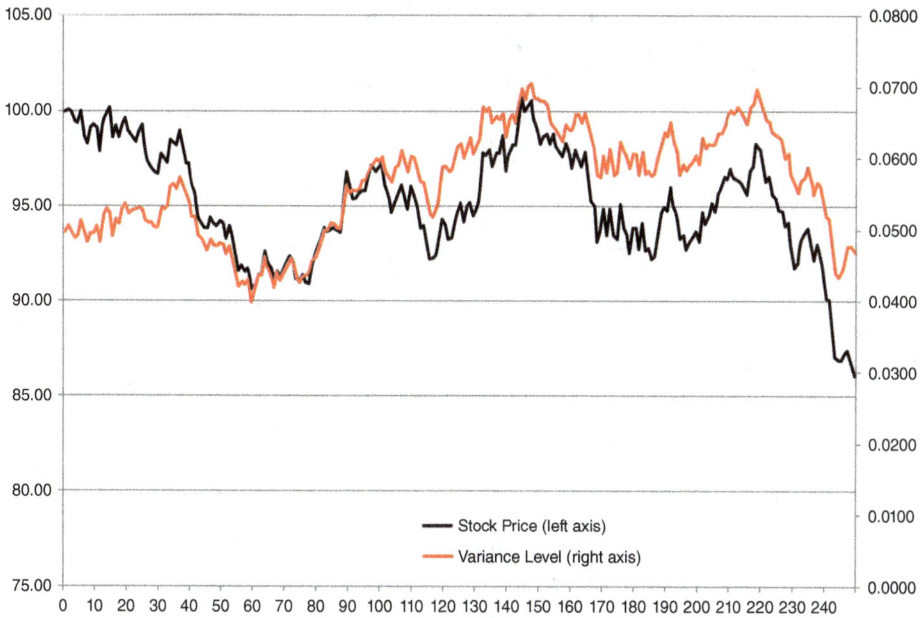

FIGURE 7.2 Stock Price and Variance under Positive Correlation

Figure 7.2, however, uses $\rho = +0.9$ and shows the opposite effect, increases in variance are associated with increasing prices, and vice versa.

Both figures can be generated with the Excel file Ch7Paths.xls. Simulation can also be used to illustrate the effect of the other Heston parameters on the stock price and the variance.

IMPLICIT MILSTEIN SCHEME

Recall that, in Equation (7.10) for Milstein discretization of dX_t, the coefficients $\mu_t = \mu(X_t)$ and $\sigma_t = \sigma(X_t)$ are the drift and volatility of the process for X_t and are functions of X_t itself. In the Milstein drift-implicit scheme, or simply implicit scheme, the drift coefficient μ_t is specified to be a function of X_{t+dt}. Hence, under this scheme, the drift coefficient is known only implicitly, and not explicitly, as is the case when it depends on X_t. Under the Itō version of this scheme, Equation (7.10) becomes

$$X_{t+dt} = X_t + \mu_{t+dt}dt + \sigma_t\sqrt{dt}Z + \frac{1}{2}\sigma_t'\sigma_t dt(Z^2 - 1), \qquad (7.15)$$

where $\mu_{t+dt} = \mu(X_{t+dt})$. See Kloeden and Platen (1992) for details. It is also possible to interpolate between explicit and implicit Milstein schemes by taking a weighted average of μ_t and μ_{t+dt}. The weighted implicit-explicit Milstein scheme is therefore

$$X_{t+dt} = X_t + [\alpha\mu_t + (1-\alpha)\mu_{t+dt}]dt + \sigma_t\sqrt{dt}Z + \frac{1}{2}\sigma_t'\sigma_t dt(Z^2 - 1), \qquad (7.16)$$

where $\alpha \in (0, 1)$ is the weight. The explicit Milstein scheme corresponds to $\alpha = 1$, and the implicit Milstein scheme to $\alpha = 0$.

To apply the implicit Milstein scheme to the Heston model, in Equation (7.11) we replace the term $\kappa(\theta - v_t)dt$ with $\kappa(\theta - v_{t+dt})dt$. We then bring $\kappa v_{t+dt}dt$ over to the left-hand side of the resulting equation, and we divide by $1 + \kappa dt$ to obtain

$$v_{t+dt} = \frac{v_t + \kappa\theta dt + \sigma\sqrt{v_t}\sqrt{dt}Z_V + \frac{1}{4}\sigma^2 dt(Z_V^2 - 1)}{1 + \kappa dt}. \tag{7.17}$$

If we apply the same steps to the weighted scheme in Equation (7.16) we obtain the weighted Milstein scheme

$$v_{t+dt} = \frac{v_t + \kappa(\theta - \alpha v_t)dt + \sigma\sqrt{v_t}\sqrt{dt}Z_V + \frac{1}{4}\sigma^2 dt(Z_V^2 - 1)}{1 + (1 - \alpha)\kappa dt}. \tag{7.18}$$

The VBA function EulerMilsteinSim applies Euler (7.6), Milstein (7.11), implicit Milstein (7.17), or weighted Milstein (7.18) discretization to the variance, and simulates the log-stock price using (7.9). It allows negative variances to be overridden with either the reflection or full truncation scheme.

```
Function EulerMilsteinSim(scheme As String, ...) As Variant
' Generate the stock and volatility paths
For i = 1 To NS
    For T = 2 To NT
        ' Generate 2 dependent N(0,1) variables
        Zv = NormSInv(Rnd())
        Zs = rho * Zv + Sqr(1 - rho ^ 2) ....
        If scheme = "E" Then
            ' Euler discretization for the variance
            V(T, i) = V(T - 1, i) + kappa * (theta - V(T -
            1, i)) ...
        ElseIf scheme = "M" Then
            ' Milstein discretization for the variance.
            V(T, i) = V(T - 1, i) + kappa * (theta - V(T -
            1, i)) ...
        ElseIf scheme = "IM" Then
            ' Implicit Milstein for the variance.
            V(T, i) = (V(T - 1, i) + kappa * theta * dt ...
        ElseIf scheme = "WM" Then
            ' Weighted Explicit-Implicit Milstein Scheme
            V(T, i) = (V(T - 1, i) + kappa * (theta - alpha
            ...
        End If
        ' Apply full truncation or reflection to the variance
        If V(T, i) <= 0 Then
```

```
            If negvar = "R" Then
                ' Reflection: take -V
                V(T, i) = Abs(V(T, i))
            ElseIf negvar = "T" Then
                ' Truncation: take max(0,V)
                V(T, i) = Max(0, V(T, i))
            End If
        End If
        ' Discretize the log stock price
        S(T, i) = S(T - 1, i) * Exp((r - q - V(T - 1, i) / 2)
        ...
    Next T
Next i
```

This function is fed into the EulerMilsteinPrice function that uses the simulated price paths as input, and calculates the call or put price from the terminal prices, as in Equation (7.4).

```
Function EulerMilsteinPrice(scheme As String, ...) As Double
' Obtain the simulated stock price and simulated variance
output = EulerMilsteinSim(scheme, ...)
' Transfer output to S and V matrices
For j = 1 To NS
    For T = 1 To NT
        S(T, j) = output(T, j)
        V(T, j) = output(T, NS + j)
    Next T
Next j
' Terminal stock prices
For j = 1 To NS
    ST(j) = S(NT, j)
Next j
' Payoff vectors
For j = 1 To NS
    If PutCall = "C" Then
        Payoff(j) = Max(ST(j) - K, 0)
    ElseIf PutCall = "P" Then
        Payoff(j) = Max(K - ST(j), 0)
    End If
Next j
' Simulated price
EulerMilsteinPrice = Exp(-r * Mat) ...
End Function
```

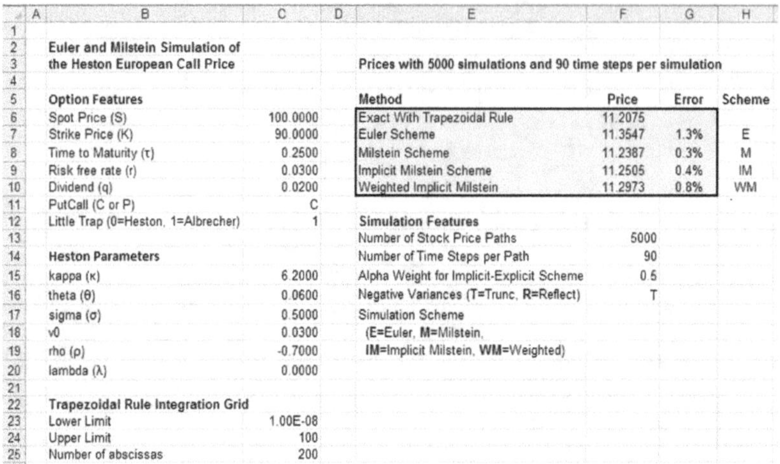

	A	B	C	D	E	F	G	H
1								
2		Euler and Milstein Simulation of						
3		the Heston European Call Price			Prices with 5000 simulations and 90 time steps per simulation			
4								
5		Option Features			Method	Price	Error	Scheme
6		Spot Price (S)	100.0000		Exact With Trapezoidal Rule	11.2075		
7		Strike Price (K)	90.0000		Euler Scheme	11.3547	1.3%	E
8		Time to Maturity (τ)	0.2500		Milstein Scheme	11.2387	0.3%	M
9		Risk free rate (r)	0.0300		Implicit Milstein Scheme	11.2505	0.4%	IM
10		Dividend (q)	0.0200		Weighted Implicit Milstein	11.2973	0.8%	WM
11		PutCall (C or P)	C					
12		Little Trap (0=Heston, 1=Albrecher)	1		Simulation Features			
13					Number of Stock Price Paths	5000		
14		Heston Parameters			Number of Time Steps per Path	90		
15		kappa (κ)	6.2000		Alpha Weight for Implicit-Explicit Scheme	0.5		
16		theta (θ)	0.0600		Negative Variances (T=Trunc, R=Reflect)	T		
17		sigma (σ)	0.5000		Simulation Scheme			
18		v0	0.0300		(E=Euler, M=Milstein,			
19		rho (ρ)	-0.7000		IM=Implicit Milstein, WM=Weighted)			
20		lambda (λ)	0.0000					
21								
22		Trapezoidal Rule Integration Grid						
23		Lower Limit	1.00E-08					
24		Upper Limit	100					
25		Number of abscissas	200					

FIGURE 7.3 Heston Call Prices under the Euler and Milstein Schemes

To illustrate, the price of a three-month European call struck at $K = 90$ on a dividend-paying stock with spot price $S = 100$ and dividend yield $q = 0.02$ is \$11.2075 when $r = 0.03$, $\kappa = 6.2$, $\theta = 0.06$, $\sigma = 0.5$, $\rho = -0.7$, and $v_0 = 0.03$. We use 5,000 stock price paths and 90 time steps for each path, and apply the reflection scheme. The results are in Figure 7.3 and indicate reasonable accuracy of the simulation schemes.

The functions presented in this section and the screen shot in Figure 7.3 are in the Excel file Ch7EulerMilstein.xls.

TRANSFORMED VOLATILITY SCHEME

One simple way to avoid negative variances is to simulate the volatility $\omega_t = \sqrt{v_t}$ rather than the variance, and then square the result. After applying Itō's Lemma, Euler discretization of the volatility produces

$$\omega_{t+dt} = \omega_t + \frac{\kappa}{2}\left[\left(\theta - \frac{\sigma^2}{4\kappa}\right)\frac{1}{\omega_t} - \omega_t\right]dt + \frac{1}{2}\sigma\sqrt{dt}Z_V, \tag{7.19}$$

while Euler discretization of the log-stock price produces

$$S_{t+dt} = S_t \exp\left(\left(r - q - \frac{1}{2}\omega_t^2\right)dt + \omega_t\sqrt{dt}Z_S\right). \tag{7.20}$$

Zhu (2010) points out that, while Euler discretization of the volatility ω_t avoids negative variances, the drawback is that the mean level $\theta_\omega = (\theta - \frac{\sigma^2}{4\kappa})/\omega_t$ in (7.19) is stochastic because of the term $1/\omega_t$. This will cause the simulation to be poorly behaved. The transformed volatility scheme proposed by Zhu (2010) rectifies this problem. The scheme is

$$\omega_{t+dt} = \omega_t + \frac{\kappa}{2}[\theta^* - \omega_t]dt + \frac{\sigma}{2}\sqrt{dt}Z_V, \tag{7.21}$$

where the mean reversion level θ_t^* is

$$\theta_t^* = \frac{\beta - \omega_t \exp(-\kappa dt/2)}{1 - \exp(-\kappa dt/2)},$$

with

$$\beta = \sqrt{(E[v_{t+dt}] - \text{Var}[\omega_{t+dt}])^+} = \sqrt{\left(\theta + (v_t - \theta)e^{-\kappa dt} - \frac{\sigma^2}{4\kappa}(1 - e^{-\kappa dt})\right)^+}.$$

Note that the β parameter is set to zero when $E[v_{t+dt}] < \text{Var}[\omega_{t+dt}]$.

The TransVolSim VBA function simulates the stock price in Equation (7.20), and the volatility in either (7.19) or (7.21). The functions use the parameters κ, θ, σ, and ρ, as in the other simulations, but the parameter for the initial volatility is $\sqrt{v_0}$.

```
Function TransVolSim(scheme As String, ...) As Variant
' Starting values for the variance and stock processes
For j = 1 To NS
    S(1, j) = S0          ' Spot price
    x(1, j) = Log(S0)     ' Log Spot price
    V(1, j) = v0          ' Heston v0 initial variance
    W(1, j) = Sqr(v0)     ' Heston initial volatility
Next j
' Generate the stock and volatility paths
For i = 1 To NS
    For t = 2 To NT
        ' Generate two dependent N(0,1) variables
        Zv = NormSInv(Rnd())
        Zx = rho * Zv + Sqr(1 - rho ^ 2)  ...
        If scheme = "E" Then
            ' Euler volatility scheme
            W(t, i) = W(t - 1, i) + 0.5 * kappa ...
        ElseIf scheme = "TV" Then
            ' Transformed Volatility scheme
            m1 = theta + (V(t - 1, i) - theta) * Exp(-kappa *
            dt)
            m2 = sigma ^ 2 / 4 / kappa * (1 - Exp(-kappa *
            dt))
            beta = Sqr(Max(0, m1 - m2))
            thetav = (beta - W(t - 1, i) * Exp(-kappa * dt /
            2)) ...
            W(t, i) = W(t - 1, i) + 0.5 * kappa * (thetav -
            W(t - 1, i)) ...
        End If
        V(t, i) = W(t, i) ^ 2
        ' Discretize the log stock price
```

```
            x(t, i) = x(t - 1, i) + (r - q - W(t - 1, i) ^ 2 /
            2) * dt ...
            S(t, i) = Exp(x(t, i))
        Next t
    Next i
    End Function
```

The simulated stock price values are then passed to the TransVolPrice function, which calculates the price of the European call or put. It is almost identical to the pricing function for the Euler and Milstein schemes presented at the end of the previous section.

```
Function TransVolPrice(scheme As String, ...) As Double
' Obtain the simulated stock price and simulated variance
output = TransVolSim(scheme, ...)
' Transfer output to S and V matrices
For j = 1 To NS
    For t = 1 To NT
        S(t, j) = output(t, j)
        V(t, j) = output(t, NS + j)
    Next t
Next j
' Terminal stock prices
For j = 1 To NS
    ST(j) = S(NT, j)
Next j
' Payoff vectors
For j = 1 To NS
    If PutCall = "C" Then
        Payoff(j) = Max(ST(j) - K, 0)
    ElseIf PutCall = "P" Then
        Payoff(j) = Max(K - ST(j), 0)
    End If
Next j
' Simulated price
TransVolPrice = Exp(-r * Mat) ...
End Function
```

In numerical experiments Zhu (2010) shows that the accuracy of his transformed volatility scheme is very high and comparable to the quadratic-exponential scheme, which we cover later in this chapter.

Continuing with the example at the end of the previous section, the closed-form call price is 11.2075. Using 5,000 stock price paths and 90 time steps per path, the price using Euler discretization of the volatility in Equation (7.19) is 11.3337. The transformed volatility in (7.21) however, produces a price of 11.3008, which is more accurate.

The functions and examples presented in this section are in the Excel file Ch7TransVol.xls.

BALANCED, PATHWISE, AND IJK SCHEMES

In this section, we describe three schemes proposed by Kahl and Jäckel (2006) for discretization of the Heston variance process. The Balanced Implicit method of Milstein et al. (1998) introduces implicitness in the diffusion term. The pathwise adapted linearization quadratic method retains terms up to $(dt)^2$ in a more general expansion for pathwise approximation. Finally, the IJK scheme uses the implicit Milstein scheme for the variance, along with an alternative discretization for the log-stock price.

The balanced implicit method is defined in Platen and Heath (2009) and Kahl and Jäckel (2006) as

$$v_{t+dt} = \frac{v_t(1 + C(v_t)) + \kappa(\theta - v_t)dt + \sigma\sqrt{v_t}\sqrt{dt}Z_V}{1 + C(v_t)}, \tag{7.22}$$

with

$$C(v_t) = \kappa dt + \frac{\sigma\sqrt{dt}|Z_V|}{\sqrt{v_t}}.$$

This scheme is able to preserve positivity of the variance process, so reflection and truncation are not needed. Unfortunately, as shown by Kahl and Jäckel (2006), the convergence of this scheme can be very poor. For details please refer to Equations (6.25) through (6.28) in their paper.

The pathwise adapted linearization quadratic method presented in Kahl and Jäckel (2006), however, has fast convergence, especially for small values of σ. This discretization scheme is given by

$$v_{t+dt} = v_t + \left(\kappa(\tilde{\theta} - v_t) + \sigma\beta_n\sqrt{v_t}\right)\left(1 + \frac{\sigma\beta_n - 2\kappa\sqrt{v_t}}{4\sqrt{v_t}}dt\right)dt, \tag{7.23}$$

where $\tilde{\theta} = \theta - \sigma^2/(4\kappa)$ and where $\beta_n = Z_V/\sqrt{dt}$. This scheme must be implemented with care, as it can lead to numerical instability for large values of σ.

Finally, the IJK scheme was also proposed by Kahl and Jäckel (2006). It involves simulating v_t with the implicit Milstein scheme from Equation (7.17), and simulating $\ln S_t$ with their IJK discretization, given by

$$\begin{aligned}\ln S_{t+dt} &= \ln S_t + \left(r - q - \frac{v_t + v_{t+dt}}{4}\right)dt + \rho\sqrt{v_t dt}Z_V \\ &\quad + \frac{1}{2}\left(\sqrt{v_t} + \sqrt{v_{t+dt}}\right)(Z_S - \rho Z_V)\sqrt{dt} + \frac{\rho\sigma dt}{2}\left(Z_V^2 - 1\right). \end{aligned} \tag{7.24}$$

Since this scheme can also produce negative variances, in (7.24) the full truncation scheme or the reflection scheme should be used. See their paper for details of the derivation.

The VBA function KahlJackelSim implements the balanced scheme in (7.22), the pathwise scheme in (7.23), and the IJK scheme in (7.17) and (7.24).

```
Function KahlJackelSim(scheme As String, ...)
For i = 1 To NS
    For t = 2 To NT
        ' Generate two dependent N(0,1) variables
        Zv = NormSInv(Rnd())
        Zs = rho * Zv + Sqr(1 - rho ^ 2) ...
        If scheme = "IJK" Then
            ' Implicit Milstein
            V(t, i) = (V(t - 1, i) + kappa * theta * dt ...
            If V(t, i) <= 0 Then
                If negvar = "R" Then
                    ' Reflection: take -V
                    V(t, i) = Abs(V(t, i))
                ElseIf negvar = "T" Then
                   ' Truncation: take max(0,V)
                    V(t, i) = Max(0, V(t, i))
                End If
            End If
            ' IJK discretization scheme for the log stock prices
            S(t, i) = S(t - 1, i) * Exp((r - q - (V(t, i) ...
        ElseIf scheme = "PW" Then
            ' Pathwise Adapated Linearization Quadratic
            theta2 = theta - sigma ^ 2 / 4 / kappa
            Bn = Zv / Sqr(dt)
            V(t, i) = V(t - 1, i) + (kappa * (theta2 - V(t -
            1, i)) ...
            If V(t, i) <= 0 Then
                If negvar = "R" Then
                    V(t, i) = Abs(V(t, i))
                ElseIf negvar = "T" Then
                    V(t, i) = Max(0, V(t, i))
                End If
            End If
            ' Euler/Milstein discretization for log stock
            price
            S(t, i) = S(t - 1, i) * Exp((r - q - V(t - 1, i) /
            2) ...
        ElseIf scheme = "B" Then
            ' Balanced Implicit scheme for the variance
```

```
                C = kappa * dt + sigma / Sqr(V(t - 1, i)) ...
                V(t, i) = (V(t - 1, i) * (1 + C) + kappa   ...
                ' Euler/Milstein discretization for the log stock
                price
                S(t, i) = S(t - 1, i) * Exp((r - q - V(t - 1, i) /
                2) ...
            End If
        Next t
    Next i
```

The KahlJackelPrice function calculates the price of a European call or put, based on paths simulated using the KahlJackelSim function, but it is not presented here.

We continue with the example in earlier sections that use 5,000 simulation paths, each with 90 time steps. Recall that the closed-form price is 11.2075. The IJK scheme produces 11.2108, the pathwise scheme produces 11.2013, and the balanced scheme produces 11.1511. These errors are small, and none of the schemes generated negative variances.

All of the functions and examples in this section are in the Excel file Ch7KJ.xls.

QUADRATIC-EXPONENTIAL SCHEME

It is well known that the value of v_{t+dt}, conditional on a realized value v_t, follows the noncentral chi-square distribution (see, for example, Cox et al., 1985, or Brigo and Mercurio, 2006, among others.) Andersen (2008) suggests sampling from an approximation to this distribution, depending on whether the noncentrality parameter is large or small. This sampled value is the foundation for the quadratic-exponential (QE) discretization scheme for the variance process.

The QE scheme makes use of the following quantities:

- The conditional mean and variance of the variance process is:

$$\begin{aligned} m &= E[v_{t+dt}|v_t] = \theta + (v_t - \theta)e^{-\kappa dt} \\ s^2 &= \mathrm{Var}[v_{t+dt}|v_t] = \frac{v_t\sigma^2 e^{-\kappa dt}}{\kappa}(1 - e^{-\kappa dt}) + \frac{\theta\sigma^2}{2\kappa}(1 - e^{-\kappa dt})^2. \end{aligned} \tag{7.25}$$

- The parameters a and b, defined as

$$b = \left(\frac{2}{\psi} - 1 + \sqrt{\frac{2}{\psi}\left(\frac{2}{\psi} - 1\right)}\right)^{\frac{1}{2}} \quad \text{and} \quad a = \frac{m}{1 + b^2}, \tag{7.26}$$

where $\psi = s^2/m^2$.

- The parameters p and β, defined as

$$p = \frac{\psi - 1}{\psi + 1} \quad \text{and} \quad \beta = \frac{1-p}{m}. \tag{7.27}$$

- The inverse function $\Psi^{-1}(u)$, defined as

$$\Psi^{-1}(u) = \begin{cases} 0 & \text{for } 0 \le u \le p \\ \dfrac{1}{\beta} \ln \dfrac{1-p}{1-u} & \text{for } p \le u \le 1. \end{cases} \tag{7.28}$$

Note that b is only defined when $\psi \le 2$, and that $0 \le p \le 1$. Note also that the condition $p \ge 0$ requires that $\psi \ge 1$. We thus have the restriction that $1 \le \psi \le 2$. The value of ψ stipulates which approximation to use. Indeed, the first approximation requires $\psi \le 2$, while the second requires $\psi \ge 1$. This implies that a critical level $\psi_c \in [1,2]$ ought to be defined as a threshold to switch between the two approximations. Andersen (2008) uses $\psi_c = 1.5$.

The QE scheme is implemented as follows:

- Given v_t, obtain m and s^2 from Equation (7.25) using estimates of θ and κ, and define $\psi = s^2/m^2$.
- Draw a uniform random number $u \in [0,1]$ and compute $\Psi^{-1}(u)$ from (7.28).
- Case 1. If $\psi \le \psi_c$ obtain a and b from (7.26) and compute $Z_V = \Phi^{-1}(u)$ where $\Phi^{-1}(\cdot)$ is the inverse standard normal CDF. Set $v_{t+dt} = a(b + Z_V)^2$.
- Case 2. If $\psi > \psi_c$ obtain β and p from (7.27). Set $v_{t+dt} = \Psi^{-1}(u)$.

Hence, the updated value v_{t+dt} is obtained as either $a(b + Z_V)^2$ or as $\Psi^{-1}(u)$, depending on the value of ψ.

Andersen (2008) proposes a discretization scheme for $\ln S_t$ that overcomes the problem of "leaky" correlation brought on by Euler discretization. The scheme for $\ln S_{t+dt}$ is

$$\ln S_{t+dt} = \ln S_t + (r-q)dt + K_0 + K_1 v_t + K_2 v_{t+dt} + \sqrt{K_3 v_t + K_4 v_{t+dt}} Z_V, \tag{7.29}$$

where

$$K_0 = -\frac{\kappa\rho\theta}{\sigma} dt, \quad K_1 = \left(\frac{\kappa\rho}{\sigma} - \frac{1}{2}\right)\gamma_1 dt - \frac{\rho}{\sigma}, \quad K_2 = \left(\frac{\kappa\rho}{\sigma} - \frac{1}{2}\right)\gamma_2 dt + \frac{\rho}{\sigma}$$
$$K_3 = (1-\rho^2)\gamma_1 dt, \quad K_4 = (1-\rho^2)\gamma_2 dt.$$

The constants γ_1 and γ_2 in these expressions are arbitrary. Setting $\gamma_1 = 1$ and $\gamma_2 = 0$ produces the Euler-type scheme, while $\gamma_1 = \gamma_2 = \frac{1}{2}$ produces a central discretization. With these values, the algorithm to generate a value of S_{t+dt}, given the values S_t, v_t, and v_{t+dt} is evident.

Under the risk-neutral measure $\mathbb{Q}$, the discounted asset price will be a martingale in continuous time. However, the discretized stock price,

$$S_{t+dt} = S_t \exp\left((r-q)dt + K_0 + K_1 v_t + K_2 v_{t+dt} + \sqrt{K_3 v_t + K_4 v_{t+dt}} Z_V\right), \quad (7.30)$$

will not be a martingale. The resulting bias is minor, since the drift away from the martingale can be controlled by reducing the size of the time increment, dt. Nonetheless, Andersen (2008) shows that the martingale property can be satisfied simply by replacing, in Equation (7.30), K_0 with K_0^* given by

$$K_0^* = -\ln M - \left(K_1 + \frac{1}{2}K_3\right) v_t. \quad (7.31)$$

The martingale correction makes use of the term $A = K_2 + \frac{1}{2}K_4$, along with a and b defined in Equation (7.26), and with p and β defined in (7.27). Again, two cases must be dealt with separately.

- When $\psi \le \psi_c$, we can implement the martingale correction provided that $A < 1/(2a)$, and the expression for M is

$$M = \frac{\exp\left(\dfrac{Ab^2a}{1-2Aa}\right)}{\sqrt{1-2Aa}}. \quad (7.32)$$

- When $\psi > \psi_c$, we can implement the martingale correction provided that $A < \beta$, and the expression for M is

$$M = p + \frac{\beta(1-p)}{\beta - A}. \quad (7.33)$$

For a more detailed description of the QE method, see Andersen (2008) or Rouah (2013). Simulation of stock price and variance paths under the QE scheme is implemented with the QESim function.

```
Function QESim(params As Variant, ...) As Variant
For i = 1 To NS
    For t = 2 To NT
        ' Generate two dependent N(0,1) variables
        Zv = NormSInv(Rnd())
        Zs = rho * Zv + Sqr(1 - rho ^ 2) ...
        ' Equations (17) through (19)
        m = theta + (V(t - 1, i) - theta) * E
        s2 = V(t - 1, i) * sigma ^ 2 * E / kappa * (1 - E) ...
        phi = s2 / m ^ 2
        Uv = Rnd()
        If phi <= phic Then
            ' Equations (27) and (28)
            b = Sqr(2 / phi - 1 + Sqr(2 / phi * (2 / phi - 1)))
            a = m / (1 + b ^ 2)
```

```
            If icdf = 1 Then
                ' Built-in Excel function for inverse normal CDF
                Zv = NormSInv(Uv)
            ElseIf icdf = 2 Then
                ' Wichura (1988) algorithm for inverse normal CDF
                Zv = normICDF(Uv)
            End If
            V(t, i) = a * (b + Zv) ^ 2      ' Equation (23)
            ' Martingale correction: Define new K0 if possible
            If (MC = 1) And bigA < (1 / (2 * a)) Then
                bigM = Exp(bigA * b ^ 2 * a / (1 - 2 * a * bigA))
                ...
                K0 = -Log(bigM) - (K1 + K3 / 2) * V(t - 1, i)
            End If
            ' Equation (36)
            S(t, i) = S(t - 1, i) * Exp((r - q) * dt + K0 ...
        Else
            p = (phi - 1) / (phi + 1)        ' Equations (29) & (30)
            beta = (1 - p) / m
            If (0 <= Uv) & (Uv <= p) Then   ' Equation (25)
                phiinv = 0
            ElseIf (p < Uv) & (Uv <= 1) Then
                phiinv = 1 / beta * Log((1 - p) / (1 - Uv))
            End If
            V(t, i) = phiinv
            ' Martingale correction: Define new K0 if possible
            If MC = 1 And bigA < beta Then
               bigM = p + beta * (1 - p) / (beta - bigA)
               K0 = -Log(bigM) - (K1 + K3 / 2) * V(t - 1, i)
            End If
            ' Equation (36)
            S(t, i) = S(t - 1, i) * Exp((r - q) * dt + K0 ...
        End If
    Next t
Next i
End Function
```

The function calls the built-in Excel file NormSInv for finding the inverse standard normal CDF. This function, however, is slow. To rectify this problem we create the VBA function normICDF, which implements the approximation algorithm of Wichura (1988). The function is an adaptation of Fortran code AS241 downloaded from StatLib (lib.stat.cmu.edu), a software and data repository hosted by the Department of Statistics at Carnegie Mellon University.

```
Function normICDF(p As Double) As Double
' Coefficients for p close to 0.5
a0 = 3.3871328727963
a1 = 133.14166789178
' Coefficients for p not close to 0, 0.5, or 1
```

```
c0 = 1.4234371107496
c1 = 4.6303378461565
' Coefficients for p near 0 or 1
e0 = 6.6579046435011
e1 = 5.4637849111641
q = p - 0.5
If (q) < 0.425 Then
    ' For p close to 0.5
    r = 0.180625 - q ^ 2
    y = q * (((((((a7 * r + a6) * r + a5) ...
Else
    If (q < 0) Then
        r = p
    Else
        r = 1 - p
    End If
    If (r <= 0) Then
        y = 0
    End If
    r = Sqr(-Log(r))
    If (r <= 5) Then
        ' For p not close to 0, 0.5, or 1
        r = r - 1.6
        y = (((((((c7 * r + c6) * r + c5) * r + c4) * r + c3) ...
    Else
        ' For p near 0 or 1
        r = r - 5
        y = (((((((e7 * r + e6) * r + e5) * r + e4) * r + e3) ...
    End If
    If (q < 0) Then
        y = -y
    End If
End If
End Function
```

Price of the call under the QE algorithm is obtained using the VBA function QEPrice. This function is similar to others encountered throughout this chapter and is not presented.

Using the same settings as the example throughout this chapter, we obtain 11.3662 and 11.3821 for the prices with and without the martingale correction, respectively.

ALFONSI SCHEME FOR THE VARIANCE

Alfonsi (2010) proposes a simulation scheme that performs well under the Heston model and that avoids negative variances. Define

$$\Psi = \frac{1 - \exp(-\kappa dt/2)}{\kappa}$$

and define

$$K_2 = \exp(\kappa dt/2)\left[\left(\frac{\sigma^2}{4} - \kappa\theta\right)\Psi + \left(\sqrt{e^{\kappa dt/2}\left(\frac{\sigma^2}{4} - \kappa\theta\right)\Psi} + \frac{\sigma}{2}\sqrt{3dt}\right)^2\right]$$

when $\sigma^2 > 4\kappa\theta$, and $K_2 = 0$ when $\sigma^2 \leq 4\kappa\theta$. At each simulation step we compare v_t to K_2, and we have a different updated value v_{t+dt} depending on the results of the comparison.

Case 1, $v_t > K_2$. Updating to v_{t+dt} requires two steps. In the first step we simulate a discrete random variable $Y \in \{0, \sqrt{3}, -\sqrt{3}\}$ with probabilities 2/3, 1/6, and 1/6 respectively. In the second step, we update to v_{t+dt} using

$$v_{t+dt} = \exp(-\kappa dt/2)\left(\sqrt{\left(\kappa\theta - \frac{\sigma^2}{4}\right)\Psi + e^{-\kappa dt/2}v_t} + \frac{\sigma^2}{2}\sqrt{dt}Y\right)^2 + \left(\kappa\theta - \frac{\sigma^2}{4}\right)\Psi.$$

Case 2, $v_t \leq K_2$. This also requires two steps. Obtain the mean and variance of v_{t+dt}, conditional on v_t, by

$$u_1 = E[v_{t+dt} \mid v_t] = \theta + (v_t - \theta)e^{-\kappa dt}$$

and

$$s^2 = \mathrm{Var}[v_{t+dt} \mid v_t] = \frac{v_t\sigma^2 e^{-\kappa dt}}{\kappa}(1 - e^{-\kappa dt}) + \frac{\theta\sigma^2}{2\kappa}(1 - e^{-\kappa dt})^2.$$

Obtain the second conditional moment, $u_2 = E[v_{t+dt}^2 \mid v_t]$ as $u_2 = s^2 + u_1^2$. Define the quantity

$$\pi = \frac{1}{2} - \frac{1}{2}\sqrt{1 - \frac{u_1^2}{u_2}}.$$

In the first step, we simulate a uniform random variable U on (0, 1). In the second step, we update to v_{t+dt} by comparing U to π so that

$$v_{t+dt} = \frac{u_1}{2\pi} \qquad \text{if } U \leq \pi$$

$$v_{t+dt} = \frac{u_1}{2(1-\pi)} \qquad \text{if } U > \pi.$$

The VBA function CIRmoments calculates the moments u_1 and u_2.

```
Function CIRmoments(...) As Double
' E[vt | vs];
u1 = theta + (vs - theta) * Exp(-kappa * dt)
' Var[vt | vs]
s2 = vs * sigma ^ 2 * Exp(-kappa * dt) / kappa ...
' E[vt^2 | vs]
u2 = s2 + u1 ^ 2
If Moment = 1 Then
    CIRmoments = u1         ' Return E[vt | vs]
ElseIf Moment = 2 Then
    CIRmoments = u2         ' Return E[vt^2 | vs]
End If
End Function
```

The algorithm to update v_t is implemented with the VBA function AlfonsiV.

```
Function AlfonsiV(...) As Double
phi = (1 - Exp(-kappa * dt / 2)) / kappa
S = (sigma ^ 2 / 4 - theta * kappa)
E = Exp(kappa * dt / 2)
' K2 parameter
If sigma ^ 2 > 4 * kappa * theta Then
    K2 = E * (S * phi + (Sqr(E * S * phi) ...
Else
    K2 = 0
End If
' Update the variance
If vt >= K2 Then
    If u <= 1 / 6 Then
        y = Sqr(3)
    ElseIf u <= 1 / 3 Then
        y = -Sqr(3)
    Else
        y = 0
    End If
    phi = (1 - Exp(-kappa * dt / 2)) / kappa
    S = (theta * kappa - sigma ^ 2 / 4)
    E = Exp(-kappa * dt / 2)
    newV = E * (Sqr(S * phi + E * vt) + sigma ...
Else
    u1 = CIRmoments(..., 1)
    u2 = CIRmoments(..., 2)
    pi = 0.5 - 0.5 * Sqr(1 - u1 ^ 2 / u2)
    If u <= pi Then
```

```
        newV = u1 / 2 / pi
    ElseIf u > pi Then
        newV = u1 / 2 / (1 - pi)
    End If
End If
AlfonsiV = newV
End Function
```

The AlfonsiV function is used in the AlfonsiSim function, which simulates the stock price in accordance with the Predictor-Corrector scheme and simulates the variance using the Alfonsi scheme.

```
Function AlfonsiSim(...) As Variant
' Starting values for the variance and stock processes
For j = 1 To NS
    S(1, j) = S0          ' Spot price
    V(1, j) = v0          ' Heston v0 initial variance
Next j
' Generate the stock and volatility paths
For i = 1 To NS
    For T = 2 To NT
        ' Alfonsi discretization
        V(T, i) = AlfonsiV(params, V(T - 1, i), dt)
        ' Predictor-Corrector for the stock price
        B = NormSInv(Rnd())

        logS = Log(Exp(-r * T * dt) * S(T - 1, i)) ...
        S(T, i) = Exp(logS) * Exp(r * (T + 1) * dt)
    Next T
Next i
' Output the stock price path and the volatility path
For j = 1 To NS
    For T = 1 To NT
        output(T, j) = S(T, j)
        output(T, NS + j) = V(T, j)
    Next T
Next j
AlfonsiSim = output
End Function
```

Finally, the output of the AlfonSim function is passed to the AlfonsiPrice function, which returns the price of a European call or put.

```
Function AlfonsiPrice(...) As Variant
' Transfer output to S and V matrices
For j = 1 To NS
    For T = 1 To NT
        S(T, j) = output(T, j)
        V(T, j) = output(T, NS + j)
    Next T
Next j
For j = 1 To NS          ' Terminal stock prices
    ST(j) = S(NT, j)
Next j
For j = 1 To NS          ' Payoff vectors
    If PutCall = "C" Then
        Payoff(j) = Max(ST(j) - K, 0)
    ElseIf PutCall = "P" Then
        Payoff(j) = Max(K - ST(j), 0)
    End If
Next j
' Simulated price
AlfonsiPrice = Exp(-r * Mat) * Average(Payoff)
End Function
```

Using the same settings as in the examples throughout this chapter, the Alfonsi scheme returns a price of 11.5009. The VBA code and example in this section are in the Excel file Ch7Alfonsi.xls.

MOMENT-MATCHING SCHEME

Andersen and Brotherton-Ratcliffe (2005) propose a moment-matched discretization scheme that generates positive variances only. The scheme produces a variance that is distributed as lognormal, so a natural choice of parameterization is one that matches the first two moments of the discretized process to lognormal moments. This produces a discretization of the form

$$v_{t+dt} = (\theta + (v_t - \theta)e^{-\kappa dt}) \exp\left(-\frac{1}{2}\Gamma_t^2 + \Gamma_t Z_V\right), \tag{7.34}$$

where

$$\Gamma_t = \ln\left(1 + \frac{\sigma^2 v_t (1 - e^{-2\kappa dt})}{2\kappa(\theta + (v_t - \theta)e^{-\kappa dt})^2}\right).$$

The MM scheme is implemented with the functions MMSim and MMPrice, but this latter function is not presented here.

```
Function MMSim(params As Variant, ...) As Variant
For i = 1 To NS
    For t = 2 To NT
        ' Generate two dependent N(0,1) variables
        Zv = NormSInv(Rnd())
        Zs = rho * Zv + Sqr(1 - rho ^ 2) ...
        ' Matched moment lognormal approximation
        Num = 0.5 * sigma ^ 2 * V(t - 1, i)  ...
        Den = (Exp(-kappa * dt) * V(t - 1, i)   ...
        Gam = Log(1 + Num / Den)
        V(t, i) = (Exp(-kappa * dt) * V(t - 1, i) ...
        ' Euler/Milstein discret. for log stock price
        S(t, i) = S(t - 1, i) * Exp((r - q -  ...
    Next t
Next i
End Function
```

Using the same settings as the example in this chapter, we obtain a price of 10.2851 under the moment-matching method. The call prices obtained from the QE and MM methods are displayed in Figure 7.4.

All of the examples, screen shots, and VBA code for the QE and MM methods are in the Excel file Ch7QE-MM.xls.

Table 7.1 suggests that the IJK and pathwise adapted schemes are among the most accurate, with most of the other schemes showing reasonable accuracy. The prices of Table 7.1, however, are based on 5,000 simulated paths and 90 time steps per path only and are for illustrative purposes only. In practice, the number of simulations would be much larger.

	A	B	C	D	E	F	G
1							
2		**Quadratic-Exponential and Moment-Matching Simulation of the Heston European Call Price**					
3							
4		**Option Features**			**Prices with 90 simulations and 5000 time steps per simulation**		
5		Spot Price (S)	100.0000				
6		Strike Price (K)	90.0000		**Method**	**Price**	**Error**
7		Time to Maturity (τ)	0.2500		Exact With Trapezoidal Rule	11.2075	
8		Risk free rate (r)	0.0300		Q-E Scheme with Martingale Correction	11.3662	1.4%
9		Dividend (q)	0.0200		Q-E Scheme without Martingale Correction	11.3821	1.6%
10		PutCall (C or P)	C		Moment-Matching Scheme	10.2851	-8.2%
11		Little Trap (0=Heston, 1=Albrecher)	1				
12							
13		**Heston Parameters**			**Simulation Features**		
14		kappa (κ)	6.2000		Number of Stock Price Paths	5000	
15		theta (θ)	0.0600		Number of Time Steps per Path	90	
16		sigma (σ)	0.5000		Alpha Weight for Implicit-Explicit Scheme	0.5	
17		v0	0.0300		Negative Variances (T=Trunc, R=Reflect)	T	
18		rho (ρ)	-0.7000		(T=Truncation, R=Reflection)		
19		lambda (λ)	0.0000				
20					**Trapezoidal Rule Integration Grid**		
21		**Parameters for the QE Algorithm**			Lower Limit	1.00E-08	
22		Gamma1	0.5000		Upper Limit	100	
23		Gamma2	0.5000		Number of abscissas	200	
24		Cut-off for low and high V(t) regimes	1.5000				
25		Inverse CDF (1=Built-in VBA, 2=Wichura)	2				

FIGURE 7.4 Heston Call Prices under the QE and MM Schemes

TABLE 7.1 European Call Prices Using Simulation

Scheme	Price	Percent Error
Exact	11.2087	—
Euler	11.3527	1.3
Milstein	11.2387	0.3
Implicit Milstein	11.2505	0.4
Weighted implicit Milstein	11.2973	0.8
Zhu Euler	11.3337	1.1
Zhu transformed volatility	11.3008	0.8
IJK	11.2108	0.0
Pathwise adapted	11.2013	−0.1
Balanced Implicit	11.1511	−0.5
QE with MC	11.3662	1.4
QE without MC	11.3821	1.6
Alfonsi	11.5009	2.6
MM	10.2851	−8.2

CONCLUSION

In this chapter, we have described several popular simulation schemes for the bivariate system (S_t, v_t) or $(\ln S_t, v_t)$ of the Heston model. Some of these schemes are traditional schemes that are applied to the Heston model, while others are developed specifically for the model to address the problem of slow convergence and negative variances.

The exact simulation scheme of Broadie and Kaya (2006) is not covered in this chapter. It is an important scheme from a theoretical standpoint, but it is difficult to implement in practice. See Van Haastrecht and Pelsser (2010) for an explanation. Other notable methods not covered in this chapter include those by Smith (2007), Van Haastrecht and Pelsser (2010), Chan and Joshi (2010a), and additional schemes by Kahl and Jäckel (2006).

One of the most important applications of simulated stock prices is for the calculation of American option prices using the Least-Squares Monte Carlo approach of Longstaff and Schwartz (2001). We describe this method as part of the next chapter on American option valuation in the Heston model.

CHAPTER 8

American Options

Abstract

We present methods to value American options in the Heston model. We first present the simulation algorithm of Longstaff and Schwartz (2001). Next, we present a finite difference method, the explicit method, for American options. We present the bivariate tree of Beliaeva and Nawalkha (2010), an adaptation of the trinomial tree in which the stock price and the volatility to evolve is along separate trees. We also cover the method of Medvedev and Scaillet (2010), which approximates the American option price using an analytic expansion and is, thus, able to produce option prices very quickly. Finally, we present the method of Chiarella and Ziogas (2006) for the valuation of American calls.

Least-Squares Monte Carlo, explicit method, bivariate tree, expansion, barrier, early exercise boundary

In this chapter, we present methods to value American options in the Heston model. We first present the simulation algorithm of Longstaff and Schwartz (2001). Next, we present a finite difference method, the explicit method, for American options. This method will be presented in its entirety in Chapter 10. We present the bivariate tree of Beliaeva and Nawalkha (2010), an adaptation of the trinomial tree in which the stock price and the volatility to evolve is along separate trees. We also cover the method of Medvedev and Scaillet (2010), which approximates the American option price using an analytic expansion and is, thus, able to produce option prices very quickly. Finally, we present the method of Chiarella and Ziogas (2006) for the valuation of American calls.

LEAST-SQUARES MONTE CARLO

The Least-Squares Monte Carlo (LSM) algorithm was developed by Longstaff and Schwartz (2001) as a way to price American options using simulation. The algorithm can be applied to any stock price stochastic process that lends itself to simulation. It is especially useful for multidimensional processes for which high-dimension trees are difficult to construct. In this section, we implement the method for the Heston model.

Denote by $C(\omega, s; t, T)$ the set of cash flows generated by the option along the stock price path ω, conditional on the option not being exercised prior to time t, and on the holder following the optimal stopping strategy at all times s, $s < t \le T$. Longstaff and Schwartz (2001) assume that the American option can be exercised only at K discrete times $0 < t_1 \le t_2 \le \cdots \le t_K = T$, where T is the time to maturity. At time t_k, the value $F(\omega, t_k)$ of continuing to hold the option, as opposed to immediate exercise, is the discounted expectation of the remaining cash flows, under all stock price paths and using the risk-neutral measure, $\mathbb{Q}$. Assuming a constant rate of interest r, the value of continuation is therefore

$$F(\omega, t_k) = e^{-r(T-t_k)} E^{\mathbb{Q}} \left[\sum_{j=k+1}^{K} C(\omega, t_j; t_k, T) \middle| \mathcal{F}_{t_k} \right]. \tag{8.1}$$

The American option is valued by comparing the value of immediate exercise, which is known, with $F(\omega, t_k)$, which is unknown. Longstaff and Schwartz (2001) estimate $F(\omega, t_k)$ using least squares on a set of basis functions, which they select to be the weighted Laguerre polynomials we encountered in Chapter 5

$$\begin{aligned} L_0(x) &= e^{-x/2}, \\ L_1(x) &= e^{-x/2}(1-x), \\ L_2(x) &= e^{-x/2}(1 - 2x + x^2/2), \cdots, \\ L_M(x) &= e^{-x/2} \sum_{r=0}^{M} \frac{(-1)^r}{r!} \binom{M}{r} x^r. \end{aligned} \tag{8.2}$$

Using the first M basis functions, $F(\omega, t_k)$ can be approximated by

$$F_M(\omega, t_k) = \sum_{j=0}^{M} a_j L_j(S_k), \tag{8.3}$$

where $S_k = S_k(\omega)$ is the value of the underlying stock price at time t_k along the price path ω. The coefficients a_j are constants that are estimated using least squares. Equation (8.3) can be written in matrix form, as $\mathbf{F} = \mathbf{La}$, where

$$\underset{K\times 1}{\mathbf{F}} = \begin{pmatrix} F_M(\omega, t_1) \\ F_M(\omega, t_2) \\ \vdots \\ F_M(\omega, t_K) \end{pmatrix}, \quad \underset{K\times N}{\mathbf{L}} = \begin{pmatrix} L_0(S_1) & L_1(S_1) & \cdots & L_M(S_1) \\ L_0(S_2) & L_1(S_2) & \cdots & L_M(S_2) \\ \vdots & \vdots & & \vdots \\ L_0(S_K) & L_1(S_K) & \cdots & L_M(S_K) \end{pmatrix}, \quad \underset{N\times 1}{\mathbf{a}} = \begin{pmatrix} a_0 \\ a_1 \\ \vdots \\ a_M \end{pmatrix}, \tag{8.4}$$

with $N = M + 1$. Longstaff and Schwartz (2001) emphasize that other basis functions are possible.

The cash flows at an arbitrary time t_k depend on whether or not exercise occurs at t_{k+1}. If exercise occurs, the cash flows going forward will change, so it is not possible to determine the cash flows at t_k by going forward. Consequently, Longstaff and Schwartz (2001) apply the LSM algorithm to approximate the cash flows backward, from t_{K-1} to t_1. At time $t_K = T$, the cash flow is simply the payoff. At each time t_k $(2 \leq k \leq K-1)$, we find all stock price paths that are in-the-money and discount by one period the cash flows at t_{k+1} along the in-the-money paths. We then estimate the $M+1$ coefficients $a_0, \cdots, a_M$ of Equation (8.3) by regression

$$\hat{\mathbf{a}} = (\mathbf{L}'\mathbf{L})^{-1}\mathbf{L}'\mathbf{F}. \tag{8.5}$$

See, for example, Kutner et al. (2004). Next, we form the predicted continuation value $\widehat{F}(\omega, t_{k-1})$ as the fitted values from the regression

$$\widehat{F}(\omega, t_{k-1}) = \hat{a}_0 L_0(S_{k-1}) + \hat{a}_1 L_1(S_{k-1}) + \cdots + \hat{a}_M L_M(S_{k-1}). \tag{8.6}$$

We compare the predicted continuation to the value of exercise, and replace the current cash flows (at time t_k) in those stock paths where it is optimal. We repeat until time t_1 and form the American option value by discounting the time t_1 cash flows by a single period.

The accuracy of the American option value can be improved by using the control variate technique. If we assume that the error in LSM pricing of an American option from its true value is the same as the error in LSM pricing of a European option from its true value, then we can write

$$\text{American Error} = \text{European Error}$$
$$\text{American Price}_{\text{True}} - \text{American Price}_{\text{LSM}} = \text{European Price}_{\text{True}} - \text{European Price}_{\text{LSM}}.$$

The control variate price of the American option is, therefore,

$$\begin{aligned}\text{American Put}_{\text{CV}} = {} & \text{European Price}_{\text{True}} \\ & + (\text{American Price}_{\text{LSM}} - \text{European Price}_{\text{LSM}}).\end{aligned} \tag{8.7}$$

Note that (8.7) amounts to adding the early exercise premium estimated by the LSM algorithm to the closed form European price. See Hull and White (1988) for a discussion of the control variate technique for pricing American options.

The VBA function LSM implements the Longstaff-Schwartz (2001) algorithm and returns American and European prices. The function requires a matrix of simulated Heston stock prices as input. The LSM function uses the MMsim algorithm presented in Chapter 7 for this purpose.

```
Function LSM(S0 As Double, ...,EuroAmer As String) As Double
' Generate Stock price paths
' Rows = stock price dimension, cols = Time dimension
S = MMSim(params, S0, T, rf, q, NT, NS)
' Set the last cash flows to the intrinsic value.
```

```
For j = 1 To NS
    If PutCall = "P" Then
        CF(j, NT) = Max(K - S(j, NT), 0)
Next j
' European price
For j = 1 To NS
    EuroPrice = EuroPrice + Exp(-rf * T) * CF(j, NT) / NS
Next j
' Work backwards through the stock prices until time t=2.
For i = NT - 1 To 2 Step -1
    ' Indices for stock paths in-the-money at time i
    For j = 1 To NS
        Ind(j) = 0
        If (((PutCall = "P") And (S(j, i) < K)) Or ... K))) Then
            Ind(j) = 1
    Next j
    ' Stock paths in-the-money at time i (X)
    For j = 1 To NS
        If Ind(j) = 1 Then
            NI = NI + 1
            X(NI) = S(j, i)
            Xi(NI) = j
    Next j
    ' Design matrix for predicted cash flows
    For j = 1 To NI
        Y(j) = CF(Xi(j), i + 1) * Exp(-rf * dt)
        Z(j, 1) = 1
        Z(j, 2) = 1 - X(j)
        Z(j, 3) = (2 - 4 * X(j) - X(j) ^ 2) / 2
    Next j
    ' Regression parameters and predicted CF
    betas = Beta(Z, Y)
    For j = 1 To NI
        PredCF(j) = betas(1, 1) * Z(j, 1) + betas(2, 1) ...
    Next j
    ' Indices for stock paths where immediate exercise is optimal
    For j = 1 To NI
        If (PutCall = "P" And (K - X(j) > 0 And K - X(j) > PredCF(j))) Or_
            NE = NE + 1
            Count = Count + 1
            JJ(Count) = j
            E(Count) = Xi(j)
    Next j
    ' All other paths, continuation is optimal
    For j = 1 To NS
        All(j) = j
    Next j
    ' C contains indices for continuation paths
    NC = NS - NE
```

```
    For j = 1 To NS
        D(j) = j
    Next j
    For j = 1 To NS
        For r = 1 To NE
            If All(j) = JJ(r) Then
                D(E(r)) = 0
        Next r
    Next j
    For j = 1 To NS
        If D(j) <> 0 Then
            Count = Count + 1
            C(Count) = D(j)
    Next j
    ' Replace cash flows with exercise value where exercise is optimal
    If NE >= 1 Then
        For j = 1 To NE
            If PutCall = "P" Then
                CF(E(j), i) = Max(K - X(JJ(j)), 0)
    If NC >= 1 Then
        For j = 1 To NC
            CF(C(j), i) = Exp(-rf * dt) * CF(C(j), i + 1)
        Next j
Next i
' Calculate the cash flow at time 2
For j = 1 To NS
    Op(j) = CF(j, 2)
Next j
' Calculate the American price
AmerPrice = Exp(-rf * dt) * VMean(Op)
' Output the American or European Prices
If EuroAmer = "A" Then
    LSM = AmerPrice
ElseIf EuroAmer = "E" Then
    LSM = EuroPrice
End If
End Function
```

The LSM function uses the VBA function Beta to obtain the parameter estimates (8.5).

```
Function Beta(X As Variant, Y As Variant) As Variant
' Calculate the required matrices
Xt = MTrans(X, N, K)
XtXinv = MInvLU(MMMult(Xt, X))
XtY = MVMult(Xt, Y)
' Parameter estimates
```

```
For i = 1 To K
    For j = 1 To K
        params(i, 1) = params(i, 1) + XtXinv(i, j) * XtY(j, 1)
    Next j
Next i
End Function
```

The Beta function makes use of several functions for matrix operations, such as multiplication and inversion, but these are not presented here. They are available in the Excel file Ch8MatrixOps.xls.

To illustrate, we implement the example of Clarke and Parrott (1999), which uses the settings $K = 10$, $r = 0.1$, and $T = 0.25$ years, with parameter values $\kappa = 5$, $\theta = 0.16$, $\sigma = 0.9$, $\rho = 0.1$, and $v_0 = 0.0625$, and spot prices 8 through 12. We use the value of American puts computed by Ikonen and Toivanen (2008) for the Clarke and Parrott (1999) settings, namely 2.0000, 1.107064, 0.520030, 0.213668, and 0.082036. We use 2,000 stock price paths and 10 time steps per path. The results are in Figure 8.1.

The prices obtained using the control variate technique with the LSM algorithm are reasonably close to the prices obtained by Ikonen and Toivanen (2008). The LSM prices are also very close but slightly less. Note that we used only 2,000 stock price paths. In practice, the number of paths would be much higher. The functions and examples in this section, along with the screen shot in Figure 8.1, are in the Excel file Ch8LSM.xls.

THE EXPLICIT METHOD

In Chapter 10, we will encounter methods to obtain the Heston price of European options by approximating with finite differences, the partial differential equation (PDE), that these options satisfy. It is straightforward to adapt one of these

Longstaff-Schwartz LSM Algorithm for American Options

Option Features	
Strike Price (K)	10.0000
Time to Maturity (τ)	0.2500
Risk free rate (r)	0.1000
Dividend (q)	0.0000
PutCall (C or P)	P
Little Trap (0=Heston, 1=Albrecher)	1
Heston Parameters	
kappa (κ)	5.0000
theta (θ)	0.1600
sigma (σ)	0.9000
v0	0.0625
rho (ρ)	0.1000
lambda (λ)	0.0000
Simulation Features	
Number of Stock Price Paths	2000
Number of Time Steps per Path	10

Prices with 10 simulations and 2000 time steps per simulation

Spot	TruePrice	LSM Amer	CV Amer	ClosedEuro	LSM Euro
8	2.000000	1.983506	1.975004	1.838868	1.847370
9	1.107064	1.086856	1.100822	1.048347	1.034382
10	0.520030	0.520447	0.591111	0.501466	0.430802
11	0.213668	0.172474	0.223156	0.208187	0.157505
12	0.082036	#VALUE!	#VALUE!	0.080429	#VALUE!

TruePrice	True American option price from Clarke and Parrott (1999)
LSM Amer	American option price using the LSM algorithm
CV Amer	American option price using the LSM algorithm and Control Variate Technique
ClosedEuro	European option price using the trapezoidal rule
LSM Euro	European option price using the LSM algorithm

Trapezoidal Rule Integration Grid

Lower Limit	1.00E-08
Upper Limit	100
Number of al	200

FIGURE 8.1 Pricing American Puts Using the LSM Algorithm

methods, the explicit method, to price American options. It can be shown that, under the Heston model, the value $U(S, v, t)$ of a derivative with maturity t satisfies the PDE:

$$\begin{aligned}\frac{\partial U}{\partial t} &= \frac{1}{2}vS^2\frac{\partial^2 U}{\partial S^2} + \rho\sigma vS\frac{\partial^2 U}{\partial v\partial S} + \frac{1}{2}\sigma^2 v\frac{\partial^2 U}{\partial v^2} - rU, \\ &+ (r-q)S\frac{\partial U}{\partial S} + \kappa(\theta - v)\frac{\partial U}{\partial v},\end{aligned} \tag{8.8}$$

where we have defined $\lambda = 0$. See Gatheral (2006), Musiela and Rutkowski (2011), or Rouah (2013), among many others. We will see in Chapter 10 that the first step in solving the PDE with finite differences is to build discrete grids for the stock price, volatility, and maturity. Denote by $U^n_{i,j} = U(S_i, v_j, t_n)$ the value of the European derivative when the stock price and volatility are at points i and j, respectively, of their grids, and when the maturity is at the point n, for $i = 0, \ldots, N_S$, $j = 0, \ldots, N_V$, and $n = 0, \ldots, N_T$. The explicit method defines the value of the derivative at maturity point $n + 1$ as

$$\begin{aligned}U^{n+1}_{i,j} &= U^n_{i,j} + dt\left[\frac{1}{2}v_j S_i^2\frac{\partial^2}{\partial S^2} + \frac{1}{2}\sigma^2 v_i\frac{\partial^2}{\partial v^2}\right. \\ &+ \left.\rho\sigma v_j S_i\frac{\partial^2}{\partial v\partial S} + (r-q)S_i\frac{\partial}{\partial S} + \kappa(\theta - v_j)\frac{\partial}{\partial v} - r\right]U^n_{i,j}.\end{aligned} \tag{8.9}$$

To evaluate $U^{n+1}_{i,j}$ we need to substitute finite difference approximations of the derivatives in (8.9). When a uniform grid is constructed, namely, one that uses equidistant spacing between successive values of the stock price and volatility, the expression for $U^{n+1}_{i,j}$ reduces to a very simple form. A nonuniform grid, however, leads to greater accuracy with fewer grid points, but also to an expression for $U^{n+1}_{i,j}$ that is more complicated.

Since the explicit method works backward in time, we start with the value $U^0_{i,j}$, namely, the value of the derivative at maturity. To price a European put option, we use

$$U^0_{i,j} = \max(K - S_i, 0). \tag{8.10}$$

This quantity is identical for all points $j = 0, \ldots, N_V$ in the v-direction. We then obtain $U^1_{i,j}, U^2_{i,j}, \ldots$ in succession until we reach the last maturity point, representing zero time to maturity. To price an American put, at each time step we add the early exercise condition

$$U^{n+1}_{i,j} = \max\left(K - S_i, U^{n+1}_{i,j}\right) \text{ for } j = 0, \ldots, N_V. \tag{8.11}$$

Finally, to price the option we need boundary conditions on the maximum and minimum values of S and v. Please refer to Chapter 10 for these boundary conditions.

The VBA function HestonExplicitPDE calculates the Heston price of an American call or put using the explicit method and a uniform grid. The first part of the function builds the uniform grid using the BuildGrid function and defines the payoff of the option at maturity. The BuildGrid function will be presented in Chapter 10.

```
Function HestonExplicitPDE(params As Variant, ...) As Double
' Build uniform grids
Spot = BuildGrid(Smin,  ..., "Uniform", "Spot")
Vol  = BuildGrid(Smin,  ..., "Uniform", "Vol")
Mat  = BuildGrid(Smin,  ..., "Uniform", "Mat")
' Boundary condition for t = Maturity
For i = 1 To NS
    For j = 1 To NV
        If PutCall = "C" Then
            U(i, j) = Max(Spot(i) - Strike, 0)
        ElseIf PutCall = "P" Then
            U(i, j) = Max(Strike - Spot(i), 0)
        End If
    Next j
Next i
```

The middle part of the function loops through time and updates the option value in accordance with Equation (8.9), the derivatives of which are approximated with finite differences.

```
For t = 1 To NT - 1
    ' Boundary condition for Smin and Smax
    For v = 1 To NV - 1
        U(NS, v) = Max(0, Smax - Strike)
    Next v
    ' Boundary condition for Vmax
    For s = 1 To NS
        U(s, NV) = Max(0, Spot(s) - Strike)
    Next s
    ' Update the temporary grid u(s,t) with the boundary conditions
    For s = 1 To NS
        smallU(s, v) = U(s, v)
    Next s
    ' Boundary condition for Vmin.
    ' Previous time step values are in temporary grid u(s,t)
    For s = 2 To NS - 1
        ' PDE Points on the middle of grid (non boundary)
        DerV = (smallU(s, 2) - smallU(s, 1)) / dv
```

```
        ' Central difference for dU/dS
        DerS = (smallU(s + 1, 1) - smallU(s - 1, 1)) / 2 / ds
        U(s, 1) = smallU(s, 1) * (1 - r * dt ...
    Next s
    ' Update temporary grid u(s,t) with boundary conditions
    For s = 1 To NS
        For v = 1 To NV
            smallU(s, v) = U(s, v)
        Next v
    Next s
    ' Interior points of the grid (non boundary).
    For s = 2 To NS - 1
        For v = 2 To NV - 1
            C1 = (1 - dt * (s - 1) ^ 2 * (v - 1) * dv ...
            C6 = 1 / 4 * dt * sigma * (s - 1) * (v - 1)
            ' The PDE
            U(s, v) = C1 * smallU(s, v) + C2 * smallU(s - 1, v) ...
        Next v
    Next s
```

Finally, the last part of the function applies the condition in Equation (8.11) at each time step to determine whether or not early exercise is optimal.

```
    If EuroAmer = "A" Then
        For s = 1 To NS
            For v = 1 To NV
                If PutCall = "C" Then
                    U(s, v) = Max(U(s, v), Spot(s) - K)
                ElseIf PutCall = "P" Then
                    U(s, v) = Max(U(s, v), K - Spot(s))
                End If
            Next v
        Next s
    End If
Next t
' Interpolate the discretized PDE, "U", at the points (Si,Vi)
U = MTrans(U, NS, NV)
HestonExplicitPDE = interp2(Spot, Vol, U, Si, Vi)
End Function
```

The function returns the entire grid at maturity, namely, $U_{i,j}^{N_T}$ for $i = 0, \ldots, N_S$, and $j = 0, \ldots, N_V$. The VBA function interp2 employs two-dimensional interpolation to obtain the price of the option for values of (S, v) that lie in between points on the grid. We do not present this function here.

	A	B	C	D	E	F	G	H	I	J
1										
2		**Explicit PDE Method for Clarke and Parrott (1999) American Puts**								
3						**True**	**Price by PDE**		**$ Error**	
4		**Option Features**			**Spot Price**	**Price**	**Uniform**	**Non-Uniform**	**Uniform**	**Non-Uniform**
5		Strike Price (K)	10.0000		8	2.000000	2.014046	2.000000	0.014046	0.000000
6		Time to Maturity (τ)	0.2500		9	1.107641	1.152318	1.109270	0.044677	0.001629
7		Risk free rate (r)	0.1000		10	0.520030	0.502333	0.519086	-0.017697	-0.000944
8		Dividend (q)	0.0000		11	0.213668	0.127102	0.211600	-0.086566	-0.002068
9		PutCall (C or P)	P		12	0.082036	0.009702	0.079837	-0.072334	-0.002199
10		European or American (E or A)	A							
11		Little Trap (0=Heston, 1=Albrecher)	1		**Number of Steps in Each Dimension**					
12					Stock Price	65				
13		**Heston Parameters**			Volatility	35				
14		kappa (κ)	5.00000		Maturity	3000				
15		theta (θ)	0.16000							
16		sigma (σ)	0.90000		**Boundary Values for Stock Price, Volatility, and Maturity**					
17		v0	0.06250		Minimum S	0.0000				
18		rho (ρ)	0.10000		Maximum S	20				
19		lambda (λ)	0.00000		Minimum V	0				
20					Maximum V	1				
21		**Trapezoidal Rule Integration Grid**			Minimum T	0				
22		Lower Limit	1.00E-10		Maximum T	0.25				
23		Upper Limit	150							
24		Number of abscissas	500							

FIGURE 8.2 Pricing American Puts Using the Explicit Method

To illustrate, we continue the numerical example of Clarke and Parrott (1999) and Ikonen and Toivanen (2008) described in the previous section. We obtain prices using both types of grid. The results are shown in Figure 8.2.

As expected, using a nonuniform grid produces more accurate results. The functions and examples presented in this section, along with the screen shot in Figure 8.2, are in the Excel file Ch8Explicit.xls.

BELIAEVA-NAWALKHA BIVARIATE TREE

Beliaeva and Nawalkha (2010) have developed a path-independent two-dimensional tree for the Heston model. In their approach, separate trees for the stock price and the variance are constructed independently of one another, and then recombined. Nawalkha (2010) construct the uncorrelated bivariate process (Y_t, v_t), where

$$Y_t = \ln S_t - \frac{\rho}{\sigma} v_t - h_t \tag{8.12}$$

and

$$h_t = \left(r - \frac{\rho \kappa \theta}{\sigma} \right) t. \tag{8.13}$$

Given a value Y_t, the stock price can be recovered by inverting (8.12):

$$S_t = \exp\left(Y_t + \frac{\rho}{\sigma} v_t + h_t \right). \tag{8.14}$$

Beliaeva and Nawalkha (2010) built a trinomial tree for the transformed variance x_t defined as

$$x_t = \frac{2\sqrt{v_t}}{\sigma}. \tag{8.15}$$

They recover the variance v_t through the inverse transformation

$$v_t = \frac{1}{4}x_t^2\sigma^2. \tag{8.16}$$

The fact that (Y_t, v_t) is uncorrelated is crucial because that allows for the construction of trees for Y_t and v_t separately. A trinomial tree for the transformed variance x_t is constructed first and transformed into a tree for the variances v_t by using (8.16). Next, a tree for the transformed stock price Y_t is constructed, and transformed into a tree for the stock price S_t by using (8.14). Finally, the trees are combined to form a bivariate tree on which American options can be priced. In the following sections, we explain how this is done.

Trinomial Tree for the Variance

Beliaeva and Nawalkha (2010) first construct a tree for the transformed variance x_t. At time $t > 0$, given that the process is at node x_t, there are two sets of moves, depending on whether $x_t > 0$ or $x_t = 0$.

Case 1. If $x_t > 0$, the up, middle, and down moves at time $t + dt$ are

$$\begin{aligned} x^{\mathrm{u}}_{t+dt} &= x_t + b(J+1)\sqrt{dt}, \\ x^{\mathrm{m}}_{t+dt} &= x_t + bJ\sqrt{dt}, \\ x^{\mathrm{d}}_{t+dt} &= x_t + b(J-1)\sqrt{dt}. \end{aligned} \tag{8.17}$$

The probability of each move is

$$\begin{aligned} p^{\mathrm{u}}_v &= \frac{1}{2b^2} - \frac{J}{2} + \frac{1}{2b}\mu(x_t, t)\sqrt{dt}, \\ p^{\mathrm{m}}_v &= 1 - \frac{1}{b^2}, \\ p^{\mathrm{d}}_v &= \frac{1}{2b^2} + \frac{J}{2} - \frac{1}{2b}\mu(x_t, t)\sqrt{dt}, \end{aligned} \tag{8.18}$$

where

$$\mu(x_t, t) = \frac{1}{x_t}\left(\frac{2\kappa\theta}{\sigma^2} - \frac{\kappa x_t^2}{2} - \frac{1}{2}\right). \tag{8.19}$$

Case 2. If $x_t = 0$, the up move x^{u}_{t+dt} is defined identically to that in Equation (8.17), the down move is $x^{\mathrm{d}}_{t+dt} = 0$, and the middle move x^{m}_{t+dt} is not used. The probabilities in this case are

$$p^{\mathrm{u}}_v = \frac{\kappa\theta dt}{v^{\mathrm{u}}_{t+dt}}, p^{\mathrm{m}}_v = 0, p^{\mathrm{d}}_v = 1 - p^{\mathrm{u}}_v, \tag{8.20}$$

where v^{u}_{t+dt} is obtained by substituting x^{u}_{t+dt} into (8.16). The preceding equations use the quantities J and b. For their definition and additional detail, see Beliaeva and Nawalkha (2010) or Rouah (2013).

The trinomial tree for x_t and v_t are each truncated below zero (they can be truncated above an arbitrary value also, to reduce computation time). The b parameter is defined within the range $1 \leq b \leq \sqrt{2}$ and serves to contract or expand the tree to ensure that the last row of the tree for x_t is exactly zero. The trinomial tree for v_t is obtained through the inverse transformation (8.16).

Trinomial Tree for the Stock Price

In the trinomial tree for the transformed stock price Y_t defined in Equation (8.12), jumps across multiple nodes are allowed. High values of v_t cause Y_t to jump up and down across multiple nodes, while low values of v_t allow for jumps across single nodes only. Beliaeva and Nawalkha (2010) define the node span as $k_t \sigma_Y(0)\sqrt{dt}$, which represents the distance between nodes for values of Y_{t+dt}, given that the process is at the node Y_t. The case $k_t = 1$ represents a jump across a single node, while $k_t > 1$ represents a jump across multiple nodes. This parameter is defined as

$$k_t = \begin{cases} \text{Ceiling}\left(\sqrt{v_t/v_0}\right) & \text{if } v_t > 0, \\ 1 & \text{otherwise.} \end{cases} \tag{8.21}$$

Multiple jumps in Y_t are illustrated in Figure 8.3, which reproduces Exhibit 3 of Beliaeva and Nawalkha (2010). The left panel is for the case $k_t = 1$ is analogous to an ordinary trinomial tree. The right panel illustrates the case $k_t = 2$. Note that in both cases, the tree recombines at every time step.

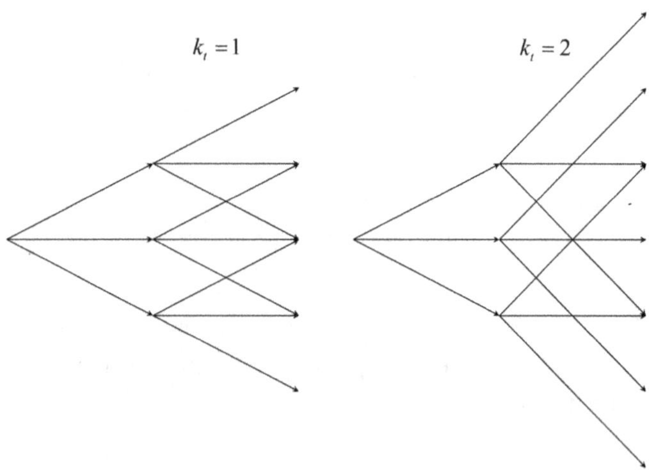

FIGURE 8.3 Jumps in the Transformed Stock Price

The time-zero value of the tree at the initial node is given by Y_0, obtained by setting $t = 0$ in Equations (8.12) an (8.13). Conditional on Y_t, the up, middle, and down values of Y_{t+dt} are

$$\begin{aligned} Y^{u}_{t+dt} &= Y_t + (I+1) \cdot k_t \sigma_Y(0)\sqrt{dt}, \\ Y^{m}_{t+dt} &= Y_t + I \cdot k_t \sigma_Y(0)\sqrt{dt}, \\ Y^{d}_{t+dt} &= Y_t + (I-1) \cdot k_t \sigma_Y(0)\sqrt{dt}, \end{aligned} \tag{8.22}$$

where I is the integer closest in absolute value to

$$\frac{\mu_Y(t)\sqrt{dt}}{k_t \sigma_Y(0)},$$

and where

$$\mu_Y(t) = \left(\frac{\rho\kappa}{\sigma} - \frac{1}{2}\right) v_t, \sigma_Y(t) = \sqrt{1-\rho^2}\sqrt{v_t}. \tag{8.23}$$

The probabilities of up, middle, and down moves are given by

$$\begin{aligned} p^{u}_{Y} &= \frac{1}{2}\frac{\sigma^2_Y(t)dt + e_m e_d}{(k_t\sigma_Y(0))^2 dt}, \\ p^{m}_{Y} &= -\frac{\sigma^2_Y(t)dt + e_u e_d}{(k_t\sigma_Y(0))^2 dt}, \\ p^{d}_{Y} &= \frac{1}{2}\frac{\sigma^2_Y(t)dt + e_u e_m}{(k_t\sigma_Y(0))^2 dt}, \end{aligned} \tag{8.24}$$

where

$$\begin{aligned} e_u &= Y^{u}_{t+dt} - Y_t - \mu_Y(t)dt = (I+1) \cdot k_t\sigma_Y(0)\sqrt{dt} - \mu_Y(t)dt, \\ e_m &= Y^{m}_{t+dt} - Y_t - \mu_Y(t)dt = I \cdot k_t\sigma_Y(0)\sqrt{dt} - \mu_Y(t)dt, \\ e_d &= Y^{d}_{t+dt} - Y_t - \mu_Y(t)dt = (I-1) \cdot k_t\sigma_Y(0)\sqrt{dt} - \mu_Y(t)dt. \end{aligned} \tag{8.25}$$

When the number of time steps is large, I approaches zero and the expressions in (8.24) take on the simpler form given in Equation (18) of Beliaeva and Nawalkha (2010). The tree for the stock price S_t is obtained by applying the inverse transformation (8.14) at every node of the tree for Y_t. Note that since Y_t depends on k_t, and since k_t depends on v_t, the tree for the variance must be constructed before the tree for the stock price.

Combining the Trinomial Trees

The final step in the approach of Beliaeva and Nawalkha (2010) is to mesh the trinomial trees for v_t and S_t into a single tree. At time zero there is a single node for (S_0, v_0). At each subsequent node (S_t, v_t) of the tree S_t and v_t each evolve to one of three possible values (up, middle, or down). Hence, each node branches out to $3 \times 3 = 9$ potential new nodes. Since these nodes recombine, however, the actual number of nodes does not increase by a factor of nine at each time step. Rather, the number of nodes depends on the values of k_t at the nodes; higher values of k_t require more nodes. The number of nodes can increase very rapidly, but the fact that the tree for Y_t recombines mitigates this increase substantially. In Exhibit 11 of Beliaeva and Nawalkha (2010), for example, there are 35 nodes at the second time step.

Each node (S_t, v_t) branches out to nine nodes. Since the trees for Y_t and v_t are uncorrelated, the joint probabilities of these branches are the product of the three marginal probabilities from each tree, defined in Equations (8.18) and (8.24):

$$\begin{aligned}
p_{\text{uu}} &= p_{\text{Y}}^{\text{u}} \times p_v^{\text{u}}, p_{\text{mu}} = p_{\text{Y}}^{\text{m}} \times p_v^{\text{u}}, p_{\text{du}} = p_{\text{Y}}^{\text{d}} \times p_v^{\text{u}}, \\
p_{\text{um}} &= p_{\text{Y}}^{\text{u}} \times p_v^{\text{m}}, p_{\text{mm}} = p_{\text{Y}}^{\text{m}} \times p_v^{\text{m}}, p_{\text{dm}} = p_{\text{Y}}^{\text{d}} \times p_v^{\text{m}}, \\
p_{\text{ud}} &= p_{\text{Y}}^{\text{u}} \times p_v^{\text{d}}, p_{\text{md}} = p_{\text{Y}}^{\text{m}} \times p_v^{\text{d}}, p_{\text{dd}} = p_{\text{Y}}^{\text{d}} \times p_v^{\text{d}}.
\end{aligned} \tag{8.26}$$

With the tree for the stock price S_t and the joint probabilities, pricing American options is done exactly as in an ordinary trinomial tree, by working backward in time from the maturity where the payoff is known, and at each node comparing the value of the American option with the value of immediate exercise. Hence, the price of the American put at time t is

$$\begin{aligned}
U(S_t, v_t) = e^{-r \times dt} \max \big(K - S_t,& \\
p_{\text{uu}} U(S^{\text{u}}_{t+dt}, v^{\text{u}}_{t+dt}) + p_{\text{um}} U(S^{\text{m}}_{t+dt}, v^{\text{u}}_{t+dt}) &+ \cdots + p_{\text{dd}} U(S^{\text{d}}_{t+dt}, v^{\text{d}}_{t+dt})\big).
\end{aligned} \tag{8.27}$$

Beliaeva and Nawalkha (2010) also compute the price of American puts using the control variate technique

$$\begin{aligned}
\text{American Put}_{\text{CV}} = &\text{ European Put}_{\text{True}} \\
&+ (\text{American Put}_{\text{Bivariate Tree}} - \text{European Put}_{\text{Bivariate Tree}}).
\end{aligned} \tag{8.28}$$

In (8.28), we use the American and European puts obtained from the tree, and we use the closed form using the original Heston (1993) formulation with 32-point Gauss-Laguerre integration.

For additional details, see Beliaeva and Nawalkha (2010) or Rouah (2013).

Implementation in VBA

The VBA function BuildVolTree builds the trees for the transformed variance x_t and the variance v_t. The first part of the function computes the b parameter, finds the number of required rows (NR) and the middle row (M) where the first node x_0 is placed, and initializes the first two columns of the tree, corresponding to time zero and time one, respectively.

```
Function BuildVolTree(kappa As Double, ...) As Variant
' Initial quantities
X0 = 2 * Sqr(V0) / sigma
be = X0 / Sqr(dt) / Int(X0 / Sqr(1.5 * dt))
bc = X0 / Sqr(dt) / Int(X0 / Sqr(1.5 * dt) + 1)
If Abs(bc - Sqr(1.5)) < Abs(be - Sqr(1.5)) Then
    bb = bc
Else
    bb = be
End If
' Initialize the X-matrix and V-matrix
NR = 2 * NT - 1
M = (NR + 1) / 2
X(M, 1) = X0
' Time 1 node for X
muX = 1 / X0 * (0.5 * kappa * (4 * theta / sigma ...
J = Int(muX * Sqr(dt) / bb + 1 / bb ^ 2)
X(M - 1, 2) = X(M, 1) + bb * (J + 1) * Sqr(dt)
X(M + 0, 2) = X(M, 1) + bb * (J + 0) * Sqr(dt)
X(M + 1, 2) = X(M, 1) + bb * (J - 1) * Sqr(dt)
```

The second part of the function creates the remaining nodes x^{u}_{t+dt}, x^{m}_{t+dt} and x^{d}_{t+dt}, based on the current node x_t and using Equation (8.17). Values of x_t smaller than a user-defined threshold are assumed to be zero. Next, a parameter (RBound) is created that identifies the row at which x_t becomes zero. Finally, the tree for the variances v_t is constructed using (8.16).

```
' Remaining nodes for X
For t = 2 To M - 1
    For n = M - t + 1 To M + t - 1
        If X(n, t) < threshold Then
            X(n, t) = threshold * 0.95
        End If
        muX = 1 / X(n, t) * (0.5 * kappa * (4 * theta ...
        J = Int(muX * Sqr(dt) / bb + 1 / bb ^ 2)
        ' Nodes where X > 0
        If (X(n, t) > threshold) And (X(n, t) ^ 2  ...) Then
            X(n - 1, t + 1) = X(n, t) + bb * (J + 1) * Sqr(dt)
            X(n + 0, t + 1) = X(n, t) + bb * (J + 0) * Sqr(dt)
            X(n + 1, t + 1) = X(n, t) + bb * (J - 1) * Sqr(dt)
```

```
        ' Nodes where X = 0
        Else
            X(n - 1, t + 1) = X(n - 1, t)
            X(n + 0, t + 1) = X(n + 0, t)
            X(n + 1, t + 1) = X(n + 1, t)
        End If
    Next n
Next t
' Replace 0.95*threshold values of X(n,t) with zero
For t = 2 To M
    For n = M - t + 1 To M + t - 1
        If X(n, t) = threshold * 0.95 Then
            X(n, t) = 0
        End If
    Next n
Next t
' Identify row of the tree where X = 0
RBound = 1
While (X(RBound, M) >= threshold And RBound < NR)
    RBound = RBound + 1
Wend
' Build the volatility tree V(n,t)
For t = 1 To NT
    For n = 1 To NR
        V(n, t) = X(n, t) * X(n, t) * sigma ^ 2 / 4
        If V(n, t) < threshold Then
            V(n, t) = 0
        End If
        If X(n, t) < threshold Then
            X(n, t) = 0
        End If
    Next n
Next t
```

The probabilities for v_t are calculated using the VBA function probV. The function applies Equation (8.18) for the case $x_t > 0$ and (8.20) for the case $x_t = 0$.

```
Function probV(X As Double, ...) As Variant
' Initial quantities
be = X0 / Sqr(dt) / Int(X0 / Sqr(1.5 * dt))
bc = X0 / Sqr(dt) / Int(X0 / Sqr(1.5 * dt) + 1)
If Abs(bc - Sqr(1.5)) < Abs(be - Sqr(1.5)) Then
    bb = bc
Else
    bb = be
End If
```

```
' Equations (22) and (30)
muX = 1 / X * (0.5 * kappa * (4 * theta / sigma ^ 2 - X ^ 2) ...
J = Int(muX * Sqr(dt) / bb + 1 / bb ^ 2)
If X > 0 Then
    ' Probabilities where X > 0 (Equation 28)
    pu = 1 / 2 / bb ^ 2 - J / 2 + 1 / 2 / bb * muX * Sqr(dt)
    pm = 1 - 1 / bb ^ 2
    pd = 1 / 2 / bb ^ 2 + J / 2 - 1 / 2 / bb * muX * Sqr(dt)
Else
    ' Probabilities where X = 0 (Equation 33)
    Xu = X + bb * (J + 1) * Sqr(dt)
    Vu = Xu ^ 2 * sigma ^ 2 / 4
    pu = kappa * theta * dt / Vu
    pm = 0
    pd = 1 - pu
End If
End Function
```

The probabilities for S_t are calculated using the VBA function probY, which applies Equation (8.24).

```
Function probY(Vt As Double, ...) As Variant
' Equation 11
If Vt > 0 Then
    k = Cceil(Sqr(Vt / V0))
End If
' Equations 9 and 6
muy = (rho / sigma * kappa - 0.5) * Vt
sigmayt = Sqr(1 - rho ^ 2) * Sqr(Vt)
sigmay0 = Sqr(1 - rho ^ 2) * Sqr(V0)
' Calculate the Yu, Ym, Yd from Equation 13
II = (Round(muy / k / sigmay0 * Sqr(dt)))
Yu = Yt + (II + 1) * k * sigmay0 * Sqr(dt)
Ym = Yt + (II + 0) * k * sigmay0 * Sqr(dt)
Yd = Yt + (II - 1) * k * sigmay0 * Sqr(dt)
' Equation 17
eu = Yu - Yt - muy * dt
em = Ym - Yt - muy * dt
ed = Yd - Yt - muy * dt
' Equation 16
pu = 0.5 * (sigmayt ^ 2 * dt + em * ed) / k ^ 2 ...
pm = -(sigmayt ^ 2 * dt + eu * ed) / k ^ 2 ...
pd = 0.5 * (sigmayt ^ 2 * dt + eu * em) / k ^ 2 ...
End Function
```

The transformed stock price tree Y_t, the stock prices S_t and the American and European prices are all built using the BuildBivariateTree function. The structure of Y_t is upper triangular and constructed by placing Y_0 in the top left-hand corner of the matrix for Y_t. The values at the first time step are placed in the first nine rows of the second column of the matrix, the values at the second time step are placed in the third column starting from the top row, and so on.

The first part of the function generates the tree for the variance using the BuildVolTree function, finds the value of k_t at each node of v_t, and finds the number of rows needed at each time step based on the maximum value of k_t and the number of variance nodes at that step. The value of k_t at each node is obtained from Equation (8.21).

```
Function BuildBivariateTree(S0 As Double, ...) As Double
' Generate the volatility trees
NR = 2 * NT - 1
X = BuildVolTree(..., "X")
V = BuildVolTree(..., "V")
M = BuildVolTree(..., "M")
RBound = BuildVolTree(..., "R")
' Find column where tree changes from triangular to rectangular
ColChange = RBound - M + 2
' The values of k(t) from Equation (11) and I(t) from (14)
For t = 1 To NT
    For n = M - (t - 1) To M + (t - 1)
        If V(n, t) > 0 Then
            k(n, t) = Cceil(Sqr(V(n, t) / V0))
        End If
    Next n
Next t
' Find dimensions of the tree
For t = 1 To NT
    For n = 1 To 2 * NT - 1
        Temp(n) = k(n, t)
    Next n
    maxK(t) = Max(Temp)    ' Column maxima of k
Next t
numY(1) = 1
numY(2) = 3
numV(1) = 1
numV(2) = 3
numRows(1) = 1
numRows(2) = 9
For t = 3 To NT
    numY(t) = numY(t - 1) + 2 * maxK(t)
    numV(t) = 2 * t - 1
    numRows(t) = numV(t) * numY(t)
Next t
NR = Max(numRows)
```

The next part of the function finds the nine branch indices at each node. The indices depend on the current values of Y_t and k_t. In Exhibit 11 of Beliaeva and Nawalkha (2010), for example, at the first time step the top node (denoted V_{11}, Y_{11} in their exhibit) has a jump size $k_{11} = 2$. This node therefore branches out to nodes 1, 3, 5 for V_{21}, to nodes 8, 10, 12 for V_{22}, and to nodes 15, 17, and 19 for V_{23}. These nodes are placed two steps apart. The last node at the first time step (denoted V_{13}, Y_{13}) has a jump size $k_{13} = 1$. The node therefore branches out to nodes 17, 18, 19 to nodes 25, 26, 27, and to nodes 32, 33, and 34. These nodes are placed one step apart.

```
' Find the branch indices
For t = 1 To 9
    Branch(1, t) = t
Next t
For t = 2 To NT - 1
    nY = numY(t)
    First = maxK(t) + 1
    For r = M - (t - 1) To M + (t - 1)
        bigK(Count) = k(r, t)
    Next r
    For n = 1 To numRows(t)
        a = Cceil(n / nY)
        b = (n - 1) Mod nY
        ' Find the middle-to-middle branches
        Branch(n, 9 * (t - 1) + 2) = First + (a - 1) ...
        Branch(n, 9 * (t - 1) + 5) = Branch(n, 9 * (t - 1) + 2) ...
        Branch(n, 9 * (t - 1) + 8) = Branch(n, 9 * (t - 1) + 2) ...
        ' Find the rest of the branches
        Branch(n, 9 * (t - 1) + 1) = Branch(n, 9 * (t - 1) + 2) ...
        Branch(n, 9 * (t - 1) + 3) = Branch(n, 9 * (t - 1) + 2) ...
        ...
        Branch(n, 9 * (t - 1) + 9) = Branch(n, 9 * (t - 1) + 8) ...
    Next n
Next t
' Adjust the last branch upward
For t = ColChange To NT - 1
    For r = 9 * (t - 1) + 7 To 9 * (t - 1) + 9
        Branch(numRows(t), r) = Branch(numRows(t) - 1, r)
    Next r
Next t
```

The next part of the function creates the tree for Y_t, based on the branch indices defined earlier, and creates the joint probabilities in Equation (8.26). At each node defined by time ("t" loop), volatility ("j" loop), and transformed stock price ("r" loop), several quantities are needed: the current values of Y_t, x_t, v_t, and k_t, the values of $\mu(x_t, t)$ and I, and the branch indices to where Y_t evolves to Y_{t+dt}. At each node, nine future values of Y_{t+dt} are created whenever $Y_t > 0$; if $Y_t = 0$ then no branches evolve from that node, and a probability of zero is assigned to each joint probability. In Exhibit 11 of Beliaeva and Nawalkha (2010) at the second time step, no branches originate from nodes (V_{24}, Y_{21}), (V_{24}, Y_{27}), (V_{25}, Y_{21}), or (V_{25}, Y_{27}). In our notation, these are rows number 22, 28, 29, and 35 in the third column of the matrix for Y_t.

```
' Log stock tree (Yt), stock price tree (St), and probabilities (Prob)
Y0 = Log(S0) - rho * V0 / sigma
Yt(1, 1) = Y0
X0 = X(M, 1)
For t = 1 To NT - 1
    For i = -(t - 1) To (t - 1)
        J(Count) = i
    Next i
    For i = 1 To numV(t)
        For r = 1 To numY(t)
            Vt = V(M + J(i), t)        ' Volatility
            Xt = X(M + J(i), t)        ' Transformed volatility
            Kt = k(M + J(i), t)        ' Node jump k(t)
            For s = 9 * (t - 1) + 1 To 9 * (t - 1) + 9
                NewBranch(Count) = Branch(n, s)
            Next s
            muy = (rho * kappa / sigma - 0.5) * Vt
            II = Round(muy / Kt / sigmay0 * Sqr(dt))
            If Yt(n, t) > 0 Then
                For s = 1 To 9
                    If s = 2 Or s = 5 Or s = 8 Then
                        ' Middle node
                        Yt(NewBranch(s), t + 1) = Yt(n, t) + (II + 0) ...
                    ElseIf s = 1 Or s = 4 Or s = 7 Then
                        ' Up node
                        Yt(NewBranch(s), t + 1) = Yt(n, t) + (II + 1) ...
                    ElseIf s = 3 Or s = 6 Or s = 9 Then
                        ' Down node
                        Yt(NewBranch(s), t + 1) = Yt(n, t) + (II - 1) ...
                    End If
                Next s
            End If
            If Yt(n, t) > 0 Then       ' Construct the joint probabilities
                pv = probV(Xt, X0, dt, kappa, theta, sigma)
                py = probY(Vt, V0, Yt(n, t), dt, rho, sigma, kappa)
                p(1) = pvu * pyu
                ...
                p(9) = pvd * pyd
                For s = 9 * (t - 1) + 1 To 9 * (t - 1) + 9
                    Prob(n, s) = p(Count)
                Next s
            End If
        Next r
    Next i
Next t
```

The last part of the function calculates the European and American prices in the usual fashion, by working backward from maturity where the payoff is known. At each time step, the probabilities are needed to calculate the option price, and the branches are needed to link the option prices from the previous step. The function produces the price of an American option by calculating the value of S_t at each node, and comparing the value of the option with the value of immediate exercise, in accordance with Equation (8.27).

```
' Last column for the stock price
t = NT
ht = (rf - rho * kappa * theta / sigma) * (t - 1) * dt
For i = -(t - 1) To (t - 1)
    JJ(Count) = i
Next i
For i = 1 To numV(t)
    For r = 1 To numY(t)
        Vt = V(M + JJ(i), t)
        If Yt(n, t) > 0 Then
            ST(n) = Exp(Yt(n, t) + rho / sigma * Vt + ht)
        End If
    Next r
Next i
' Payoff at maturity
For n = 1 To NR
    Euro(n, NT) = Max(ST(n) - Strike, 0)
    Amer(n, NT) = Max(ST(n) - Strike, 0)
Next n
For t = NT - 1 To 1 Step -1
    ht = (rf - rho * kappa * theta / sigma) * (t - 1) * dt
    For i = -(t - 1) To (t - 1)
        J(Count) = i
    Next i
    For i = 1 To numV(t)
        For r = 1 To numY(t)
            Vt = V(M + J(i), t)
            If Yt(n, t) > 0 Then
                ' Stock price through transformation of Y(t)
                SSt = Exp(Yt(n, t) + rho / sigma * Vt + ht)
                For s = 9 * (t - 1) + 1 To 9 * (t - 1) + 9
                    bigP(Count) = Prob(n, s)
                    bigB(Count) = Branch(n, s)
                    Count = Count + 1
                Next s
                ' European and American prices
                Euro(n, t) = bigP(1) * Euro(bigB(1), t + 1) ...
                Euro(n, t) = Exp(-rf * dt) * Euro(n, t)
                Amer(n, t) = bigP(1) * Amer(bigB(1), t + 1) ...
                Amer(n, t) = Exp(-rf * dt) * Amer(n, t)
```

```
                    If PutCall = "C" Then
                        Amer(n, t) = Max(SSt - Strike, Amer(n, t))
                    ElseIf PutCall = "P" Then
                        AmerTemp = Amer(n, t)
                        Amer(n, t) = Max(Strike - SSt, AmerTemp)
                    End If
                End If
            Next r
        Next i
    Next t
    EuroPrice = Euro(1, 1)
    AmerPrice = Amer(1, 1)
    End Function
```

Finally, the preceding functions require a function for the ceiling of a number. This is accomplished using the VBA function Cceil.

```
Function Cceil(X As Double) As Double
    Cceil = Int(X) - (X - Int(X) > 0)
End Function
```

To illustrate, we reproduce the American put prices of Clarke and Parrott (1999) and Ikonen and Toivanen (2008). The results are shown in Figure 8.4.

The VBA functions presented in this section, and the screen shot in Figure 8.4, are from the Excel file Ch8ClarkeParrott.xls. An additional example is in the Excel file Ch8BN.xls.

	A	B	C	D	E	F	G	H	I
1									
2		**Beliaeva-Nawalkha Bivariate Tree for the Heston model**							
3		**Uses put prices from Clarke and Parrott (1999)**				**Prices Using 35 Time Steps**			
4						**True Price**	**Closed**	**Tree**	**Tree**
5		**Option Features**			**Spot**	**Amer**	**Euro**	**Euro**	**Amer**
6		Spot Price (S)	10.0000		8	2.000000	1.8389	1.8417	2.0000
7		Strike Price (K)	10.0000		9	1.107641	1.0483	1.0442	1.1017
8		Time to Maturity (τ)	0.2500		10	0.520030	0.5015	0.4909	0.5087
9		Risk free rate (r)	0.1000		11	0.213668	0.2082	0.1993	0.2044
10		Dividend (q)	0.0000		12	0.082036	0.0804	0.0749	0.0764
11		PutCall (C or P)	P						
12		Little Trap (0=Heston, 1=Albrecher)	1						
13					**Heston Parameters**				
14		**Tree Settings**			kappa (κ)	5.0000			
15		Threshold	1.00E-02		theta (θ)	0.1600			
16		Number of Time Steps	35		sigma (σ)	0.9000			
17		Time increment (dt)	0.00714		v0	0.0625			
18					rho (ρ)	0.1000			
19		**Trapezoidal Rule Integration Grid**			lambda (λ)	0.0000			
20		Lower Limit	1.00E-06						
21		Upper Limit	100						
22		Number of abscissas	200						

FIGURE 8.4 Put Prices Using the Beliaeva and Nawalkha Tree

MEDVEDEV-SCAILLET EXPANSION

Medvedev and Scaillet (2010) develop a method in which the American put price can be expressed analytically, as an asymptotic expansion. Their method is applicable to a wide class of stochastic volatility models. In this section, we first introduce their method for American puts under the Black-Scholes model, and then present their expansion for the Heston model. The advantage of their method is that the American put price is available in an expansion that involves analytic terms only. Hence, the method is able to generate Black-Scholes and Heston American option prices very quickly.

Medvedev-Scaillet for Black-Scholes

Medvedev and Scaillet (2010) denoted by $P(\theta, \tau)$, the American put price, where τ is the maturity and where

$$\theta = \frac{\ln(K/S)}{\sigma\sqrt{\tau}} \tag{8.29}$$

is the normalized moneyness. The main result of Medvedev and Scaillet (2010) is that the American put price can be approximated by the expansion

$$P(\theta, \tau) = \sum_{n=1}^{\infty} P_n(\theta)\tau^{n/2}. \tag{8.30}$$

The terms inside the sum are defined as

$$\begin{aligned} P_n(\theta) &= C_n\left[p_n^0(\theta)\Phi(\theta) + q_n^0(\theta)\phi(\theta)\right] + p_n^1(\theta)\Phi(\theta) + q_n^1(\theta)\phi(\theta) \\ &= C_n P_n^0(\theta) + P_n^1(\theta), \end{aligned} \tag{8.31}$$

where $\Phi(\theta)$ and $\phi(\theta)$ denote the standard normal cumulative distribution function and density, respectively. To obtain the American put price $P(\theta, \tau)$, we first find the polynomials p_n^0, q_n^0, p_n^1 and q_n^1, and the coefficients C_n. We then find non-negative values of the barrier $\tilde{y} \geq \theta$ as

$$\tilde{y} = \arg\max_{y\geq\theta, y\geq 0} P(\theta, \tau, y), \tag{8.32}$$

where $P(\theta, \tau, y)$ is the American put price $P(\theta, \tau)$, but with the extra argument to emphasize the dependence of $P(\theta, \tau)$ on y through C_n. The approximation of Medvedev and Scaillet (2010) for the price of an American put, $P(\theta, \tau, \tilde{y})$, given p_n^0, q_n^0, p_n^1, q_n^1, and C_n is the following:

- Construct $P(\theta, \tau, y)$ using Equation (8.30).
- Find $\tilde{y}$ using (8.32), under the constraint $\tilde{y} \geq \theta$.

- Substitute $\tilde{y}$ into C_n so that $C_n = C_n(\tilde{y})$. Substitute in $P(\theta, \tau, \tilde{y})$ to find the price, using (8.30) and (8.31).

For details of the derivation, see Medvedev and Scaillet (2010) or Rouah (2013). The coefficients C_n are obtained by solving

$$C_n\left[p_n^0(\tilde{y})\Phi_0 + q_n^0(\tilde{y})\phi_0\right] + p_n^1(\tilde{y})\Phi_0 + q_n^1(\tilde{y})\phi_0 = (-1)^{n+1}\frac{K}{n!}\sigma^n\tilde{y}^n \tag{8.33}$$

for C_n. In Equation (8.33) $\Phi_0 = \Phi(\tilde{y})$ and $\phi_0 = \phi(\tilde{y})$ are the standard normal distribution and density, respectively, evaluated at $\theta = \tilde{y}$, the optimized value from (8.32). For example, when $n = 1$ we have that $p_1^0 = \theta$, $q_1^0 = 1$, and $p_1^1 = q_1^1 = 0$. Hence, C_1 is obtained as

$$C_1 = \frac{Ky\sigma}{\tilde{y}\Phi_0 + \phi_0}. \tag{8.34}$$

The coefficients p_n^0, q_n^0, p_n^1 and q_n^1 are defined in Medvedev and Scaillet (2010). Rouah (2013) provides code to generate these coefficients automatically.

To implement the approximation of Medvedev and Scaillet (2010), we first construct the VBA function MSPutBS, which constructs the expansion in Equation (8.30) for a general value of y. We use $n = 5$ terms in the expansion.

```
Function MSPutBS(y As Double, ...) As Double
' The "C" coefficients evaluated at theta = y
cdf = normcdf(y)
pdf = normpdf(y)
C1 = sigma * y * K / (y * cdf + pdf)
C2 = -1 / 2 * (cdf * sigma ^ 2 * C1 ...
...
C5 = 1 / 1920 * (16 * sigma ^ 9 * y ^ 5 * K + ...
' Set 1 polynomials
p01 = theta
p11 = 0
q01 = 1
q11 = 0
' Set 2 polynomials
p02 = theta ^ 2 + 1
p12 = -1 / 2 * (-sigma ^ 2 + 2 * mu) * C1 / sigma
q02 = theta
q12 = 0
' Set 3 polynomials
p03 = theta ^ 3 + 3 * theta
p13 = -theta * (-sigma ^ 2 * C2 + 2 * C2 * mu + r * C1 ...
q03 = theta ^ 2 + 2
q13 = -1 / 8 * (-8 * sigma ^ 3 * C2 + 16 * C2 * mu...
' Set 4 polynomials
```

```
p04 = theta ^ 4 + 6 * theta ^ 2 + 3
p14 = -1 / 2 * (2 * r * C2 * sigma - 3 * C3 ...
q04 = theta ^ 3 + 5 * theta
q14 = -1 / 48 * (-72 * sigma ^ 4 * C3 + 144 ...
' Set 5 polynomials
p05 = theta ^ 5 + 10 * theta ^ 3 + 15 * theta
p15 = -(r * C3 * sigma - 2 * C4 * sigma ^ 2 ...
q05 = theta ^ 4 + 9 * theta ^ 2 + 8
q15 = -1 / 384 * (-sigma ^ 8 * C1 + 8 * sigma ^ 6 ...
' The Black-Scholes American put approximation
cdf = normcdf(theta)
pdf = normpdf(theta)
MSPutBS = (C1 * (p01 * cdf + q01 * pdf) + p11 ...
End Function
```

The MSPriceBS function finds the barrier $\tilde{y}$ using the bisection algorithm, and feeds this specific value $\tilde{y}$ into the expansion function MSPutBS. The function returns the approximation to the Black-Scholes American put price.

```
Function MSPriceBS(S As Double, ...) As Variant
theta = Log(K / S) / sigma / Sqr(T)
' Find the barrier, optimal value y~
y = Bisection(y, dy, theta, ...)
' American put Black Scholes price
Price = MSPutBS(y, theta, K, sigma, r, q, T)
End Function
```

The Bisection function is used to find the barrier $\tilde{y}$.

```
Function Bisection(y As Double, ...) As Double
' Positive and negative differences
lowCdif  = MSPutBSdiff(a, ...)
highCdif = MSPutBSdiff(b, ...)
y = 0
' Return error value of -999 if endpoints are not correct
If (lowCdif * highCdif > 0) Then
    y = -999
Else
    ' Bisection algorithm
    For x = 0 To MaxIter
        midP = (a + b) / 2
```

```
            midCdif = MSPutBSdiff(midP, ...)
            If (Abs(midCdif) < Tol) Then
                Exit For
            Else
                If (midCdif > 0) Then
                    a = midP
                Else
                    b = midP
                End If
            End If
            y = midP
        Next x
    End If
    Bisection = y
    End Function
```

The Bisection function uses the objective function MSPutBSdiff, which is based on finite differences.

```
Function MSPutBSdiff(y As Double, ...) As Double
MSPutBSdiff = (MSPutBS(y + dy, ...) - MSPutBS(y - dy, ...)) / 2 / dy
End Function
```

To illustrate, we reproduce Table 2 of Medvedev and Scaillet (2010). The settings are $S = 40$, $r = 0.0488$, and $q = 0$ for various values of volatility (σ) and maturity (τ). We benchmark the results to the American put prices obtained using a trinomial tree with 500 steps. European puts are obtained using the Black-Scholes formula. The results are shown in Figure 8.5.

	A	B	C	D	E	F	G	H	I	J	K	L	M	N
1														
2		**Table 2 of Medvedev and Scaillet (2010)**				**Prices of American and European Puts Under Black-Scholes**								
3						Sigma = 0.2			Sigma = 0.3			Sigma = 0.4		
4		**Option Features**			Volatility	0.2	0.2	0.2	0.3	0.3	0.3	0.4	0.4	0.4
5		Spot Price (S)	40.0000		Maturity	0.0833	0.3333	0.5833	0.0833	0.3333	0.5833	0.0833	0.3333	0.5833
6		Risk free rate (r)	0.0488		Strike	35	35	35	35	35	35	35	35	35
7		Dividend (q)	0.0000		Euro Put	0.006	0.196	0.417	0.077	0.687	1.189	0.246	1.330	2.113
8					MS Put	0.006	0.200	0.432	0.077	0.697	1.218	0.247	1.345	2.153
9		**Trinomial Tree Settings**			Tree Put	0.006	0.200	0.433	0.077	0.698	1.220	0.247	1.346	2.155
10		Number of steps (N)	500		Strike	40	40	40	40	40	40	40	40	40
11		Put or Call (PutCall)	P		Euro Put	0.840	1.522	1.881	1.299	2.428	3.063	1.758	3.334	4.247
12		European or American	A		MS Put	0.852	1.578	1.987	1.310	2.481	3.166	1.768	3.386	4.349
13					Tree Put	0.852	1.580	1.990	1.310	2.482	3.169	1.768	3.387	4.352
14		**Settings for the Bisection Method**			Strike	45	45	45	45	45	45	45	45	45
15		Maximum Iterations	500		Euro Put	4.840	4.780	4.840	4.980	5.529	5.972	5.236	6.377	7.165
16		Tolerance	1.00E-10		MS Put	5.021	5.085	5.261	5.059	5.702	6.237	5.286	6.506	7.377
17		Increment (dt)	1.00E-05		Tree Put	5.000	5.088	5.267	5.060	5.706	6.243	5.287	6.510	7.383
18		Upper Limit (b)	3											
19					Euro Put	Black-Scholes closed form European Put Price								
20					MS Put	Fifth-order MS (2010) American Put Expansion								
21					Tree Put	Trinomial Tree American Put with 500 Steps								

FIGURE 8.5 American Put Prices under Black-Scholes

The VBA function Trinomial implements the trinomial tree.

```
Function Trinomial(Spot As Double, ...) As Double
' Tree probabilities
pu = (Exp(r * dt / 2) - Exp(-v * Sqr(dt / 2))) ^ 2 ...
pd = (Exp(v * Sqr(dt / 2)) - Exp(r * dt / 2)) ^ 2 ...
pm = 1 - pu - pd
' Tree for stock price minus P.V. of dividends
S(1, 1) = Spot
For j = 2 To (n + 1)
    For i = 1 To (2 * j - 1)
        S(i, j) = S(1, 1) * u ^ j * d ^ i
    Next i
Next j
' Calculate Terminal Price for Calls and Puts
For i = 1 To (2 * n + 1)
Select Case PutCall
    Case "C": Op(i, n + 1) = Max(S(i, n + 1) - K, 0)
     Case "P": Op(i, n + 1) = Max(K - S(i, n + 1), 0)
End Select
Next i
' Calculate Remaining entries for Calls and Puts
For j = n To 1 Step -1
    For i = 1 To (2 * j - 1)
    Select Case EuroAmer
    Case "A":
        If PutCall = "C" Then
            Op(i, j) = Max(S(i, j) - K, Exp(-r * dt) ...
        ElseIf PutCall = "P" Then
            Op(i, j) = Max(K - S(i, j), Exp(-r * dt) ...
        End If
    Case "E":
            Op(i, j) = Exp(-r * dt) * (pu * Op(i, j + 1) ...
    End Select
    Next i
Next j
Trinomial = Op(1, 1)
End Function
```

The functions presented in this section, along with the screen shot in Figure 8.5, are in the Excel file Ch8MS.xls.

Finally, Medvedev and Scaillet (2010) note that the limiting value $y = \infty$ produces European put prices rather than American prices. In the Excel file Ch8Barrier.xls, we set $y = 1E + 50$ and recover European prices. This file is not presented here.

Medvedev-Scaillet for Heston

The Medvedev and Scaillet (2010) approximation of the American put price under the Heston (1993) model is identical in form to that for the Black-Scholes model in Equation (8.30):

$$P(\theta, \tau, v) = \sum_{n=1}^{\infty} P_n(\theta, v)\tau^{n/2}. \tag{8.35}$$

The terms inside the sum are defined as

$$\begin{aligned} P_n(\theta, v) &= C_n(v)\left[p_n^0(\theta)\Phi(\theta) + q_n^0(\theta)\phi(\theta)\right] + p_n^1(\theta, v)\Phi(\theta) + q_n^1(\theta, v)\phi(\theta) \\ &= C_n(v)P_n^0(\theta) + P_n^1(\theta, v). \end{aligned} \tag{8.36}$$

Note that the polynomials superscripted with 1 now depend on v as well as on θ, and that the C_n coefficients depend on v. To simplify the notation, we write the polynomials as $p_n^1 = p_n^1(\theta, v)$, $q_n^1 = q_n^1(\theta, v)$, $p_n^0 = p_n^0(\theta)$, $q_n^0 = q_n^0(\theta)$, and the coefficients $C_n = C_n(v)$. Rouah (2013) provides code to generate the polynomials automatically. The coefficients $C_n(v)$ are obtained by solving the following equation for C_n:

$$C_n(v)\left[p_n^0(\tilde{y})\Phi_0 + q_n^0(\tilde{y})\phi_0\right] + p_n^1(\tilde{y}, v)\Phi_0 + q_n^1(\tilde{y}, v)\phi_0 = \frac{(-1)^{n+1}K}{n!}v^{n/2}\tilde{y}^n. \tag{8.37}$$

As in the Black-Scholes case the coefficients C_n are evaluated at the barrier $\theta = \tilde{y}$ given by

$$\tilde{y} = \arg\max_{y \geq \theta, y \geq 0} P(\theta, \tau, v, y). \tag{8.38}$$

The first approximation of Medvedev and Scaillet (2010) for the price of an American put, $P(\theta, \tau, v, \tilde{y})$, is analogous to that in the Black-Scholes case.

Approximation 1:

- Construct $P(\theta, \tau, v, y)$ using (8.35).
- Find $\tilde{y}$ using (8.38) under the constraint $\tilde{y} \geq \theta$.
- Use $C_n = C_n(v, \tilde{y})$ in $P(\theta, \tau, v, \tilde{y})$ to find the price.

Medvedev and Scaillet (2010) point out that, as in the Black-Scholes case described in the previous section, an infinite barrier, $\tilde{y} = \infty$, corresponds to a European put. They recommend obtaining the price of an American put as the European put obtained using a closed form, such as those covered in Chapters 1, 3, and 4, plus the early exercise premium. Their second approximation for the American put is the control variate price.

Approximation 2:

- Find the price of the European put $P(K)$ using a closed-form solution.
- Find $\tilde{y}$ as in the first approximation.

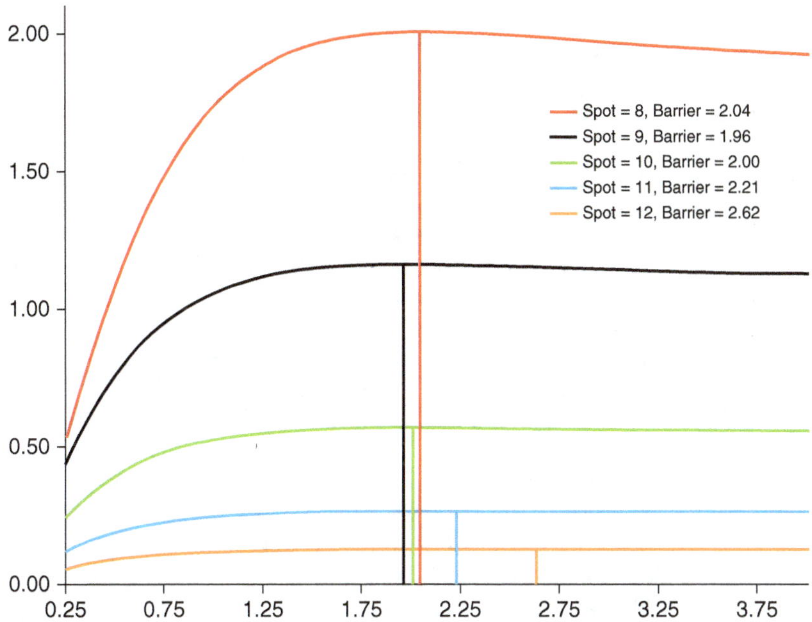

FIGURE 8.6 Barrier Levels for the Medvedev-Scaillet Approximation

- Obtain the early exercise premium as $\varepsilon = P(\theta, \tau, v, \tilde{y}) - P(\theta, \tau, v, \infty)$.
- Obtain the American put price as $P_A(K) = P(K) + \varepsilon$.

For a detailed derivation of the expansion, see Rouah (2013).

We illustrate the maximization problem in Equation (8.38) in Figure 8.6 by plotting $P(\theta, \tau, v, y)$ over various values of y, using the settings of Clarke and Parrott (1999) for the spot prices 8 through 12. The optimal values $\tilde{y}$ are represented by dashed lines and all lie within the vicinity $\tilde{y} \approx 2$. The curves have been rescaled so to make the graph more illustrative. The figure is in the Excel file Ch8Figure.xls.

The implementation in VBA of the Medvedev and Scaillet (2010) approximation for the Heston model is similar to that for the Black-Scholes model in the previous section. The VBA function MSPutHeston constructs the expansion in Equation (8.35) for a general value of y. We use $n = 3$ terms in the expansion.

```
Function MSPutHeston(y As Double, ...) As Double
' Coefficients
pi21 = 1 / 2 * (v - 2 * mu) * y * K / (y * cdf + pdf)
qi21 = 1 / 4 * rho * sigma * y * K / (y * cdf + pdf)
pi31 = -1 / 4 * y * K / v ^ (1 / 2) * (2 * cdf * v ^ 2 ...
qi31 = 1 / 32 * rho ^ 2 * sigma ^ 2 / v ^ (1 / 2) * y * K ...
qi32 = -1 / 24 * (-48 * qi31 * v ^ (1 / 2) * y * cdf ...
qi33 = -1 / 16 * (-y ^ 3 * cdf * rho ^ 2 * sigma ^ 2 ...
```

```
' First set of polynomials
p11 = 0
q11 = 0
p01 = theta
q01 = 1
C1 = v ^ (1 / 2) * y * K / (y * cdf + pdf)
' Second set of polynomials
p12 = 1 / 2 * (v - 2 * mu) * y * K / (y * cdf + pdf)
q12 = 1 / 4 * rho * sigma * theta * y * K / (y * cdf + pdf)
p02 = theta ^ 2 + 1
q02 = theta
C2 = -1 / 4 * y * K * (2 * v * cdf - 4 * cdf * mu ...
' Third set of polynomials
p13 = -1 / 4 * y * K / v ^ (1 / 2) * (2 * v ^ 2 ...
q13 = 1 / 32 * rho ^ 2 * sigma ^ 2 / v ^ (1 / 2) ...
p03 = theta ^ 3 + 3 * theta
q03 = theta ^ 2 + 2
c3 = (2 * cdf ^ 2 * y * mu ^ 2 + 1 / 2 * cdf ^ 2 ...
' The Heston American put approximation
cdf = normcdf(theta)
pdf = normpdf(theta)
MSPutHeston = (C1 * (p01 * cdf + q01 * pdf) + p11 * cdf + q11 * pdf) ...
End FunctionT
```

The MSPrice function finds the barrier $\tilde{y}$ using the bisection algorithm, and feeds this specific value $\tilde{y}$ into the expansion function MSPutHeston. The function returns the approximation to the Black-Scholes American put price.

```
Function MSPrice(S As Double, ...) As Variant
' Closed-form European put
EuroPutClosed = HestonPriceTrapezoidal("P", ...)
' Moneyness
theta = Log(K / S) / Sqr(v0) / Sqr(T)
' Find the barrier level, y~, using the Bisection method
y = Bisection(a, b, ..., dy)
' Euro and Amer put by MS expansion
EuroPutMS = MSPutHeston(yinf, ...)
AmerPutMS = MSPutHeston(y, ...)
' Find the early exercise premium
EEP = AmerPutMS - EuroPutMS
' American put terms
AmerPut = EuroPutClosed + EEP
End Function
```

	A	B	C	D	E	F	G	H	I	J	K
1											
2		**Medvedev and Scaillet (2010) Price of American Puts Under Heston**									
3		**Uses True Put Prices from Clarke and Parrott, and 3 Expansion Terms**									
4											
5		**Option Features**			**Spot**	**True Price**	**MS Price**	**Barrier**	**Moneyness**	**$Error**	**%Error**
6		Strike Price (K)	10.0000		8	2.000000	2.008878	2.0385	1.7851	-0.0089	0.44%
7		Risk free rate (r)	0.1000		9	1.107641	1.161388	1.9625	0.8429	-0.0537	4.85%
8		Dividend (q)	0.0000		10	0.520030	0.567316	1.9993	0.0000	-0.0473	9.09%
9		Maturity (τ)	0.2500		11	0.213668	0.265075	2.2072	-0.7625	-0.0514	24.06%
10		Trap (0=Heston, 1=Albrecher)	1		12	0.082036	0.127242	2.6206	-1.4586	-0.0452	55.10%
11											
12		**Hard Coded Heston Parameters**			True Price	Price from Clarke and Parrott (1999)					
13		kappa (κ)	5		MS Price	Price from Medvedev and Scaillet (2010) with 3 Expansion Terms					
14		theta (θ)	0.16								
15		sigma (σ)	0.9		**Integration Grid for Trapezoidal Rule**						
16		v0	0.0625		Lower Limit	1.00E-08					
17		rho (ρ)	0.1		Upper Limit	150.00					
18		lambda (λ)	0		# of abscissas	500					
19		Trap (0=Albrecher, 1=Heston)	1								

FIGURE 8.7 American Puts Using Medvedev-Scaillet Expansion

As in the Black-Scholes case, the barrier $\tilde{y}$ is found using the bisection algorithm. The algorithm uses the objective function MSPutdiff, which is based on finite differences.

```
Function MSPutDiff(y As Double, ...) As Double
MSPutDiff = (MSPutHeston(y + dy) - MSPutHeston(y - dy)) / 2 / dy
End Function
```

To illustrate, we continue with the example of Clarke and Parrott (1999) and Ikonen and Toivanen (2008), using $n = 3$ terms in the expansion. The results are shown in Figure 8.7.

The VBA functions presented in this book and the screen shot in Figure 8.7 are in the Excel file Ch8Heston.xls.

The prices obtained using the methods described earlier in this chapter are resumed in Table 8.1. For comparison, the last row contains the European put prices, obtained from the trapezoidal rule.

The results point to varying accuracy of the pricing methods. In particular, the LSM algorithm cannot calculate the deep out-of-the-money put (for $S_t = 12$). Note also that the explicit method erroneously produces American prices that are often lower than the European price.

TABLE 8.1 Clarke and Parrott (1999) American Put Prices under Various Models

	$S_t = 8$	$S_t = 9$	$S_t = 10$	$S_t = 11$	$S_t = 12$
Clarke-Parrott Price	2.0000	1.1076	0.5200	0.2137	0.0820
LSM	1.9750	1.1008	0.5911	0.2232	—
Explicit Method	1.8323	1.0375	0.4964	0.2105	0.0836
Bivariate Tree	2.0000	1.1097	0.5490	0.2494	0.1069
MS Approximation	2.0088	1.1614	0.5673	0.2651	0.1272
European Put Price	1.8388	1.0483	0.5015	0.2082	0.0804

CHIARELLA AND ZIOGAS AMERICAN CALL

In this section, the last of this chapter, we present the method of Chiarella and Ziogas (2006) for pricing American calls in the Heston (1993) model. Their method requires an estimate of the early exercise boundary. The early exercise boundary and other features of American options are discussed in Kwok (2008), for example.

Early Exercise Boundary Approximation

We encountered the Heston partial differential equation (PDE) in Equation (8.8). For an American call option, $C_A(S, v, \tau)$, the PDE is

$$\begin{aligned}\frac{\partial C_A}{\partial \tau} &= \frac{1}{2}vS^2\frac{\partial^2 C_A}{\partial S^2} + \rho\sigma vS\frac{\partial^2 C_A}{\partial v\partial S} + \frac{1}{2}\sigma^2 v\frac{\partial^2 C_A}{\partial v^2},\\ &\quad - rC_A + (r-q)S\frac{\partial C_A}{\partial S} + \left[\kappa(\theta - v) - \lambda v\right]\frac{\partial C_A}{\partial v},\end{aligned} \tag{8.39}$$

where τ is the time until maturity. The PDE holds for $0 \le \tau < T$, where T is the maturity calendar time, and for $0 < S \le b(v, \tau)$, where $b(v, \tau)$ is the early exercise boundary. Building on the work of Tzavalis and Wang (2003), Chiarella and Ziogas (2006) approximate the early exercise boundary $b(v, \tau)$ with the log-linear function

$$b(v, \tau) \approx \exp(b_0(\tau) + b_1(\tau)v_0). \tag{8.40}$$

In the following section, we explain how $b(v, \tau)$ is estimated and how the American call price is obtained.

The American Call Price

To implement the method of Chiarella and Ziogas (2006), we need to introduce an additional time variable t into the characteristic function, by replacing τ with $\tau - t$, and an additional integration variable ψ. They write the characteristic function f_2 as

$$f_2(\phi, \psi; x_0, v_0, \tau - t) = \exp(C_2(\tau - t, \phi, \psi) + D_2(\tau - t, \phi, \psi)v_0 + i\phi x_0), \tag{8.41}$$

where the coefficients are

$$\begin{aligned}C_2(\tau - t, \phi, \psi) &= (r-q)i\phi(\tau - t)\\ &\quad + \frac{a}{\sigma^2}\left[(b_2 - \rho\sigma i\phi + d_2)(\tau - t) - 2\ln\left(\frac{1 - g_2 e^{d_2(\tau - t)}}{1 - g_2}\right)\right],\\ D_2(\tau - t, \phi, \psi) &= i\psi + \frac{b_2 - \rho\sigma i\phi - \sigma^2 i\psi + d_2}{\sigma^2}\left(\frac{1 - e^{d_2(\tau - t)}}{1 - g_j e^{d_2(\tau - t)}}\right).\end{aligned} \tag{8.42}$$

The required quantities are

$$g_2 = \frac{b_2 - \rho\sigma i\phi - \sigma^2 i\psi + d_2}{b_2 - \rho\sigma i\phi - \sigma^2 i\psi - d_2}, \quad d_2 = \sqrt{(\rho\sigma i\phi - b_2)^2 - \sigma^2(2u_2 i\phi - \phi^2)}. \tag{8.43}$$

Note that, when $t = \psi = 0$, the coefficients reduce to those of the original Heston (1993) model. As before, we have $b_2 = \kappa + \lambda$, $u_2 = -\frac{1}{2}$, and $a = \kappa\theta$. The characteristic function f_1 is

$$f_1(\phi, \psi; x_0, v_0, \tau - t) = \exp(-x_0 - (r - q)(\tau - t)) \times f_2(\phi - i, \psi; x_0, v_0, \tau - t), \tag{8.44}$$

where $x_0 = \ln S_0$ the log spot price, and v_0 is the initial variance. Obtaining the European call price $C(x_0, v_0, \tau)$ is straightforward, by setting $\psi = 0$ and $t = 0$ into the characteristic functions. The calculation is identical to that in the original Heston (1993) model,

$$C(x_0, v_0, \tau) = S_0 e^{-q\tau} P_1 - K e^{-r\tau} P_2, \tag{8.45}$$

where, for $j = 1, 2$,

$$P_j = \frac{1}{2} + \frac{1}{\pi} \int_0^\infty \text{Re}\left(\frac{e^{-i\phi \ln K}}{i\phi} f_j(\phi, 0; x_0, v_0, \tau) \right) d\phi. \tag{8.46}$$

Chiarella and Ziogas (2006) show that the early exercise premium $V(x_0, v_0, \tau)$ on an American call with strike K and maturity is τ is

$$\begin{aligned} V(x_0, v_0, \tau) &= \frac{1}{2}[S_0 (1 - e^{-q\tau}) - K (1 - e^{-r\tau})] \\ &+ \frac{S_0}{\pi} q e^{-q\tau} \int_0^\tau \int_0^\infty e^{qt} \text{Re}\left(\frac{\exp(-b_0(t)i\phi)}{i\phi} f_1(\phi, -b_1(t)\phi; x_0, v_0, \tau - t) \right) d\phi dt \\ &- \frac{K}{\pi} r e^{-r\tau} \int_0^\tau \int_0^\infty e^{rt} \text{Re}\left(\frac{\exp(-b_0(t)i\phi)}{i\phi} f_2(\phi, -b_1()\phi; x_0, v_0, \tau - t) \right) d\phi dt. \end{aligned} \tag{8.47}$$

Finally, the price of an American call is obtained by adding the early exercise premium to the price of the European call:

$$C_A(S_0, v_0, \tau) = C(x_0, v_0, \tau) + V(x_0, v_0, \tau). \tag{8.48}$$

To evaluate the integral for the European call $C(x_0, v_0, \tau)$, we can use Gauss-Laguerre quadrature. To evaluate the double integrals in the early exercise premium $V(x_0, v_0, \tau)$, we can use either composite Gauss-Legendre quadrature or the composite trapezoidal rule, both of which were presented in Chapter 5.

The VBA function CZCharFun implements the characteristic functions in Equations (8.41) and (8.44).

```
Function CZCharFun(S0 As Double, ...) As Variant
If funNum = 2 Then
    d = cSqr(cAdd(Term1, Term2))
    g = cDiv(Num, Den)
    bigG = cDiv(Num, Den)
    bigC = cAdd(Term1, Term2)
    bigF = cDiv(Num, Den)
    bigD = cAdd(Term1, Term2)
    ' The second characteristic function.
    ' f2 = exp(C + D*v0 + i*phi*x);
    f2 = cExp(Term3)
ElseIf funNum = 1 Then
    d = cSqr(cAdd(Term1, Term2))
    g = cDiv(Num, Den)
    bigG = cDiv(Num, Den)
    bigC = cAdd(Term1, Term2)
    bigF = cDiv(Num, Den)
    bigD = cAdd(Term1, Term2)
    ' The second characteristic function with phi = phi-i
    ' F2 = exp(C + D*v0 + i*(phi-i)*x);
    bigF2 = cExp(Term3)
    ' The first characteristic function
    ' y = 1/S0 * exp(-(rf-q)*(tau-t)) * bigF2;
    f1 = cProd(T1, bigF2)
End If
End Function
```

The first part of the function calculates the coefficients $C_2(\tau - t, \phi, \psi)$ and $D_2(\tau - t, \phi, \psi)$, and returns the second characteristic function, f_2. The second part of the function calculates $C_2(\tau - t, \phi - i, \psi)$ and $D_2(\tau - t, \phi - i, \psi)$, and returns the first characteristic function, f_1. The function is identical to that for the characteristic functions of the Heston (1993) model, except for the additional integration variable and the fact that τ is replaced by $\tau - t$.

The function CZEuroCall calculates the European call price in Equation (8.45). The first part of the function sets $\psi = t = 0$ in the characteristic functions, as required by (8.46), and calculates the European call price exactly as in the original Heston (1993) model.

```
Function CZEuroCall(S0 As Double, ...)
' Create the integrands
For j = 1 To N
    phi = X(j)
    weight = w(j)
```

```
    ' Int1(k) = w(k) * real(exp(-i*phi*log(K)) ...
    CF = CZCharFun(S0, ...,1)
    Int1(j) = weight * cReal(cProd(CharFun, Coeff))
    ' Int2(k) = w(k) * real(exp(-i*phi*log(K)) ...
    CF = CZCharFun(S0, ...,2)
    Int2(j) = weight * cReal(cProd(CharFun, Coeff))
Next j
P1 = 0.5 + (1 / pi) * Sum(Int1)
P2 = 0.5 + (1 / pi) * Sum(Int2)
' The call price
CZEuroCall = S0 * Exp(-q * tau) * P1 - K ...
End Function
```

The function CZEarlyExercise implements the early exercise premium in Equation (8.47) using either composite Gauss-Legendre quadrature or the composite trapezoidal rule. The arguments (a, b) represent the integration domain for time, and (c, d) represent the integration domain for the stock price. The function can invoke either composite Gauss-Legendre quadrature or the composite trapezoidal rule.

```
Function CZEarlyExercise(S0 As Double, ...) As Double
' The integrals
If DoubleType = "GL" Then
      ' Composite Gauss-Legendre
      Int1 = DoubleGaussLegendre(S0, ...,1)
      Int2 = DoubleGaussLegendre(S0, ...,2)
ElseIf DoubleType = "Trapz" Then
      ' Composite trapezoidal
      ht = (b - a) / Nt
      hs = (d - c) / Nt
      For j = 1 To Nt + 1
            T(j) = a + (j - 1) * ht
            X(j) = c + (j - 1) * hs
      Next j
      Int1 = DoubleTrapezoidal(params, ...,1)
      Int2 = DoubleTrapezoidal(params, ...,2)
End If
' The early exercise premium
V1 = S0 * (1 - Exp(-q * tau)) / 2 + (1 / pi) * S0 ...
V2 = K * (1 - Exp(-rf * tau)) / 2 + (1 / pi) * K ...
CZEarlyExercise = V1 - V2
End Function
```

The function CZAmerCall adds the early exercise premium to the European call to obtain the American call.

```
Function CZAmerCall(S0 As Double, ...) As Double
' European price
Euro = CZEuroCall(S0, tau, params, K, rf, q, xs, ws)
Premium = CZEarlyExercise(S0, ... ,DoubleType)
' American price
Amer = Euro + Premium
If EuroAmer = "A" Then
    CZAmerCall = Amer
ElseIf EuroAmer = "E" Then
    CZAmerCall = Euro
End If
End Function
```

The preceding function calls the function CZEuroCall, which returns the Heston European price.

```
Function CZEuroCall(S0 As Double, ...)
For j = 1 To N
    phi = X(j)
    weight = w(j)
    ' Int1(k) = w(k) * real(exp(-i*phi*log(K)) ...
    CF = CZCharFun(S0, ... ,1)
    Int1(j) = weight * cReal(cProd(CharFun, Coeff))
    ' Int2(k) = w(k) * real(exp(-i*phi*log(K))  ...
    CF = CZCharFun(S0, ... ,2)
    Int2(j) = weight * cReal(cProd(CharFun, Coeff))
Next j
' Define the probabilities
P1 = 0.5 + (1 / pi) * Sum(Int1)
P2 = 0.5 + (1 / pi) * Sum(Int2)
CZEuroCall = S0 * Exp(-q * tau) * P1 - K ...
End Function
```

Estimating the Early Exercise Boundary

The early exercise premium $V(x_0, v_0, \tau)$ requires estimates of the two unknowns, $b_0(\tau)$ and $b_1(\tau)$, in (8.40). Using two distinct values $v_0 = v_0(\tau)$ and $v_1 = v_1(\tau)$ of the variance, along with the boundary condition for the call at $b(v, \tau)$, Chiarella and Ziogas (2006) obtain the following system of two equations,

$$\begin{aligned} C_A(b(v_0, \tau), v, \tau) &= \exp(b_0(\tau) + b_1(\tau)v_0(\tau)) - K \\ C_A(b(v_1, \tau), v, \tau) &= \exp(b_0(\tau) + b_1(\tau)v_1(\tau)) - K, \end{aligned} \tag{8.49}$$

and use an iterative method to solve this system for $b_0(\tau)$ and $b_1(\tau)$. The time interval $(0, T)$ is divided into N subintervals of increasing length $\tau_1, \ldots, \tau_N$, where $\tau_n = n \cdot d\tau$, $n = 1, \ldots, N$ and $d\tau = \tau/N$ is the time increment. Denote $b_0^n = b_0(\tau_n)$, $b_1^n = b_1(\tau_n)$, $v_0^n = v_0(\tau_n)$, and $v_1^n = v_1(\tau_n)$. The coefficients b_0^n and b_1^n are updated iteratively, by obtaining a successive set of coefficients $b_{0,k}^n$ and $b_{1,k}^n$ that are the roots of the nonlinear equations g_1 and g_0 defined as

$$\begin{aligned} g_1\left(b_{1,k}^n\right) &= \frac{1}{v_0^n}\left\{\ln\left[C_A\left(\exp\left(b_{0,k-1}^n + v_0^n b_{1,k}^n\right), v_0^n, \tau\right) + K\right] - b_{0,k-1}^n\right\} - b_{0,k-1}^n \\ g_0\left(b_{0,k}^n\right) &= \ln\left[C_A\left(\exp\left(b_{0,k}^n + v_1^n b_{1,k}^n\right), v_1^n, \tau\right) + K\right] - v_1^n b_{1,k}^n - b_{0,k}^n. \end{aligned} \tag{8.50}$$

The values of $b_0(\tau)$ and $b_1(\tau)$ are the values at the last time step, so that $b_0(\tau) = b_0^N$ and $b_1(\tau) = b_1^N$. For details, see Chiarella and Ziogas (2006) or Rouah (2013).

The function CZNewton uses Newton's method to find the roots of the functions g_1 or g_0 defined in (8.50). The derivatives required of Newton's method are obtained with central differences.

```
Function CZNewton(start As Double, ...) As Double
' Newton's method
While (Abs(diff) > tol)
    If gNum = 1 Then
        ' First set of functions and derivative
        CallA1 = CZAmerCall(Exp(b0 + b * v0), ...)
        g0 = (Log(CallA1 + K) - b0) / v0 - b
        CallA1 = CZAmerCall(Exp(b0 + (b + db) * v0), ...)
        g = (Log(CallA1 + K) - b0) / v0 - (b + db)
        CallA1 = CZAmerCall(Exp(b0 + (b - db) * v0), ...)
        g_ = (Log(CallA1 + K) - b0) / v0 - (b - db)
    Else
        ' Second set of functions and derivatives
        CallA0 = CZAmerCall(Exp(b + b1 * V1), ...)
        g0 = (Log(CallA0 + K) - V1 * b1) - b
        CallA0 = CZAmerCall(Exp(b + db + b1 * V1), ...)
        g = (Log(CallA0 + K) - V1 * b1) - (b + db)
        CallA0 = CZAmerCall(Exp(b - db + b1 * V1), ...)
        g_ = (Log(CallA0 + K) - V1 * b1) - (b - db)
    End If
    ' The derivative
```

```
        dg = (g - g_) / 2 / db
        ' Newton's method
        b_new = b - g0 / dg
        diff = b_new - b
        b = b_new
    Wend
    CZNewton = b
    End Function
```

The findB function loops through the time steps and applies the iterative procedure to the functions g_1 and g_0 at each time step. It returns the vectors b_0^n and b_1^n for $n = 0, \ldots, N$.

```
Function findBB(tau As Double, ...) As Variant
For j = 2 To Ntau
    ' Maturity
    mat = j * dtau
    ' Variances
    Evt(j) = EV(v0t, theta, kappa, tau, mat)
    v0(j) = Evt(j) + sigma / kappa * Sqr(kappa * theta / 2)
    V1(j) = Evt(j) - sigma / kappa * Sqr(kappa * theta / 2)
    ' Starting values for Newton's method
    b0k_ = b0(j - 1)
    b1k_ = b1(j - 1)
    ' Set the counter and the initial differences
    diff0 = 1.1 * tol0
    diff1 = 1.1 * tol1
    ' Loop until Newton's method returns bk & bk(-1) to tol.
    While (diff0 > tol0) And (diff1 > tol1)
        counter = counter + 1
        b1k = CZNewton(b1k_, v0(j), V1(j), ...)
        b0k = CZNewton(b0k_, v0(j), V1(j), ...)
        b0(j) = b0k
        b1(j) = b1k
        diff0 = Abs(b0k_ - b0k)
        diff1 = Abs(b1k_ - b1k)
        b0k_ = b0k
        b1k_ = b1k
    Wend
Next j
End Function
```

	A	B	C	D	E	F	G	H	I	J	K	L	M	N
1														
2		**Chiarella Ziogas Algorithm for American Calls**								**Early Exercise Boundary**				
3														**Early Ex.**
4		**Option Features**				**b0(*N*)**	**b1(*N*)**			**n**	**Time**	**b0(*n*)**	**b1(*n*)**	**Boundary**
5		Spot Price (S)	100.0000		Boundary Points	4.7237	0.1674			1	0.01	4.6052	0.0000	100.00
6		Strike Price (K)	100.0000							2	0.02	4.6229	0.6122	104.31
7		Time to Maturity (τ)	0.2500					**American**		3	0.03	4.6275	0.6832	105.09
8		Risk free rate (r)	0.0100			**European**	**American**	**Control Variate**		4	0.04	4.6325	0.7247	105.79
9		Dividend (q)	0.1200		Closed Form	3.5058				5	0.05	4.6415	0.6793	106.55
10		PutCall (C or P)	C		Chiarella-Ziogas	3.5058	3.6256	3.6255		6	0.06	4.6458	0.7053	107.12
11		Little Trap (0=Heston, 1=Albrecher)	1							7	0.07	4.6505	0.7148	107.67
12		European or American (E or A)	A							8	0.08	4.6555	0.7117	108.20
13										9	0.09	4.6641	0.6298	108.78
14		**Heston Parameters**			**Settings for Volterra-Like Algorithm**					10	0.10	4.6682	0.6322	109.23
15		kappa (κ)	4.0000		First tolerance (tol0)			0.005		11	0.11	4.6726	0.6218	109.67
16		theta (θ)	0.0900		Second tolerance (tol1)			0.005		12	0.12	4.6772	0.6021	110.09
17		sigma (σ)	0.1000		Number of Maturity steps (Ntau)			25		13	0.13	4.6819	0.5757	110.50
18		v0	0.0400		Steps Tolerance (Ntol)			1.00E-08		14	0.14	4.6866	0.5448	110.87
19		rho (ρ)	0.0000		Time increment (dt)			0.01		15	0.15	4.6911	0.5110	111.23
20		lambda (λ)	0.0000							16	0.16	4.6955	0.4754	111.55
21					**Starting Values for FindB() Function**					17	0.17	4.6997	0.4389	111.86
22		**Points for Double Trapezoidal Rule**	15		EVt			0.07161		18	0.18	4.7036	0.4023	112.13
23					V00			0.08221		19	0.19	4.7072	0.3659	112.38
24		**Integration Limits for Maturity and Stock Price**			V10			0.06100		20	0.20	4.7106	0.3302	112.60
25		Maturity, Lower (ALim)	1.00E-10		b00			4.60517		21	0.21	4.7138	0.2954	112.80
26		Maturity, Higher (BLim)	0.25		b10			0.00000		22	0.22	4.7167	0.2616	112.97
27		Stock Price, Lower (CLim)	1.00E-10							23	0.23	4.7193	0.2289	113.12
28		Stock Price, Higher (DLim)	100		**Double Integration Type ("GL" or Trapz")**			GL		24	0.24	4.7216	0.1975	113.24
29										25	0.25	4.7237	0.1674	113.34
30														

FIGURE 8.8 Boundary Points and American Call Price

To illustrate, we use the settings $S = K = 100$, a maturity of three months, $r = 0.01$, $q = 0.12$, along with the parameter values $\kappa = 4$, $\theta = 0.09$, $\sigma = 0.1$, $v_0 = 0.04$, and $\rho = 0$. The results are in Figure 8.8.

The findB function returns $b_0(\tau) = 4.7237$ and $b_1(\tau) = 0.1674$. The control variate American call price, using these values, is 3.6255. The Heston European put price is 3.5058. The right portion of Figure 8.8 contains the early exercise boundary. A plot of the boundary appears in Figure 8.9.

The VBA functions presented in this section, along with the examples and figures, are in the Excel file Ch8CZ.xls.

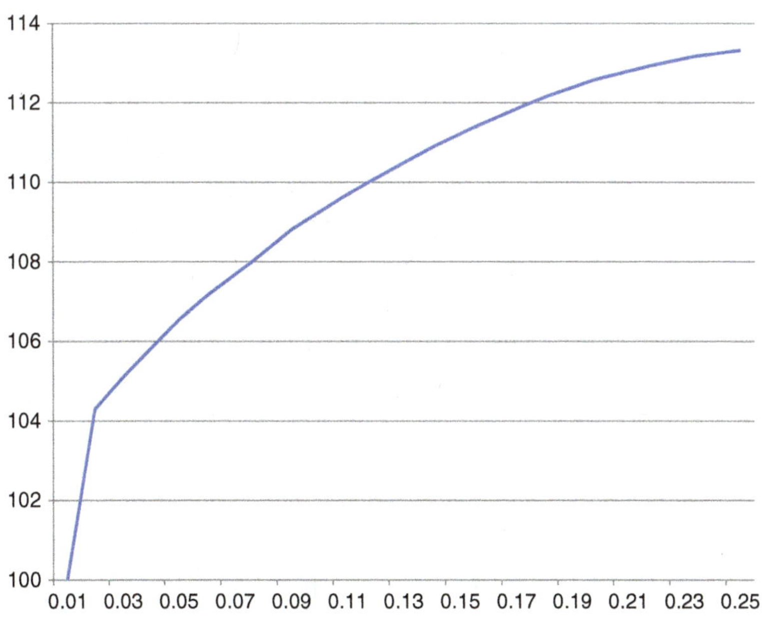

FIGURE 8.9 Early Exercise Boundary

CONCLUSION

In this chapter, we have presented several methods to value American options in the Heston model. The Least-Squares Monte Carlo (LSM) algorithm can be applied to the model in this regard and, as will be shown in Chapter 12, to the double Heston model of Christoffersen et al. (2009) as well. The explicit method, which will be covered in Chapter 10 when we present finite difference methods, can easily be adapted to handle American options also.

In this chapter, we have reviewed the bivariate tree of Beliaeva and Nalwalkha (2010). Other multivariate trees for pricing American options in a stochastic volatility framework are those of Ruckdeschel et al. (2013) and Vellekoop and Nieuwenhuis (2009), which are designed for the Heston model, and Leisen (2000), which can handle more general models. Finally, Zhylyevskyy (2010) extends the Geske and Johnson (1984) approximation to the Heston model. We also reviewed the approximation of Medvedev and Scaillet (2010), which is able to produce option prices very quickly, and the method of Chiarella and Ziogas (2006), which is designed for American calls and borrows from the method of Tzavalis and Wang (2003). In a recent paper, AitSahlia et al. (2012) adapt the method of Chiarella and Ziogas (2006) to American puts.

All of the methods presented so far have assumed the Heston parameters to be static, as in the original formulation of Heston (1993). As shown in Chapter 6, however, the Heston model with static parameters is sometimes unable to provide a good fit to the volatility surface at short maturities. A number of researchers have modified the original Heston (1993) model to allow for parameters to be time dependent. This enrichment of the model makes it more flexible and better able to fit the volatility surface at all maturities. We introduce the Heston model with time-dependent parameters in the next chapter.

CHAPTER 9

Time-Dependent Heston Models

Abstract

The Heston model is often unable to provide a good fit to short-maturity market implied volatilities. One common remedy to this problem is to enrich the model with additional parameters by specifying a more realistic volatility process, which is the approach of the double Heston model. Another approach is to allow the parameters to be time dependent. This latter approach is the one adopted by Mikhailov and Nögel (2003), Elices (2009), Benhamou et al. (2010), and others. Here, we present these time-dependent models. First, we introduce a generalization of the Riccati equation from that allows for nonzero initial conditions. Then we introduce the bivariate characteristic function, and we show that the generalization of the Riccati equation arises as a special case. We then present the models with time-dependent parameters.

time-dependent parameters, piecewise constant parameters, affine model, generalized Riccati equation, bivariate characteristic function, Mikhailov-Nögel, Elices, Benhamou-Miri-Gobet

The Heston model is often unable to provide a good fit to short-maturity market implied volatilities. One common remedy to this problem is to enrich the model with additional parameters by specifying a more realistic volatility process, which is the approach of the double Heston model covered in Chapter 12. Another approach is to allow the parameters to be time dependent. This latter approach is the one adopted by Mikhailov and Nögel (2003), Elices (2009), Benhamou et al. (2010), and others. In this chapter, we present these time-dependent models. First, we introduce a generalization of the Riccati equation from Chapter 1 that allows for nonzero initial conditions. Then we introduce the bivariate characteristic function, and we show that the generalization of the Riccati equation arises as a special case. We then present the models with time-dependent parameters.

GENERALIZATION OF THE RICCATI EQUATION

The coefficients $D_j(\phi, \tau)$ and $C_j(\phi, \tau)$ of the Heston characteristic function were obtained in Chapter 1 under the initial conditions $D_j(\phi, 0) = 0$ and $C_j(\phi, 0) = 0$, and at expiry $\tau = 0$ as

$$D_j(\phi, \tau) = \frac{b_j - \rho\sigma i\phi + d_j}{\sigma^2}\left(\frac{1 - e^{d_j\tau}}{1 - g_j e^{d_j\tau}}\right), \tag{9.1}$$

$$C_j(\phi, \tau) = (r - q)i\phi\tau + \frac{a}{\sigma^2}\left[(b_j - \rho\sigma i\phi + d_j)\tau - 2\ln\left(\frac{1 - g_j e^{d_j\tau}}{1 - g_j}\right)\right]. \tag{9.2}$$

Suppose that instead of the initial conditions $C_j(\phi, 0) = D_j(\phi, 0) = 0$, we use the general nonzero initial conditions

$$C_j(\phi, 0) = C_j^0, \quad D_j(\phi, 0) = D_j^0. \tag{9.3}$$

These conditions produce the general coefficients

$$\widetilde{D}_j(\phi, \tau) = \frac{(b_j - \rho\sigma i\phi + d_j) - (b_j - \rho\sigma i\phi - d_j)\tilde{g}_j e^{d_j\tau}}{\sigma^2(1 - \tilde{g}_j e^{d_j\tau})}, \tag{9.4}$$

$$\widetilde{C}_j(\phi, \tau) = (r - q)i\phi\tau + \frac{a}{\sigma^2}\left[(b_j - \rho\sigma i\phi + d_j)\tau - 2\ln\left(\frac{1 - \tilde{g}_j e^{d_j\tau}}{1 - \tilde{g}_j}\right)\right] + C_j^0. \tag{9.5}$$

The notation $\widetilde{D}_j(\phi, \tau)$ and $\widetilde{C}_j(\phi, \tau)$ distinguishes these coefficients from their static counterparts $D_j(\phi, \tau)$ and $C_j(\phi, \tau)$ in (9.1) and (9.2). Setting $C_j^0 = D_j^0 = 0$ in (9.4) and (9.5) reduces $\widetilde{D}_j(\phi, \tau)$ and $\widetilde{C}_j(\phi, \tau)$ to $D_j(\phi, \tau)$ and $C_j(\phi, \tau)$, respectively.

See Rouah (2013) for the $\tilde{g}_j$ coefficients and a detailed derivation of (9.4) and (9.5).

BIVARIATE CHARACTERISTIC FUNCTION

In Chapter 1, the characteristic function of the log-stock price at maturity, $x_T = \ln S_T$, was presented in the following form (dropping the j subscripts on f_j, $C_j(\tau, \phi)$ and $D_j(\tau, \phi)$ for notational convenience)

$$f(\phi, \tau; x_t, v_t) = E\left[\exp(i\phi x_T)\right] = \exp(C(\tau, \phi) + D(\tau, \phi)v_t + i\phi x_t). \tag{9.6}$$

The initial conditions $C(0, \phi) = D(0, \phi) = 0$ were used to find analytic expressions for $C(\tau, \phi)$ and $D(\tau, \phi)$. The bivariate characteristic function of the joint process (x_T, v_T) is defined as

$$\begin{aligned} f(\phi_1, \phi_2; v_t, x_t) &= E\left[\exp\left(i\phi_1 x_T + i\phi_2 v_T\right)\right] \\ &= \exp(A(\tau, \phi_1, \phi_2) + B(\tau, \phi_1, \phi_2)x_t + C(\tau, \phi_1, \phi_2)v_t), \end{aligned} \tag{9.7}$$

where $\tau = T - t$ is the time remaining until expiry. Using the results of Duffie et al. (2000) and Singleton (2001), the Heston model can be written in terms of two independent Brownian motions $B_{1,t}$ and $B_{2,t}$ as

$$d\mathbf{x}_t = \boldsymbol{\mu}(\mathbf{x}_t)dt + \boldsymbol{\sigma}(\mathbf{x}_t)d\mathbf{B}_t, \tag{9.8}$$

where

$$\boldsymbol{\mu}_t = \begin{pmatrix} r - \frac{1}{2}v_t \\ \kappa(\theta - v_t) \end{pmatrix}, \quad \boldsymbol{\sigma}(\mathbf{x}_t) = \begin{pmatrix} \sqrt{v_t} & 0 \\ \sigma\rho\sqrt{v_t} & \sigma\sqrt{1-\rho^2}\sqrt{v_t} \end{pmatrix}, \quad d\mathbf{B}_t = \begin{pmatrix} dB_{1,t} \\ dB_{2,t} \end{pmatrix}. \tag{9.9}$$

Both the drift $\boldsymbol{\mu}$ and the matrix $\boldsymbol{\sigma}\boldsymbol{\sigma}^T$ in the Heston model can be written in the affine form,

$$\begin{aligned} \boldsymbol{\mu}(\mathbf{x}_t) &= \mathbf{K}_0 + \mathbf{K}_1 x_t + \mathbf{K}_2 v_t \\ \boldsymbol{\sigma}(\mathbf{x}_t)\boldsymbol{\sigma}(\mathbf{x}_t)^T &= \mathbf{H}_0 + \mathbf{H}_1 x_t + \mathbf{H}_2 v_t, \end{aligned} \tag{9.10}$$

with

$$\mathbf{K}_0 = \begin{pmatrix} r \\ \kappa\theta \end{pmatrix}, \ \mathbf{K}_1 = \begin{pmatrix} 0 \\ 0 \end{pmatrix}, \ \mathbf{K}_2 = \begin{pmatrix} -\frac{1}{2} \\ -\kappa \end{pmatrix}, \ \mathbf{H}_0 = \mathbf{H}_1 = \begin{pmatrix} 0 & 0 \\ 0 & 0 \end{pmatrix}, \ \mathbf{H}_2 = \begin{pmatrix} 1 & \rho\sigma \\ \rho\sigma & \sigma^2 \end{pmatrix}.$$

The result of Duffie et al. (2000) is that the characteristic function has the log-linear form in Equation (9.7). Moreover, the coefficients of the characteristic function can be obtained by solving the system of Riccati equations,

$$\begin{aligned} \frac{\partial A}{\partial t} &= -\mathbf{K}_0^T\boldsymbol{\beta} - \frac{1}{2}\boldsymbol{\beta}^T\mathbf{H}_0\boldsymbol{\beta}, \\ \frac{\partial B}{\partial t} &= -\mathbf{K}_1^T\boldsymbol{\beta} - \frac{1}{2}\boldsymbol{\beta}^T\mathbf{H}_1\boldsymbol{\beta}, \\ \frac{\partial C}{\partial t} &= -\mathbf{K}_2^T\boldsymbol{\beta} - \frac{1}{2}\boldsymbol{\beta}^T\mathbf{H}_2\boldsymbol{\beta}, \end{aligned} \tag{9.11}$$

subject to the boundary conditions $B(0) = i\phi_1$, $C(0) = i\phi_2$, and $A(0) = 0$, and where $\boldsymbol{\beta}^T = (B, C)$. The resulting coefficients are

$$\begin{aligned} A(\tau, \phi_1, \phi_2) &= (r-q)i\phi_1\tau + \frac{\kappa\theta}{\sigma^2}\left[(\kappa - \rho\sigma i\phi_1 + d_2)\tau - 2\ln\left(\frac{1-\tilde{g}_2 e^{d_2\tau}}{1-\tilde{g}_2}\right)\right] \\ B(\tau, \phi_1, \phi_2) &= i\phi_1 \\ C(\tau, \phi_1, \phi_2) &= \frac{(\kappa - \rho\sigma i\phi_1 + d_2) - (\kappa - \rho\sigma i\phi_1 - d_2)\tilde{g}_2 e^{d_2\tau}}{\sigma^2(1-\tilde{g}_2 e^{d_2\tau})}. \end{aligned} \tag{9.12}$$

The coefficients of the univariate characteristic function (9.6) arise as a special case of (9.12). See Rouah (2013) for details.

LINKING THE BIVARIATE CF AND THE GENERAL RICCATI EQUATION

The univariate characteristic function for x_T in the Heston model is Equation (9.6):

$$f(\phi, \tau; x_t, v_t) = E\left[\exp(i\phi x_T)\right] = \exp(C(\tau, \phi) + D(\tau, \phi)v_t + i\phi x_t), \qquad (9.13)$$

with coefficients defined in Equations (9.1) and (9.2). The bivariate characteristic function for (x_T, v_T), on the other hand, is (9.7)

$$\begin{aligned} f(\phi_1, \phi_2; v_t, x_t) &= E\left[\exp\left(i\phi_1 x_T + i\phi_2 v_T\right)\right] \\ &= \exp(A(\tau, \phi_1, \phi_2) + B(\tau, \phi_1, \phi_2)x_t + C(\tau, \phi_1, \phi_2)v_t), \end{aligned} \qquad (9.14)$$

with coefficients defined in (9.12). The two characteristic functions are clearly similar in form, but with different coefficients. The difference arises from the choice of initial conditions for the general solution of the Riccati equation in (9.4) and (9.5). To obtain the univariate characteristic function, we set $D_j^0 = 0$ and $C_j^0 = 0$ in Equation (9.3) but to obtain the bivariate characteristic function we set $C_j^0 = 0$ and $D_j^0 = i\phi_2$.

If we set $\phi_2 = 0$ and write $\phi = \phi_1$ in the bivariate characteristic function (9.14) we obtain $f(\phi, 0; x, v) = E\left[\exp(i\phi x_T)\right]$, which is the univariate characteristic function $f_2(\phi; x, v)$ for x_T, and we also obtain $D_j^0 = 0$. Hence, we recover the coefficients of the univariate characteristic function $f_2(\phi; x, v)$ and we obtain

$$A(\tau, \phi, 0) = C_2(\tau, \phi), \quad C(\tau, \phi, 0) = D_2(\tau, \phi). \qquad (9.15)$$

Finally, the coefficients of the bivariate characteristic function can be written in an equivalent form that is consistent with the "Little Trap" formulation of Albrecher et al. (2007), as in Kahl (2008). Indeed, it can be shown that $C(\tau, \phi_1, \phi_2)$ in Equation (9.12) can be written as Equation (2.117) of Kahl:

$$C(\tau, \phi_1, \phi_2) = \frac{(\kappa - \rho\sigma i\phi_1 - d_2) - (\kappa - \rho\sigma i\phi_1 + d_2)\tilde{c}_2 e^{-d_2\tau}}{\sigma^2(1 - \tilde{c}_2 e^{-d_2\tau})}. \qquad (9.16)$$

Similarly, $A(\tau, \phi_1, \phi_2)$ in (9.12) can be written

$$A(\tau, \phi_1, \phi_2) = (r - q)i\phi_1\tau + \frac{\kappa\theta}{\sigma^2}\left[(\kappa - \rho\sigma i\phi_1 - d_2)\tau - 2\ln\left(\frac{1 - \tilde{c}_2 e^{-d_2\tau}}{1 - \tilde{c}_2}\right)\right], \qquad (9.17)$$

which is Equation (2.118) of Kahl (2008).

The bivariate characteristic function is implemented using the VBA function HestonBivariateCF. The first two arguments to the function are complex.

```
Function HestonBivariateCF(phi1, phi2, ...) As Variant
d = cSqr(cSub(Term1, cProd(Term2, Term3)))
g = cDiv(Num, Den)
c = cDiv(one, g)
bigB = cProd(i, phi1)
' Little Trap formulation in Kahl (2008)
bigG = cDiv(Num, Den)
bigA = cAdd(Term1, Term2)
bigC = cDiv(cDiv(Term1, Term2), Term3)
' The characteristic function.
' y = exp(A + B*x0 + C*v0);
y = cExp(cAdd(cAdd(bigA, Term1), Term2))
' Output real and imaginary parts separately
output(1) = cReal(y)
output(2) = cImag(y)
HestonBivariateCF = output
End Function
```

This function can be passed to the HestonPriceGaussLaguerre function, which illustrates that the call price can be identically obtained with either the univariate or bivariate characteristic function. This is accomplished by setting the second argument to zero in the HestonBivariateCF function.

```
Function HestonPriceGaussLaguerreBivariate(...) As Double
For j = 1 To N
    phi = x(j)
    weight = w(j)
    ' Characteristic functions and integrands
    f2 = HestonBivariateCF(u2, ...)
    int2(j) = weight * cReal(cDiv(cProd(expKf, CharFun2), ...)
    f1 = HestonBivariateCF(u1, ...)
    int1(j) = weight * cReal(cDiv(cProd(expKf, CharFun1), ...)
Next j
P1 = 0.5 + 1 / pi * Sum(int1)
P2 = 0.5 + 1 / pi * Sum(int2)
End Function
```

To illustrate, we obtain call prices using the univariate and bivariate characteristic functions. The results in Figure 9.1 show that these prices are identical.

The VBA code presented in this section, and the screen shot in Figure 9.1, are in the Excel file Ch9BivariateCF.xls.

	B	C	E	F	G
1					
2	**Heston Price With Univariate and Bivariate Characteristic Functions**				
3				**Price**	
4	**Option Features**		**Strike**	**Univariate C.F.**	**Bivariate C.F.**
5	Spot Price (S)	100.0000	90	13.9774	13.9774
6	Time to Maturity (τ)	0.2500	91	13.3540	13.3540
7	Risk free rate (r)	0.0300	92	12.7477	12.7477
8	Dividend (q)	0.0700	93	12.1586	12.1586
9	Trap (0=Heston, 1=Albrecher)	1	94	11.5869	11.5869
10	Put or Call ("P" or "C")	C	95	11.0324	11.0324
11			96	10.4954	10.4954
12	**Heston Parameters**		97	9.9758	9.9758
13	kappa (κ)	0.2000	98	9.4736	9.4736
14	theta (θ)	0.0500	99	8.9886	8.9886
15	sigma (σ)	0.3000	100	8.5209	8.5209
16	v0	0.2200	101	8.0702	8.0702
17	rho (ρ)	-0.8000	102	7.6364	7.6364
18	lambda (λ)	0.0000	103	7.2194	7.2194
19			104	6.8189	6.8189
20			105	6.4346	6.4346
21			106	6.0664	6.0664
22			107	5.7140	5.7140
23			108	5.3769	5.3769
24			109	5.0550	5.0550
25			110	4.7479	4.7479

FIGURE 9.1 Call Prices Using Different Characteristic Functions

MIKHAILOV AND NÖGEL MODEL

This model introduces time dependency in the Heston model by allowing the parameters in the model to be piecewise constant. We denote the coefficients of the characteristic function by $\widetilde{C}_j(\phi, \tau_1; \Theta)$ and $\widetilde{D}_j(\phi, \tau_1; \Theta)$ to emphasize their dependence on the parameters $\Theta = (\kappa, \theta, \sigma, v_0, \rho)$.

Suppose we are given the N maturities $0 < T_1 < T_2 < \cdots < T_N < \infty$. Divide the time axis $[0, T_N]$ into the maturity increments $\tau_1, \tau_2, \ldots, \tau_N$, where $\tau_k = T_k - T_{k-1}$ for $k = 2, \ldots, N$, and with $\tau_1 = T_1$. The idea is to obtain expressions for $\widetilde{C}_j$ and $\widetilde{D}_j$ recursively. In first estimation step, we obtain $\widetilde{C}_j(\phi, \tau_1; \Theta)$ and $\widetilde{D}_j(\phi, \tau_1; \Theta)$ for the first maturity τ_1 using the static initial conditions $C_j^0 = 0$ and $D_j^0 = 0$, exactly as in the ordinary Heston model. We then construct the characteristic functions and the Heston model option prices, and estimate Θ. This produces the first set of estimates $\Theta_1 = (\kappa^{(1)}, \theta^{(1)}, \sigma^{(1)}, v_0^{(1)}, \rho^{(1)})$ corresponding to the first maturity τ_1. In the second estimation step, substitute Θ_1 into the expressions for $\widetilde{C}_j$ and $\widetilde{D}_j$ to produce the second set of initial conditions C_j^1 and D_j^1. Then construct $\widetilde{C}_j(\phi, \tau_2; \Theta)$ and $\widetilde{D}_j(\phi, \tau_2; \Theta)$ for the second maturity τ_2, construct the characteristic functions and the Heston model option price, and produce the parameter estimate $\Theta_2 = (\kappa^{(2)}, \theta^{(2)}, \sigma^{(2)}, v_0^{(2)}, \rho^{(2)})$. We continue in this recursive fashion until the last maturity, τ_N. The following steps summarize this recursive method:

Step 1. Use $C_j^0 = D_j^0 = 0$ to form $C_j(\phi, \tau_1; \Theta)$ and $D_j(\phi, \tau_1; \Theta)$, and obtain the characteristic functions f_j $(j = 1, 2)$ at time τ_1

$$f_j(\phi; x, v, \Theta) = \exp(\widetilde{C}_j(\phi, \tau_1; \Theta) + \widetilde{D}_j(\phi, \tau_1; \Theta)v_0 + i\phi x),$$

where $x = \ln S_0$, the log spot price. Form the Heston option prices, and use them or the Heston implied volatilities to obtain $\Theta_1 = (\kappa^{(1)}, \theta^{(1)}, \sigma^{(1)}, v_0^{(1)}, \rho^{(1)})$, the set of parameter estimates for maturity τ_1. In this first step, the estimation of Θ is exactly the same as that for the ordinary Heston model, using the maturity τ_1.

Step $k \geq 2$. Substitute the parameter estimates $\Theta_{k-1} = (\kappa^{(k-1)}, \theta^{(k-1)}, \sigma^{(k-1)}, v_0^{(k-1)}, \rho^{(k-1)})$ from the previous step into the expressions for $\widetilde{C}_j$ and $\widetilde{D}_j$ to obtain the next initial conditions $C_j^{k-1} = \widetilde{C}_j(\phi, \tau_{k-1}; \Theta_{k-1})$ and $D_j^{k-1} = \widetilde{D}_j(\phi, \tau_{k-1}; \Theta_{k-1})$, using Equations (9.5) and (9.4), respectively. Construct $\widetilde{C}_j(\phi, \tau_k; \Theta)$ and $\widetilde{D}_j(\phi, \tau_k; \Theta)$ for the maturity τ_k, again using (9.5) and (9.4):

$$\begin{aligned}
\widetilde{C}_j(\phi, \tau_k; \Theta) &= (r - q)i\phi\tau_k + \frac{a}{\sigma^2}\left[(b_j - \rho\sigma i\phi + d_j)\tau_k - 2\ln\left(\frac{1 - \tilde{g}_j e^{d_j\tau_k}}{1 - \tilde{g}_j}\right)\right] + C_j^{k-1}, \\
\widetilde{D}_j(\phi, \tau_k; \Theta) &= \frac{(b_j - \rho\sigma i\phi + d_j) - (b_j - \rho\sigma i\phi - d_j)\tilde{g}_j \exp(d_j\tau_k)}{\sigma^2(1 - \tilde{g}_j \exp(d_j\tau_k))}.
\end{aligned} \tag{9.18}$$

Use the characteristic function

$$f_j(\phi; x, v, \Theta) = \exp\left(\widetilde{C}_j(\phi, \tau_k; \Theta) + \widetilde{D}_j(\phi, \tau_k; \Theta)v_0 + i\phi x\right)$$

to form the integrand for the probabilities P_1 and P_2, obtain the Heston prices with maturity τ_k, and obtain the parameter estimates $\Theta_k = (\kappa^{(k)}, \theta^{(k)}, \sigma^{(k)}, v_0^{(k)}, \rho^{(k)})$.

Final step. At the final time τ_N we have the estimates $\Theta_N = (\kappa^{(N)}, \theta^{(N)}, \sigma^{(N)}, v_0^{(N)}, \rho^{(N)})$, which we use to form the characteristic function

$$f_j(\phi; x, v, \Theta_N) = \exp\left(\widetilde{C}_j(\phi, \tau_N; \Theta_N) + \widetilde{D}_j(\phi, \tau_N; \Theta_N)v_0^{(N)} + i\phi x\right). \tag{9.19}$$

We use this characteristic function to form the integrand for the probabilities P_1 and P_2, and obtain the Heston prices with maturity τ_N.

Note that the estimation in Step $k \geq 2$ is for the current parameter set Θ only. The parameter set from the previous iteration, Θ_{k-1}, is fixed and used in the initial conditions C_j^{k-1} and D_j^{k-1}. Hence, the initial conditions do not impact the estimation of Θ directly. Note, however, that even though the initial conditions are not functions of the current parameter set Θ, they are functions of the integration variable ϕ. For the purpose of integration, the initial conditions cannot be treated as constants.

The VBA function MNProb implements the integrand for the time-dependent Heston model of Mikhailov and Nögel (2003). The function accepts as inputs a vector of parameter estimates obtained in the prior time steps, stored in the matrix param0, with the parameter estimates arranged in rows. The estimates from the most recent time step are in the top row, and the oldest estimates are in the bottom row. It also accepts vector of prior maturities (tau0), with the most recent maturity on top, and the oldest at the bottom. The function returns the integrand for the probabilities P_1 and P_2.

```
Function MNProb(phi As Double, params As Variant, params0 As Variant,_
               tau As Double, tau0 As Variant, ...) As Double
' Create the past Cj and Dj values corresponding to the old maturities
For j = 1 To N
    kappa = params0(j, 1)
    theta = params0(j, 2)
    sigma = params0(j, 3)
    v0 = params0(j, 4)
    rho = params0(j, 5)
    T = tau0(j)
    If (j = 1) Then
        D0 = zero
        C0 = zero
    Else
        D0 = D
        C0 = C
    End If
    Cfun = Ct(phi, ..., C0, D0)
    Dfun = Dt(phi, ..., C0, D0)
Next j
' Cj and Dj values for a single maturity
kappa = params(1)
theta = params(2)
sigma = params(3)
v0 = params(4)
rho = params(5)
T = tau
If N = 0 Then
    D0 = zero
    C0 = zero
Else
    D0 = D
    C0 = C
End If
```

```
Cfun = Ct(phi, ..., C0, D0)
Dfun = Dt(phi, ..., C0, D0)
' The characteristic function.
f = cExp(cAdd(cAdd(C, T1), T2))
' Return the real part of the integrand.
y = cReal(cDiv(Num, Den))
MNProb = y
End Function
```

The MNProb function makes use of the VBA functions Ct and Dt, which construct $\widetilde{C}_j(\phi, \tau_k; \Theta)$ and $\widetilde{D}_j(\phi, \tau_k; \Theta)$, respectively, from (9.18).

```
Function Ct(phi As Double, ...) As Variant
D = cSqr(cSub(Term1, Term2))
g = cDiv(Num, Den)
bigG = cDiv(Num, Den)
bigC = cAdd(cAdd(Term1, Term2), C0)
' Output real and imaginary parts separately
output(1) = cReal(bigC)
output(2) = cImag(bigC)
Ct = output
End Function
```

```
Function Dt(phi As Double, ...) As Variant
D = cSqr(cSub(Term1, Term2))
g = cDiv(Num, Den)
bigG = cDiv(Num, Den)
bigD = cDiv(Num, Den)
' Output the real and imaginary parts separately
output(1) = cReal(bigD)
output(2) = cImag(bigD)
Dt = output
End Function
```

Finally, the MNProb function is passed to the MNPriceGaussLaguerre function, which uses Gauss-Laguerre integration to obtain the call price.

```
Function MNPriceGaussLaguerre(...) As Double
' Numerical integration
For j = 1 To N
    phi = x(j)
    weight = w(j)
    int1(j) = weight * MNProb(phi, ..., 1)
    int2(j) = weight * MNProb(phi, ..., 2)
Next j
P1 = 0.5 + 1 / pi * Sum(int1)
P2 = 0.5 + 1 / pi * Sum(int2)
CallPrice = S * Exp(-q * tau) * P1 - K ...
' The option price
If PutCall = "C" Then
    MNPriceGaussLaguerre = CallPrice
Else
    MNPriceGaussLaguerre = CallPrice - S * Exp(-q * tau) ...
End If
End Function
```

To illustrate, we reproduce Table 1 of Mikhailov and Nögel (2003). They use $S = 1$, $r = 0$ and a maturity of $T = 5$ years. The parameters $\theta = v_0 = 0.1$, $\sigma = 0.2$, $\rho = -0.3$ are fixed, and κ varies from $\kappa = 1, 2, 4$ in the three periods, which we assume to be equal in length. This is implemented with the following code. The results are shown in Figure 9.2.

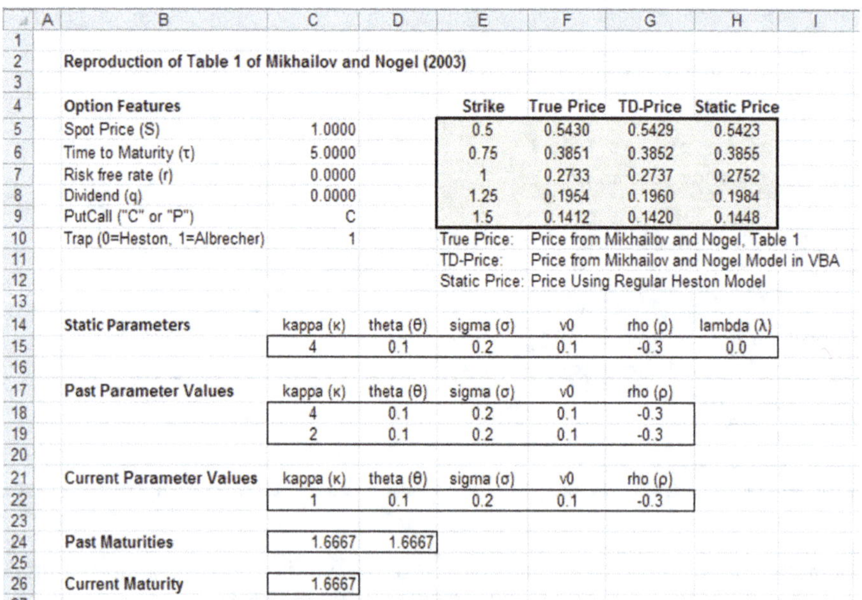

	A	B	C	D	E	F	G	H
1								
2		Reproduction of Table 1 of Mikhailov and Nogel (2003)						
3								
4		Option Features			Strike	True Price	TD-Price	Static Price
5		Spot Price (S)	1.0000		0.5	0.5430	0.5429	0.5423
6		Time to Maturity (τ)	5.0000		0.75	0.3851	0.3852	0.3855
7		Risk free rate (r)	0.0000		1	0.2733	0.2737	0.2752
8		Dividend (q)	0.0000		1.25	0.1954	0.1960	0.1984
9		PutCall ("C" or "P")	C		1.5	0.1412	0.1420	0.1448
10		Trap (0=Heston, 1=Albrecher)	1		True Price:	Price from Mikhailov and Nogel, Table 1		
11					TD-Price:	Price from Mikhailov and Nogel Model in VBA		
12					Static Price:	Price Using Regular Heston Model		
13								
14		Static Parameters	kappa (κ)	theta (θ)	sigma (σ)	v0	rho (ρ)	lambda (λ)
15			4	0.1	0.2	0.1	-0.3	0.0
16								
17		Past Parameter Values	kappa (κ)	theta (θ)	sigma (σ)	v0	rho (ρ)	
18			4	0.1	0.2	0.1	-0.3	
19			2	0.1	0.2	0.1	-0.3	
20								
21		Current Parameter Values	kappa (κ)	theta (θ)	sigma (σ)	v0	rho (ρ)	
22			1	0.1	0.2	0.1	-0.3	
23								
24		Past Maturities	1.6667	1.6667				
25								
26		Current Maturity	1.6667					

FIGURE 9.2 Mikhailov and Nögel Option Prices

The true prices in column F are taken from Table 1 of Mikhailov and Nögel (2003). The prices obtained using the VBA function MNPriceLaguerre are in column G and are close to the true prices. The VBA functions presented in this section, and the screen shot in Figure 9.2, are from the Excel file Ch9MN.xls.

ELICES MODEL

The time-dependent models of both Elices (2009) and Mikhailov and Nögel (2003) make use of a recursive calculation on the bivariate characteristic function, presented in Afshani (2010) and Kahl and Lord (2010). In Elices (2009), however, this calculation is more clearly illustrated. Recall from Equations (9.7) and (9.14) that the time-t bivariate characteristic function for (x_T, v_T) is

$$\begin{aligned} f(\phi_1, \phi_2, \tau, x_t, v_t) &= E[\exp(i\phi_1 x_T + i\phi_2 v_T) | \mathcal{F}_t] \\ &= \exp(A(\tau, \phi_1, \phi_2) + i\phi_1 x_t + C(\tau, \phi_1, \phi_2) v_t), \end{aligned} \tag{9.20}$$

where $\tau = T - t$ is the time to maturity. As before, suppose that we are given N maturities $0 < T_1 < T_2 < \cdots < T_N < \infty$ and that the time axis $[0, T_N]$ is divided into the maturity increments $\tau_1, \tau_2, \ldots, \tau_N$, where $\tau_k = T_k - T_{k-1}$ for $k = 2, \ldots, N$ and with $\tau_1 = T_1$. Define x_k, v_k and $\mathcal{F}_k$ to represent x_t, v_t and $\mathcal{F}_t$, but each evaluated at T_k. Lord and Kahl (2010) apply the law of iterated expectations by conditioning on the information set at T_{N-1} to obtain the characteristic function for x_N as

$$E[\exp(i\phi_1 x_N)] = \exp(A(\tau_N, \phi_1, 0)) E\left[\exp\left(i\phi_1 x_{N-1} + i\phi_2^{N-1} v_{N-1}\right)\right], \tag{9.21}$$

where $\phi_2^{N-1} = -iC(\tau_N, \phi_1, 0)$. Recognizing that the second argument of the bivariate characteristic can be written in this form, is the trick that makes the recursive calculation possible. Now apply the law of iterated expectations again to the last term of the last equation in (9.21), conditioning this time on $\mathcal{F}_{N-2}$. We obtain

$$E[e^{i\phi_1 x_N}] = \exp\left(A(\tau_N, \phi_1, 0) + A\left(\tau_{N-1}, \phi_1, \phi_2^{N-1}\right)\right) E\left[\exp\left(i\phi_1 x_{N-2} + i\phi_2^{N-2} v_{N-2}\right)\right],$$

where $\phi_2^{N-2} = -iC(\tau_{N-1}, \phi_1, \phi_2^{N-1})$. Continuing in this manner, by repeated application of the law of iterated expectations and the trick, the characteristic function for $x_N = x_{T_N}$ can be written as

$$\begin{aligned} f(\phi_1, x_0, v_0) &= E\left[\exp(i\phi_1 x_N)\right] \\ &= \exp\left(\sum_{k=0}^{N-1} A\left(\tau_{N-k}, \phi_1, \phi_2^{N-k}\right)\right) \exp\left(i\phi_1 x_0 + C\left(\tau_1, \phi_1, \phi_2^0\right) v_0\right), \end{aligned} \tag{9.22}$$

with $\phi_2^{N-k} \equiv -iC(\tau_{N-k+1}, \phi_1, \phi_2^{N-k+1})$ and $\phi_2^N \equiv 0$.

As explained in Chapter 2, we use $f(\phi, x_0, v_0)$ in (9.22) directly for the second characteristic function, but for the first characteristic function we must use $f(\phi - i, x_0, v_0)/(Se^{(r-q)T_N})$.

Elices (2009) estimates v_0 at the first maturity, and restricts this parameter to remain constant throughout the remaining maturities. The other parameters are piecewise constant and change their value at the maturities. Denote by $\Theta_k = (\kappa^{(k)}, \theta^{(k)}, \sigma^{(k)}, \rho^{(k)})$, the parameter set estimated in time increment (T_{k-1}, T_k). The model of Elices (2009) is implemented from the first maturity to the last, using the following steps.

Step 1. Construct the characteristic function at the first maturity, which depends on the parameter set Θ_1, as

$$\exp\left(A(\tau_1, \phi_1, 0; \Theta_1)\right) \times \exp(i\phi_1 x_0 + C(\tau_N, \phi_1, 0; \Theta_1)v_0).$$

Obtain the parameter estimates v_0 and Θ_1 by minimizing the loss function using market prices or implied volatilities at the first maturity.

Step 2. Construct the characteristic function at the second maturity, which depends on the parameter sets Θ_1 and Θ_2, as

$$\exp\left(A(\tau_2, \phi_1, 0; \Theta_2) + A\left(\tau_1, \phi_1, \phi_2^1; \Theta_1\right)\right) \times \exp\left(i\phi_1 x_0 + C\left(\tau_1, \phi_1, \phi_2^0; \Theta_1\right)v_0\right),$$

where $\phi_2^1 = -iC(\tau_2, \phi_1, 0; \Theta_2)$ and $\phi_2^0 = -iC(\tau_1, \phi_1, \phi_2^1; \Theta_1)$. Obtain the parameter estimates Θ_2 by minimizing the loss function using prices or volatilities at the second maturity, keeping Θ_1 and v_0 fixed.

Step *k*. Construct the characteristic function at maturity k, which depends on the parameter sets set $\Theta_1, \Theta_2, \ldots, \Theta_k$, as

$$\begin{aligned}&\exp\left(A(\tau_k, \phi_1, 0; \Theta_k) + A\left(\tau_{k-1}, \phi_1, \phi_2^{k-1}; \Theta_{k-1}\right) + \cdots + A\left(\tau_1, \phi_1, \phi_2^1; \Theta_1\right)\right)\\ &\times \exp\left(i\phi_1 x_0 + C\left(\tau_1, \phi_1, \phi_2^0; \Theta_1\right)v_0\right)\end{aligned}$$

where

$$\begin{aligned}\phi_2^k &= 0\\ \phi_2^{k-1} &= -iC(\tau_k, \phi_1, \phi_2^k; \Theta_k)\\ &\vdots\\ \phi_2^1 &= -iC(\tau_2, \phi_1, \phi_2^2; \Theta_2)\\ \phi_2^0 &= -iC(\tau_1, \phi_1, \phi_2^1; \Theta_1).\end{aligned}$$

Obtain the estimates Θ_k by minimizing the loss function using prices or volatilities at the kth maturity, keeping $\Theta_1, \Theta_2, \ldots, \Theta_{k-1}$ and v_0 fixed.

At the final step, we have the characteristic function in Equation (9.22) at the last maturity, written here to emphasize its dependence on the parameter sets $\Theta_1, \Theta_2, \ldots, \Theta_N$:

$$\begin{aligned}f(\phi_1, x_0, v_0) = \exp&\left(\sum_{k=0}^{N-1} A\left(\tau_{N-k}, \phi_1, \phi_2^{N-k}; \Theta_{N-k}\right)\right),\\ &\times \exp\left(i\phi_1 x_0 + C\left(\tau_1, \phi_1, \phi_2^0; \Theta_1\right)v_0\right).\end{aligned} \tag{9.23}$$

The coefficients $A(\tau_j, \phi_1, \phi_2^j; \Theta_j)$ and $C(\tau_j, \phi_1, \phi_2^j; \Theta_j)$ are implemented with the VBA functions bigA and bigC, respectively.

```
Function bigA(phi1 As cNum, phi2 As cNum, ...) As Variant
d = cSqr(cSub(Term1, Term2))
num = cSub(cAdd(cSub(T1, rhosigmaiphi1), d), T2)
den = cSub(cSub(cSub(T1, rhosigmaiphi1), d), T2)
' Ensure denominator for g remains > 0
If cReal(den) = 0 And cImag(den) = 0 Then
    den = Complex(0.01, 0)
End If
G = cDiv(num, den)
AA = cAdd(Term1, Term3)
' Output real and imaginary parts separately
output(1) = cReal(AA)
output(2) = cImag(AA)
bigA = output
End Function
```

```
Function bigC(phi1 As cNum, phi2 As cNum, ...) As Variant
d = cSqr(cSub(Term1, Term2))
num = cSub(cAdd(cSub(T1, rhosigmaiphi1), d), T2)
den = cSub(cSub(cSub(T1, rhosigmaiphi1), d), T2)
' Ensure denominator for g remains > 0
If cReal(den) = 0 And cImag(den) = 0 Then
    den = Complex(0.01, 0)
End If
G = cDiv(num, den)
CC = cDiv(Term1, Term2)
output(1) = cReal(CC)
output(2) = cImag(CC)
bigC = output
End Function
```

These are used in the VBA function ElicesCF, which calculates the characteristic function in Equation (9.23). The parameters for the current maturity are passed in the vector param, while the parameters of the prior maturities are passed in the matrix paramfixed. The initial variance parameter estimate is passed as an argument to the function. The maturity increments are passed in the vector tau, with the increment for the shortest maturity in the top position of the vector. The first portion of the function calculates the coefficients ϕ_2^k recursively, going backwards from the last maturity value $\phi_2^N = 0$.

```
Function ElicesCF(phi1, param, paramfixed, ...) As Variant
' phi2(N) coefficients vector.
If N >= 2 Then
    phi2(N - 1) = cProd(im, CC)
End If
If N >= 3 Then
    For x = N - 2 To 1 Step -1
        phi2(x) = cProd(im, CC)
    Next x
End If
If N >= 2 Then
    phi20 = cProd(im, CC)
ElseIf N = 1 Then
    phi20 = cProd(im, CC)
End If
' A coefficients.  Last maturity at last position in vector.
AA = bigA(phi1, zero, param, v0, ttau, r, q)
Ah(N) = Complex(AA(1), AA(2))
If N >= 2 Then
    For x = N - 1 To 1 Step -1
        ' Ah(x) = A(phi1,phi2(x),paramfixed(x,:),tau(x),r,q);
        AA = bigA(phi1, phi2(x), ParamTemp, v0, ttau, r, q)
        Ah(x) = Complex(AA(1), AA(2))
    Next x
End If
' C coefficient
If N >= 2 Then
    C = bigC(phi1, phi20, ParamTemp, v0, ttau, S)
Else
    C = bigC(phi1, phi20, param, v0, ttau, S)
End If
' Sum the vector Ah(N)
sumAh = Complex(Sum(1), Sum(2))
phi1x0i = cProd(Complex(x0, 0), cProd(phi1, i))
Chv0 = cProd(Ch, Complex(v0, 0))
' z = exp(sum(Ah) + i*phi1*x0 + Ch*v0);
z = cExp(cAdd(cAdd(sumAh, phi1x0i), Chv0))
' Return real and imaginary parts separately
output(1) = cReal(z)
output(2) = cImag(z)
ElicesCF = output
End Function
```

The function ElicesPrice uses the characteristic function to produce the Heston call or put price with time-dependent parameters. The current parameters are in the vector param, while the fixed parameters from the previous periods are in the matrix paramfixed. Note that to allow for missing fixed parameters, as is the case during the first period, we use the Optional keyword for the argument of paramfixed in the function declaration.

```
Function ElicesPrice(..., Optional ByVal paramfixed As Variant = 0)
For j = 1 To Nx
    ' f2(k) = ElicesCF(phi,...);
    phi = Complex(x(j), 0)
    weight = w(j)
    cf = ElicesCF(phi,...)
    ' f1(j) = ElicesCF(phi-i,...) / (S*exp((r-q)*Mat));
    cf = ElicesCF(phi_i,...)
    f1 = Complex(cf(1) / den, cf(2) / den)
    int2(j) = cReal(cDiv(cProd(explogK, f2),...)) * weight
    int1(j) = cReal(cDiv(cProd(explogK, f1),...)) * weight
Next j
' Call and put price
P1 = 0.5 + 1 / pi * Sum(int1)
P2 = 0.5 + 1 / pi * Sum(int2)
HestonC = S * Exp(-q * Mat) * P1 - K * Exp(-r * Mat) * P2
HestonP = HestonC - S * Exp(-q * Mat) + K * Exp(-r * Mat)
End Function
```

To illustrate, we use the DJIA puts from the Excel file Ch6DIA introduced in Chapter 6 to estimate the time dependent parameters in the Elices (2009) model.[1] The results are shown in Figure 9.3 and indicate a good fit of the implied volatilities derived from prices generated with time-dependent parameters to the market implied volatilities.

The VBA code and the plots in Figure 9.3 presented in this section are in the Excel file Ch9Elices.xls.

BENHAMOU-MIRI-GOBET MODEL

Benhamou, Gobet, and Miri (BGM, 2010) use a volatility of variance expansion similar to the one employed by Lewis (2000) to derive an expression for the European put price that is not only very fast but also allows for the parameters θ_t, σ_t, and ρ_t to be piecewise constant. The remaining two parameters, v_0 and κ, are assumed constant. Denote the time-t log forward price by $X_t = \ln(Se^{(r-q)\tau})$, where $\tau = T - t$

[1] Parameter estimation with the Elices (2009) is not covered in this book, but is covered in Rouah (2013).

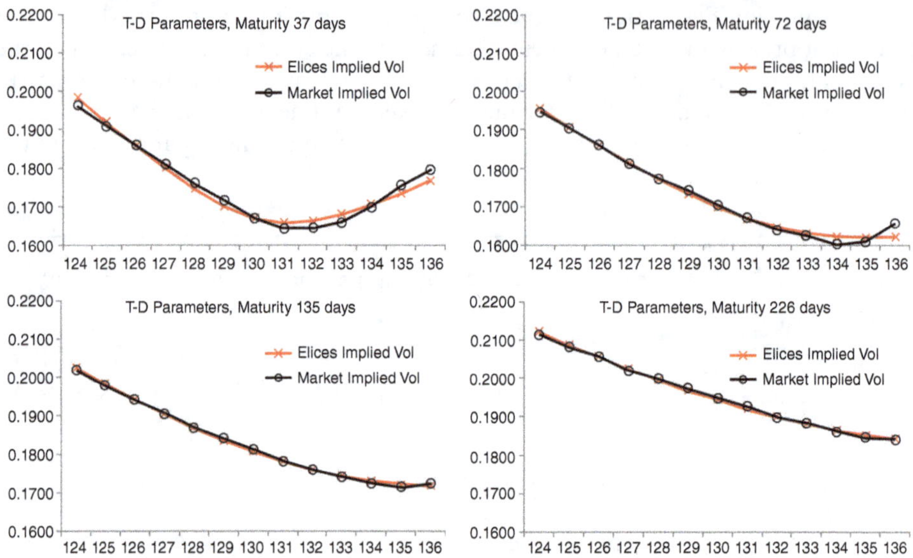

FIGURE 9.3 Implied Volatility from the Elices (2009) Model

is the time to maturity. Applying Itō's Lemma, the bivariate process for the time-dependent Heston model of BGM (2010) is

$$\begin{aligned} dX_t &= -\frac{v_t}{2}dt + \sqrt{v_t}dW_{1,t} \\ dv_t &= \kappa(\theta_t - v_t)dt + \sigma_t\sqrt{v_t}dW_{2,t}, \\ E^{\mathbb{Q}}\left[dW_{1,t}dW_{2,t}\right] &= \rho_t dt \end{aligned} \tag{9.24}$$

where v_0 is the initial variance. Note that in (9.24) only the parameters θ, σ, and ρ are allowed to vary; κ is assumed constant, and v_0 is an unobserved state variable.

BGM (2010) show that the Heston put price can be expressed as the sum of Black-Scholes put price and a set of correction terms, involving derivatives of the put. Assuming a constant rate of interest and dividend yield, the put price can be expressed in terms of the total variance $y = \sigma^2\tau$ and the log-spot price $x = \ln S$ as [2]

$$P_{BS}(x, y) = Ke^{-r\tau}\Phi(f(x, y)) - Se^{-q\tau}\Phi(g(x, y)), \tag{9.25}$$

where

$$\begin{aligned} f(x, y) &= \frac{1}{\sqrt{y}}\left[-x + \ln K - (r - q)T\right] + \frac{\sqrt{y}}{2}, \\ g(x, y) &= \frac{1}{\sqrt{y}}\left[-x + \ln K - (r - q)T\right] - \frac{\sqrt{y}}{2}. \end{aligned}$$

[2] BGM (2010) uses a time-varying interest rate and dividend yield, but we assume that these are constant, for notational simplicity. The generalization to the time-varying versions is straightforward.

The put price in the model appears in Theorem 2.2 of BGM (2010) as

$$\begin{aligned} e^{-r\tau}E^{\mathbb{Q}}[(K-e^{r\tau+X_T})^+] &= P_{BS}(x,\hat{w}_T)+a_{1,T}\frac{\partial^2 P_{BS}}{\partial x\partial y}(x,\hat{w}_T)+a_{2,T}\frac{\partial^3 P_{BS}}{\partial x^2\partial y}(x,\hat{w}_T) \\ &\quad + b_{0,T}\frac{\partial^2 P_{BS}}{\partial y^2}(x,\hat{w}_T)+b_{2,T}\frac{\partial^4 P_{BS}}{\partial x^2\partial y^2}(x,\hat{w}_T), \end{aligned} \tag{9.26}$$

where

$$\hat{w}_T = \int_0^T v_{0,t}dt, \tag{9.27}$$

and

$$v_{0,t} = e^{-\kappa t}\left(v_0 + \int_0^t \theta_s \kappa e^{\kappa s} ds\right). \tag{9.28}$$

The coefficients $a_{1,T}$, $a_{2,T}$, $b_{0,T}$ and $b_{2,T}$ in Equation (9.26) are

$$\begin{aligned} a_{1,T} &= \int_0^T e^{\kappa t}\rho_t\sigma_t v_{0,t}\left(\int_t^T e^{-\kappa u}du\right)dt \\ a_{2,T} &= \int_0^T e^{\kappa t}\rho_t\sigma_t v_{0,t}\left(\int_t^T \rho_s\sigma_s\left(\int_s^T e^{-\kappa u}du\right)ds\right)dt \\ b_{0,T} &= \int_0^T e^{2\kappa t}\sigma_t^2 v_{0,t}\left(\int_t^T e^{-\kappa s}\left(\int_s^T e^{-\kappa u}du\right)ds\right)dt \\ b_{2,T} &= \frac{a_{1,T}^2}{2}. \end{aligned} \tag{9.29}$$

For details, see Benhamou, Gobet, and Miri (2010) or Rouah (2013).

Constant Parameters

If the parameters are assumed constant, then $\theta_t = \theta$, $\sigma_t = \sigma$, and $\rho_t = \rho$. Moving these parameters outside the integrals and evaluating the integrals in, produces the following expressions, which appear in Proposition 2.4 of BGM (2010):

$$\begin{aligned} a_{1,T} &= \frac{\rho\sigma e^{-\kappa T}}{\kappa^2}[v_0(-\kappa T+e^{\kappa T}-1)+\theta(\kappa T+e^{\kappa T}(\kappa T-2)+2)], \\ a_{2,T} &= \frac{\rho^2\sigma^2 e^{-\kappa T}}{2\kappa^3}[v_0(-\kappa T(\kappa T+2)+2e^{\kappa T}-2)+\theta(2e^{\kappa T}(\kappa T-3)+\kappa T(\kappa T+4)+6)], \\ b_{0,T} &= \frac{\sigma^2 e^{-2\kappa T}}{4\kappa^3}[v_0(-4e^{\kappa T}\kappa T+2e^{2\kappa T}-2)+\theta(4e^{\kappa T}(\kappa T+1)+e^{2\kappa T}(2\kappa T-5)+1)], \\ b_{2,T} &= a_{1,T}^2/2. \end{aligned} \tag{9.30}$$

Note that under constant parameters we have

$$v_{0,t} = \theta + (v_0 - \theta)e^{-kt}, \hat{w}_T = (v_0 - \theta)\left(\frac{1 - e^{-\kappa T}}{\kappa}\right) + \theta T, \tag{9.31}$$

so that $\hat{w}_T$ reduces to the form we encountered in Chapter 2. To obtain the put price, we substitute the coefficients from Equation (9.30) into (9.26), using the Black-Scholes derivatives presented at the end of this chapter. The call price is obtained by put-call parity.

As noted by BGM (2010), the put price expansion in Equation (9.26) under constant parameters is identical to the volatility of variance expansion of Lewis (2000) covered in Chapter 4. Indeed, it is straightforward to verify that $a_{1,T} = \sigma J_1(v, T)$, $a_{2,T} = \sigma^2 J_4(v, T)$, and $b_{0,T} = \sigma^2 J_3(v, T)$, and that identical put prices are produced.

The VBA function BGMApproxPrice implements the approximation to the Heston put in (9.26) assuming constant parameters. The function also returns the price of a call obtained by put-call parity.

```
Function BGMApproxPrice(params As Variant, ...) As Double
' Integrated variance
y = (v0 - theta) * (1 - Exp(-kappa * T)) / kappa + theta * T
' Black Scholes Put Price
g = y ^ (-1 / 2) * (-x + Log(Strike) - (rf - q) * T) ...
f = y ^ (-1 / 2) * (-x + Log(Strike) - (rf - q) * T) ...
BSPut = Strike * Exp(-rf * T) * NormSDist(f) ...
' Coefficients for the expansion
a1T = (rho * sigma * ekTm / K ^ 2) * (v0 * (-kT + ekT - 1) ...
a2T = (rho ^ 2 * sigma ^ 2 * ekTm / 2 / K ^ 3) ...
b0T = (sigma ^ 2 * Exp(-2 * kT) / 4 / K ^ 3) ...
b2T = a1T ^ 2 / 2
' Normal pdf evaluated at f and g
Pf = Exp(-f ^ 2 / 2) / Sqr(2 * pi)
Pg = Exp(-g ^ 2 / 2) / Sqr(2 * pi)
' Derivatives of f and g
fy = -1 / 2 / y * g
gx = fx
gy = -1 / 2 / y * f
' The cdf PHI(f) and PHI(g)
PHIf = NormSDist(f)
PHIg = NormSDist(g)
' Derivatives of the pdf phi(f)
Pfx = y ^ (-1 / 2) * f * Pf
Pfy = (1 / 2) / y * f * g * Pf
' Derivatives of the cdf PHI(f)
PHIfxy = (1 / 2) * y ^ (-3 / 2) * Pf * (1 - f * g)
...
PHIfx2y2 = (1 / 2) * ((y ^ (-2) * Pfy - 2 * y ^ (-3) * Pf) ...
```

```
' Derivatives of the pdf phi(g)
Pgx = y ^ (-1 / 2) * g * Pg
Pgy = (1 / 2) / y * f * g * Pg
' Derivatives of cdf PHI(g)
PHIgx = -Pg * y ^ (-1 / 2)
PHIgy = -(1 / 2) * f * Pg / y
...
PHIgx2y2 = (1 / 2) * ((y ^ (-2) * Pgy - 2 * y ^ (-3) * Pg) ...
' Derivatives of Black-Scholes Put
dPdxdy = Strike * Exp(-rf * T) * PHIfxy - Exp(-q * T) ...
dPdx2dy2 = Strike * Exp(-rf * T) * PHIfx2y2 - Exp(-q * T) ...
' Benhamou, Gobet, Miri expansion
PutPrice = BSPut + a1T * dPdxdy + a2T * dPdx2dy + b0T * dPdy2 ...
End Function
```

To illustrate, in Figure 9.4 we reproduce the implied volatilities in Table 3 of BGM (2010).[3] Their tables use $S = 100$, $\theta = 0.06$, $\kappa = 3$, $\sigma = 0.3$, and $\rho = 0$.

The entries in Figure 9.4 are identical to those obtained by BGM (2010) in their Table 3. The VBA code and example presented in this section are in the Excel file Ch9BGMTables34.xls.

Table 3 of Behamou, Gobet, and Miri (2010) -- Implied Volatilities

	Maturity								
Approximate	0.25	0.2306	0.2219	0.2142	0.2119	0.2138	0.2188	0.2219	0.2249
Exact GL-32	0.25	0.2306	0.2216	0.2142	0.2119	0.2138	0.2186	0.2216	0.2245
Approximate	0.5	0.2413	0.2336	0.2257	0.2198	0.2209	0.2279	0.2324	0.2365
Exact GL-32	0.5	0.2437	0.2329	0.2255	0.2199	0.2210	0.2275	0.2317	0.2360
Approximate	1	0.2476	0.2413	0.2314	0.2289	0.2306	0.2371	0.2420	0.2442
Exact GL-32	1	0.2485	0.2406	0.2315	0.2290	0.2306	0.2366	0.2414	0.2438
Approximate	2	0.2485	0.2440	0.2382	0.2361	0.2372	0.2419	0.2450	0.2478
Exact GL-32	2	0.2485	0.2436	0.2382	0.2361	0.2373	0.2416	0.2446	0.2476
Approximate	3	0.2493	0.2456	0.2410	0.2389	0.2398	0.2428	0.2455	0.2475
Exact GL-32	3	0.2495	0.2453	0.2410	0.2389	0.2398	0.2427	0.2453	0.2474
Approximate	5	0.2485	0.2457	0.2420	0.2412	0.2417	0.2439	0.2454	0.2470
Exact GL-32	5	0.2488	0.2456	0.2420	0.2412	0.2417	0.2438	0.2453	0.2469
Approximate	7	0.2510	0.2446	0.2430	0.2422	0.2427	0.2442	0.2455	0.2466
Exact GL-32	7	0.2471	0.2446	0.2430	0.2423	0.2427	0.2442	0.2454	0.2465
Approximate	10	0.2471	0.2451	0.2434	0.2430	0.2434	0.2444	0.2454	0.2462
Exact GL-32	10	0.2476	0.2451	0.2434	0.2430	0.2434	0.2444	0.2453	0.2461

FIGURE 9.4 Implied Volatility from the BGM Model

[3] Note that the prices in Tables 3 and 4 of Benhamou et al. (2010) are those of calls, not puts. We thank Emmanuel Gobet for pointing this out.

Piecewise Constant Parameters

Suppose that there are N maturities $0 = T_0 < T_1 < T_2 < \cdots < T_N < \infty$. BGM (2010) assume that κ and v_0 are constant over $[0, T_N]$, but that θ, σ, and ρ have the piecewise constant values $\theta_{i+1}, \sigma_{i+1}$ and ρ_{i+1} respectively, over the interval $[T_i, T_{i+1}]$. They provide recursive expressions for the price coefficients $a_{1,T_{i+1}}, a_{2,T_{i+1}}$ and $b_{0,T_{i+1}}$ by separating the domain of integration in Equations (9.29) over $(0, T_i)$ and (T_i, T_{i+1}). BGM (2010) thus obtain the recursive relations for the coefficients (using $T_0 = 0$):

$$\begin{aligned}
a_{1,T_{i+1}} &= a_{1,T_i} + \sum_{j=1}^{i} \rho_j\sigma_j \int_{T_{j-1}}^{T_j} e^{\kappa t} v_{0,t} \left(\int_{T_i}^{T_{i+1}} e^{-\kappa u} du \right) dt \\
&\quad + \rho_{i+1}\sigma_{i+1} \int_{T_i}^{T_{i+1}} e^{\kappa t} v_{0,t} \left(\int_{t}^{T_{i+1}} e^{-\kappa u} du \right) dt \\
a_{2,T_{i+1}} &= a_{2,T_i} + \sum_{j=1}^{i} (\rho_j\sigma_j)^2 \int_{T_{j-1}}^{T_j} e^{\kappa t} v_{0,t} \int_{t}^{T_i} \left(\int_{T_i}^{T_{i+1}} e^{-\kappa u} du \right) dsdt \\
&\quad + \sum_{j=1}^{i} (\rho_j\sigma_j)^2 \int_{T_{j-1}}^{T_j} e^{\kappa t} v_{0,t} \int_{T_i}^{T_{i+1}} \left(\int_{s}^{T_{i+1}} e^{-\kappa u} du \right) dsdt, \\
&\quad + (\rho_{i+1}\sigma_{i+1})^2 \int_{T_i}^{T_{i+1}} e^{\kappa t} v_{0,t} \int_{t}^{T_{i+1}} \left(\int_{s}^{T_{i+1}} e^{-\kappa u} du \right) dsdt \\
b_{0,T_{i+1}} &= b_{0,T_i} + \sum_{j=1}^{i} \sigma_j^2 \int_{T_{j-1}}^{T_j} e^{2\kappa t} v_{0,t} \int_{t}^{T_i} e^{-\kappa s} \left(\int_{T_i}^{T_{i+1}} e^{-\kappa u} du \right) dsdt \\
&\quad + \sum_{j=1}^{i} \sigma_j^2 \int_{T_{j-1}}^{T_j} e^{2\kappa t} v_{0,t} \int_{T_i}^{T_{i+1}} e^{-\kappa s} \left(\int_{s}^{T_{i+1}} e^{-\kappa u} du \right) dsdt \\
&\quad + \sigma_{i+1}^2 \int_{T_i}^{T_{i+1}} e^{2\kappa t} v_{0,t} \int_{t}^{T_{i+1}} e^{-\kappa s} \left(\int_{s}^{T_{i+1}} e^{-\kappa u} du \right) dsdt \\
b_{2,T_{i+1}} &= a_{1,T_{i+1}}^2 / 2.
\end{aligned} \tag{9.32}$$

In these expressions, we use the following form for $v_{0,t}$, the piecewise constant version of Equation (9.28):

$$v_{0,t} = e^{-\kappa t} \left(v_0 + \theta_{i+1} \int_0^t \kappa e^{\kappa s} ds \right) = e^{-\kappa t}(v_0 - \theta_{i+1}) + \theta_{i+1}. \tag{9.33}$$

To evaluate the put price under piecewise constant parameters, we first evaluate $a_{1,T_1}, a_{2,T_1}, b_{0,T_1}$ and b_{2,T_1} using Equations (9.30) (the constant parameter case) with parameters κ, v_0, θ_1, σ_1 and ρ_1. We then evaluate $a_{1,T_2}, a_{2,T_2}, b_{0,T_2}$ and b_{2,T_2} using Equation (9.32) with parameters κ, v_0, θ_2, σ_2 and ρ_2, and θ_1, σ_1 and ρ_1. We continue to apply (9.32) until we reach the last maturity T_N, at which point we substitute the coefficients $a_{1,T_N}, a_{2,T_N}, b_{0,T_N}$ and b_{2,T_N} into (9.26) to obtain the put price.

Recall that the parameters κ and v_0 are fixed for all maturities, but θ, σ, and ρ are allowed to vary. To order these in a vector, we choose κ and v_0 in the first two positions, and θ_j, σ_j, and ρ_j (in that order) for the remaining positions. For example, for three maturities, the vector is

$$(\kappa, v_0, \theta_1, \sigma_1, \rho_1, \theta_2, \sigma_2, \rho_2, \theta_3, \sigma_3, \rho_3). \tag{9.34}$$

To implement the price in VBA, it is convenient to break up the sums in the expressions for the coefficients $a_{1,T_{i+1}}$, $a_{2,T_{i+1}}$, and $b_{0,T_{i+1}}$ in Equations (9.32) into the first term of the sum and the remaining terms. For example, $a_{1,T_{i+1}}$ can be written as

$$\begin{aligned} a_{1,T_{i+1}} = a_{1,T_i} &+ \rho_1\sigma_1 \int_0^{T_1} e^{\kappa t} v_{0,t} \left(\int_{T_i}^{T_{i+1}} e^{-\kappa u} du \right) dt \\ &+ \sum_{j=2}^{i} \rho_j\sigma_j \int_{T_{j-1}}^{T_j} e^{\kappa t} v_{0,t} \left(\int_{T_i}^{T_{i+1}} e^{-\kappa u} du \right) dt \\ &+ \rho_{i+1}\sigma_{i+1} \int_{T_i}^{T_{i+1}} e^{\kappa t} v_{0,t} \left(\int_{t}^{T_{i+1}} e^{-\kappa u} du \right) dt. \end{aligned} \tag{9.35}$$

For details, see Benhamou, Gobet, and Miri (2010) or Rouah (2013).

The function BGMApproxPriceTD calculates the approximate put value under piecewise constant maturities. We illustrate the function with the code for the coefficient $a_{1,T_{i+1}}$ in (9.35). The code for the other coefficients is similar. The beginning of the function stacks the parameters in the order specified by (9.34) and calculates the first component of the coefficients, corresponding to the first time step. The first component is the term a_{1,T_i} in (9.35), obtained using (9.30).

```
Function BGMApproxPriceTD(params As Variant, ...) As Double
' [kappa v0 | theta(1) sigma(1) rho(1) | theta(2) sigma(2) rho(2) | etc..]
' Create a vector of all the parameters
kappa = params(1)
v0 = params(2)
For i = 3 To Nparam Step 3
    j = Floor(i / 3, 1)
    theta(j) = params(i)
    sigma(j) = params(i + 1)
    rho(j) = params(i + 2)
Next i
' First set of coefficients
a1T(1) = -rho(1) * sigma(1) * (2 * theta(1) * Exp(kappa * T(1))...
a2T(1) = -1 / 2 * rho(1) ^ 2 * sigma(1) ^ 2 * (kappa ^ 2 * v0 ...
b0T(1) = -1 / 4 * sigma(1) ^ 2 * (5 * theta(1) * Exp(kappa * T(1))...
b2T(1) = a1T(1) ^ 2 / 2
```

The second part calculates the remaining portion of the coefficients. The terms A1 correspond to the integrals in (9.35), in the same order.

```
' Remaining sets of coefficients
If NT >= 2 Then
    For i = 1 To NT - 1
        A1 = A1 + rho(j) * sigma(j) ...
        a1T(i + 1) = a1T(i) + Sum(A1)
        A2 = A2 - rho(j) ^ 2 * sigma(j) ^ 2 ...
        a2T(i + 1) = a2T(i) + A2
        B0 = B0 - 1 / 4 * sigma(j) ^ 2 * (-Exp(-2 * kappa * T(i)) ...
        b0T(i + 1) = b0T(i) + B0
        b2T(i + 1) = a1T(i + 1) * a1T(i + 1) / 2
    Next i
End If
```

The third and final part retains the last element of the arrays for the coefficients, calculates the required derivatives, and calculates the put price in Equation (9.26). The function returns the call price by put-call parity.

```
' Integrated variance
wT = (v0 - theta(NT)) * (1 - Exp(-kappa * T(NT))) ...
y = wT
' Black Scholes Put Price
g = y ^ (-1 / 2) * (-x + Log(K) - (rf - q) * T(NT)) - ...
f = y ^ (-1 / 2) * (-x + Log(K) - (rf - q) * T(NT)) + ...
BSPut = K * Exp(-rf * T(NT)) * normcdf(f) - S ...
' Derivatives of the pdf phi(g)
phigx_pdf = y ^ (-1 / 2) * g * phig_pdf
phigy_pdf = (1 / 2) / y * f * g * phig_pdf
' Benhamou, Gobet, Miri expansion
PutPrice = BSPut + AA1T * dPdxdy + AA2T * dPdx2dy ....
' Return the put or the call by put-call parity
If PutCall = "P" Then
    BGMApproxPriceTD = PutPrice
ElseIf PutCall = "C" Then
    BGMApproxPriceTD = PutPrice - K * Exp(-rf * T(NT)) ...
End If
End Function
```

To illustrate pricing with time-dependent parameters in the model of BGM (2010), we reproduce the at-the-money ($K = 100$) put prices in their Table 8.

BGM (2010) Approximate Heston Prices Under Piece-Wise Constant Parameters

Option Features	
Spot Price (S)	100
Strike Price (K)	100
Risk free rate (r)	0
Dividend (q)	0
Flavor (P or C)	C
Trap (0=Heston, 1=Albrecher)	1
Heston Parameters	
kappa (κ)	3
theta (θ)	
sigma (σ)	
v0	0.04
rho (ρ)	
Settings for Bisection Algorithm	
Lower Limit for IV	0.01
Upper Limit for IV	2
Tolerance	1.00E-04
Maximum Iterations	1000

Maturity	Heston Closed Avg. Params (a)	BGM VBA Piecewise (b)	BGM True Price Piecewise (c)
0.25	3.93	3.93	3.93
0.5	5.53	5.54	5.53
1	7.84	7.80	7.85
2	11.23	11.11	11.23
3	13.92	13.78	13.92
5	18.35	18.24	18.37
7	22.13	21.99	22.15
10	27.14	26.77	27.17

(a) Heston closed form with averaged parameters
(b) BGM (2010) model with piecewise constant parameters, values from VBA function
(c) BGM (2010) model with piecewise constant parameters, values from their paper

t	T(t)	theta(t)	sigma(t)	rho(t)	Pw Price
1	0.250	0.0400	0.3000	-0.2000	3.9265
2	0.500	0.0405	0.3050	-0.1965	5.5404
3	0.750	0.0410	0.3100	-0.1930	6.7625
4	1.000	0.0415	0.3150	-0.1895	7.7988
5	1.250	0.0420	0.3200	-0.1860	8.7229
6	1.500	0.0425	0.3250	-0.1825	9.5703
7	1.750	0.0430	0.3300	-0.1790	10.3610
8	2.000	0.0435	0.3350	-0.1755	11.1074
9	2.250	0.0440	0.3400	-0.1720	11.8177
10	2.500	0.0445	0.3450	-0.1685	12.4979
11	2.750	0.0450	0.3500	-0.1650	13.1521
12	3.000	0.0455	0.3550	-0.1615	13.7837
13	3.250	0.0460	0.3600	-0.1580	14.3951
14	3.500	0.0465	0.3650	-0.1545	14.9884
15	3.750	0.0470	0.3700	-0.1510	15.5653
16	4.000	0.0475	0.3750	-0.1475	16.1270
17	4.250	0.0480	0.3800	-0.1440	16.6747
18	4.500	0.0485	0.3850	-0.1405	17.2094
19	4.750	0.0490	0.3900	-0.1370	17.7320
20	5.000	0.0495	0.3950	-0.1335	18.2432
21	5.250	0.0500	0.4000	-0.1300	18.7437

FIGURE 9.5 Time-Varying Parameters

First, we construct the piecewise parameters across 40 time periods. This appears as columns L through P in Figure 9.5.

Column Q contains the BGM (2010) put price, using the VBA function BGMApproxPriceTD described earlier. These prices use the fixed parameters κ and v_0 in columns R and S, respectively, and past parameter values θ_t, σ_t, and ρ_t in column T and beyond. Selecting only the required maturities, we obtain the prices in column H. The prices in column G are the Heston closed-form put prices, but using the averaged parameter values in rows 27 through 31 of Figure 9.5. Finally, the prices in column I are taken directly from BGM (2010).

The VBA code in this section and the screen shot in Figure 9.5 are from the Excel file Ch9BGMTable8.xls.

BLACK-SCHOLES DERIVATIVES

To obtain the approximated put price of BGM (2010) in Equation (9.26), we need high-order derivatives of the Black-Scholes put. The derivative of the standard normal density $\phi(x) = e^{-x^2/2}/\sqrt{2\pi}$ is $\phi_x(x) = -x\phi(x)$. It is easy to verify the derivatives $f_x = g_x = -y^{-1/2}$, $g_y = -\frac{1}{2}y^{-1}f$ and $f_y = -\frac{1}{2}y^{-1}g$.

For the derivatives of $\Phi(f)$ and $\phi(f)$, we have $\Phi(f)_x = -\phi(f)y^{-1/2}$, $\phi(f)_x = y^{-1/2}f\phi(f)$, $\phi(f)_y = \frac{1}{2}y^{-1}fg\phi(f)$, $\Phi(f)_{xy} = \frac{1}{2}y^{-3/2}\phi(f)(1-fg)$, and

$$\Phi(f)_{x^2y} = \frac{1}{2y^2}\phi(f)[2f + g - f^2g],$$

$$\Phi(f)_{y^2} = \frac{1}{2y^2}\phi(f)\left(g + \frac{1}{2}f - \frac{1}{2}fg^2\right),$$

$$\Phi(f)_{y^2x^2} = \frac{1}{2}[(y^{-2}\phi_y - 2y^{-3}\phi)(2f + g - f^2g) + y^{-2}\phi(2f_y + g_y - 2f_yfg - f^2g_y)].$$

Similarly, for derivatives involving $\Phi(g)$ and $\phi(g)$, we have $\Phi(g)_x = -\phi(g)y^{-1/2}$, $\Phi(g)_y = -\frac{1}{2}f\phi(g)y^{-1}$, $\phi(g)_x = y^{-1/2}g\phi(g)$, $\phi(g)_y = \frac{1}{2}y^{-1}fg\phi(g)$, $\Phi(g)_{xy} = \frac{1}{2}y^{-3/2}\phi(g)(1-fg)$, and

$$\begin{aligned}
\Phi(g)_{x^2y} &= \frac{1}{2y^2}\phi(g)[2g+f-fg^2],\\
\Phi(g)_{y^2} &= \frac{1}{2}y^{-2}\phi(g)\left(f+\frac{1}{2}g-\frac{1}{2}f^2g\right),\\
\Phi(g)_{xy^2} &= \frac{1}{4y^2}[\phi(g)_x(2f+g-f^2g)+\phi(g)(2f_x+g_x-f_xgf-f^2g_x)],\\
\Phi(g)_{y^2x^2} &= y\frac{1}{2}[(y^{-2}\phi_y-2y^{-3}\phi)(2g+f-fg^2)+y^{-2}\phi(2g_y+f_y-2fgg_y-g^2f_y)].
\end{aligned}$$

The required derivatives of the Black-Scholes put are therefore

$$\begin{aligned}
\frac{\partial^2 P_{BS}}{\partial x\partial y} &= Ke^{-r\tau}\Phi(f)_{xy} - e^{-q\tau}e^x[\Phi(g)_y+\Phi(g)_{xy}],\\
\frac{\partial^3 P_{BS}}{\partial x^2\partial y} &= Ke^{-r\tau}\Phi(f)_{x^2y} - e^{-q\tau}e^x[\Phi(g)_y+2\Phi(g)_{xy}+\Phi(g)_{x^2y}],\\
\frac{\partial^2 P_{BS}}{\partial y^2} &= Ke^{-r\tau}\Phi(f)_{yy} - e^{-q\tau}e^x\Phi(g)_{yy},\\
\frac{\partial^4 P_{BS}}{\partial x^2\partial y^2} &= Ke^{-r\tau}\Phi(f)_{x^2y^2}\\
&\quad -e^{-q\tau}e^x[\Phi(g)_y+2\Phi(g)_{xy}+\Phi(g)_{x^2y}+\Phi(g)_{yy}+2\Phi(g)_{xy^2}+\Phi(g)_{x^2y^2}].
\end{aligned}$$

CONCLUSION

In this chapter, we have shown that the univariate characteristic function for x_T and the bivariate characteristic function for (x_T, v_T) are identical in form except for the coefficients in each function. What differentiates the coefficients is solely the initial condition for the Riccati equation that is solved to obtain them. We have also shown that the univariate characteristic function is a special case of the bivariate characteristic function. Next, we have presented the time-dependent parameter models of Mikhailov and Nögel (2003) and Elices (2009). Both of these models rely on a recursive relation on the bivariate characteristic function illustrated by Kahl and Lord (2010). Finally, we have presented the model of BGM (2010), which relies on an analytic expansion to obtain prices under time-dependent parameters. As such, it produces option prices much faster than either of the other two time-dependent models covered in this chapter.

It is possible to use market data to estimate the piecewise parameters in the models covered in this chapter. Estimation of time-varying models is slow, however, and is not covered in this book. For details, coding, and examples of time-varying parameter estimation with the models in this chapter, see Rouah (2013).

In Chapter 8, we introduced the explicit method and we explained that it is an example of methods that approximate the Heston partial differential equation (PDE) with finite differences. We also saw in that chapter that these methods produce a set of option prices along a two-dimensional grid of stock prices and volatility, and not solely for a single value of stock price and volatility. The literature on finite difference methods in option pricing is rich and varied, and we present several popular methods in the next chapter.

CHAPTER 10

Methods for Finite Differences

Abstract

In this chapter, we present methods to obtain the European call price by solving the Heston PDE along a two-dimensional grid representing the stock price and the volatility. We first show how to construct uniform and nonuniform grids for the discretization of the stock price and the volatility, and present formulas for finite difference approximations to the derivatives in the Heston PDE. We then present the weighted method, a popular method that includes the implicit scheme, explicit scheme, and Crank-Nicolson scheme as special cases. We encountered the explicit scheme earlier, when we applied this method to the pricing of American options. Next, we explain the boundary conditions of the PDE for a European call. Finally, we present the alternating direction implicit (ADI) method, which produces accurate results with very few time points. The methods can easily be modified to allow for the pricing of European puts, which requires a reformulation of the boundary conditions. In many cases, however, it is simpler to use put-call parity to obtain the put price.

finite difference, partial differential equation, boundary condition, uniform grid, nonuniform grid, weighted method, explicit method, ADI scheme, Crank-Nicolson scheme

In this chapter, we present methods to obtain the European call price by solving the Heston PDE along a two-dimensional grid representing the stock price and the volatility. We first show how to construct uniform and nonuniform grids for the discretization of the stock price and the volatility, and present formulas for finite difference approximations to the derivatives in the Heston PDE. We then present the weighted method, a popular method that includes the implicit scheme, explicit scheme, and Crank-Nicolson scheme as special cases. We encountered the explicit scheme briefly in Chapter 8, when we applied this method to the pricing of American options. Next, we explain the boundary conditions of the PDE for a European call. Finally, we present the alternating direction implicit (ADI) method, which produces accurate results with very few time points. The methods can easily be modified to allow for the pricing of European puts, which requires a reformulation of the boundary conditions. In many cases, however, it is simpler to use put-call parity to obtain the put price.

THE PDE IN TERMS OF AN OPERATOR

The Heston partial differential equation (PDE) for the value $U(S, v, t)$ of an option on a dividend-paying stock, when the spot price is S, the volatility is v, and the maturity is t, is

$$\begin{aligned}\frac{\partial U}{\partial t} &= \frac{1}{2}vS^2\frac{\partial^2 U}{\partial S^2} + \rho\sigma vS\frac{\partial^2 U}{\partial v\partial S} + \frac{1}{2}\sigma^2 v\frac{\partial^2 U}{\partial v^2} \\ &\quad - rU + (r-q)S\frac{\partial U}{\partial S} + \kappa(\theta - v)\frac{\partial U}{\partial v}.\end{aligned} \tag{10.1}$$

Using $U(t) = U(S, v, t)$ as compact notation we can express the PDE as

$$\frac{\partial U}{\partial t} = LU(t), \tag{10.2}$$

where the operator L is defined as

$$L = \frac{1}{2}vS^2\frac{\partial^2}{\partial S^2} + \frac{1}{2}\sigma^2 v\frac{\partial^2}{\partial v^2} + \rho\sigma vS\frac{\partial^2}{\partial v\partial S} + (r-q)S\frac{\partial}{\partial S} + \kappa(\theta - v)\frac{\partial}{\partial v} - r. \tag{10.3}$$

Finite difference methods are techniques to find a numerical approximation to the PDE. To implement finite differences, we first need a discretization grid for the two state variables (the stock price and the variance), and a discretization grid for the maturity. These grids can have equally or unequally spaced increments. Second, we need discrete approximations to the continuous derivatives that appear in the PDE. Finally, we need a finite difference methodology to solve the PDE.

BUILDING GRIDS

Uniform grids are those that have equally spaced increments for the two state variables. They have two advantages: (1) they are easy to construct; and (2) since the increments are equal, the finite difference approximations to the derivatives in the PDE take on a simple form. Nonuniform grids are more complicated to construct, and the finite difference approximations to the derivatives are more complicated. They are, however, often preferable since they produce more accurate prices with fewer grid points and, consequently, with less computation time.

We denote the maximum values of (S, v, t) as $(S_{max}, v_{max}, t_{max})$ with $t_{max} = \tau$ (the maturity), and the minimum values as $(S_{min}, v_{min}, t_{min})$ with $t_{min} = 0$. We denote by $U^n_{i,j} = U(S_i, v_j, t_n)$ the value of a European call at time t_n when the stock price is S_i and the volatility is v_j. We use $N_S + 1$ points for the stock price, $N_V + 1$ points for the volatility, and $N_T + 1$ points for the maturity. For convenience, sometimes we write simply $U(S_i, v_j)$ for $U^n_{i,j}$.

Using the minimum values $S_{\min} = v_{\min} = 0$, a uniform grid for (S, v, t) can be constructed as

$$\begin{aligned} S_i &= i \times ds, \quad i = 0, 1, \ldots, N_S, \\ v_j &= j \times dv, \quad j = 0, 1, \ldots, N_V, \\ t_n &= n \times dt, \quad n = 0, 1, \ldots, N_T, \end{aligned} \tag{10.4}$$

where the increments are $ds = (S_{\max} - S_{\min})/N_S$, $dv = (v_{\max} - v_{\min})/N_V$, and $dt = (t_{\max} - t_{\min})/N_T$. The maximum values are therefore $S_{\max} = N_S ds$ and $v_{\max} = N_V dv$.

Building on the work of Clarke and Parrott (1999) and Kluge (2002), In'T Hout and Foulon (2010) describe a nonuniform grid that is finer around the strike price K and around the spot volatility $v_0 = 0$. Their grid of size $N_S + 1$ for the stock price is

$$S_i = K + c \sinh(\xi_i), \quad i = 0, 1, \ldots, N_S,$$

where they select $c = K/5$, and where $\xi_i = \sinh^{-1}(-K/c) + i\Delta\xi$, with

$$\Delta\xi = \frac{1}{N_S}\left[\sinh^{-1}\left(\frac{S_{\max} - K}{c}\right) - \sinh^{-1}\left(-\frac{K}{c}\right)\right].$$

The grid of size $N_V + 1$ for the volatility is

$$v_j = d \sinh(j\Delta\eta), \quad j = 0, 1, \ldots, N_V,$$

with $\Delta\eta = \sinh^{-1}(V_{\max}/d)/N_V$. In'T Hout and Foulon (2010) use $d = V_{\max}/500$, and a uniform grid for t. Figure 10.1 illustrates a nonuniform grid using their settings, along with $N_S = 70$, $N_V = 50$ and $K = 10$. The grid for the stock price is represented by blue lines, and the volatility by red lines. Note that in the stock price dimension,

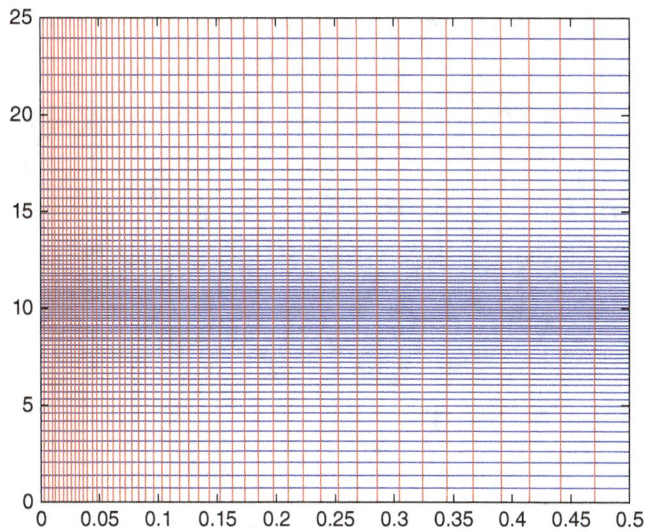

FIGURE 10.1 Nonuniform Grid

the grid is finest around the strike price, while in the volatility dimension, the grid becomes finer as we progress toward zero.

The BuildGrid function is used throughout this chapter to construct uniform and nonuniform grids.

```
Function BuildGrid(..., GridType As String, output As String)
As Variant
' Increments for the maturity, stock price, volatility
dt = (Tmax - Tmin) / (NT - 1)
ds = (Smax - Smin) / (NS - 1)
dv = (Vmax - Vmin) / (NV - 1)
' Maturity grid
For j = 0 To NT - 1
    Mat(j + 1) = j * dt
Next j
If GridType = "Uniform" Then
    ' The stock price grid
    For j = 0 To NS - 1
        Spot(j + 1) = j * ds
    Next j
    For j = 1 To NV - 1
        Vol(j + 1) = j * dv
    Next j
ElseIf GridType = "NonUniform" Then
    C = K / 5
    dz = 1 / (NS - 1) * (Asinh((Smax - K) / C) - Asinh(-K / C))
    For i = 1 To NS
        Z(i) = Asinh(-K / C) + (i - 1) * dz
        Spot(i) = K + C * Sinh(Z(i))
    Next i
    ' The volatility grid
    d = Vmax / 10
    dn = Asinh(Vmax / d) / (NV - 1)
    For j = 1 To NV
        N(j) = (j - 1) * dn
        Vol(j) = d * Sinh(N(j))
    Next j
End If
' Output the grid of choice
If output = "Spot" Then
    For j = 1 To NS
        output2(j) = Spot(j)
    Next j
ElseIf output = "Vol" Then
    For j = 1 To NV
        output2(j) = Vol(j)
    Next j
ElseIf output = "Mat" Then
    For j = 1 To NT
        output2(j) = Mat(j)
    Next j
End If
BuildGrid = output2
End Function
```

FINITE DIFFERENCE APPROXIMATION OF DERIVATIVES

Recall that we use the notation $U^n_{i,j}$, $U(S_i, v_j, t_n)$, or $U(S_i, v_j)$ to represent the value of a European option at time t_n when the stock price is S_i and the volatility is v_j. Whenever possible throughout this book, we use central difference approximations to the first- and second-order derivatives in the S and v directions in the PDE for $U^n_{i,j}$ in Equation (10.1). In general, first- and second-order derivatives of $U^n_{i,j}$ at a point (S_i, v_j) on the grid can be written in terms of sums of values of U at points adjacent to (S_i, v_j).

In the following paragraphs, we express the central difference approximation to the derivatives assuming a nonuniform grid. The approximations under a uniform grid arise as a special case and reduce the expressions to much simpler forms. We treat the approximations for the interior and boundary points of the PDE separately.

Interior points lie on the interior of the grid, so they are off the boundary. The first-order derivatives approximated with central differences for an interior point (S_i, v_j) are

$$\frac{\partial U}{\partial S}(S_i, v_j) = \frac{U^n_{i+1,j} - U^n_{i-1,j}}{S_{i+1} - S_{i-1}}, \quad \frac{\partial U}{\partial v}(S_i, v_j) = \frac{U^n_{i,j+1} - U^n_{i,j-1}}{v_{j+1} - v_{j-1}}, \tag{10.5}$$

When uniform grids are used, the denominators are replaced by $2ds$ and $2dv$, respectively. The central differences for second-order derivatives are in Table 4.1 of Kluge (2002) and also in In'T Hout and Foulon (2010). These are

$$\frac{\partial^2 U}{\partial S^2}(S_i, v_j) = \frac{U^n_{i-1,j}}{(S_i - S_{i-1})(S_{i+1} - S_{i-1})} - \frac{2U^n_{i,j}}{(S_i - S_{i-1})(S_{i+1} - S_i)} + \frac{U^n_{i+1,j}}{(S_{i+1} - S_i)(S_{i+1} - S_{i-1})},$$

and

$$\frac{\partial^2 U}{\partial v^2}(S_i, v_j) = \frac{U^n_{i,j-1}}{(v_j - v_{j-1})(v_{j+1} - v_{j-1})} - \frac{2U^n_{i,j}}{(v_j - v_{j-1})(v_{j+1} - v_j)} + \frac{U^n_{i,j+1}}{(v_{j+1} - v_j)(v_{j+1} - v_{j-1})}.$$

When uniform grids are used, the denominators are replaced by $(ds)^2$ and $(dv)^2$, respectively, and the resulting expressions are much simpler. Finally, the mixed derivative of an interior point appears in Table 4.4 of Kluge (2002) as

$$\begin{aligned}\frac{\partial^2 U}{\partial S \partial v}(S_i, v_j) &= a_{-1,-1} U^n_{i-1,j-1} + a_{-1,0} U^n_{i-1,j} + a_{-1,1} U^n_{i-1,j+1} \\ &\quad + a_{0,-1} U^n_{i,j-1} + a_{0,0} U^n_{i,j} + a_{0,1} U^n_{i,j+1} \\ &\quad + a_{1,-1} U^n_{i+1,j-1} + a_{1,0} U^n_{i+1,j} + a_{1,1} U^n_{i+1,j+1}.\end{aligned} \tag{10.6}$$

The $a_{,}$ coefficients are available in Kluge (2002) or Rouah (2013). Other, simpler expressions for the second-order derivatives also work but are not as accurate. We do not present them here.

When the grid is uniform, the mixed derivative in Equation (10.6) reduces to the much simpler form

$$\frac{\partial^2 U}{\partial S \partial v}(S_i, v_j) = \frac{U^n_{i+1,j+1} + U^n_{i-1,j-1} - U^n_{i-1,j+1} - U^n_{i+1,j-1}}{4dsdv}. \tag{10.7}$$

See Kluge (2002) or Burden and Faires (2010) for details. On the boundary points of the PDE, which are defined later in the next section, we need to use approximations that do not involve points off the grid. Hence, we can use forward or backward differences. For the first-order S-derivative, for example, the differences are, respectively,

$$\frac{\partial U}{\partial S}(S_i, v_j) = \frac{U^n_{i+1,j} - U^n_{i,j}}{S_{i+1} - S_i}, \quad \frac{\partial U}{\partial S}(S_i, v_j) = \frac{U^n_{i,j} - U^n_{i,j-1}}{S_i - S_{i-1}}. \tag{10.8}$$

The textbook by Duffy (2006) is also an excellent reference for finite difference approximations to PDEs in the context of option pricing.

BOUNDARY CONDITIONS FOR THE PDE

Boundary conditions for the PDE in Equation (10.1) for a European call are explained by Heston (1993) and by In'T Hout and Foulon (2010), among others. We describe them for a European call option as follows:

- *Boundary condition at maturity.* At maturity ($t = 0$) the value of the call is its intrinsic value (the payoff):

$$U(S_i, v_j, 0) = \max(0, S_i - K).$$

  This implies that the boundary condition for $t = 0$ is $U^0_{i,j} = (S_i - K)^+$ for $i = 0, 1, \ldots, N_S$ and $j = 0, 1, \ldots, N_V$.
- *Boundary condition for $S = S_{\min}$.* When $S = S_{\min} = 0$, the call is worthless. Hence, we have $U(0, v_j, t_n) = 0$ and the boundary condition is $U^n_{0,j} = 0$ for $n = 0, \ldots, N_T$ and $j = 0, 1, \ldots, N_V$.
- *Boundary condition for $S = S_{\max}$.* As S becomes large, delta for the call option approaches 1. Hence, for $S = S_{\max}$, we have

$$\frac{\partial U}{\partial S}(S_{\max}, v_j, t_n) = 1.$$

  The boundary condition for $S_{\max}$ is, therefore, $U^n_{N_S,j} = S_{\max}$ for $n = 0, \ldots, N_T$ and $j = 0, \ldots, N_V$.
- *Boundary condition for $v = v_{\max}$.* When v becomes large, we have $U(S_i, v_{\max}, t_n) = S_i$. The boundary condition for $v_{\max}$ is, therefore, $U^n_{i,N_V} = S_i$ for $n = 0, \ldots, N_T$, and $i = 0, \ldots, N_S$. At $v_{\max}$ we have $U = S_i$ and, therefore, $\partial U/\partial S = 1$.

- *Boundary Condition for $v = v_{\min}$.* When $v = v_{\min} = 0$, the boundary condition is a little more complicated. When $v = 0$ the PDE in (10.1) becomes

$$\frac{\partial U}{\partial t} = -rU + (r-q)S\frac{\partial U}{\partial S} + \kappa\theta\frac{\partial U}{\partial v}.$$

We can use central differences for $\partial U/\partial S$:

$$\frac{\partial U}{\partial S}(S_i, 0, t_n) = \frac{U^n_{i+1,0} - U^n_{i-1,0}}{S_{i+1} - S_{i-1}}$$

but for $\partial U/\partial v$, we must use forward differences, for example, the simple form

$$\frac{\partial U}{\partial S}(S_i, 0, t_n) = \frac{U^n_{i,1} - U^n_{i,0}}{v_1}$$

since $v_0 = 0$. Remember that in this context we are using v_0 to denote the first point on the grid for the variance, and not the Heston parameter for the spot variance.

For an explanation of how the boundary conditions affect the construction of **L** and its submatrices, see Rouah (2013).

THE WEIGHTED METHOD

This is a general method that incorporates other finite difference schemes as special cases. Recall that $U^n_{i,j}$ denotes the value of the European call at the grid points (S_i, v_j) and at maturity t_n. Since the two-dimensional grid for (S, v) is of size $N = (N_S + 1)(N_V + 1)$, at each t_n there are N possible values for $U^n_{i,j}$, as indicated in Figure 10.2.

To apply the weighted method, we must construct a vector $\mathbf{U}^n$ of size N with these values, arranged in any way we like. We choose to stack the N_V column vectors $\mathbf{u}_0, \mathbf{u}_1, \mathbf{u}_2 \ldots, \mathbf{u}_{N_V}$ in Figure 10.2 on top of one another, so that $\mathbf{U}^n =$

S-direction \ v-direction	v_0	v_1	$\cdots$	v_{N_V}
S_0	$U^n_{0,0}$	$U^n_{0,1}$	$\cdots$	U^n_{0,N_V}
S_1	$U^n_{1,0}$	$U^n_{1,1}$	$\cdots$	U^n_{1,N_V}
$\vdots$	$\vdots$	$\vdots$	$\cdots$	$\vdots$
S_{N_S}	$U^n_{N_S,0}$	$U^n_{N_S,1}$	$\cdots$	$U^n_{N_S,N_V}$

FIGURE 10.2 Value of the European Call along the Stock Price and Variance Grids

$(\mathbf{u}_0^T, \mathbf{u}_1^T, \ldots, \mathbf{u}_{N_V}^T)^T$ is our vector. The entries of $\mathbf{U}^n$ therefore correspond to the following (S_i, v_j) points

$$\underbrace{(S_0,v_0),(S_1,v_0),\ldots,(S_{NS},v_0)}_{\text{Values of } S \text{ for } v_0},\ \underbrace{(S_0,v_1),(S_1,v_1),\ldots,(S_{NS},v_1)}_{\text{Values of } S \text{ for } v_1},\ \ldots,$$
$$\underbrace{(S_0,v_{NV-1}),(S_1,v_{NV-1}),\ldots,(S_{NS},v_{NV-1})}_{\text{Values of } S \text{ for } v_{NV-1}},\ \underbrace{(S_0,v_{NV}),(S_1,v_{NV}),\ldots,(S_{NS},v_{NV})}_{\text{Values of } S \text{ for } v_{NV}}. \qquad (10.9)$$

The weighted method, also called the θ-method, is defined via the relationship

$$\frac{\mathbf{U}^{n+1} - \mathbf{U}^n}{dt} = \mathbf{L}\left(\theta\mathbf{U}^{n+1} + (1-\theta)\mathbf{U}^n\right), \qquad (10.10)$$

where $\mathbf{L}$ is a sparse matrix of dimension $N \times N$. This matrix is based on the operator defined in Equation (10.3). The initial condition $\mathbf{U}^0$ is known, since it represents the value of the call at expiry. Hence, we can work from expiry, starting with the initial value $\mathbf{U}^0$, and we use $\mathbf{L}$ to obtain $\mathbf{U}^1$, $\mathbf{U}^2$, and so forth, until we reach $\mathbf{U}^{N_T}$. This is done by solving, at each time, the system

$$\left(\mathbf{I} - \theta dt\mathbf{L}\right)\mathbf{U}^{n+1} = \left(\mathbf{I} + (1-\theta)dt\mathbf{L}\right)\mathbf{U}^n, \qquad (10.11)$$

where $\mathbf{I}$ is the identity matrix of size N. The system can be solved by taking the inverse of the matrix on the left-hand side, so that

$$\mathbf{U}^{n+1} = \left(\mathbf{I} - \theta dt\mathbf{L}\right)^{-1}\left(\mathbf{I} + (1-\theta)dt\mathbf{L}\right)\mathbf{U}^n. \qquad (10.12)$$

The composition of $\mathbf{U}^0$ depends on the option being priced. For a call option, it will contain $S - K$ in the components of $\mathbf{U}$ that correspond to $S > K$, and zero in the components that correspond to $S < K$. The order in which these appear in the vector will depend on how the components of $\mathbf{U}$ are arranged.

A number of finite difference schemes arise as a special case of Equation (10.11), depending on the value of θ. Setting $\theta = 0$ produces the explicit scheme, $\theta = \frac{1}{2}$ produces the Crank-Nicolson scheme, and $\theta = 1$ produces the implicit scheme. See Kluge (2002) for details of a general derivation of the weighted method, and a discussion of the numerical difficulties that can arise when N is large. The explicit Euler scheme is the simplest to deal with numerically because when we set $\theta = 0$ in (10.12), we no longer need to invert a matrix.

The $\mathbf{L}$ matrix is a square matrix of dimension $N = (N_S + 1)(N_V + 1)$, with rows and columns that depend on how the vector $\mathbf{U}^n$ is constructed. Since we have constructed $\mathbf{U}^n$ by stacking the N_V column vectors $\mathbf{u}_0, \mathbf{u}_1, \ldots, \mathbf{u}_{N_V}$ from Figure 10.2 on top of one another, the row and columns of $\mathbf{L}$ correspond to the entries of the vector $\mathbf{U}^n$ in (10.9).

We modify the matrix **L** for the operator L in Equation (10.3) by separating $\partial/\partial v$ in L into two components:

$$L = \frac{1}{2}vS^2\frac{\partial^2}{\partial S^2} + \frac{1}{2}\sigma^2 v\frac{\partial^2}{\partial v^2} + \rho\sigma vS\frac{\partial^2}{\partial v\partial S} + (r-q)S\frac{\partial}{\partial S} + \kappa\theta\frac{\partial}{\partial v} - \kappa v\frac{\partial}{\partial v} - r. \tag{10.13}$$

It is preferable to construct the submatrices of **L** (namely, the submatrices for the first- and second-order derivatives) without the Heston parameters, and add the parameters later when we construct **L** from its submatrices. In this way, we can construct the submatrices once, and then obtain **L** for any values of the Heston parameters we desire. Note that, to separate the Heston parameters from the construction of the submatrices, two separate matrices are required for $\partial/\partial v$, as indicated in (10.13).

To summarize, we construct the following submatrices:

$\mathbf{L}_{SS}$ for $vS^2\frac{\partial^2}{\partial S^2}$, $\mathbf{L}_{vv}$ for $v\frac{\partial^2}{\partial v^2}$, $\mathbf{L}_{vS}$ for $vS\frac{\partial^2}{\partial v\partial S}$

$\mathbf{L}_S$ for $S\frac{\partial}{\partial S}$, $\mathbf{L}_{v1}$ for $\frac{\partial}{\partial v}$, $\mathbf{L}_{v2}$ for $v\frac{\partial}{\partial v}$, and **I** for r.

Coding the submatrices of **L** in a programming language is tricky, since some values adjacent to a point (S_i, v_j) on the grid in Figure 10.2 will no longer be adjacent in the v-direction when we arrange the grid into the vector $\mathbf{U}^n$, although they will still be adjacent in the S-direction. Hence, we lose the convenient indexing of having $U^n_{i,j}$ represented in a two-dimensional grid. See Rouah (2013) for a very detailed example of how the vector $\mathbf{U}^n$ and the matrix **L** are constructed.

The VBA function BuildDerivatives is a lengthy program that creates the submatrices of **L**. It requires three grids as inputs for the stock price, volatility, and maturity, all obtained from the BuildGrid function described earlier. It assumes that these are built using uniform grids. The first section arranges the vectors into stacks and identifies the elements of **U** that correspond to boundary points for S and v.

```
Function BuildDerivatives(...) As Variant
' Build the grids
Spot = BuildGrid(..., "Uniform", "Spot")
Vol =  BuildGrid(..., "Uniform", "Vol")
Mat =  BuildGrid(..., "Uniform", "Mat")
' Identification of the boundary points
' Vmin and Vmax
For s = 1 To NS - 1
    VminB(s) = 1
Next s
For s = N - NS + 2 To N
    VmaxB(s) = 1
```

```
Next s
' Smin and Smax
For s = NS + 1 To N
    If (s Mod NS = 0) And (s <> N) Then
        SmaxB(s) = 1    ' Indices for Smax
    End If
    If (s Mod NS = 1) And (s <> 1) Then
        SminB(s) = 1    ' Indices for Smin
    End If
Next s
```

The second section identifies non-boundary points, and identifies which elements of **U** receive forward, backward, or central differences.

```
' Identification of the non-boundary points
For B = 2 To NV - 1
    For K = B * NS - (NS - 2) To B * NS - 1
        NB(K) = 1
    Next K
Next B
NB(NS) = 1
' Indices for S
For B = 2 To NV - 1
    For K = B * NS - (NS - 3) To B * NS - 2
        Cs(K) = 1  ' Central differences for S
    Next K
Next B
' Indices for V
For B = 3 To NV - 2
    For K = B * NS - (NS - 2) To B * NS - 1
        Cv(K) = 1  ' Central differences for V
    Next K
Next B
' Indices for SV
For B = 2 To NV - 1
    For K = B * NS - (NS - 2) To B * NS - 1
        Csv(K) = 1 ' Central difference for SV
    Next K
Next B
```

The next section loops through the identified points, and attributes the coefficients for central, forward, or backward differences to each of the first- and second-order matrices.

```
' NON BOUNDARY POINTS ---------------------------------
I = find2(Cs)
N = Count(I)
For K = 1 To N
    ' Create the matrix for S-derivatives with central differences
    derS(I(K), I(K) - 1) = -1 / 2 / ds * Si(I(K))      ' U(s-1,v)
    derS(I(K), I(K)) = 0                               ' U(s,v)
    derS(I(K), I(K) + 1) = 1 / 2 / ds * Si(I(K))       ' U(s+1,v)
    derSS(I(K), I(K) - 1) = 1 / ds ^ 2 * Vi(I(K)) ... ' U(s-1,v)
    derSS(I(K), I(K)) = -2 / ds ^ 2 * Vi(I(K)) *  ... ' U(s,v)
    derSS(I(K), I(K) + 1) = 1 / ds ^ 2 * Vi(I(K)) ... ' U(s+1,v)
Next K
' BOUNDARY POINTS ---------------------------------
' Boundary for Smin
I = find2(SminB)
N = Count(I)
For K = 1 To N
    derS(I(K), I(K)) = 0
    derSS(I(K), I(K)) = 0
    ...
    R(I(K), I(K)) = 0
Next K
```

The next section assigns the output.

```
If output = "derS" Then
    BuildDerivatives = derS
ElseIf output = "derSS" Then
    BuildDerivatives = derSS
...
End If
End Function
```

The BuildDerivatives function is used in the WeightedMethod function, which applies Equation (10.12) and updates **U** at every time step iteration. The value of the derivative is returned by interpolating **U** at the desired point (S_0, v_0).

```
Function WeightedMethodPrice(...) As Double
' U(0) vector - value of U(T) at maturity
For V = 1 To NV
    For s = 1 To NS
        Si(Count) = Spot(s)
    Next s
```

```
Next V
For s = 1 To N
    U(s) = Max(0, Si(s) - Strike)
Next s
' Calculate the "L" matrix
If GridType = "Uniform" Then
    derS = BuildDerivatives(..., "derS")
    ...
    R = BuildDerivatives(..., "R")
ElseIf GridType = "NonUniform" Then
    derS = BuildDerivativesNonUniform(..., "derS")
    ...
    R = BuildDerivativesNonUniform(..., "R")
End If
L = MSub(MSub(MAdd(MAdd(MAdd(MAdd(M1, M2), M4), M5), M6), M3), M7)
' Calculate the Weighted Method matrices
If thet = 0 Then
    Ainv = BuildI(N)
Else
    Ainv = MInvLU(AA)
End If
' Loop thru time, updating U(t) to U(t+1) at each step
For t = 2 To NT
    For s = 1 To N
        smallU(s) = U(s)
    Next s
    If thet = 0 Then
        U = MVMult(BB, smallU)                ' Explicit Method
    ElseIf thet = 1 Then
        U = MVMult(Ainv, smallU)              ' Implicit Method
    Else
        U = MVMult(Ainv, MVMult(BB, smallU)) ' Weighted Method
    End If
Next t
' Interpolate to get the price at S0 and v0
WeightedMethodPrice = interp2(Vol, Spot, UU, V0, S0)
End Function
```

The WeightedMethodPrice function makes use of several VBA functions for matrix operations, but these functions are not presented here.

To illustrate the weighted method, we use the parameter values defined in Case 1 of Table 1 of In'T Hout and Foulon (2010) along with a uniform grid. We use $N_S = 40$, $N_V = 20$, and $N_T = 20$. The results are in Figure 10.3.

In this example, the exact price using the Heston closed-form solution is 4.1084. The explicit, implicit, and Crank-Nicolson schemes produce prices that are off by approximately 0.05.

The VBA function BuildDerivativesNonUniform is a version of the function BuildDerivatives that accepts a nonuniform grid and returns the submatrices of **L**. For each entry of the submatrices, the divisors *ds* and *dv* are specified in accordance

	A	B	C	D	E	F	G	H
1								
2		**Comparison of Weighted Schemes**						
3								
4		**Option Features**			**Weighted Method**	**Price**	**$ Error**	**Theta**
5		Strike Price (K)	100.0000		Closed European Price	4.1084		
6		Time to Maturity (τ)	0.1500		Explicit Method	4.1061	-0.0022	0
7		Risk free rate (r)	0.0200		Implicit Method	4.0490	-0.0594	1
8		Dividend (q)	0.0500		Crank-Nicolson	4.0775	-0.0308	0.5
9		PutCall (C or P)	C					
10		Little Trap (0=Heston, 1=Albrecher)	1		**Number of Steps in Each Dimension**			
11					Stock Price	40		
12		**Values of (S,v) where to Interpolate the PDE**			Volatility	20		
13		Spot Price (Si)	101.52000		Maturity	20		
14		Volatility (Vi)	0.05412		Grid Type ("Uniform" or "NonUniform")	Uniform		
15								
16		**Heston Parameters**			**Boundary Values for Stock Price, Volatility, and Maturity**			
17		kappa (κ)	1.50000		Minimum S	0.0000		
18		theta (θ)	0.04000		Maximum S	200		
19		sigma (σ)	0.30000		Minimum V	0		
20		v0	0.05412		Maximum V	0.5		
21		rho (ρ)	-0.90000		Minimum T	0		
22		lambda (λ)	0.00000		Maximum T	0.15		
23								
24		**Trapezoidal Rule Integration Grid**						
25		Lower Limit	1.00E-10					
26		Upper Limit	150					
27		Number of abscissas	500					

FIGURE 10.3 Call Prices Using the Weighted Method and Uniform Grid

with the values of (S, v), and must respect the nonadjacent positions of successive values in the vector that stores the volatilities.

```
' NON BOUNDARY POINTS ----------------------------------
I = find2(Cs)
N = Count(I)
For K = 1 To N
    ' Create matrix for S-derivatives with central differences
    ds = Si(I(K)) - Si(I(K) - 1)
    derS(I(K), I(K) - 1) = -1 / 2 / ds * Si(I(K))        ' U(s-1,v)
    derSS(I(K), I(K) - 1) = 1 / ds ^ 2 * Vi(I(K)) ...    ' U(s-1,v)
    ds = Si(I(K) + 1) - Si(I(K))
    derS(I(K), I(K) + 1) = 1 / 2 / ds * Si(I(K))  ...    ' U(s+1,v)
    derSS(I(K), I(K) + 1) = 1 / ds ^ 2 * Vi(I(K)) ...    ' U(s+1,v)
    ds = (Si(I(K) + 1) - Si(I(K) - 1)) / 2
    derS(I(K), I(K)) = 0                          ...    ' U(s,v)
    derSS(I(K), I(K)) = -2 / ds ^ 2 * Vi(I(K)) *  ...    ' U(s,v)
Next K
' BOUNDARY POINTS ----------------------------------
' Boundary for Smin
I = find2(SminB)
N = Count(I)
For K = 1 To N
    derS(I(K), I(K)) = 0
    derSS(I(K), I(K)) = 0
    ...
    R(I(K), I(K)) = 0
Next K
```

	A	B	C	D	E	F	G	H
1								
2		**Comparison of Weighted Schemes**						
3								
4		**Option Features**			**Weighted Method**	**Price**	**$ Error**	**Theta**
5		Strike Price (K)	100.0000		Closed European Price	4.1084		
6		Time to Maturity (τ)	0.1500		Explicit Method	4.1736	0.0653	0
7		Risk free rate (r)	0.0200		Implicit Method	4.1035	-0.0048	1
8		Dividend (q)	0.0500		Crank-Nicolson	4.1385	0.0302	0.5
9		PutCall (C or P)	C					
10		Little Trap (0=Heston, 1=Albrecher)	1		**Number of Steps in Each Dimension**			
11					Stock Price	20		
12		**Values of (S,v) where to Interpolate the PDE**			Volatility	20		
13		Spot Price (Si)	101.52000		Maturity	20		
14		Volatility (Vi)	0.05412		Grid Type ("Uniform" or "NonUniform")	NonUniform		
15								
16		**Heston Parameters**			**Boundary Values for Stock Price, Volatility, and Maturity**			
17		kappa (κ)	1.50000		Minimum S	0.0000		
18		theta (θ)	0.04000		Maximum S	200		
19		sigma (σ)	0.30000		Minimum V	0		
20		v0	0.05412		Maximum V	0.5		
21		rho (ρ)	-0.90000		Minimum T	0		
22		lambda (λ)	0.00000		Maximum T	0.15		
23								
24		**Trapezoidal Rule Integration Grid**						
25		Lower Limit	1.00E-10					
26		Upper Limit	150					
27		Number of abscissas	500					

FIGURE 10.4 Call Prices Using the Weighted Method and Nonuniform Grid

To illustrate, we use the same settings as in the example under the uniform case but use a smaller grid size. The results are shown in Figure 10.4.

Even with a reduced grid size, the nonuniform grid produces prices that are comparable to those generated with a uniform grid.

The VBA code, examples, and screen shots presented in this section are in the Excel file Ch10Weighted.xls.

EXPLICIT SCHEME

The explicit scheme is a special case of the weighted method that arises by setting $\theta = 0$ in Equation (10.11), reproduced here for convenience:

$$\mathbf{U}^{n+1} = (\mathbf{I} + dt\mathbf{L})\mathbf{U}^{n}. \tag{10.14}$$

Hence, given the matrix $\mathbf{L}$, we can obtain $\mathbf{U}^{n+1}$ directly from $\mathbf{U}^{n}$, without requiring matrix inversion. The element of $\mathbf{U}^{n+1}$ corresponding to $U_{i,j}^{n+1}$ is

$$\begin{aligned} U_{i,j}^{n+1} = U_{i,j}^{n} + dt \Bigg[& \frac{1}{2} v_j S_i^2 \frac{\partial^2}{\partial S^2} + \frac{1}{2}\sigma^2 v_j \frac{\partial^2}{\partial v^2} \\ & + \rho\sigma v_j S_i \frac{\partial^2}{\partial v \partial S} + (r-q) S_i \frac{\partial}{\partial S} + \kappa(\theta - v_j)\frac{\partial}{\partial v} - r \Bigg] U_{i,j}^{n}. \end{aligned} \tag{10.15}$$

This is the same expression for $U_{i,j}^{n+1}$ that we encountered in Chapter 8, when we used the explicit method to price American options. When we use a uniform grid for (S_i, v_j) the expression for $U^n_{i,j}$ can be reduced to a simple expression that involves only the parameters, the index values, points adjacent to $U^n_{i,j}$, and the increments. We substitute the approximations to the derivatives under a uniform grid, noting that $S_i = i \times ds$ and $v_j = j \times dv$, and obtain

$$\begin{aligned} U^{n+1}_{i,j} &= \left[1 - dt\left(i^2 j dv + \frac{\sigma^2 j}{dv} + r\right)\right] U^n_{i,j} \\ &+ \left[\frac{idt}{2}(ijdv - r + q)\right] U^n_{i-1,j} + \left[\frac{idt}{2}(ijdv + r - q)\right] U^n_{i+1,j} \\ &+ \left[\frac{dt}{2dv}(\sigma^2 j - \kappa(\theta - jdv)\right] U^n_{i,j-1} + \left[\frac{dt}{2dv}(\sigma^2 j + \kappa(\theta - jdv)\right] U^n_{i,j+1}, \\ &+ \frac{ijdt\sigma}{4}\left(U^n_{i+1,j+1} + U^n_{i-1,j-1} - U^n_{i-1,j+1} - U^n_{i+1,j-1}\right). \end{aligned} \tag{10.16}$$

The VBA function HestonExplicitPDE returns the matrix that contains all the elements $U^{N_T}_{i,j}$ from the explicit method and a uniform grid. All the intermediate time values $U^t_{i,j}$ for $t < N_T$ are discarded. The function requires as inputs the grids for S, v, and t.

```
Function HestonExplicitPDE(params As Variant,...) As Double
For t = 1 To NT - 1
    ' Boundary condition for Smin and Smax
    For v = 1 To NV - 1
        U(1, v) = 0
        U(NS, v) = Max(0, Smax - Strike)
    Next v
    ' Boundary condition for Vmax
    For s = 1 To NS
        U(s, NV) = Max(0, Spot(s) - Strike)
    Next s
    ' Boundary condition for Vmin.
    ' Previous time step values are in the temporary grid u(s,t)
    For s = 2 To NS - 1
        ' PDE Points on the middle of the grid (non boundary)
        DerV = (smallU(s, 2) - smallU(s, 1)) / dv
        ' Central difference for dU/dS
        DerS = (smallU(s + 1, 1) - smallU(s - 1, 1)) / 2 / ds
        U(s, 1) = smallU(s, 1) * (1 - r * dt - kappa * theta  ...
    Next s
    ' Update temporary grid u(s,t) with boundary conditions
    For s = 1 To NS
        For v = 1 To NV
            smallU(s, v) = U(s, v)
        Next v
    Next s
    ' Interior points of the grid (non boundary).
```

```
    For s = 2 To NS - 1
        For v = 2 To NV - 1
            C1 = (1 - dt * (s - 1) ^ 2 * (v - 1) * dv - sigma ^ 2 ...
            C2 = (1 / 2 * dt * (s - 1) ^ 2 * (v - 1) * dv - 1 / 2 ...
            ...
            C6 = 1 / 4 * dt * sigma * (s - 1) * (v - 1)
            ' The PDE
            U(s, v) = C1 * smallU(s, v) + C2 * smallU(s - 1, v) ...
        Next v
    Next s
Next t
' Interpolate the discretized PDE, "U", at the points (Si,Vi)
HestonExplicitPDE = interp2(Spot, Vol, U, Si, Vi)
End Function
```

When we use a nonuniform grid, simplification of Equation (10.15) to (10.16) is not possible, and we work with (10.15) directly. This is implemented with the VBA function HestonExplicitPDENonUniformGrid.

```
Function HestonExplicitPDENonUniform(params As Variant,...) As Double
For t = 1 To NT - 1
    ' Boundary condition for Vmin.
    ' Previous time step values are in the temporary grid u(s,t)
    For s = 2 To NS - 1
        DerV = (smallU(s, 2) - smallU(s, 1)) / (Vol(2) - Vol(1))
        DerS = (smallU(s + 1, 1) - smallU(s - 1, 1)) ...
        LHS = -r * smallU(s, 1) + (r - q) * Spot(s) ...
        U(s, 1) = LHS * dt + smallU(s, 1)
    Next s
    ' Interior points. Previous time step values in temp grid u(s,t)
    For s = 2 To NS - 1
        For v = 2 To NV - 1
            ' Central difference for dU/dS and dU/dV
            DerS = (smallU(s + 1, v) - smallU(s - 1, v)) ...
            DerV = (smallU(s, v + 1) - smallU(s, v - 1)) ...
            derSS = ((smallU(s + 1, v) - smallU(s, v))   ...
            derVV = ((smallU(s, v + 1) - smallU(s, v))   ...
            derSV = (smallU(s + 1, v + 1) - smallU(s - 1, v + 1) ...
            L = 0.5 * Vol(v) * Spot(s) ^ 2 * derSS ...
            U(s, v) = L * dt + smallU(s, v)
        Next v
    Next s
Next t
' Interpolate the discretized PDE, "U", at the points (Si,Vi)
U = MTrans(U, NS, NV)
HestonExplicitPDENonUniform = interp2(Spot, Vol, U, Si, Vi)
End Function
```

	A	B	C	D	E	F	G
1							
2		**The Explicit Method with Uniform and NonUniform Grids**					
3							
4		**Option Features**			**Method**	**Price**	**$ Error**
5		Strike Price (K)	100.0000		Closed European Price	4.1084	
6		Time to Maturity (τ)	0.1500		European Price, Uniform Grid	4.2740	0.1656
7		Risk free rate (r)	0.0200		European Price, Non-Uniform Grid	4.1064	-0.0019
8		Dividend (q)	0.0500				
9		PutCall (C or P)	C		**Number of Steps in Each Dimension**		
10		Little Trap (0=Heston, 1=Albrecher)	1		Stock Price	30	
11					Volatility	30	
12		**Values of (S,v) where to Interpolate the PDE**			Maturity	1500	
13		Spot Price (Si)	101.52000				
14		Volatility (Vi)	0.05412		**Boundary Values for Stock Price, Volatility, and Maturity**		
15					Minimum S	0.0000	
16		**Heston Parameters**			Maximum S	200	
17		kappa (κ)	1.50000		Minimum V	0	
18		theta (θ)	0.04000		Maximum V	0.5	
19		sigma (σ)	0.30000		Minimum T	0	
20		v0	0.05412		Maximum T	0.15	
21		rho (ρ)	-0.90000				
22		lambda (λ)	0.00000				
23							
24		**Trapezoidal Rule Integration Grid**					
25		Lower Limit	1.00E-10				
26		Upper Limit	150				
27		Number of abscissas	500				
28							

FIGURE 10.5 Call Prices Using the Explicit Method

Although we can use the nonuniform grid function with a uniform grid, the function made for a uniform grid is slightly faster. The VBA functions HestonExplicitPDE and HestonExplicitPDENonUniformGrid both return the grid $U_{i,j}^{N_T}$ of terminal values, corresponding to values S_i and v_j along the grids. At the last step, to obtain a value of U^{N_T} between points on the grid, we apply the VBA function interp2 for two-dimensional interpolation. This function is not presented here.

To illustrate, we use the same settings as those in the examples of Figures 10.3 and 10.4. We wish to obtain the price at the spot $S_0 = 101.52$ when the volatility is $v = 0.05412$. The results are shown in Figure 10.5.

The exact price, using the closed-form solution, is 4.1084. The uniform grid produces a price of 4.2740, while the nonuniform grid produces a price of 4.1064, which is much more accurate. Even with 10,000 time points, the accuracy of the uniform grid does not improve much. To increase the accuracy of the uniform grid, we must use larger grid sizes for the stock price and volatility, which increases computational time.

The VBA code, examples, and screen shots presented in this section are in the Excel file Ch10Explicit.xls.

ADI SCHEMES

Alternating Direction Implicit (ADI) schemes have the advantage of being stable and showing good convergence for a small number of time points. The idea behind ADI schemes is that the components of the matrix **L** are treated separately, so that certain components are treated explicitly and others implicitly. We decompose $\mathbf{L}$ into three matrices $\mathbf{A}_0$, $\mathbf{A}_1$, and $\mathbf{A}_2$ each of size $N \times N$, so that

$$\mathbf{L} = \mathbf{A}_0 + \mathbf{A}_1 + \mathbf{A}_2. \tag{10.17}$$

The matrices are

$$\begin{aligned}
\mathbf{A}_0 &= \rho\sigma v S \left(\frac{\partial U}{\partial S \partial v}\right)_{N\times N} \\
\mathbf{A}_1 &= (r-q)S\left(\frac{\partial U}{\partial S}\right)_{N\times N} + \frac{1}{2}vS^2\left(\frac{\partial^2 U}{\partial S^2}\right)_{N\times N} - \frac{1}{2}r(U)_{N\times N}, \\
\mathbf{A}_2 &= \kappa(\theta - v)\left(\frac{\partial U}{\partial v}\right)_{N\times N} + \frac{1}{2}\sigma^2 v\left(\frac{\partial^2 U}{\partial v^2}\right)_{N\times N} - \frac{1}{2}r(U)_{N\times N}.
\end{aligned} \tag{10.18}$$

From Equation (10.2), we can write

$$\mathbf{U}'(t) = \mathbf{L}\mathbf{U}(t). \tag{10.19}$$

This system of equations can be solved using various ADI schemes that all work iteratively, by updating a given $\mathbf{U}_{t-1} = \mathbf{U}(t-1)$ to a new value $\mathbf{U}_t$. All the schemes require an initial value $\mathbf{U}_0$. For the call option, this initial value is exactly the same as that described in previous sections of this chapter. Denote by $\mathbf{I}$ the identity matrix of dimension N. The schemes covered by In'T Hout and Foulon (2010) are the following:

- *Douglas scheme.* This is the simplest ADI scheme under consideration. Given $\mathbf{U}_{t-1}$, we update to $\mathbf{U}_t$ using the following steps:

  Step 1. $\mathbf{Y}_0 = [\mathbf{I} + dt\mathbf{L}]\mathbf{U}_{t-1}$.
  Step 2. $\mathbf{Y}_k = [\mathbf{I} - \theta dt\mathbf{A}_k]^{-1}[\mathbf{Y}_0 - \theta dt\mathbf{A}_k\mathbf{U}_{t-1}]$ for $k = 1, 2$.
  Step 3. Set $\mathbf{U}_t = \mathbf{Y}_2$.

- *Craig-Sneyd scheme.* This scheme is similar to the Douglas scheme, except that two additional steps are added:

  Step 1. $\mathbf{Y}_0 = [\mathbf{I} + dt\mathbf{L}]\mathbf{U}_{t-1}$.
  Step 2. $\mathbf{Y}_k = [\mathbf{I} - \theta dt\mathbf{A}_k]^{-1}[\mathbf{Y}_{k-1} - \theta dt\mathbf{A}_k\mathbf{U}_{t-1}]$ for $k = 1, 2$.
  Step 3. $\widetilde{\mathbf{Y}}_0 = \mathbf{Y}_0 + \frac{1}{2}dt[\mathbf{A}_0\mathbf{Y}_2 - \mathbf{A}_0\mathbf{U}_{t-1}]$.
  Step 4. $\widetilde{\mathbf{Y}}_k = [\mathbf{I} - \theta dt\mathbf{A}_k]^{-1}[\widetilde{\mathbf{Y}}_{k-1} - \theta dt\mathbf{A}_k\mathbf{U}_{t-1}]$.
  Step 5. Set $\mathbf{U}_t = \widetilde{\mathbf{Y}}_2$.

- *Modified Craig-Sneyd scheme:*

  Step 1. $\mathbf{Y}_0 = [\mathbf{I} + dt\mathbf{L}]\mathbf{U}_{t-1}$.
  Step 2. $\mathbf{Y}_k = [\mathbf{I} - \theta dt\mathbf{A}_k]^{-1}[\mathbf{Y}_{k-1} - \theta dt\mathbf{A}_k\mathbf{U}_{t-1}]$.
  Step 3. $\hat{\mathbf{Y}}_0 = \mathbf{Y}_0 + \theta dt[\mathbf{A}_0\mathbf{Y}_2 - \mathbf{A}_0\mathbf{U}_{t-1}]$.

Step 4. $\widetilde{\mathbf{Y}}_0 = \widehat{\mathbf{Y}}_0 + (\frac{1}{2} - \theta)dt[\mathbf{LY}_2 - \mathbf{LU}_{t-1}]$.
Step 5. $\widetilde{\mathbf{Y}}_k = [\mathbf{I} - \theta dt\mathbf{A}_k]^{-1}[\widetilde{\mathbf{Y}}_{k-1} - \theta dt\mathbf{A}_k\mathbf{U}_{t-1}]$.
Step 6. Set $\mathbf{U}_t = \widetilde{\mathbf{Y}}_2$.

- *Hundsdorfer-Verwer scheme:*

Step 1. $\mathbf{Y}_0 = [\mathbf{I} + dt\mathbf{L}]\mathbf{U}_{t-1}$.
Step 2. $\mathbf{Y}_k = [\mathbf{I} - \theta dt\mathbf{A}_k]^{-1}[\mathbf{Y}_{k-1} - \theta dt\mathbf{A}_k\mathbf{U}_{t-1}]$.
Step 3. $\widetilde{\mathbf{Y}}_0 = \mathbf{Y}_0 + \frac{1}{2}dt[\mathbf{LY}_2 - \mathbf{LU}_{t-1}]$.
Step 4. $\widetilde{\mathbf{Y}}_k = [\mathbf{I} - \theta dt\mathbf{A}_k]^{-1}[\widetilde{\mathbf{Y}}_{k-1} - \theta dt\mathbf{A}_k\mathbf{Y}_2]$.
Step 5. $\widetilde{\mathbf{Y}}_2 = [\mathbf{I} - \theta dt\mathbf{A}_2]^{-1}[\widetilde{\mathbf{Y}}_1 - \theta dt\mathbf{A}_2\mathbf{Y}_2]$.
Step 6. Set $\mathbf{U}_t = \widetilde{\mathbf{Y}}_2$.

The parameter θ controls the type of weighing being implemented, exactly as in the weighted method. Hence, an ADI scheme is specified by the scheme itself and the value of the parameter θ.

Once the $\mathbf{L}$ matrix is constructed, it is straightforward to implement the ADI schemes. This is done with the ADIPrice function. The first part of the function builds the required matrices of derivatives, which can be constructed with either a uniform or nonuniform grid. The functions used to build the matrices are the same that were used for the weighted method presented earlier in this chapter.

```
Function ADIPrice(scheme As String,...) As Double
' Build the grids
Spot = BuildGrid(..., GridType, "Spot")
Vol =  BuildGrid(..., GridType, "Vol")
Mat =  BuildGrid(..., GridType, "Mat")
' Build the matrices for the derivatives and other matrices
If GridType = "Uniform" Then
    derS = BuildDerivatives(..., "derS")
    derSS = BuildDerivatives(..., "derSS")
    ...
    R = BuildDerivatives(..., "R")
ElseIf GridType = "NonUniform" Then
    derS = BuildDerivativesNonUniform(..., "derS")
    derSS = BuildDerivativesNonUniform(..., "derSS")
    ...
    R = BuildDerivativesNonUniform(..., "R")
End If
```

The second part uses the derivatives matrices to construct the matrices $\mathbf{A}_0$, $\mathbf{A}_1$, and $\mathbf{A}_2$, in accordance with (10.18), creates a vector stock prices from the grid, and initializes the vector $\mathbf{U}^n$ as the value of the European call at maturity. The function uses the VBA function BuildI function for constructing the identity matrix.

```
' The "A" matrices
A0 = MCMult(derSV, rho * sigma)
A1 = MAdd(MAdd(M1, M2), M3)
A2 = MAdd(MAdd(MAdd(M1, M2), M3), M4)
A012 = MAdd(MAdd(A0, A1), A2)
' Initialize the u vector, create identity matrix
' smallU plays the role of u(t-1)
Id = BuildI(N)
For V = 1 To NV
    For s = 1 To NS
        Si(Count) = Spot(s)
    Next s
Next V
' U(0) vector - value of U(T) at maturity
For s = 1 To N
    U(s) = Max(0, Si(s) - Strike)
Next s
```

Finally, the last part of the function loops through time and applies the desired ADI scheme. It then rearranges the vector $\mathbf{U}^n$ into a matrix, and interpolates the matrix to find the European call price at the desired values of S_0 and v_0.

```
For t = 2 To NT
    ' Vectors common to all schemes
    Y0 = MVMult(M1, smallU)
    Y1 = MVMult(MInvLU(M1), V2)
    Y2 = MVMult(MInvLU(M1), V2)
    If scheme = "DO" Then ' Douglas
        U = CopyVector(Y2)
    ElseIf scheme = "CS" Then ' Craig-Sneyd
        Y0_ = VAdd(Y0, V4)
        Y1_ = MVMult(MInvLU(M1), V2)
        Y2_ = MVMult(MInvLU(M1), V2)
        U = CopyVector(Y2_)
    ElseIf scheme = "MCS" Thenv ' Modified Craig-Sneyd
        Y0h = VAdd(Y0, V2)
        Y0_ = VAdd(Y0h, V2)
        Y1_ = MVMult(MInvLU(M1), V3)
        Y2_ = MVMult(MInvLU(M1), V3)
        U = CopyVector(Y2_)
```

```
        ElseIf scheme = "HV" Then ' Hundsdorfer-Verwer
            Y0_ = VAdd(Y0, V2)
            Y1_ = MVMult(MInvLU(M1), V3)
            Y2_ = MVMult(MInvLU(M1), V3)
            U = CopyVector(Y2_)
        End If
    Next t
    ' Restack the U vector to output a matrix
    For j = 1 To NV
        For s = 1 To NS
            UU(s, j) = U(Count)
            Count = Count + 1
    Next j
    ' Interpolate to get the price at S0 and v0
    ADIPrice = interp2(Vol, Spot, UU, v00, S00)
    End Function
```

We continue with the example earlier in this chapter, using $N_T = 10$ time steps and a nonuniform grid with $N_S = 20$ and $N_V = 15$. The results are shown in Figure 10.6.

To save on computation time, we have used few time steps and small grids. In practice, these would be higher and produce more accurate results.

The VBA code, examples, and screen shots in this section are from the Excel file Ch10ADI.xls.

	B	C	E	F	G	H
1						
2	**Comparison of ADI Schemes**					
3						
4	**Option Features**		**ADI Method**	**Price**	**$ Error**	**Theta**
5	Strike Price (K)	100.0000	Closed European Price	4.1083		
6	Time to Maturity (τ)	0.1500	Douglas Scheme	4.1209	0.0126	0.5
7	Risk free rate (r)	0.0200	Craig-Sneyd Scheme	4.0996	-0.0088	0.5
8	Dividend (q)	0.0500	Modified Craig-Sneyd Scheme	4.0996	-0.0088	0.5
9	PutCall (C or P)	C	Hundsdorfer-Verwer Scheme	4.0994	-0.0089	0.5
10	Little Trap (0=Heston, 1=Albrecher)	1				
11			**Number of Steps in Each Dimension**			
12	**Values of (S,v) where to Interpolate the PDE**		Stock Price	20		
13	Spot Price (Si)	101.52000	Volatility	15		
14	Volatility (Vi)	0.05412	Maturity	10		
15			Grid Type ("Uniform" or "NonUniform")	NonUniform		
16	**Heston Parameters**					
17	kappa (κ)	1.50000	**Boundary Values for Stock Price, Volatility, and Maturity**			
18	theta (θ)	0.04000	Minimum S	0.0000		
19	sigma (σ)	0.30000	Maximum S	200		
20	v0	0.05412	Minimum V	0		
21	rho (ρ)	-0.90000	Maximum V	0.5		
22	lambda (λ)	0.00000	Minimum T	0		
23			Maximum T	0.15		
24	**Trapezoidal Rule Integration Grid**					
25	Lower Limit	1.00E-04				
26	Upper Limit	150				
27	Number of abscissas	500				

FIGURE 10.6 Call Prices Using ADI Schemes

CONCLUSION

In this chapter, we have presented some of the finite difference methods that are commonly used to obtain European prices in the Heston model. Pricing models that employ finite differences are varied and have been applied in a stochastic volatility framework by Clarke and Parrott (1999), In'T Hout and Foulon (2010), and Ikonen and Toivanen (2008), among many others. Please see Tavella and Randall (2000) and Duffy (2006) for an overview of finite differences for pricing European and American options.

All of the methods we have encountered up to this chapter have dealt with either the European or American price. Central to option pricing theory, however, are the option price sensitivities to the inputs used in the price: the Greeks. This is the subject of the next chapter.

CHAPTER 11

The Heston Greeks

Abstract

Here, we present the option sensitivities, the Greeks, from the Heston model. We first derive analytic expressions for the most popular Greeks. We illustrate the Heston Greeks by comparing them to Greeks from Black-Scholes prices that are close to the Heston prices. We show that finite differences produce very good approximations to analytic Greeks, at the expense of increased computation time. We do this not only with Greeks obtained from the original Heston (1993) model, but also with Greeks obtained from the Attari (2004), Lewis (2000, 2001), and Carr and Madan (1999) formulations. We show that fast Fourier transform (FFT) of Carr and Madan (1999) and that the fractional FFT of Chourdakis (2005) are able to very quickly produce a set of Greeks across a wide range of strikes, in the same way that these methods produce prices. Finally, we show that Greeks of American options can be obtained from simulation methods, from the explicit method, and from the Medvedev and Scaillet (2010) method.

Greek, delta, gamma, theta, rho, vega, vanna, volga, finite difference, American Greek

In this chapter, we present the option sensitivities, the Greeks, from the Heston model. We first derive analytic expressions for the most popular Greeks. We illustrate the Heston Greeks by comparing them to Greeks from Black-Scholes prices that are close to the Heston prices. We show that finite differences produce very good approximations to analytic Greeks, at the expense of increased computation time. We do this not only with Greeks obtained from the original Heston (1993) model, but also with Greeks obtained from the Attari (2004), Lewis (2000, 2001), and Carr and Madan (1999) formulations. We show that fast Fourier transform (FFT) of Carr and Madan (1999) and that the fractional FFT of Chourdakis (2005) are able to very quickly produce a set of Greeks across a wide range of strikes, in the same way that these methods produce prices. Finally, we show that Greeks of American options can be obtained from simulation methods, from the explicit method, and from the Medvedev and Scaillet (2010) method.

ANALYTIC EXPRESSIONS FOR EUROPEAN GREEKS

The prices of European calls and puts in the Heston model are available in closed form. It is therefore possible to differentiate the call or put price and obtain expressions for most of the Greeks in closed form also. Recall that the call and put price are, respectively,

$$C(K) = S_t e^{-q\tau} P_1 - K e^{-r\tau} P_2, \quad P(K) = C(K) + K e^{-r\tau} - S_t e^{-q\tau}, \tag{11.1}$$

where

$$P_j = \frac{1}{2} + \frac{1}{\pi} \int_0^\infty \text{Re}\left[\frac{e^{-i\phi \ln K} f_j(\phi; x_t, v_t)}{i\phi}\right] d\phi. \tag{11.2}$$

Hence, the sensitivity of calls and puts to a parameter or input y usually involves first- and second-order derivatives of the in-the-money probabilities P_j:

$$\frac{\partial P_j}{\partial y} = \frac{1}{\pi} \int_0^\infty \text{Re}\left[\frac{\partial f_j}{\partial y} \times \frac{e^{-i\phi \ln K}}{i\phi}\right] d\phi, \quad \frac{\partial^2 P_j}{\partial y^2} = \frac{1}{\pi} \int_0^\infty \text{Re}\left[\frac{\partial^2 f_j}{\partial y^2} \times \frac{e^{-i\phi \ln K}}{i\phi}\right] d\phi. \tag{11.3}$$

In the following sections, we use (11.3) to derive analytic expressions for most of the popular first- and second-order Greeks.

Delta, Gamma, Rho, Theta, and Vega

Delta, gamma, rho, and theta are obtained by differentiating Equation (11.1) and applying (11.3) when required. Vega is more arbitrary, since there are several parameters that affect the volatility smile in the Heston model. The second-order volatility Greeks vanna and volga will be covered in the next section.

As explained by Bakshi et al. (1997), Reiss and Wystup (2000), and Bakshi and Madan (2000), and others, delta for the call and put and are given by, respectively,

$$\Delta_C = \frac{\partial C}{\partial S} = e^{-q\tau} P_1 \quad \text{and} \quad \Delta_P = \frac{\partial P}{\partial S} = e^{-q\tau}(P_1 - 1). \tag{11.4}$$

We can express gamma as

$$\Gamma = \frac{\partial^2 C}{\partial S^2} = e^{-q\tau} \frac{\partial P_1}{\partial S} = \frac{e^{-q\tau}}{\pi S_t} \int_0^\infty \text{Re}\left[e^{-i\phi \ln K} f_1(\phi; x_t, v_t)\right] d\phi. \tag{11.5}$$

For calls and puts, rho is, respectively,

$$\rho_C = \frac{\partial C}{\partial r} = K e^{-r\tau} \tau P_2 \quad \text{and} \quad \rho_P = \frac{\partial P}{\partial r} = K e^{-r\tau} \tau (P_2 - 1). \tag{11.6}$$

For calls and puts, theta is, respectively,

$$\begin{aligned}\Theta_C &= -\frac{\partial C}{\partial \tau} = -S_t e^{-q\tau}\left(-qP_1 + \frac{\partial P_1}{\partial \tau}\right) + Ke^{-r\tau}\left(-rP_2 + \frac{\partial P_2}{\partial \tau}\right),\\ \Theta_P &= -\frac{\partial P}{\partial \tau} = \Theta_C + Kre^{-r\tau} - qS_t e^{-q\tau},\end{aligned} \tag{11.7}$$

where

$$\frac{\partial f_j}{\partial \tau} = \exp(C_j + D_j v_t + i\phi x_t)\left(\frac{\partial C_j}{\partial \tau} + \frac{\partial D_j}{\partial \tau} v_t\right), \tag{11.8}$$

and

$$\begin{aligned}\frac{\partial C_j}{\partial \tau} &= (r-q)\phi i + \frac{\kappa\theta}{\sigma^2}\left[b_j - \rho\sigma\phi i + d_j + \frac{2g_j d_j e^{d_j\tau}}{1 - g_j e^{d_j\tau}}\right],\\ \frac{\partial D_j}{\partial \tau} &= \frac{b_j - \rho\sigma\phi i + d_j}{\sigma^2} \times \frac{(g_j - 1)d_j e^{d_j\tau}}{(1 - g_j e^{d_j\tau})^2}.\end{aligned} \tag{11.9}$$

In Equation (11.8), $x_t = \ln S_t$ is the log spot price, and v_t is the initial variance, which is unobserved and estimated as the parameter v_0. The quantities b_j, g_j, and d_j are given in Chapter 1 for $j = 1, 2$.

Vega is defined as the derivative of the call and put price with respect to the implied volatility. In the Black-Scholes model, the implied volatility is represented by the volatility parameter σ_{BS}, so vega for the call is readily obtained as $\partial C_{BS}/\partial \sigma_{BS}$, where C_{BS} is the Black-Scholes call price. In the Heston model, both v_0 and θ influence variance, so to create measures of sensitivity to volatility, Zhu (2010) defines two vegas, $\mathcal{V}_1$ based on $\upsilon = \sqrt{v_0}$ and $\mathcal{V}_2$ based on $\omega = \sqrt{\theta}$. The vegas for the call are

$$\mathcal{V}_1 = \frac{\partial C}{\partial \upsilon} = \frac{\partial C}{\partial v_0} 2\sqrt{v_0} \quad \text{and} \quad \mathcal{V}_2 = \frac{\partial C}{\partial \omega} = \frac{\partial C}{\partial \theta} 2\sqrt{\theta}. \tag{11.10}$$

The first vega is

$$\mathcal{V}_1 = Se^{-q\tau}\frac{\partial P_1}{\partial v_0} 2\sqrt{v_0} - Ke^{-r\tau}\frac{\partial P_2}{\partial v_0} 2\sqrt{v_0}, \tag{11.11}$$

where

$$\frac{\partial P_j}{\partial v_0} = \frac{1}{\pi}\int_0^\infty \text{Re}\left[\frac{e^{-i\phi\ln K} f_j(\phi; x_t, v_t) D_j(\tau, \phi)}{i\phi}\right] d\phi. \tag{11.12}$$

The second vega is

$$\mathcal{V}_2 = Se^{-q\tau}\frac{\partial P_1}{\partial \theta}2\sqrt{\theta} - Ke^{-r\tau}\frac{\partial P_2}{\partial \theta}2\sqrt{\theta}, \tag{11.13}$$

where

$$\frac{\partial P_j}{\partial \theta} = \frac{1}{\pi}\int_0^\infty \text{Re}\left[\frac{e^{-i\phi \ln K} f_j(\phi; x_t, v_t)\partial C_j/\partial \theta}{i\phi}\right] d\phi, \tag{11.14}$$

and

$$\frac{\partial C_j}{\partial \theta} = \frac{\kappa}{\sigma^2}\left[(b_j - \rho\sigma i\phi + d_j)\tau - 2\ln\left(\frac{1 - g_j e^{d_j\tau}}{1 - g_j}\right)\right]. \tag{11.15}$$

By examination of Equation (11.1), it is easy to verify that $\mathcal{V}_1$ and $\mathcal{V}_2$ for the put are the same as those for the call.

Vanna, Volga, and Other Greeks

The most popular second-order Greeks are vanna and volga. In this subsection, we focus only the first vega, $\mathcal{V}_1$ in Equation (11.11). Vanna and volga are

$$\text{Vanna} = \frac{\partial^2 C}{\partial \upsilon \partial S} = \frac{\partial^2 C}{\partial v_0 \partial S}2\sqrt{v_0} \quad \text{and} \quad \text{Volga} = \frac{\partial^2 C}{\partial \upsilon^2}, \tag{11.16}$$

where $\upsilon = \sqrt{v_0}$. Vanna can be obtained from delta as

$$\text{Vanna} = \frac{\partial}{\partial \upsilon}\left(\frac{\partial C}{\partial S}\right) = 2e^{-q\tau}\sqrt{v_0}\frac{\partial P_1}{\partial v_0}. \tag{11.17}$$

Volga can be obtained from vega, by using (11.10)

$$\text{Volga} = \frac{\partial \mathcal{V}_1}{\partial \upsilon} = Se^{-q\tau}\frac{\partial^2 P_1}{\partial \upsilon^2} - Ke^{-r\tau}\frac{\partial^2 P_2}{\partial \upsilon^2}, \tag{11.18}$$

where

$$\begin{aligned}\frac{\partial^2 P_j}{\partial \upsilon^2} &= 4\left(\frac{\partial^2 P_j}{\partial v_0^2}v_0 + \frac{1}{2}\frac{\partial P_j}{\partial v_0}\right)\\ &= \frac{1}{\pi}\int_0^\infty \text{Re}\left[\frac{e^{-i\phi\ln K}}{i\phi}2D_j(\tau,\phi)f_j(\phi;x_t,v_t)\left(2D_j(\tau,\phi)v_0 + 1\right)\right] d\phi.\end{aligned} \tag{11.19}$$

Equivalently,

$$\text{Volga} = \frac{\partial \mathcal{V}_1}{\partial v_0} 2\sqrt{v_0} = 4\sqrt{v_0}\left(\frac{\partial^2 C}{\partial v_0^2}\sqrt{v_0} + \frac{\mathcal{V}_1}{4v_0}\right) = 4\left(\frac{\partial^2 C}{\partial v_0^2} v_0 + \frac{1}{2}\frac{\partial C}{\partial v_0}\right). \tag{11.20}$$

We need the second-order derivative

$$\frac{\partial^2 C}{\partial v_0^2} = Se^{-q\tau}\frac{\partial^2 P_1}{\partial v_0^2} - Ke^{-r\tau}\frac{\partial^2 P_2}{\partial v_0^2} \tag{11.21}$$

from Equation (11.12),

$$\frac{\partial^2 P_j}{\partial v_0^2} = \frac{1}{\pi}\int_0^\infty \text{Re}\left[\frac{e^{-i\phi \ln K} f_j(\phi; x_t, v_t) D_j(\tau, \phi)^2}{i\phi}\right] d\phi, \tag{11.22}$$

We have defined vega ($\mathcal{V}_1$), vanna, and volga all in terms of the spot volatility, $v = \sqrt{v_0}$. However, the Heston PDE for the option price $U(S_t, v_t, t)$, which we encountered in Chapter 1, contains derivatives expressed in terms of the variance, v_0. If we redefine vega, vanna, and volga in terms of v_0 instead of v, then we can substitute the Greeks into the Heston PDE and show that it is satisfied. Hence, we obtain

$$\begin{aligned} &\Theta + \frac{1}{2}v_0 S_0^2 \Gamma + (r-q)S_0\Delta - rU \\ &\rho\sigma v_0 S_0 \text{Vanna} + \frac{1}{2}\sigma^2 v_0 \text{Volga} + \kappa(\theta - v_0)\text{Vega}_1 = 0, \end{aligned} \tag{11.23}$$

where we have set $\lambda(S_t, v_t, t) = 0$ and where S_0 is the spot price. The first line in (11.23) is the Black-Scholes PDE, and the second line adds correction terms for stochastic volatility. It is easy to verify that the PDE with Greeks holds for both the Black-Scholes and Heston models, provided that vega, vanna, and volga are constructed in terms of variance rather than in terms of volatility. This is accomplished with the VBA functions BlackScholesPDE and HestonPDE. The latter function makes use of the HestonGreeks function, which we introduce later in this chapter.

```
Function BlackScholesPDE(...) As Double
'Calculate the prices and the Greeks
Price = BSPrice(...)
Delta = BSGreeks(..., "Delta")
Gamma = BSGreeks(..., "Gamma")
theta = BSGreeks(..., "Theta")
' Return the value of the PDE, which should be zero
BlackScholesPDE = theta + 0.5 * sigma ^ 2 ...
End Function

Function HestonPDE(...) As Double
' Calculate the price and the Greeks
```

```
Price = HestonPriceGaussLaguerre(...)
Delta = HestonGreeks(..., "Delta")
Gamma = HestonGreeks(..., "Gamma")
Thet  = HestonGreeks(..., "Theta")
Vega1 = HestonGreeks(..., "Vega1") / (2 * Sqr(v0))
Vanna = HestonGreeks(..., "Vanna") / (2 * Sqr(v0))
Volga = HestonGreeks(..., "Volga")
Volga = (1 / 4 / Sqr(v0) * Volga - Vega1 / 2 ...
' Return the value of the PDE, which should be zero
HestonPDE = Thet + 0.5 * v0 * S ^ 2 ...
End Function
```

The results of these functions are in Figure 11.1. The values of the PDEs are both close to zero, as expected.

See Zhu (2010) for a further discussion of the Heston PDE with Greeks. The VBA code and examples for the PDEs, and the screen shot in Figure 11.1, are in the Excel file Ch11PDE.xls.

As mentioned in Chapter 2, the correlation ρ and the volatility of variance σ, control the slope and curvature, respectively, of the Heston implied volatility, while κ controls the speed of reversion to the mean level of volatility. The sensitivity of the call price to these parameters is

$$\frac{\partial C}{\partial \xi} = Se^{-q\tau}\frac{\partial P_1}{\partial \xi} - Ke^{-r\tau}\frac{\partial P_2}{\partial \xi}, \tag{11.24}$$

	A	B	C	D	E	F	G
1							
2		**Heston and Black-Scholes PDEs Using Closed Form and Finite Differences**					
3							
4		**Option Features**				**Price**	**PDE**
5		Spot Price (S)	100.0000		**Heston**	9.4951	0.0000508
6		Strike Price (K)	100.0000		**Black-Scholes**	9.4115	0.0000000
7		Time to Maturity (τ)	1.0000				
8		Risk free rate (r)	0.0500				
9		Dividend (q)	0.0300				
10		PutCall ("C" or "P")	C				
11							
12		**Heston Parameters**					
13		kappa (κ)	5.0000				
14		theta (θ)	0.0500				
15		sigma (σ)	0.2200				
16		v0	0.0500				
17		rho (ρ)	-0.8000				
18		lambda (λ)	0.0000				
19		Trap (0=Heston, 1=Albrecher)	1				

FIGURE 11.1 Black-Scholes and Heston PDEs

with

$$\frac{\partial P_j}{\partial \xi} = \frac{1}{\pi} \int_0^\infty \text{Re}\left[\frac{\partial f_j}{\partial \xi} \times \frac{e^{-i\phi \ln K}}{i\phi} \right] d\phi, \tag{11.25}$$

and

$$\frac{\partial f_j}{\partial \xi} = \exp\left(C_j + D_j v_t + i\phi x_t\right) \left(\frac{\partial C_j}{\partial \xi} + \frac{\partial D_j}{\partial \xi} v_j \right), \tag{11.26}$$

where $\zeta \in \{\rho, \sigma, \kappa\}$. By examination of (11.1) it is easy to verify that the sensitivities of the put to ρ, σ, and κ are the same as those for the call.

FINITE DIFFERENCES FOR THE GREEKS

In the previous section, we derived analytic expressions for the Greeks from the Heston call or put price. Alternatively, we can apply finite differences to find the Greeks and other option sensitivities. When this approach is used, however, the computation time is increased because the option price must be calculated more than once, multiple times in the case of the second-order Greeks. For the first-order Greeks, delta (Δ), theta (Θ), rho (ρ), vega1 ($\mathcal{V}_1$), and vega2 ($\mathcal{V}_2$), as well as for the first-order sensitivities $\partial U/\partial \xi$, for $\xi \in (\rho, \sigma, \kappa)$, the sensitivity of the option price to a parameter or variable can be approximated with first-order central differences. For example, delta for the call $C(S, v_0, t)$ is approximated as

$$\Delta_C \approx \frac{C(S + dS, v_0, t) - C(S - dS, v_0, t)}{2dS}.$$

For the second-order Greeks, gamma (Γ) and volga, we can use the second-order central differences for a single variable. Hence, for example, gamma is approximated as

$$\Gamma \approx \frac{C(S + dS, v_0, t) - 2C(S, v_0, t) + C(S - dS, v_0, t)}{(dS)^2}.$$

For volga, which we express in terms of $\upsilon = \sqrt{v_0}$, we first approximate the following second order derivative in v_0 as

$$\left.\frac{\partial^2 C}{\partial v^2}\right|_{v=v_0} \approx \frac{C(S, v_0 + dv, t) - 2C(S, v_0, t) + C(S, v_0 - dv, t)}{(dv)^2}. \tag{11.27}$$

We then approximate $\mathcal{V}_1$ and substitute it along with (11.27) into (11.20). Finally, for vanna, we use the second-order central difference in two variables. We first approximate the second-order derivative in (11.16), and then multiply by $2\sqrt{v_0}$.

Hence, vanna is approximated as

$$\begin{aligned}\text{Vanna} \approx 2\sqrt{v_0}[C(S+dS, v_0+dv, t) - C(S+dS, v_0-dv, t)\\ -C(S-dS, v_0+dv, t) + C(S-dS, v_0-dv, t)]/(4dSdv).\end{aligned} \tag{11.28}$$

NUMERICAL IMPLEMENTATION OF THE GREEKS

The VBA function HestonGreeksProb contains the integrands to compute the Greeks in closed analytic form. The first part of the function calculates the coefficients $C_j(\tau,\phi)$ and $D_j(\tau,\phi)$, and calculates the characteristic functions $f_j(\phi)$ in the usual way. The second part of the function returns the integrands. Delta in Equation (11.4) and rho in (11.6) require P_j, so the function simply returns the integrand for P_j.

```
Function HestonGreeksProb(phi,...,Greek) As Double
' The characteristic function.
f = cExp(cAdd(cAdd(bigC, Dv0), phixi))
' The integrands for the various Greeks
If Greek = "Delta" Or Greek = "Rho" Then
    ' y = real(exp(-i*phi*log(K))*f/i/phi);
    y = cReal(cDiv(t1, t2))
```

Gamma requires the integrand specified in (11.5).

```
ElseIf Greek = "Gamma" Then
'     y = real(exp(-i*phi*log(K))*f);
    y = cReal(cProd(expiphilogK, f))
```

Theta is slightly more complicated because the derivatives for $C_j(\tau,\phi)$ and $D_j(\tau,\phi)$ in (11.9) needs to be obtained.

```
ElseIf Greek = "Theta" Then
    ' dP/dtau
    dD = cDiv(cProd(cProd(t1, t2), t3), t4)
    ' dC/tau
    dC = cAdd(rqphi, t5)
    ' df = f*(dC + dD*v0);
    df = cProd(f, cAdd(dC, dDv))
    ' y = real(exp(-i*phi*log(K))*df/i/phi);
    y = cReal(cDiv(t1, t2))
```

The first vega ($\mathcal{V}_1$) is straightforward, also since only the integrand in (11.12) is required.

```
ElseIf Greek = "Vega1" Then
    ' y = real(exp(-i*phi*log(K))*f*D/i/phi);
    y = cReal(cDiv(t1, t2))
```

The second vega ($\mathcal{V}_2$) is straightforward also, and uses the integrand in (11.15), and allows for the "Little Trap" formulation of Albrecher et al. (2007).

```
ElseIf Greek = "Vega2" Then
    If trap = 1 Then
        dC = cProd(t1, cSub(t2, t3))
    ElseIf trap = 0 Then
        dC = cProd(t1, cSub(t2, t3))
    End If
    ' y = real(exp(-i*phi*log(K))*df/i/phi);
    y = cReal(cDiv(t1, t2))
```

Finally, volga in Equation (11.18) requires the integrand in (11.22).

```
ElseIf Greek = "Volga" Then
    ' y = real(exp(-i*phi*log(K))*df/i/phi);
    y = cReal(cDiv(t1, t2))
End If
End Function
```

To calculate the Greeks in closed form, the HestonGreeksProb function is then passed to the HestonGreeks function, which performs the required integration using Gauss-Laguerre integration, and returns the desired Greek. To conserve space, not all of the Greeks are presented.

```
Function HestonGreeks(..., Greek) As Double
If Greek = "Delta" Then
    For j = 1 To N
        int1(j) = weight * HestonGreeksProb(..., "Delta")
    Next j
    P1 = 1 / 2 + 1 / pi * Sum(int1)
    If PutCall = "C" Then
        y = Exp(-q * T) * P1
    End If
```

```
ElseIf Greek = "Vega1" Then
    For j = 1 To N
        int1(j) = weight * HestonGreeksProb(..., 1, "Vega1")
        int2(j) = weight * HestonGreeksProb(..., 2, "Vega1")
    Next j
    dP1 = 1 / pi * Sum(int1) * 2 * Sqr(v0)
    dP2 = 1 / pi * Sum(int2) * 2 * Sqr(v0)
    y = S * Exp(-q * T) * dP1 - K * Exp(-r * T) * dP2
End If
HestonGreeks = y
End Function
```

Calculation of the Greeks using finite differences is much simpler. This is accomplished with the VBA function HestonGreeksFD. Again, to conserve space, only a few Greeks are presented.

```
Function HestonGreeksFD(..., Greek) As Double
If Greek = "Delta" Then
    Hu = HestonPriceGaussLaguerre(S + dS,...)
    Hd = HestonPriceGaussLaguerre(S - dS,...)
    y = (Hu - Hd) / 2 / dS
ElseIf Greek = "Vanna" Then
    params(4) = v0 + dV
    Huu = HestonPriceGaussLaguerre(S + dS,...)
    Hdu = HestonPriceGaussLaguerre(S - dS,...)
    params(4) = v0 - dV
    Hud = HestonPriceGaussLaguerre(S + dS,...)
    Hdd = HestonPriceGaussLaguerre(S - dS,...)
    y = (Huu - Hud - Hdu + Hdd) / 4 / dV / dS ...
ElseIf Greek = "Correlation" Then
    params(5) = rho + dR
    Hu = HestonPriceGaussLaguerre(...)
    params(5) = rho - dR
    Hd = HestonPriceGaussLaguerre(...)
    y = (Hu - Hd) / 2 / dR
End Function
```

To illustrate the calculation of the Greeks, recall from Chapter 1 that when we set $\sigma = 0$ and $\theta = v_0$ in the Heston model, then we retrieve the Black-Scholes model exactly. We also saw in that chapter that we cannot simply set $\sigma = 0$ in the Heston characteristic function, since that will entail division by zero. We can, however, set σ to be small, and set $\theta = v_0$. We will then obtain Heston prices that are close to Black-Scholes prices, and we can compare the Heston Greeks with the Black-Scholes Greeks, which are all available in closed form, in Haug (2006), for example. The

Heston and Black-Scholes Greeks Using Closed Form and Finite Differences

Option Features	
Spot Price (S)	100.0000
Strike Price (K)	100.0000
Time to Maturity (τ)	0.5000
Risk free rate (r)	0.0500
Dividend (q)	0.0300
PutCall ("C" or "P")	C

Heston Parameters	
kappa (κ)	0.0000
theta (θ)	0.0700
sigma (σ)	0.0000
v0	0.0700
rho (ρ)	-0.8000
lambda (λ)	0.0000
Trap (0=Heston, 1=Albrecher)	1
Black Scholes Volatility	0.2646

	Heston Greek		
Greek	Exact	FD	Black-Scholes
Delta	0.5501	0.5501	0.5501
Gamma	0.0208	0.0208	0.0208
Rho	23.6031	23.6031	23.6030
Theta	-7.9833	-7.9837	-7.9834
Vega1	27.4908	27.4908	27.4909
Vanna	0.0589	0.0589	0.0589
Volga	-0.6153	-0.6152	-0.6123

Other Greeks by Finite Difference	
Vega2	17.4217
Correlation	0.0726
Kappa	0.0169
Sigma	-0.4895

Price	
Heston	Black-Scholes
7.8057	7.8057

FIGURE 11.2 Heston and Black-Scholes Greeks

Black-Scholes Greeks are implemented with the VBA function BSGreeks, but this function is not presented here.

We use the following settings: $S = K = 100$, $r = 0.05$, $q = 0.03$, and a maturity of six months. In addition, we set $\kappa = 0$, $\theta = v_0 = 0.07$, $\rho = -0.8$, and $\sigma = 0.0001$. The Heston and Black-Scholes price of a call with these features are each 7.8057. The Heston Greeks obtained using their closed forms, the Heston Greeks by finite differences, and the Black-Scholes Greeks are all presented in Figure 11.2.

The three sets of Greeks are all very close, which suggests that the closed form expressions and their finite difference equivalence are sensible. The VBA code and examples in this section are from the Excel file Ch11Heston.xls.

It is informative to present visual illustrations of the Greeks. Figures 11.3 and 11.4 present a plot of gamma and theta, respectively, from the Heston model. The skew in the surfaces is driven by the nonzero value of the correlation, namely, $\rho = -0.8$.

The figures are in the Excel file Ch11EuroPlot.xls.

GREEKS UNDER THE ATTARI AND CARR-MADAN FORMULATIONS

It is possible to derive analytic expressions for the Greeks under formulations other than that by Heston (1993), such as those encountered in previous chapters. For example, it is straightforward to obtain delta and gamma using the Attari (2004) expression for the call price, as explained by Zhu (2010). Recall from Chapter 3 that the call price in this model is given by

$$C(K) = S_t - \frac{1}{2}Ke^{-r\tau} - \frac{Ke^{-r\tau}}{\pi}\int_0^\infty A(u)du.$$

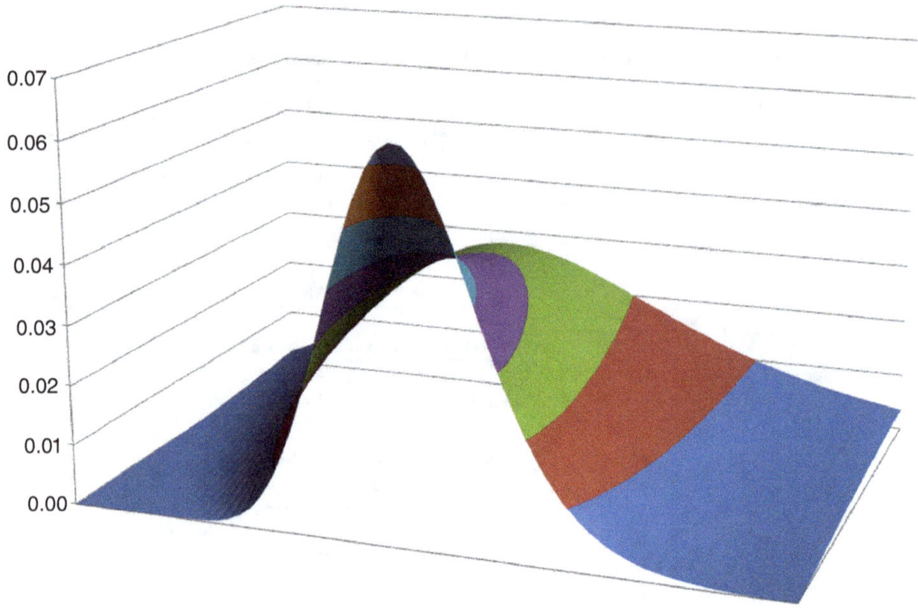

FIGURE 11.3 Gamma from the Heston Model

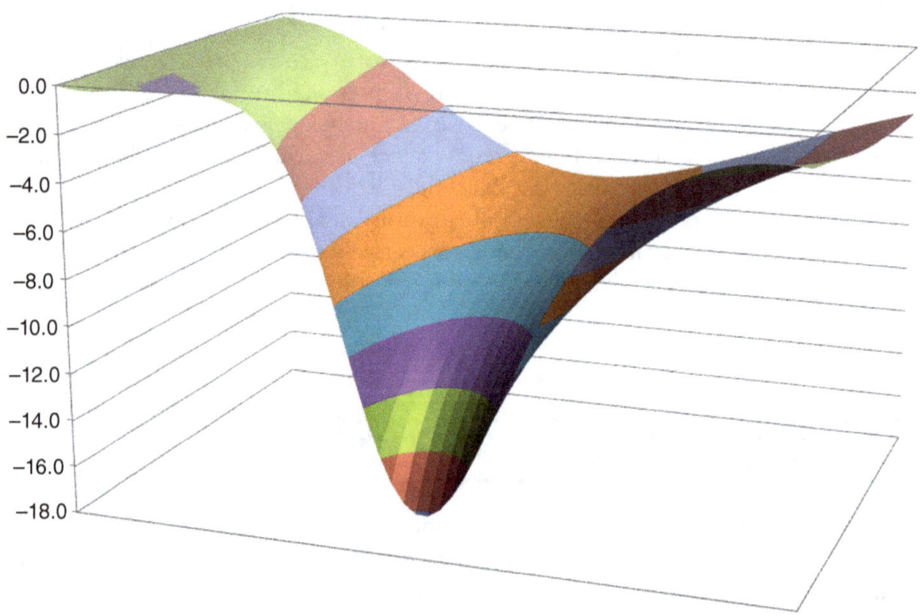

FIGURE 11.4 Theta from the Heston Model

The integrand is

$$
\begin{aligned}
A(u) &= \frac{\left(R_2 + \frac{I_2}{u}\right)\cos(\ell u) + \left(I_2 - \frac{R_2}{u}\right)\sin(\ell u)}{1+u^2} \\
&= \frac{F(u)\cos(\ell u) + G(u)\sin(\ell u)}{1+u^2},
\end{aligned}
\tag{11.29}
$$

where $\ell = \ln(Ke^{-r\tau}/S_t)$. In the integrand (11.29), $R_2 = \mathrm{Re}\left[\varphi_2(u)\right]$ and $I_2 = \mathrm{Im}\left[\varphi_2(u)\right]$ denote the real and imaginary parts, respectively, of the Attari (2004) characteristic function $\varphi_2(u)$ given by

$$
\varphi_2(u) = \exp\left(C_2(\tau,u) + D_2(\tau,u)v_0 - iur\tau\right). \tag{11.30}
$$

It is straightforward to derive the expression for delta for the call:

$$
\Delta_C = 1 - \frac{Ke^{-r\tau}}{\pi}\int_0^\infty \frac{\partial A(u)}{\partial S}du. \tag{11.31}
$$

By applying the chain rule, we obtain the integrand in (11.31) as

$$
\frac{\partial A(u)}{\partial S} = \frac{-F(u)\sin(\ell u) + G(u)\cos(\ell u)}{1+u^2} \times \left(-\frac{u}{S}\right), \tag{11.32}
$$

since $\partial(\ell u)/\partial S = -u/S$. Gamma is given by

$$
\Gamma = -\frac{Ke^{-r\tau}}{\pi}\int_0^\infty \frac{\partial^2 A(u)}{\partial S^2}du, \tag{11.33}
$$

with integrand

$$
\begin{aligned}
\frac{\partial^2 A(u)}{\partial S^2} &= \frac{-F(u)\left(\cos(\ell u)u + \sin(\ell u)\right) + G(u)\left(-\sin(\ell u)u + \cos(\ell u)\right)}{1+u^2} \\
&\quad \times \left(\frac{u}{S^2}\right).
\end{aligned}
\tag{11.34}
$$

In the Attari (2004) formulation of the call price, delta and gamma are easily obtained in closed form because $\varphi_2(u)$ does not depend on the spot price S_t. It is not practical to obtain the other Greeks in this manner, because the parameter for the Greek will appear in $\varphi_2(u)$. We can still obtain the Greeks in the model using finite differences, however.

The VBA function AttariProbGreeks calculates the integrand required for delta and gamma in Equations (11.32) and (11.34). It is very similar to the AttariProb function presented in Chapter 3.

```
Function AttariProbGreeks(..., Greek) As Double
' The characteristic function for Attari.
f = cExp(cAdd(bigC, cSub(Dv, iphirtau)))
' The "L" function
L = Log(Exp(-r * tau) * K / S)
' The coefficients
FF = (cReal(f) + cImag(f) / phi)
GG = (cImag(f) - cReal(f) / phi)
' Return the integrand for the chosen Greek
If Greek = "Delta" Then
    AttariProbGreeks = (FF * Sin(L * phi) ...
ElseIf Greek = "Gamma" Then
    y = (-FF * (Cos(L * phi) * phi + Sin(L * phi)) ...
    AttariProbGreeks = y * phi / S ^ 2 / ...
End If
End Function
```

This function is then passed to the AttariGreeks function, which uses numerical integration to calculate delta using Equation (11.31) or gamma using (11.33).

```
Function AttariGreeks(Greek,...) As Double
For j = 1 To N
    If Greek = "Delta" Then
        a(j) = weight * AttariProbGreeks(..., "Delta")
    ElseIf Greek = "Gamma" Then
        a(j) = weight * AttariProbGreeks(..., "Gamma")
    End If
Next j
Integral = Sum(a)
If Greek = "Gamma" Then
    AttariGreeks = -Exp(-r * T) * K / pi * Integral
ElseIf Greek = "Delta" Then
    If PutCall = "C" Then
        AttariGreeks = 1 - Exp(-r * T) * K / pi * Integral
    Else
        AttariGreeks = -Exp(-r * T) * K / pi * Integral
    End If
End If
End Function
```

Using finite difference approximations, it is easy to verify that the AttariGreeks function produces values of delta and gamma that are quite accurate. This can be accomplished with the VBA function AttariGreeksFD.

```
Function AttariGreeksFD(...,Greek As String) As Double
Ah = AttariPriceGaussLaguerre(S0 + dS,...)
Am = AttariPriceGaussLaguerre(S0,...)
Ad = AttariPriceGaussLaguerre(S0 - dS,...)
If Greek = "Delta" Then
    AttariGreeksFD = (Ah - Ad) / 2 / dS
ElseIf Greek = "Gamma" Then
    AttariGreeksFD = (Ah - 2 * Am + Ad) / dS ^ 2
End If
End Function
```

To illustrate, we use the same settings as in the example of Figure 11.2. The results are in Figure 11.5.

The VBA functions and example in this section are in the Excel file Ch11Attari.xls.

We can also derive closed-form expressions for the Greeks under the Carr and Madan (1999) formulation of the call price, which we first encountered in Chapter 3. Recall that the call price under their formulation is

$$C(k) = \frac{e^{-\alpha k}}{\pi} \int_0^\infty \text{Re}\left[e^{-ivk} \frac{e^{-r\tau} f_2(v - (\alpha+1)i)}{\alpha^2 + \alpha - v^2 + iv(2\alpha+1)} \right] dv, \tag{11.35}$$

where α is the damping factor, k is the logarithm of the strike price, and f_2 is the Heston (1993) characteristic function for $x_T = \ln S_T$. To obtain the Greeks, we simply differentiate f_2, substitute into (11.35) and evaluate the integral. Theta and rho are

	A	B	C	D	E	F	G	H	I
1									
2		**Delta and Gamma for the Attari (2004) Model**							
3						Delta		Gamma	
4		**Option Features**			Strike	Exact	Finite Diff	Exact	Finite Diff
5		Spot Price (S)	100.0000		95	0.6682	0.6533	0.0192	0.0192
6					96	0.6478	0.6330	0.0197	0.0197
7		Time to Maturity (τ)	0.5000		96	0.6478	0.6330	0.0197	0.0197
8		Risk free rate (r)	0.0500		98	0.6066	0.5917	0.0203	0.0203
9		Dividend (q)	0.0300		99	0.5858	0.5709	0.0206	0.0206
10		PutCall (C or P)	C		100	0.5650	0.5501	0.0208	0.0208
11					101	0.5443	0.5294	0.0209	0.0209
12		**Heston Parameters**			102	0.5236	0.5087	0.0210	0.0210
13		kappa (κ)	0.0000		103	0.5031	0.4882	0.0210	0.0210
14		theta (θ)	0.0700		104	0.4828	0.4680	0.0210	0.0210
15		sigma (σ)	0.0000		105	0.4628	0.4479	0.0209	0.0209
16		v0	0.0700						
17		rho (ρ)	-0.8000						
18		lambda (λ)	0.0000						
19		Trap (0=Heston, 1=Albrecher)	1						
20									

FIGURE 11.5 Delta and Gamma under the Attari Formulation

slightly more complicated, because we need to apply the product rule to $e^{-r\tau}f_2$ in (11.35). Theta, for example, is obtained as

$$\Theta_C = -\frac{e^{-\alpha k}}{\pi}\int_0^\infty \text{Re}\left[e^{-ivk}\frac{e^{-r\tau}(-rf_2 + \partial f_2/\partial\tau)}{\alpha^2+\alpha-v^2+iv(2\alpha+1)}\right]dv, \tag{11.36}$$

where f_2 and $\partial f_2/\partial\tau$ are both evaluated at $v-(\alpha+1)i$. To calculate volga for $v=\sqrt{v_0}$, note that an application of the chain rule produces $\partial^2 f_2/\partial v^2 = 2D_2 f_2(2D_2 v_0 + 1)$, where $D_2 = D_2(\tau, v)$ is the coefficient for the Heston characteristic function.

The VBA function HestonCFGreek returns the derivative of f_2, which is required to obtain the Greeks for the Carr and Madan (1999) call price. The function also returns the call price, if desired, by returning f_2 itself rather than a derivative. It is similar to the HestonGreeksProb function defined earlier in this chapter.

```
Function HestonCFGreek(phi,..., Greek) As Variant
' The characteristic function.
f = cExp(cAdd(cAdd(bigC, Dv0), phixi))
' Derivatives of f required for the Greeks
If Greek = "Price" Then
    df = f
ElseIf Greek = "Delta" Then
    df = cProd(cProd(iphi, f), Complex(1 / S, 0))
ElseIf Greek = "Vega1" Then
    df = cProd(f, bigD)
ElseIf Greek = "Volga" Then
    df = cProd(Term1, Term2)
End If
' Ouput real and imag parts of df separately
output(1, 1) = cReal(df)
output(2, 1) = cImag(df)
End Function
```

The derivatives are then passed to the CarrMadanGreeks function, which uses numerical integration and returns delta, gamma, theta, rho, vega1, vanna, and volga, or the call price. Both functions can be easily modified to return additional option sensitivities.

```
Function CarrMadanGreeks(...,Greek As String) As Double
For j = 1 To N
    Inte = cDiv(cProd(cProd(cProd(Term1, Term2), ...)
    bigI(j) = cReal(Inte)
Next j
```

```
If Greek = "Delta" Or Greek = "Gamma" Or Greek = "Rho" Or _
   Greek = "Theta" Or Greek = "Volga" Or Greek = "Price" Then
     CarrMadanGreeks = Exp(-alpha * Log(K)) ...
 ElseIf Greek = "Vega1" Or Greek = "Vanna" Then
     CarrMadanGreeks = Exp(-alpha * Log(K)) ...
End If
End Function
```

It is straightforward to verify that the Greeks calculated with this function produce values that are close to their finite difference approximations. This is illustrated in Figure 11.6.

The VBA code and example in this section are in the Excel file Ch11CM.xls.

GREEKS UNDER THE LEWIS FORMULATIONS

Recall from Chapter 4 that the Lewis (2000) expressions for the call price can be written in terms of the fundamental transform $\hat{H}(k, v, \tau)$ as

$$C_1(K) = -\frac{Ke^{-r\tau}}{\pi}\int_0^\infty \text{Re}\left[\frac{e^{-ikX}}{k^2 - ik}\hat{H}(k, v, \tau)\right] dk, \tag{11.37}$$

for $1 < k_i < \beta$, and as

$$C_2(K) = S_t e^{-q\tau} - \frac{Ke^{-r\tau}}{\pi}\int_0^\infty \text{Re}\left[\frac{e^{-ikX}}{k^2 - ik}\hat{H}(k, v, \tau)\right] dk, \tag{11.38}$$

	A	B	C	D	E	F	G	H
1								
2		**Carr-Madan Greeks Using Closed Form and Finite Differences**						
3								
4		**Option Features**				**Closed Form**	**Finite Difference**	**Error**
5		Spot Price (S)	100.0000		**Price**	5.0837	----	----
6		Strike Price (K)	100.0000		**Delta**	0.5833	0.5833	3.60E-04
7		Time to Maturity (τ)	0.2500		**Gamma**	0.0347	0.0347	4.99E-04
8		Risk free rate (r)	0.0500		**Theta**	-11.4004	-11.4004	-1.56E-06
9		Dividend (q)	0.0000		**Rho**	13.3127	13.3127	3.19E-09
10		PutCall ("C" or "P")	C		**Vega1**	15.3909	15.3909	-3.01E-07
11					**Vanna**	-0.1257	-0.1257	1.22E-02
12		**Heston Parameters**			**Volga**	15.4273	15.4273	6.11E-05
13		kappa (κ)	2.0000		**Theta**	-11.4004	-11.4004	-1.56E-06
14		theta (θ)	0.0500					
15		sigma (σ)	0.1000					
16		v0	0.0500					
17		rho (ρ)	-0.9000					
18		lambda (λ)	0.0000					
19		Trap (0=Heston, 1=Albrecher)	1					
20								
21		**Dampening Factor (α)**	1.7500					

FIGURE 11.6 Greeks under the Carr-Madan Formulation

for $\max(0,\alpha) < k_i < \min(1,\beta)$ and where $X = \ln(S_t/K) + (r-q)\tau$. We can readily differentiate the integrands for $C_1(K)$ and $C_2(K)$ to obtain analytical expressions for the Greeks, as we did in the previous sections. Gamma, for example, is given by

$$\Gamma = \frac{Ke^{-r\tau}}{\pi S^2}\int_0^\infty \text{Re}\left[e^{-ikX}\hat{H}(k,v,\tau)\right]dk, \tag{11.39}$$

The VBA function LewisIntegrandGreek is a modification of the function Lewis-Integrand from Chapter 4 and returns the integrand required for the calculation of Greeks using either $C_1(K)$ or $C_2(K)$. It also returns the integrand for the price itself.

```
Function LewisIntegrandGreek(k As cNum,...) As Double
' The fundamental transform, H(k,S,t)
bigH = cExp(cAdd(bigC, Dv0))
' The term exp(-X*i*k - r*tau) / (k^2 - i*k) * H
expHk = cDiv(cProd(expXik, bigH), Den)
' Return the real part of the integrand for each Greek
If Greek = "Price" Then
    y = cReal(expHk)
ElseIf Greek = "Delta" Then
    y = cReal(cProd(expHk, cProd(ik, Complex(-1 / S, 0))))
ElseIf Greek = "Gamma" Then
    y = -cReal(cProd(cProd(expXik, bigH), ...))
ElseIf Greek = "Vega1" Then
    y = cReal(cProd(cProd(expHk, bigD), ...))
ElseIf Greek = "Vanna" Then
    y = cReal(cProd(expHk, Term2))
End If
LewisIntegrandGreek = y
End Function
```

The function is then passed to the VBA function HestonLewisGreekPrice to produce the Greeks. The function allows for numerical integration using either the trapezoidal rule or the Gauss-Laguerre rule.

```
Function HestonLewisGreekPrice(...) As Double
If IntRule = 1 Then
    ' Trapezoidal Rule and weights
    For j = 2 To Nphi
        phi(j) = phi(j - 1) + dphi
    Next j
    For j = 2 To Nphi - 1
        wt(j) = dphi
```

```
        Next j
        For j = 1 To Nphi
            inte(j) = wt(j) * LewisIntegrandGreek(u,...,Greek)
        Next j
        Integral = Sum(inte)
    Else
        ' Gauss Laguerre integration
        ...
    End If
    ' Compute the Greeks
    If Greek = "Price" Then
        If form = 2 Then
            ' C2(S,K,t) Equation (2.10) page 41 of Lewis (2000)
            y = S * Exp(-q * tau) - (Strike / pi) * Integral
        Else
            ' C1(S,K,t) Equation (2.8) page 40 of Lewis (2000)
            y = -(Strike / pi) * Integral
        End If
    ElseIf Greek = "Theta" Then
        If form = 2 Then
            y = q * S * Exp(-q * tau) + (Strike / pi) * Integral
        Else
            y = (Strike / pi) * Integral
        End If
    End If
    HestonLewisGreekPrice = y
    End Function
```

The Greeks using the Lewis (2000) formulation are illustrated in Figure 11.7.

The VBA function HestonLewisGreekFD is used to obtain the Lewis (2000) Greeks with finite differences, but this function is not presented here. The VBA code and example in this section are in the Excel file Ch11LewisFT.xls.

The option price $C(S_t)$ derived by Lewis (2001), that uses Parseval's identity, was also covered in Chapter 4. The form that uses $k_i = \frac{1}{2}$ is Equation (3.11) of Lewis (2001):

$$C(S_t) = S_t e^{-q\tau} - \frac{\sqrt{K}}{\pi} \int_0^\infty \text{Re}\left[\frac{K^{-iu} e^{-r\tau} f_2\left(u - \frac{1}{2}i\right)}{u^2 + \frac{1}{4}} \right] du,$$

where X is defined after (11.38). We have used the fact from Chapter 4 that $\varphi(u) = f_2(u)e^{-iuY}$, where $Y = \ln S_t + (r - q)\tau$ and f_2 is the Heston (1993) characteristic function. The VBA function LewisGreeks311 is used to implement the Greeks for the call price $C(S_t)$ from Equation (3.11) of Lewis (2001). This function is not presented here, but the results are in Figure 11.8.

Heston Greeks Using the Lewis (2000) Fundamental Transform

Option Features			C1(K)		C2(K)	
			Analytic	Finite Difference	Analytic	Finite Difference
Spot Price (S)	100.0000					
Strike Price (K)	100.0000	**Price**	5.0749	5.0749	5.0680	5.0680
Time to Maturity (τ)	0.2500	**Delta**	0.5666	0.5666	0.5666	0.5666
Risk free rate (r)	0.0500	**Gamma**	0.0353	0.0353	0.0353	0.0353
Dividend (q)	0.0000	**Theta**	-11.3464	-11.3464	-11.3465	-11.3466
		Rho	12.8969	12.8969	12.8975	12.8975
Heston Parameters		**Vega1**	15.4812	15.4812	15.4812	15.4812
kappa (κ)	2.0000	**Vanna**	0.0516	0.0516	0.0517	0.0516
theta (θ)	0.0500	**Volga**	15.7285	15.7285	15.7295	15.7285
sigma (σ)	0.1000	ki	1.5		0.5	
v0	0.0500	Form	1		2	
rho (ρ)	-0.9000	Rule	2		2	
lambda (λ)	0.0000					
Integration Settings Trapezoidal Rule						
Lower Limit of Integration	1.00E-10					
Upper Limit of Integration	150.00					
Number of Points	500					

FIGURE 11.7 Greeks under the Lewis (2000) Formulation

Heston Greeks Using the Approach of Lewis (2001), Equation 3.11

Option Features			Lewis Greek, Equation 3.11	
			Analytic	Finite Difference
Spot Price (S)	100.0000			
Strike Price (K)	100.0000	**Price**	5.0790	5.0790
Time to Maturity (τ)	0.2500	**Delta**	0.5833	0.5833
Risk free rate (r)	0.0500	**Gamma**	0.0347	0.0347
Dividend (q)	0.0000	**Theta**	-11.4009	-11.4009
		Rho	13.3133	13.3133
Heston Parameters		**Vega1**	15.3915	15.3915
kappa (κ)	2.0000	**Vanna**	-0.1257	-0.1257
theta (θ)	0.0500	**Volga**	15.4055	15.4054
sigma (σ)	0.1000			
v0	0.0500			
rho (ρ)	-0.9000			
lambda (λ)	0.0000			
Trap (0=Heston, 1=Albrecher)	1			

FIGURE 11.8 Greeks under the Lewis (2001) Formulation

The VBA function Lewis311GreekFD is used to obtain the Lewis (2001) Greeks with finite differences, but this function is not presented here. The VBA code and example in this section are in the Excel file Ch11Lewis311.xls.

GREEKS USING THE FFT AND FRFT

We saw in Chapter 5 that the fast Fourier transform (FFT) and fractional fast Fourier transform (FRFT) are both able to produce call prices very quickly and for a wide range of strikes simultaneously. It is straightforward to adapt these methods to produce the Greeks in the same manner. Recall from Chapter 5 that to implement the FFT on the call price, we construct the integration grid $\{v_j\}_{j=1}^N$ and the log-strike grid $\{k_u\}_{u=1}^N$, and calculate the points $x_j = \exp\left(i(b - \ln S_t)v_j\right) \psi(v_j)w_j$ for $j = 1, \cdots, N$. We then obtain $\hat{x}_u = C(k_u)$, the call price evaluated at the log-strike point k_u, as the sum

$$\hat{x}_u = \frac{\eta e^{-\alpha k_u}}{\pi} \sum_{j=1}^{N} \text{Re}\left[e^{-i\frac{2\pi}{N}(j-1)(u-1)}x_j\right] \text{ for } u = 1, \cdots, N. \tag{11.40}$$

To obtain a set of Greeks with the FFT, in x_j we simply replace the term

$$\psi(v_j) = \frac{e^{-r\tau} f_2(v_j - (\alpha+1)i)}{\alpha^2 + \alpha - v_j^2 + iv_j(2\alpha+1)} \tag{11.41}$$

with a modified version that uses the derivative of f_2 instead of f_2, such as that for theta in Equation (11.36), for example. We use this modification to obtain the Greeks under the FRFT also.

Implementing the Greeks with the FFT requires a slight modification of the code presented in Chapter 5. The VBA function HestonCallFFTGreek is nearly identical to the HestonCallFFT function from that chapter, except that it uses the function HestonCFGreek for the characteristic function.

```
Function HestonCallFFTGreek(..., Greek) As Variant
For u = 1 To N
    For j = 1 To N
        charfun = HestonCFGreek(..., Greek)
        psi(j) = Complex(charfun(1, 1), charfun(2, 1))
        phi(j) = cDiv(Num, Den)
        x(j) = cProd(t1, t2)
        e(j) = cReal(cProd(t1, x(j)))
    Next j
    CallFFT(u) = eta * Exp(-alpha * K(u)) / pi ...
Next u
' Output the strikes and the FFT call prices
For j = 1 To N
    output(j, 1) = bigK(j)
    output(j, 2) = CallFFT(j)
Next j
End Function
```

The VBA function HestonCallFRFTGreek is similar to the preceding function, but it is used to implement the fractional FFT Greeks.

```
Function HestonCallFRFTGreek(..., Greek) As Variant
' Implement the FRFT Part 1
For j = 1 To N
    psi(j) = Complex(charfun(1, 1), charfun(2, 1))
    phi(j) = cDiv(Num, Den)
    x(j) = cProd(t1, t2)
    xReal(j) = cReal(x(j))
    xImag(j) = cImag(x(j))
Next j
' Implement the FRFT Part 2
For j = 1 To N
    y(j) = Complex(FRFTvec(j, 1), FRFTvec(j, 2))
Next j
' Implement the FRFT Part 3
For u = 1 To N
    ' Calls = eta * Exp(-alpha * k(u)) * y(u) / pi
    Calls = cProd(y(u), Complex(temp1, 0))
    CallFRFT(u) = cReal(Calls)
Next u
' Output the strikes and the FRFT call prices
For j = 1 To N
    output(j, 1) = bigK(j)
    output(j, 2) = CallFRFT(j)
Next j
End Function
```

Figures 11.9 and 11.10 illustrate the FFT and FRFT Greeks, respectively.

The VBA code for the FFT Greeks and the example in Figure 11.9 are in the Excel file Ch11FFT.xls, while those for the FRFT Greeks are in the Excel file Ch11FRFT.xls.

Heston Greeks Using the Fast Fourier Transform

Option Features	
Spot Price (S)	50.0000
Time to Maturity (τ)	0.5000
Risk free rate (r)	0.0300
Dividend (q)	0.0500
Little Trap (0=Heston, 1=Albrecher)	1
Heston Parameters	
kappa (κ)	0.2000
theta (θ)	0.0500
sigma (σ)	0.3000
v0	0.0500
rho (ρ)	-0.7000
lambda (λ)	0.0000
Trap (0=Heston, 1=Albrecher)	0
FFT Settings	
Number of points	256
Dampening factor	1.5
Upper Limit of integration	100
Integration(T=Trapezoidal, S=Simpson's)	T

Strike	Price	Delta	Gamma	Theta	Rho	Vega1	Vanna	Volga
41.4102	8.6381	0.8706	0.0171	-2.8364	17.4465	14.0522	-1.4000	26.6931
44.0956	6.4761	0.8029	0.0265	-3.2832	16.8351	19.8376	-1.5640	21.6688
46.9551	4.4454	0.7012	0.0387	-3.5384	15.3073	25.9244	-1.2879	9.5169
50.0000	2.6782	0.5580	0.0524	-3.3922	12.6103	30.2234	-0.1244	-2.4152
53.2424	1.3267	0.3757	0.0619	-2.7042	8.7299	29.0667	2.2457	12.7374
56.6950	0.5018	0.1891	0.0525	-1.6420	4.4772	19.8988	4.2020	66.3946
60.3716	0.1424	0.0657	0.0257	-0.7209	1.5709	8.7004	3.0472	72.5743

Greeks using Finite Differences

Strike	Price	Delta	Gamma	Theta	Rho	Vega1	Vanna	Volga
41.4102	--	0.8704	0.0173	-0.6597	17.4407	6.2872	-0.6061	27.6355
44.0956	--	0.8029	0.0263	-1.2753	16.8339	8.8542	-0.7091	21.6802
46.9551	--	0.7014	0.0388	-1.7862	15.3132	11.6078	-0.5797	8.9438
50.0000	--	0.5579	0.0525	-1.9975	12.6078	13.5205	-0.0478	-2.1289
53.2424	--	0.3756	0.0618	-1.7643	8.7265	12.9869	1.0044	13.0241
56.6950	--	0.1893	0.0524	-1.1694	4.4803	8.8989	1.8730	66.1373
60.3716	--	0.0658	0.0258	-0.5572	1.5737	3.9036	1.3629	72.2709

FIGURE 11.9 Greeks under the Fast Fourier Transform

Heston Greeks Using the Fractional FFT

Option Features	
Spot Price (S)	50.0000
Time to Maturity (τ)	0.5000
Risk free rate (r)	0.0300
Dividend (q)	0.0500
Little Trap (0=Heston, 1=Albrecher)	1
Heston Parameters	
kappa (κ)	0.2000
theta (θ)	0.0500
sigma (σ)	0.3000
v0	0.0500
rho (ρ)	-0.7000
lambda (λ)	0.0000
Trap (0=Heston, 1=Albrecher)	0
FRFT Settings	
Number of points	1024
Dampening factor	1.5
Upper Limit of integration	100
Integration (T=Trapezoidal, S=Simpson's)	T

Strike	Price	Delta	Gamma	Theta	Rho	Vega1	Vanna	Volga
48.5223	3.4438	0.5764	0.0483	-3.1160	12.6889	26.0895	0.7650	28.9842
49.0099	3.1949	0.5522	0.0486	-3.0512	12.2079	25.9333	0.8995	30.1180
49.5025	2.9556	0.5279	0.0487	-2.9808	11.7193	25.7092	1.0291	31.2097
50.0000	2.7261	0.5035	0.0487	-2.9052	11.2248	25.4191	1.1530	32.2518
50.5025	2.5066	0.4792	0.0486	-2.8248	10.7259	25.0654	1.2706	33.2370
51.0101	2.2971	0.4549	0.0484	-2.7398	10.2245	24.6508	1.3814	34.1584
51.5227	2.0976	0.4308	0.0480	-2.6509	9.7222	24.1781	1.4849	35.0095

Greeks Using Finite Differences

Strike	Price	Delta	Gamma	Theta	Rho	Vega1	Vanna	Volga
48.5223	---	0.6318	0.0460	-1.9463	14.0565	12.8004	-0.3636	2.0097
49.0099	---	0.6083	0.0482	-1.9744	13.6056	13.0893	-0.2720	0.2437
49.5025	---	0.5836	0.0504	-1.9916	13.1226	13.3319	-0.1670	-1.1812
50.0000	---	0.5579	0.0525	-1.9975	12.6078	13.5205	-0.0478	-2.1289
50.5025	---	0.5311	0.0546	-1.9916	12.0617	13.6475	0.0860	-2.4445
51.0101	---	0.5033	0.0565	-1.9738	11.4853	13.7049	0.2343	-1.9596
51.5227	---	0.4746	0.0582	-1.9438	10.8803	13.6848	0.3968	-0.4985

FIGURE 11.10 Greeks under the Fractional Fast Fourier Transform

AMERICAN GREEKS USING SIMULATION

The Least-Squares Monte Carlo (LSM) algorithm of Longstaff and Schwartz (2001) can be modified to calculate American Greeks. For this to work, we must store the values of the correlated normal random variables used to generate the stock price and volatility paths and apply these same random variables when we generate the paths under the shifted values of the inputs. This ensures that any differences between the original paths and the shifted paths are due to the shifts themselves, and not due to simulation noise.

It is straightforward to modify the simulation functions of Chapter 7 to obtain Greeks for American options with the LSM algorithm. The first task is to create matrices of simulated correlated random variables outside of the functions, and pass these matrices as function arguments. The VBA function MMSimGreeks is a simple modified version of the MMSim function encountered in Chapter 7 for the moment-matching simulation scheme of Andersen and Brotherton-Ratcliffe (2005). The only difference is that the correlated random variables Z_S and Z_V are generated outside the function and passed to the function in its argument.

The following code snippets are in the Excel file Ch11LSMGreeks.xls.

```
Function MMSimGreeks(..., Zv As Variant, Zs As Variant) As Variant
' Generate the stock and volatility paths
For i = 1 To NS
    For j = 2 To NT
        ' Matched moment lognormal approximation
        Num = 0.5 * sigma ^ 2 * V(j - 1, i) * (1 - Exp(-2 * kappa * dT)) ...
        Den = (Exp(-kappa * dT) * V(j - 1, i) + (1 - Exp(-kappa * dT)) ...
        Gam = Log(1 + Num / Den)
        V(j, i) = (Exp(-kappa * dT) * V(j - 1, i) + (1 - Exp(-kappa * dT)) ...
        S(j, i) = S(j - 1, i) * Exp((r - q - V(j - 1, i) / 2) * dT ...
    Next j
Next i
```

```
' Output the stock price paths, transposed for the LSM algorithm
St = MTrans(S, NT, NS)
MMSimGreeks = St
End Function
```

To calculate the Greeks, we generate the matrices of correlated random variables, and we generate a series of stock price paths using the same random variables but using shifted values of the inputs. This is accomplished with the VBA functions LSMGreeks and LSMGreeksCalc. The LSMGreeks function generates the correlated variables and invokes the LSMGreeksCalc function for the actual calculations of the Greeks.

```
Function LSMGreeks(...) As Variant
' Generate correlated N(0,1) standard normal random variables
For i = 1 To NS
    For j = 1 To NT
        Randomize
        Zv(i, j) = NormSInv(Rnd())
        Randomize
        Zs(i, j) = Rho * Zv(i, j) + Sqr(1 - Rho ^ 2)...
    Next j
Next i
' Output the results
output = LSMGreeksCalc(..., Zv, Zs)
LSMGreeks = output
End Function
```

The LSMGreeksCalc function requires the correlated random variables Z_V and Z_S as inputs. It returns the option price, along with the six Greeks calculated using the moment-matching simulation scheme through the MMSimGreeks function and the LSM method.

```
Function LSMGreeksCalc(..., Zv As Variant, Zs As Variant) As Variant
' Calculation of Price, Delta, Gamma
Spathsm = MMSimGreeks(params0, Spot - dS,..., Zv, Zs)
Spaths0 = MMSimGreeks(params0, Spot,..., Zv, Zs)
Spathsp = MMSimGreeks(params0, Spot + dS,..., Zv, Zs)
ym = LSM(Spathsm, ...)
y0 = LSM(Spaths0, ...)
yp = LSM(Spathsp, ...)
Price = y0
Delta = (yp - ym) / 2 / dS
Gamma = (yp - 2 * y0 + ym) / dS ^ 2
' Calculation of Vega1
paramsp(4) = v0 + dV
```

```
paramsm(4) = v0 - dV
Spathsm = MMSimGreeks(paramsm, ..., Zv, Zs)
Spathsp = MMSimGreeks(paramsp, ..., Zv, Zs)
ym = LSM(Spathsm, ...)
yp = LSM(Spathsp, ...)
Vega1 = (yp - ym) / 2 / dV * 2 * Sqr(v0)
paramsp(4) = v0
paramsm(4) = v0
' Output the results
output(1) = Price
output(2) = Delta
...
output(7) = Vanna
LSMGreeksCalc = output
End Function
```

The LSMGreeks function depends on the LSM function to generate the LSM algorithm. The LSM function was presented in Chapter 8 and is therefore not presented here.

To illustrate, we run the LSM algorithm on American puts, using the settings in Clarke and Parrott (1999) with the prices computed by Ikonen and Toivanen (2008), namely $K = 10$, $\tau = 0.25$, $r = 0.1$, $\kappa = 5$, $\theta = 0.16$, $\sigma = 0.9$, and $\rho = 0.1$, with spot price running from 8 to 12. The results are in Figure 11.11.

The results in Figure 11.11 are in the Excel file Ch11LSMGreeks.xls. Note that the parameter in cell C12 allows for the calculation of European Greeks. It is simpler, however, to calculate those Greeks using finite differences or other methods encountered earlier.

AMERICAN GREEKS USING THE EXPLICIT METHOD

Recall from Chapter 10 that when the Heston PDE is solved with finite differences, a matrix in the stock price and volatility dimensions is obtained that contains a complete set of option prices. Hence, the matrix contains shifted values of the call

Longstaff-Schwartz LSM Algorithm for European and American options

Option Features	
Strike Price (K)	10.0000
Time to Maturity (τ)	0.2500
Risk free rate (r)	0.1000
Dividend (q)	0.0000
PutCall (C or P)	P
Trap (0=Heston, 1=Albrecher)	1
Euro or American ("E" or "A")	A
Heston Parameters	
kappa (κ)	5.0000
theta (θ)	0.1600
sigma (σ)	0.9000
v0	0.0625
rho (ρ)	0.1000
lambda (λ)	0.0000

Spot	TruePrice	Price	Delta	Gamma	Theta	Rho	Vega1	Vanna	Number of Time steps per path	Number of Stock price paths
8.0	2.000000	2.0493	-0.9754	-0.6477	-0.1963	1.9625	0.3458	-2.3028	90	1000
9.0	1.107064	1.1089	-0.8189	0.5608	-0.1754	1.7544	0.7350	0.2286	90	1000
10.0	0.520030	0.5500	-0.4651	-0.3425	-1.0686	10.6857	1.3645	1.4502	90	1000
11.0	0.213668	#VALUE!	#VALUE!	#VALUE!	#VALUE!	#VALUE!	#VALUE!	#VALUE!	90	1000
12.0	0.082036	#VALUE!	#VALUE!	#VALUE!	#VALUE!	#VALUE!	#VALUE!	#VALUE!	90	1000

FIGURE 11.11 American Greeks Using the LSM Algorithm

value in price and volatility, and finite differences can readily be applied to obtain the Greeks. This requires two-dimensional interpolation to obtain the call prices at the shifted values. In this manner, all the Greeks representing sensitivities in S and v_0 can be obtained, namely, delta, gamma, vega1, vanna, and volga. The VBA function GreeksPDE uses the VBA functions HestonExplicitPDE and HestonExplicit PDENonUniform defined in Chapter 10 for uniform and nonuniform grids, respectively, to obtain the Greeks.

```
Function GreeksPDE(...GridType As String) As Variant
' Build the grids
If GridType = "Uniform" Then
    ' Matrix U(S,v,T), dimension NV x Ns
    U  = HestonExplicitPDE(..., "U")
    ' Matrix U(S,v,T-dt), dimension Nv x NS
    Us = HestonExplicitPDE(..., "Us")
    ' Vector of spot prices, dimension NS
    Spot = HestonExplicitPDE(..., "Spot")
    ' Vector of volatilities, dimension NV
    Vol  = HestonExplicitPDE(..., "Vol")
ElseIf GridType = "NonUniform" Then
    U    = HestonExplicitPDENonUniform(..., "U")
    Us   = HestonExplicitPDENonUniform(..., "Us")
    Spot = HestonExplicitPDENonUniform(..., "Spot")
    Vol  = HestonExplicitPDENonUniform(..., "Vol")
End If
' Option Price
Price = interp2(Spot, Vol, U, Si, Vi)
' Delta and Gamma
yp = interp2(..., Si + dS)
ym = interp2(..., Si - dS)
y0 = interp2(..., Si)
Delta = (yp - ym) / 2 / dS
Gamma = (yp - 2 * y0 + ym) / dS / dS
' Theta
T1 = interp2(..., U,  Si, Vi)     ' U(S,v,T)
T2 = interp2(..., Us, Si, Vi)     ' U(S,v,T-dt)
dt = (Tmax - Tmin) / (NT - 1)
ThetaPDE = -(T1 - T2) / dt
End Function
```

The function uses the VBA function interp2 for two-dimensional interpolation. Note that theta can be obtained by recognizing that the VBA functions HestonExplicitPDE and HestonExplicitPDENonUniform both retain the value of $U(S, v, t)$ in the previous time step, $U(S, v, t - dt)$, but overwrite this value only at maturity. This provides the time-shifted value of the derivative that is required for a finite difference approximation to theta. These functions were introduced in Chapter 10 and are not presented here.

The GreeksPDE function returns both American and European Greeks. We can use finite differences to verify the accuracy of European Greeks obtained with the explicit method. This is accomplished with the VBA function HestonGreeksPDE.

```
Function HestonGreeksFD(..., Greek) As Double
If Greek = "Delta" Then
    Hu = HestonPriceTrapz(..., S + dS)
    Hd = HestonPriceTrapz(..., S - dS)
    Y = (Hu - Hd) / 2 / dS
ElseIf Greek = "Volga" Then
    ' Find Vega1
    params(4) = v0 + dV
    Hu = HestonPriceTrapz(...)
    params(4) = v0 - dV
    Hd = HestonPriceTrapz(...)
    Vega1FD = (Hu - Hd) / 2 / dV * 2 * Sqr(v0)
    ' Find second derivative
    params(4) = v0
    Hm = HestonPriceTrapz(...)
    dC2 = (Hu - 2 * Hm + Hd) / (dV ^ 2)
    ' Volga
    Y = 4 * Sqr(v0) * (dC2 * Sqr(v0) + Vega1FD ...
End If
HestonGreeksFD = Y
End Function
```

We use the settings of Clarke and Parrott (1999) and the prices of Ikonen and Toivanen (2008) that are used throughout this chapter, along with a stock price grid size of 60, a volatility grid size of 30, and 3,000 time steps. The results are in Figure 11.12.

The VBA function and screen shot example in Figure 11.12 are in the Excel file Ch11Explicit.xls.

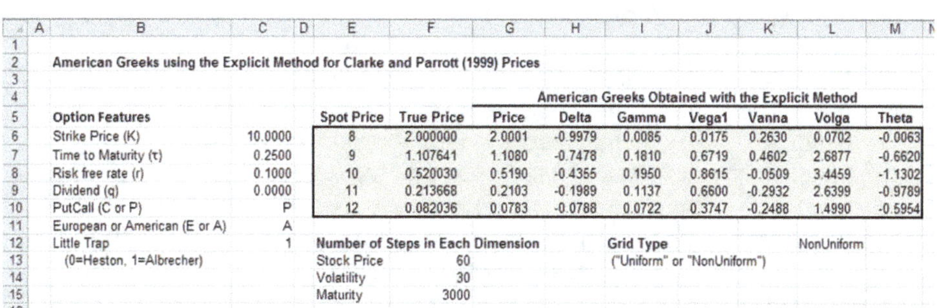

American Greeks using the Explicit Method for Clarke and Parrott (1999) Prices

Option Features		Spot Price	True Price	Price	Delta	Gamma	Vega1	Vanna	Volga	Theta
				American Greeks Obtained with the Explicit Method						
Strike Price (K)	10.0000	8	2.000000	2.0001	-0.9979	0.0085	0.0175	0.2630	0.0702	-0.0063
Time to Maturity (τ)	0.2500	9	1.107641	1.1080	-0.7478	0.1810	0.6719	0.4602	2.6877	-0.6620
Risk free rate (r)	0.1000	10	0.520030	0.5190	-0.4355	0.1950	0.8615	-0.0509	3.4459	-1.1302
Dividend (q)	0.0000	11	0.213668	0.2103	-0.1989	0.1137	0.6600	-0.2932	2.6399	-0.9789
PutCall (C or P)	P	12	0.082036	0.0783	-0.0788	0.0722	0.3747	-0.2488	1.4990	-0.5954
European or American (E or A)	A									
Little Trap	1	Number of Steps in Each Dimension				Grid Type			NonUniform	
(0=Heston, 1=Albrecher)		Stock Price	60			("Uniform" or "NonUniform")				
		Volatility	30							
		Maturity	3000							

FIGURE 11.12 American Greeks Using the Explicit Method

AMERICAN GREEKS FROM MEDVEDEV AND SCAILLET

In Chapter 8, we presented the American put approximation of Medvedev and Scaillet (2010) and noted that one key advantage of this method is its ability to generate American put prices very quickly. Hence, calculating the Greeks with finite differences does not require excessive computation time. This is accomplished with the VBA function MSGreeks, which uses the MSPrice function for the Medvedev and Scaillet (2010) expansion presented in Chapter 8. As usual, parts of the function have been omitted.

```
Function MSGreeksFD(params0,..., Greek) As Double
' Delta and Gamma
yp = MSPrice(S + ds, ...)
y0 = MSPrice(S, ...)
ym = MSPrice(S - ds, ...)
Delta = (yp - ym) / ds / 2
Gamma = (yp - 2 * y0 + ym) / ds / ds
' Theta
yp = MSPrice(S, K, T + dt, ...)
ym = MSPrice(S, K, T - dt, ...)
Theta2 = -(yp - ym) / dt / 2
' Vega1 and Volga
paramsp(4) = v0 + dv
paramsm(4) = v0 - dv
yp = MSPrice(S, K, T, r, q, paramsp, ...)
y0 = MSPrice(S, K, T, r, q, params0, ...)
ym = MSPrice(S, K, T, r, q, paramsm, ...)
Vega1 = (yp - ym) / 2 / dv * 2 * Sqr(v0)
dC2 = (yp - 2 * y0 + ym) / dv / dv
Volga = 4 * Sqr(v0) * (dC2 * Sqr(v0) + Vega1 / 4 / v0)
' Rho
paramsp(4) = v0
paramsm(4) = v0
yp = MSPrice(S, K, T, r + dr, ...)
ym = MSPrice(S, K, T, r - dr, ...)
Rho2 = (yp - ym) / dr / 2
' Output the results
If Greek = "Delta" Then MSGreeksFD = Delta
If Greek = "Gamma" Then MSGreeksFD = Gamma
If Greek = "Theta" Then MSGreeksFD = Theta2
If Greek = "Vega1" Then MSGreeksFD = Vega1
If Greek = "Volga" Then MSGreeksFD = Volga
If Greek = "Vanna" Then MSGreeksFD = Vanna
If Greek = "Rho" Then MSGreeksFD = Rho2
End Function
```

Medvedev and Scaillet (2010) Price of American Puts Under Heston
Uses True Put Prices from Clarke and Parrott, and 3 Expansion Terms

Option Features		Spot	True Price	MS Price	Delta	Gamma	Vega1	Vanna	Volga	Theta
Strike Price (K)	10.0000	8.0	2.000000	1.981347	-0.9907	0.1950	-0.1435	-0.1435	-0.1435	0.1088
Risk free rate (r)	0.1000	9.0	1.107641	1.106377	-0.7414	0.2972	0.6024	-0.1435	-0.1435	-0.6809
Dividend (q)	0.0000	10.0	0.520030	0.518822	-0.4349	0.2900	0.8974	-0.1435	-0.1435	-1.1497
Maturity (τ)	0.2500	11.0	0.213668	0.211618	-0.1995	0.1744	0.7007	-0.1435	2.4586	-0.9962
Trap (0=Heston, 1=Albrecher)	1	12.0	0.082036	0.080826	-0.0788	0.0762	0.3940	-0.1435	2.0774	-0.6158

FIGURE 11.13 Greeks from Medvedev-Scaillet Model

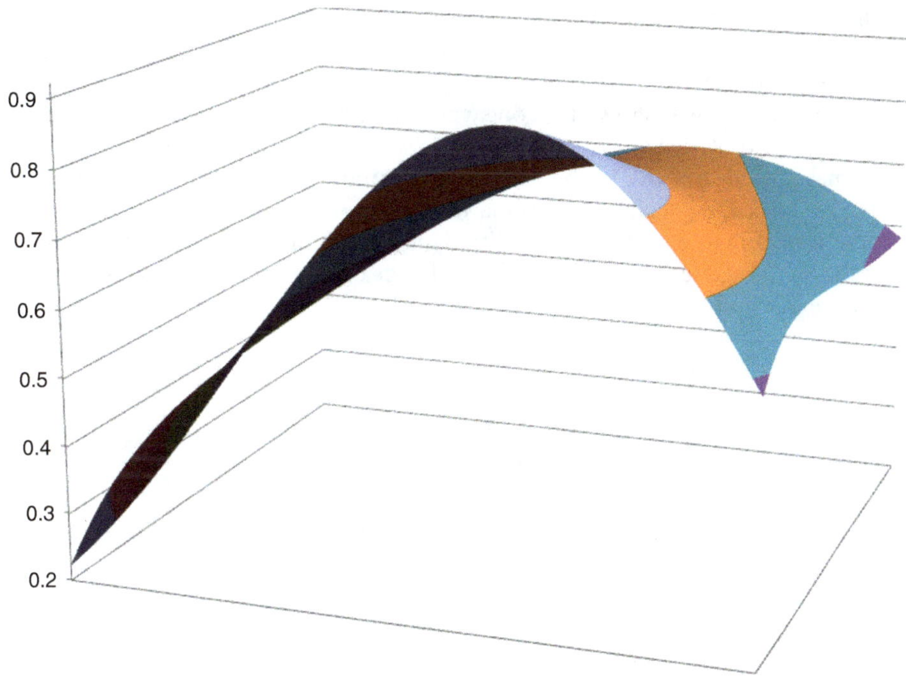

FIGURE 11.14 Vega from Medvedev-Scaillet Model

To illustrate, we use the settings of Clarke and Parrott (1999) that are used in Figure 11.12. Three terms are used in the expansion. The results are in Figure 11.13.

The results are comparable to those generated with the explicit method and presented in Figure 11.12, especially for those Greeks that do not require second-order derivatives. Increasing the number of terms in the Medvedev and Scaillet (2010) would increase the accuracy of the results in Figure 11.13.

We continue with the settings of Clarke and Parrott (1999) to generate the surface for the first vega ($\mathcal{V}_1$). This plot appears as Figure 11.14. Three terms are used in the Medvedev and Scaillet (2010) expansion.

CONCLUSION

In this chapter, we have presented formulas for the Greeks of the Heston (1993) model. All of the closed-form pricing formulas can be differentiated analytically to yield Greeks. The fast Fourier transform and its fractional counterpart can both produce a large set of Greeks very quickly. In addition, it is straightforward to obtain Greeks from American options with the explicit finite difference method. In this chapter, we have also used the LSM algorithm to obtain American Greeks. Glasserman (2003), however, cautions that obtaining Greeks with simulation can cause difficulties for all but the simplest derivatives. Other methods to compute Greeks include the pathwise method and likelihood ratio method of Broadie and Glasserman (1996) described in Glasserman (2003) and Chan and Joshi (2010b). Broadie and Kaya (2004) obtain pathwise and likelihood ratio Greeks under their exact simulation scheme (Broadie and Kaya, 2006). Benhamou (2002) and Davis and Johansson (2005), among others, apply Malliavin calculus to obtain simulation-based Greeks in the Heston model.

In Chapter 9, it was shown that one way to make the Heston model more flexible is to introduce time-dependent parameters. It was shown also that these models can sometimes provide a better fit to the implied volatility surface than the original Heston (1993) model, especially at short maturities. Another way to introduce flexibility into the model is to enrich the volatility dynamics in the model so that the model allows for two regimes of volatility. This is the idea behind the double Heston model that we review in the final chapter.

CHAPTER 12

The Double Heston Model

Abstract

The original Heston (1993) model is not always able to fit the implied volatility smile very well, especially at short maturities. The remedy is to add further parameters, which allows the model to be more flexible. This can be accomplished by allowing the parameters to be time dependent. Another approach is to enrich the variance process. One simple way to do this is to specify a two-factor structure for the volatility. This is the approach of Christoffersen et al. (2009) in their double Heston model.

We first present the multidimensional Feynman-Kac theorem. The fact that the double Heston model is affine, in the sense of Duffie et al. (2000), allows us to easily obtain the characteristic function of the model. This shows that the double Heston model is a simple extension of its univariate counterpart and that its extra parameters allow for a better fit of the implied volatility smile at multiple maturities. We show that the "Little Trap" formulation of the characteristic function of Albrecher et al. (2007) can be applied to the double Heston model. Finally, we present different simulation schemes that can be applied to the double Heston model.

double Heston model, Feynman-Kac theorem, characteristic function, simulation, American options

The original Heston (1993) model is not always able to fit the implied volatility smile very well, especially at short maturities. The remedy is to add additional parameters, which allows the model to be more flexible. This can be accomplished by allowing the parameters to be time dependent, as was illustrated by the methods covered in Chapter 9. Another approach is to enrich the variance process. One simple way to do this is to specify a two-factor structure for the volatility. This is the approach of Christoffersen et al. (2009) in their double Heston model, which we present in this chapter.

We first present the multidimensional Feynman-Kac theorem. The fact that the double Heston model is affine in the sense of Duffie et al. (2000) allows us to easily obtain the characteristic function of the model. This shows that the double Heston model is a simple extension of its univariate counterpart, and that its extra parameters allow for a better fit of the implied volatility smile at multiple maturities. We show that the "Little Trap" formulation of the characteristic function of Albrecher et al. (2007) can be applied to the double Heston model. Finally, we present different simulation schemes that can be applied to the double Heston model. Most of these schemes are straightforward extensions of the univariate schemes presented in Chapter 7.

MULTIDIMENSIONAL FEYNMAN-KAC THEOREM

The bivariate version of this theorem was presented in Chapters 2 and 9. In this section, we state the multidimensional version. Suppose that the vector $\mathbf{x}_t$ follows the n-dimensional stochastic process

$$d\mathbf{x}_t = \boldsymbol{\mu}(\mathbf{x}_t, t) + \boldsymbol{\sigma}(\mathbf{x}_t, t)d\mathbf{B}_t^{\mathbb{Q}}, \tag{12.1}$$

where $\mathbf{x}_t$ and $\boldsymbol{\mu}(\mathbf{x}_t, t)$ are each vectors of dimension n, $\mathbf{B}_t^{\mathbb{Q}}$ is a vector of m-dimension independent $\mathbb{Q}$-Brownian motion, and $\boldsymbol{\sigma}(\mathbf{x}_t, t)$ is a volatility matrix of size $n \times m$. Analogous to the univariate case, the generator $\mathcal{A}$ of the process is defined as the operator

$$\mathcal{A} = \sum_{i=1}^{n} \mu_i \frac{\partial}{\partial x_i} + \frac{1}{2} \sum_{i=1}^{n} \sum_{j=1}^{n} (\boldsymbol{\sigma}\boldsymbol{\sigma}^T)_{ij} \frac{\partial^2}{\partial x_i \partial x_j}, \tag{12.2}$$

where, for notational convenience, $\mu_i = \mu_i(\mathbf{x}_t, t)$, $\boldsymbol{\sigma} = \boldsymbol{\sigma}(\mathbf{x}_t, t)$, and $(\boldsymbol{\sigma}\boldsymbol{\sigma}^T)_{ij}$ is element (i, j) of the matrix $\boldsymbol{\sigma}\boldsymbol{\sigma}^T$ of size $n \times n$. The multidimensional version of the Feynman-Kac theorem states that the partial differential equation of a function $f(\mathbf{x}_t, t)$ is given by

$$\frac{\partial f}{\partial t} + \mathcal{A}f(\mathbf{x}_t, t) - r(\mathbf{x}_t, t)f(\mathbf{x}_t, t) = 0, \tag{12.3}$$

and with boundary condition $f(\mathbf{x}_T, T)$, has the solution

$$f(\mathbf{x}_t, t) = E^{\mathbb{Q}} \left[\exp\left(-\int_t^T r(\mathbf{x}_u u)du \right) f(\mathbf{x}_T, T) | \mathcal{F}_t \right].$$

In the following section, we use this result to obtain the PDE and characteristic function of the double Heston model, and the double Heston call price.

DOUBLE HESTON CALL PRICE

The double Heston model proposed by Christoffersen et al. (2009) introduces a second factor for the variance, driven by its own stochastic differential equation (SDE):

$$\begin{aligned} dS &= (r - q)Sdt + \sqrt{v_1}SdW_1 + \sqrt{v_2}SdW_2 \\ dv_1 &= \kappa_1(\theta_1 - v_1)dt + \sigma_1\sqrt{v_1}dZ_1 \\ dv_2 &= \kappa_2(\theta_2 - v_2)dt + \sigma_2\sqrt{v_2}dZ_2. \end{aligned} \tag{12.4}$$

The following correlation structure is specified:

$$
\begin{aligned}
E[dW_1 dZ_1] &= \rho_1 dt \\
E[dW_2 dZ_2] &= \rho_2 dt \\
E[dW_1 dW_2] &= E[dZ_1 dZ_2] = E[dW_1 dZ_2] = E[dW_2 dZ_1] = 0.
\end{aligned}
\tag{12.5}
$$

Note that we have suppressed the time subscript for notational simplicity. The idea behind this model is that the additional volatility factor provides more flexibility in modeling the volatility surface. In the single-factor Heston model, the single correlation ρ is constant over time, which means that the model has trouble providing an adequate fit to market implied volatilities when the slope of the smile varies substantially across maturities, although it does a good job when the slopes are all relatively flat or all relatively steep. Incorporating a second volatility factor allows for two different correlations and, hence, for two different regimes of volatility.

The double Heston system of equations in (x, v_1, v_2) can be written in the affine form described in Chapter 9. We can therefore use the result of Duffie et al. (2000) that the characteristic function for $(x_T, v_{1,T}, v_{2,T})$ has the log linear form

$$
\begin{aligned}
f(\phi_0, \phi_1, \phi_2; x_t, v_{1,t}, v_{2,t}) &= E[\exp(i\phi_0 x_T + i\phi_1 v_{1,T} + i\phi_2 v_{2,T})] \\
&= \exp(A(\tau) + B_0(\tau)x_t + B_1(\tau)v_{1,t} + B_2(\tau)v_{2,t}),
\end{aligned}
\tag{12.6}
$$

where $\tau = T - t$ is the time remaining until expiry. In this expression, the coefficients A, B_0, B_1, and B_2 depend not only on τ but also on ϕ_0, ϕ_1, and ϕ_2 but this has been omitted for notational convenience. Since we are interested in the characteristic function for x_T only, and not in the joint characteristic function for $(x_T, v_{1,T}, v_{2,T})$, we set $\phi_1 = \phi_2 = 0$ in Equation (12.6). The initial conditions become $B_1(0) = B_2(0) = 0$, while $B_0(0) = i\phi$ and $A(0) = 0$ remain unchanged (we write ϕ for ϕ_0). Hence, the Ricatti equations for B_1 and B_2 are identical to their univariate counterparts, so their solutions are

$$
B_j(\tau, \phi) = \frac{\kappa_j - \rho_j \sigma_j \phi i + d_j}{\sigma_j^2} \left[\frac{1 - e^{d_j \tau}}{1 - g_j e^{d_j \tau}} \right],
$$

where

$$
g_j = \frac{\kappa_j - \rho_j \sigma_j \phi i + d_j}{\kappa_j - \rho_j \sigma_j \phi i - d_j}, \quad d_j = \sqrt{(\kappa_j - \rho_j \sigma_j \phi i)^2 + \sigma_j^2 \phi(\phi + i)}.
$$

Note that d_j and g_j both refer to the second form for d and g, corresponding to the second characteristic function f_2. In this chapter, the subscript on d_j and g_j refers to that of the volatility v_j.

The solution for $A(\tau, \phi)$ is

$$
A(\tau, \phi) = (r - q)\phi i \tau + \sum_{j=1}^{2} \frac{\kappa_j \theta_j}{\sigma_j^2} \left[(\kappa_j - \rho_j \sigma_j \phi i + d_j)\tau - 2 \ln \left(\frac{1 - g_j e^{d_j \tau}}{1 - g_j} \right) \right].
$$

See Rouah (2013) for a detailed derivation.

By defining $c_j = 1/g_j$, we can also use the "Little Trap" formulation of Albrecher et al. (2007), which expresses the coefficients of the characteristic function in terms of $\exp(-d_j\tau)$ rather than $\exp(d_j\tau)$, as in Gauthier and Possamaï (2010). This produces the alternate forms of the coefficients

$$B_j(\tau, \phi) = \frac{\kappa_j - \rho_j\sigma_j\phi i - d_j}{\sigma_j^2}\left[\frac{1 - e^{-d_j\tau}}{1 - c_j e^{-d_j\tau}}\right]$$

and

$$A(\tau, \phi) = (r - q)\phi i\tau + \sum_{j=1}^{2}\frac{\kappa_j\theta_j}{\sigma_j^2}\left[(\kappa_j - \rho_j\sigma_j\phi i - d_j)\tau - 2\ln\left(\frac{1 - c_j e^{-d_j\tau}}{1 - c_j}\right)\right].$$

As in the univariate case, this formulation avoids the discontinuity problems that can arise with the original formulation. Once the coefficients are obtained, either with the original formulation or the "Little Trap" formulation, the characteristic function is

$$f(\phi; x_t, v_{1,t}, v_{2,t}) = \exp(A(\tau, \phi) + i\phi x_t + B_1(\tau, \phi)v_{1,t} + B_2(\tau, \phi)v_{2,t}), \quad (12.7)$$

where x_t is the log spot price of the underlying, and $v_{1,t}$ and $v_{2,t}$ are the initial variances, which can be estimated as the parameters v_{01} and v_{02}, as in the univariate case. The call price is obtained in the usual fashion

$$C(K) = S_t e^{-q\tau}P_1 - Ke^{-r\tau}P_2, \quad (12.8)$$

where

$$P_1 = \frac{1}{2} + \frac{1}{\pi}\int_0^\infty \text{Re}\left[\frac{e^{-i\phi\ln K}f(\phi - i; x_t, v_{1,t}, v_{2,t})}{i\phi S_t e^{(r-q)\tau}}\right]d\phi,$$

$$P_2 = \frac{1}{2} + \frac{1}{\pi}\int_0^\infty \text{Re}\left[\frac{e^{-i\phi\ln K}f(\phi; x_t, v_{1,t}, v_{2.t})}{i\phi}\right]d\phi. \quad (12.9)$$

Implementing the double Heston model is only slightly more complicated than implementing its univariate counterpart. In the VBA code, we order the parameters as

$$\Theta = (\kappa_1, \theta_1, \sigma_1, v_{10}, \rho_1, \kappa_2, \theta_2, \sigma_2, v_{20}, \rho_2). \quad (12.10)$$

The VBA function DoubleHestonCF returns the characteristic function for the double Heston model.

```
Function DoubleHestonCF(phi As cNum, ...) As Variant
' The coefficients
d1 = cSqr(cAdd(Term1, Term2))
d2 = cSqr(cAdd(Term1, Term2))
g1 = cDiv(Num, Den)
g2 = cDiv(Num, Den)
B1 = cDiv(cDiv(cProd(Term1, Term2), Term3), Term4)
B2 = cDiv(cDiv(cProd(Term1, Term2), Term3), Term4)
X1 = cDiv(Term1, Term2)
X2 = cDiv(Term1, Term2)
A = cAdd(cAdd(Term1, Term2), Term3)
' The characteristic function.
' y = exp(A + B1*v01 + B2*v02 + i*phi*x0);
y = cExp(cAdd(cAdd(cAdd(A, Term1), Term2), Term3))
' Output the real and imaginary parts separately
output(1) = cReal(y)
output(2) = cImag(y)
DoubleHestonCF = output
End Function
```

The VBA function DoubleHestonPriceTrapezoidal calculates the call price using the trapezoidal rule, and returns either the call price itself, or the put price by put-call parity.

```
Function DoubleHestonPriceTrapezoidal(...) As Double
' The integrands
For j = 1 To N
    u = Complex(x(j), 0)
    weight = w(j)
    CF = DoubleHestonCF(u, params, T, S, rf, q)
    f2(j) = Complex(CF(1), CF(2))
    CF = DoubleHestonCF(v, params, T, S, rf, q)
    f1(j) = Complex(CF(1), CF(2))
    coeff = cExp(cProd(Complex(-Log(K), 0), cProd(i, u)))
    int2(j) = weight * cReal(...)
    int1(j) = weight * cReal(...) / S / Exp((rf - q) * T)
Next j
' The ITM probabilities
P1 = 1 / 2 + 1 / pi * Sum(int1)
P2 = 1 / 2 + 1 / pi * Sum(int2)
' The Double Heston call price
HestonC = S * Exp(-q * T) * P1 - K * Exp(-rf * T) * P2
' The put price by put-call parity
HestonP = HestonC - S * Exp(-q * T) + K * Exp(-rf * T)
End Function
```

	A	B	C	D	E	F	G	H	I
1									
2		Double Heston Price, Example from Table 3 of Gauthier and Possamai							
3								Gauss-Laguerre	Trapezoidal
4		Option Features			Percent	Strike	Maturity	Call Price	Call Price
5		Spot Price (S)	61.9000		1.0	61.90	1	19.4538	19.4538
6		Risk free rate (r)	0.0300		1.0	61.90	10	41.3942	41.3940
7		Dividend (q)	0.0000		0.7	43.33	1	27.6047	27.6047
8		PutCall ("C" or "P")	C		0.7	43.33	10	45.2796	45.2793
9					1.3	80.47	1	13.9276	13.9276
10		Double Heston Parameters			1.3	80.47	10	38.2718	38.2719
11		kappa1 (κ)	0.9000						
12		theta1 (θ)	0.1000		Trapezoidal Rule Settings				
13		sigma1 (σ)	0.1000		Lower Limit		1.00E-10		
14		v01	0.36		Upper Limit		150.00		
15		rho1 (ρ)	-0.5000		Number of Abscissas		1000		
16		kappa2 (κ)	1.2000						
17		theta2 (θ)	0.1500						
18		sigma2 (σ)	0.2000						
19		v02	0.49						
20		rho2 (ρ)	-0.5000						

FIGURE 12.1 The Double Heston Model

The VBA function DoubleHestonPriceGaussLaguerre calculates the call price using Gauss-Laguerre quadrature. It is nearly identical to the above function and is not presented here.

To illustrate the double Heston model, we reproduce Table 3 of Gauthier and Possamaï (2010). The call prices using the trapezoidal rule are presented in Figure 12.1 and are almost identical to those of Gauthier and Possamaï.

In practice, we use Gauss-Laguerre quadrature, since this is almost as accurate as the trapezoidal rule but much faster. The VBA code and example in this section are in the Excel file Ch12GPTable3.xls.

DOUBLE HESTON GREEKS

In this section, we derive analytic expressions for the Greeks in the double Heston model. We saw in Chapter 11 that many of the Greeks for the Heston (1993) model are available analytically, by straightforward differentiation of the call price. We also saw that by using finite difference approximations to the Greeks, it is easy to verify the accuracy of the analytic Greeks. This approach can be used with the double Heston model as well, by differentiation of the call price in (12.8). The Greeks in the double Heston model are straightforward generalizations of their univariate counterparts. Gamma, for example, is $\Gamma = e^{-q\tau}\partial P_1/\partial S$, where, from Equation (12.9),

$$\frac{\partial P_1}{\partial S} = \frac{1}{\pi}\int_0^\infty \text{Re}\left[\frac{e^{-i\phi \ln K} f(\phi - i; x_t, v_{1,t}, v_{2,t})}{S_t^2 e^{(r-q)\tau}}\right] d\phi.$$

Theta requires

$$\frac{\partial P_1}{\partial \tau} = \frac{1}{\pi}\int_0^\infty \text{Re}\left[\frac{e^{-i\phi \ln K}}{i\phi S_t e^{(r-q)\tau}}\left(\frac{\partial f}{\partial \tau} - (r-q)f\right)\right] d\phi,$$

where f and its τ-derivative are both evaluated at $\phi - i$. It also requires

$$\frac{\partial P_2}{\partial \tau} = \frac{1}{\pi}\int_0^\infty \text{Re}\left[\frac{e^{-i\phi \ln K}}{i\phi}\left(\frac{\partial f}{\partial \tau}\right)\right] d\phi,$$

where the τ-derivative of f is evaluated at ϕ. The expression for theta is identical to that in Chapter 11. In the derivatives of P_1 and P_2, we have

$$\frac{\partial f}{\partial \tau} = \exp(A + i\phi x_t + B_1 v_{1,t} + B_2 v_{2,t})\left(\frac{\partial A}{\partial \tau} + \frac{\partial B_1}{\partial \tau}v_{1,t} + \frac{\partial B_2}{\partial \tau}v_{2,t}\right),$$

where the τ-derivative of $A(\tau, \phi)$ is analogous to that for $C(\tau, \phi)$ in Chapter 11, and where the τ-derivative of $B_1(\tau, \phi)$ and $B_2(\tau, \phi)$ both correspond to that for $D(\tau, \phi)$. Recall that $v_{1,t}$ and $v_{2,t}$ are the initial variances, which are estimated as the parameters v_{01} and v_{02}.

We saw in Chapter 11 that Zhu (2010) defines the first vega $\mathcal{V}_1$ to be based on $\upsilon = \sqrt{v_0}$. Since there are two initial variance parameters in the double Heston model, there are two such vegas, $\mathcal{V}_{11}$ based on $\upsilon_1 = \sqrt{v_{01}}$, and $\mathcal{V}_{12}$ based on $\upsilon_2 = \sqrt{v_{02}}$. These can be easily obtained, by noting that since $\partial f/\partial v_{0j} = f \times B_j$, we have the derivatives

$$\begin{aligned}\frac{\partial P_1}{\partial v_{0j}} &= \frac{1}{\pi}\int_0^\infty \text{Re}\left[\frac{e^{-i\phi \ln K}}{i\phi S_t e^{(r-q)\tau}} f(\phi - i; x_t, v_{1,t}, v_{2,t}) B_j(\tau, \phi - i)\right] d\phi, \\ \frac{\partial P_2}{\partial v_{0j}} &= \frac{1}{\pi}\int_0^\infty \text{Re}\left[\frac{e^{-i\phi \ln K}}{i\phi} f(\phi; x_t, v_{1,t}, v_{2,t}) B_j(\tau, \phi)\right] d\phi.\end{aligned} \tag{12.11}$$

The two vegas are identical to the form derived in Chapter 11:

$$\mathcal{V}_{1j} = Se^{-q\tau}\frac{\partial P_1}{\partial v_{0j}}2\sqrt{v_{0j}} - Ke^{-r\tau}\frac{\partial P_2}{\partial v_{0j}}2\sqrt{v_{0j}}, \tag{12.12}$$

for $j = 1, 2$. Similarly, the two volgas are obtained with $\partial^2 f/\partial v_{0j}^2 = f \times B_j^2$. Using the relationship derived in Chapter 11, $\partial^2 P_1/\partial \upsilon_j^2$ is

$$\begin{aligned}\frac{\partial^2 P_1}{\partial \upsilon_j^2} &= 4\left(\frac{\partial^2 P_1}{\partial v_{0j}^2}v_{0j} + \frac{1}{2}\frac{\partial P_1}{\partial v_{0j}}\right) \\ &= \frac{1}{\pi}\int_0^\infty \text{Re}\left[\frac{e^{-i\phi \ln K}}{i\phi S_t e^{(r-q)\tau}} 2B_1 f\,(2B_1 v_{0j} + 1)\right] d\phi,\end{aligned}$$

where f and B_1 are both evaluated at $\phi - i$. The expression for $\partial^2 P_2/\partial v_j^2$ is identical, except that $S_t e^{(r-q)\tau}$ is not included in the denominator and f and B_1 are both evaluated at ϕ. The volgas are then

$$\text{Volga}_j = Se^{-q\tau}\frac{\partial^2 P_1}{\partial v_j^2} - Ke^{-r\tau}\frac{\partial^2 P_2}{\partial v_j^2}. \tag{12.13}$$

There are also two vannas, based on v_1 and v_2:

$$\text{Vanna}_j = 2e^{-q\tau}\sqrt{v_{0j}}\frac{\partial P_1}{\partial v_{0j}}. \tag{12.14}$$

The VBA function DoubleHestonGreeks calculates the analytical Greeks of the double Heston model. The function calls the B function to calculate the coefficients $B_1(\tau,\phi)$ and $B_2(\tau,\phi)$ required for vega, vanna, and volga, as well as the DiffTau function to calculate the τ-derivatives of $A(\tau,\phi)$, $B_1(\tau,\phi)$, and $B_2(\tau,\phi)$ required for theta. To conserve space, most of the function has been omitted. The first part of the function creates the integrands for the selected Greek.

```
Function DoubleHestonGreeks(..., Greek As String) As Double
For j = 1 To N
    CF = DoubleHestonCF(u, ...)
    f2 = Complex(CF(1), CF(2))
    CF = DoubleHestonCF(v, ...)
    f1 = Complex(CF(1), CF(2))
    If Greek = "Price" Then
        int2(j) = weight * cReal(...))
        int1(j) = weight * cReal(...) / Exp((rf - q) * T) / S
    ElseIf Greek = "Delta" Then
        int1(j) = weight * cReal(...) / Exp((rf - q) * T) / S
    ElseIf Greek = "Vanna1" Or Greek = "Vanna2" Then
        If Greek = "Vanna1" Then
            v0choice = 1
        Else
            v0choice = 2
        End If
        BF = B(v, params, T, v0choice)
        B1 = Complex(BF(1), BF(2))
        df1 = cProd(f1, B1)
        dint1(j) = weight * cReal(...) / Exp((rf - q) * T) / S
    End If
Next j
```

The second part of the function calculates the integrals and returns the price or the Greek.

```
If Greek = "Price" Then
        P1 = 0.5 + 1 / pi * Sum(int1)
        P2 = 0.5 + 1 / pi * Sum(int2)
        y = S * Exp(-q * T) * P1 - K * Exp(-rf * T) * P2
ElseIf Greek = "Delta" Then
        P1 = 0.5 + 1 / pi * Sum(int1)
        y = Exp(-q * T) * P1
End If
DoubleHestonGreeks = y
End Function
```

The VBA function DiffTau returns the τ-derivatives of $A(\tau,\phi)$, $B_1(\tau,\phi)$, and $B_2(\tau,\phi)$.

```
Function DiffTau(phi As cNum, ..., output As String) As Variant
d1 = cSqr(cAdd(Term1, Term2))
d2 = cSqr(cAdd(Term1, Term2))
g1 = cDiv(Num, Den)
g2 = cDiv(Num, Den)
' Output the real and imaginary parts separately
If output = "dA" Then
     out(1) = cReal(dA)
     out(2) = cImag(dA)
ElseIf output = "dB1" Then
     out(1) = cReal(dB1)
     out(2) = cImag(dB1)
ElseIf output = "dB2" Then
     out(1) = cReal(dB2)
     out(2) = cImag(dB2)
End If
DiffTau = out
End Function
```

The VBA function B returns the coefficient $B_1(\tau,\phi)$ or $B_2(\tau,\phi)$, depending on the choice of "j" in the function argument. The function allows for the original Heston (1993) formulation, or for the "Little Trap" formulation of Albrecher et al. (2007).

```
Function B(phi As cNum, ..., v0choice As Integer) As Variant
B1 = cDiv(cDiv(cProd(Term1, Term2), Term3), Term4)
B2 = cDiv(cDiv(cProd(Term1, Term2), Term3), Term4)
If v0choice = 1 Then
    y = B1
Else
    y = B2
End If
' Output the real and imaginary parts separately
output(1) = cReal(y)
output(2) = cImag(y)
B = output
End Function
```

To illustrate the double Heston Greeks, we use the same settings as those in Figure 12.1 and generate the Greeks of the at-the-money call price with a maturity of one year. The results are in Figure 12.2.

Recall from Table 12.1 that the price with these settings is 19.4538. The analytic Greeks are all accurate, as indicated by their absolute difference with their finite difference counterparts.

We saw in Chapter 11 that the Greeks satisfy the PDE of the univariate Heston model, provided that the PDE be expressed in terms of S rather than $x = \ln S$, and that vega, vanna, and volga be in terms of the variance v_0 rather than the volatility $v = \sqrt{v_0}$. It is straightforward to demonstrate this for the PDE of the double Heston model also. Using the generator in Equation (12.2) for S along with (12.3), and

Double Heston Greeks, Closed Form and Finite Differences, and PDE

Option Features	
Spot Price (S)	61.9000
Strike Price (K)	61.9000
Risk free rate (r)	0.0300
Maturity (τ)	1.0000
Dividend (q)	0.0000
PutCall ("C" or "P")	C
Double Heston Parameters	
kappa1 (κ)	0.9000
theta1 (θ)	0.1000
sigma1 (σ)	0.1000
v01	0.36
rho1 (ρ)	-0.5000
kappa2 (κ)	1.2000
theta2 (θ)	0.1500
sigma2 (σ)	0.2000
v02	0.49
rho2 (ρ)	-0.5000

Double Heston Greeks

Greek	Analytic	Finite Difference	Abs(Error)
Price	19.4538	19.4538	3.55E-15
Delta	0.6730	0.6730	3.30E-07
Gamma	0.0075	0.0075	4.21E-09
Rho	22.2029	22.2029	5.32E-08
Theta	-7.0594	-7.0594	1.77E-06
Vega11	11.2973	11.2973	1.80E-06
Vega12	11.5147	11.5147	1.38E-06
Vanna1	0.0745	0.0745	2.59E-07
Vanna2	0.0816	0.0816	2.65E-07
Volga1	10.4625	10.4625	1.80E-07
Volga2	7.7954	7.7954	1.82E-07

Heston PDE: 1.0956E-07

FIGURE 12.2 Greeks from the Double Heston Model

substituting the Greeks for the derivatives in S, v_{01}, and v_{02} of the resulting PDE, produces

$$\begin{aligned}\Theta + (r-q)S_0\Delta + \kappa_1(\theta_1 - v_{01})\text{Vega}_1 + \kappa_2(\theta_2 - v_{02})\text{Vega}_2 \\ + \frac{1}{2}(v_{01}+v_{02})S_0^2\Gamma + \rho_1\sigma_1 v_{01}S_0\text{Vanna}_1 + \rho_2\sigma_2 v_{02}S_0\text{Vanna}_2 \\ + \frac{1}{2}\sigma_1^2 v_{01}\text{Volga}_1 + \frac{1}{2}\sigma_2^2 v_{02}\text{Volga}_2 - rC = 0. \end{aligned} \tag{12.15}$$

The VBA function DHestonPDE is used to demonstrate that the PDE in (12.15) holds.

```
Function DHestonPDE(...) As Double
' Calculate the Greeks
Price = DoubleHestonGreeks(..., "Price")
Delta = DoubleHestonGreeks(..., "Delta")
...
Volga2 = DoubleHestonGreeks(..., "Volga2")
' Modified Greeks for variance instead of volatility
Vega11p = Vega11 / (2 * Sqr(v01))
Vega12p = Vega12 / (2 * Sqr(v02))
Volga1p = (0.25 / Sqr(v01) * Volga1 - Vega11p / 2 / Sqr(v01)) / Sqr(v01)
Volga2p = (0.25 / Sqr(v02) * Volga2 - Vega12p / 2 / Sqr(v02)) / Sqr(v02)
' The Double Heston PDE
A = (rf - q) * Spot * Delta + kappa1 * (theta1 - v01) * Vega11p ....
HestonPDE = Theta + A - rf * Price
End Function
```

Note that we express the derivatives of the PDE (12.15) in terms of v_0 rather than v, before substituting these derivatives into the Heston PDE, as we did in Chapter 11. With the settings used to generate Figure 12.2, the code returns 1.1×10^{-7} for the value of the PDE.

The VBA code and examples in this section are in the Excel file Ch12Greeks.xls.

PARAMETER ESTIMATION

Christoffersen et al. (2009) estimate the volatility parameters v_{01} and v_{02} as daily spot volatilities $v_{01,t}$ and $v_{02,t}$, and the remaining parameters $\Omega = \{\kappa_j, \theta_j, \sigma_j, \rho_j\}_{j=1,2}$ on a yearly basis. In this section, we employ the simpler approach of treating v_{01} and v_{02} as fixed parameters, analogous to what is done in Chapter 6 for the univariate Heston model. As first mentioned in Chapter 6, the problem with using IVRMSE and other loss functions that use implied volatility is that the model implied volatility IV_{tk}^{Θ} must be obtained at every iteration of the optimization, which is computationally intensive. To address this issue, in Chapter 6 we introduced the Christoffersen et al. (2009) proxy

$$\frac{1}{N}\sum_{t,k} w_{tk}\left(\frac{C_{tk}-C^{\Theta}_{tk}}{\text{BSVega}_{tk}}\right)^2, \tag{12.16}$$

where C_{tk} and C^{Θ}_{tk} are the market and model call prices, respectively, and where BSVega_{tk} is the Black-Scholes vega evaluated at the strike K_k, at the maturity τ_t, and using the market implied volatility IV_{tk} as the volatility input. The Black-Scholes vega is given by

$$\text{BSVega}_{tk} = S\exp(-q\tau_t)n(d_{tk})\sqrt{\tau_t}, \tag{12.17}$$

where

$$d_{tk} = \frac{\ln(S/K_k) + (r - q + IV^2_{tk}/2)\tau_t}{IV_{tk}\sqrt{\tau_t}}, \tag{12.18}$$

and where $n(x) = \exp(-x^2/2)/\sqrt{2\pi}$ is the standard normal density. The loss function in (12.16) is implemented with the VBA function DHestonObjFun.

```
Function DHestonObjFun(...) As Variant
For i = 1 To NK
    For j = 1 To NT
        ' Heston Call price with Gauss Laguerre integration
        ModelPrice = DoubleHestonPriceGaussLaguerre(...)
        ' Select the objective function
        ...
        ElseIf ObjFun = 4 Then
            ' IVRMSE Christoffersen, Heston, Jacobs proxy
            ImpVol = MktIV(i, j)
            d = (Log(S / Strike) + (rf - q + ImpVol ^ 2 / 2) * Mat) ...
            Vega = S * Norm_S_Dist(d, 0) * Sqr(Mat)
            Errors(i, j) = (ModelPrice - MarketPrice) ^ 2 / Vega ^ 2
        End If
    Next j
Next i
```

The function also allows for MSE, IVRMSE and RMSE loss functions, and can be easily modified to accept additional loss functions.

	A	B	C	D	E	F
1						
2		**Double Heston Parameter Estimation Using DJIA Puts**				
3						
4		**Option Features**			**Parameter Estimates**	
5		Spot Price (S)	129.1400		kappa1 (κ)	0.0023
6		Risk free rate (r)	0.0000		theta1 (θ)	0.0010
7		Dividend (q)	0.0000		sigma1 (σ)	2.7621
8		PutCall	P		v01	0.0364
9		Trap (0=Heston, 1=Albrecher)	1		rho1 (ρ)	0.0536
10					kappa2 (κ)	1.1715
11		**Settings for the Nelder Mead Algorithm**			theta2 (θ)	0.0890
12		Parameter Starting Values			sigma2 (σ)	0.3336
13		kappa1 (κ)	3.000		v02	0.0057
14		theta1 (θ)	0.030		rho2 (ρ)	-0.9899
15		sigma1 (σ)	2.000		Value of Objective Function	1.09E-03
16		v01	0.030		Number of Iterations	1001
17		rho1 (ρ)	0.060			
18		kappa2 (κ)	2.000		**Settings for Bisection Algorithm**	
19		theta2 (θ)	0.060		Lower Limit for IV	0.01
20		sigma2 (σ)	0.070		Upper Limit for IV	2
21		v02	0.010		Tolerance	1.00E-04
22		rho2 (ρ)	-0.900		Maximum Iterations	1000
23		Tolerance	1.00E-15			
24		Maximum # Iterations	1000			
25		Shock for starting values	2%			
26		Objective Function	2			
27						

FIGURE 12.3 Double Heston Model Parameter Estimates

To illustrate parameter estimation under the double Heston model, we use the same Dow Jones Industrial Average implied volatilities quoted on May 10, 2012, that were used to estimate the time-dependent model of Mikhailov and Nögel (2003) in Chapter 9. The results are shown in Figure 12.3.

The estimates are consistent with a double regime of volatility described by Christoffersen et al. (2009). In particular, the first volatility factor has high variance (σ_1) and near-zero correlation, corresponding to a symmetric but highly curved implied volatility smile. The second volatility factor has low variance and highly negative correlation, corresponding to a highly negatively skewed but much flatter smile (see Figure 2.9 for the effect of these parameters on the smile).

Implied volatilities from the double Heston model, using the parameter estimates in Figure 12.3, are in Figure 12.4.

The VBA code for the double Heston model, and the screen shots in Figures 12.3 and 12.4, are in the Excel file Ch12DH_DIA.xls.

We can also extract the risk-neutral densities (RNDs) from the Heston call prices generated with the estimated parameters from Figure 12.3. These appear in Figure 12.5.

Figure 12.5 appears as part of the Excel file Ch12RND_DIA.xls.

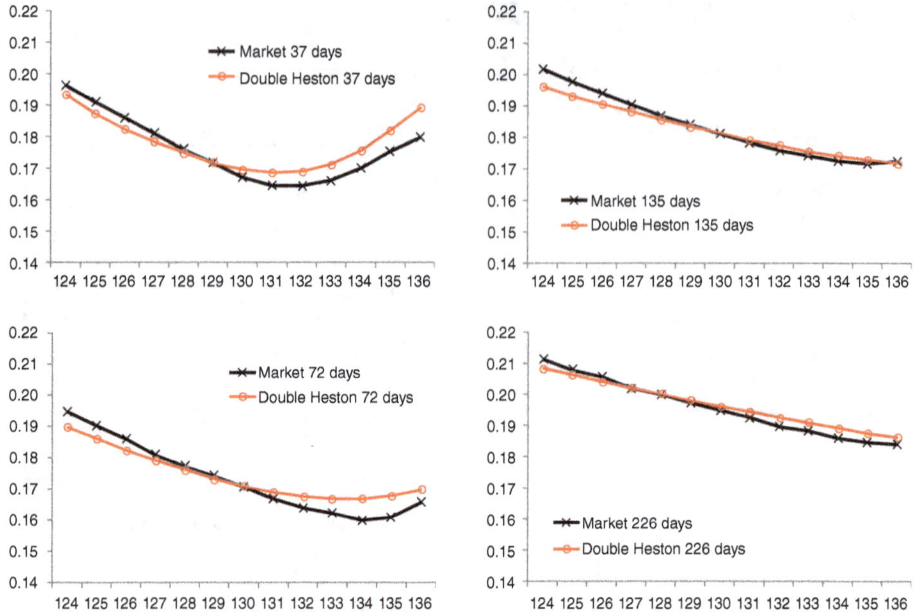

FIGURE 12.4 Implied Volatilities from Double Heston Model

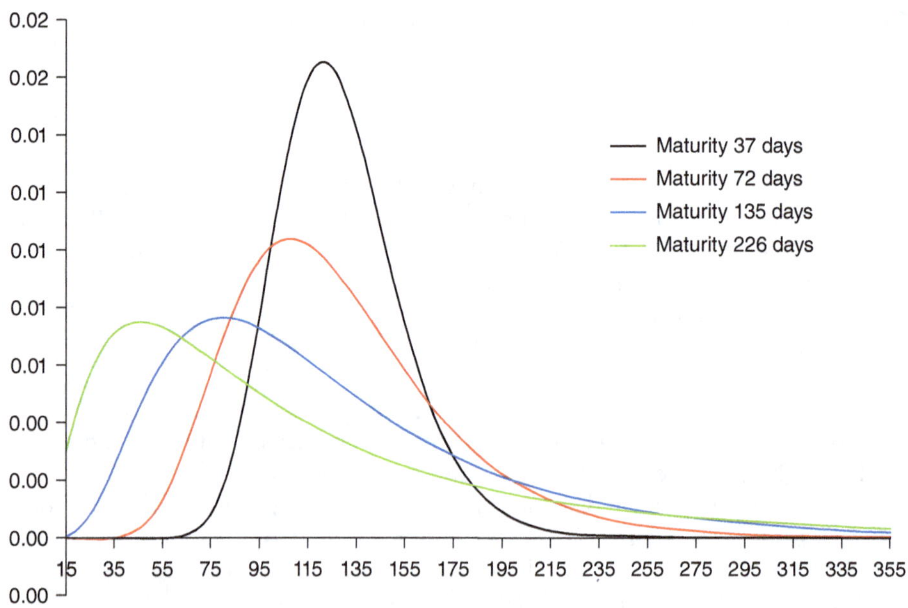

FIGURE 12.5 Risk-Neutral Densities from the Double Heston Model

SIMULATION IN THE DOUBLE HESTON MODEL

Gauthier and Possamaï (2010) adapt many of the simulation schemes for the Heston model that we encountered in Chapter 7 to the double Heston model. In this section, we present a few of these simulation schemes. In most cases, the generalization of the scheme from the Heston model to the double Heston model is straightforward and intuitive. The notation must be updated with "j" subscripts, for $j = 1, 2$, to reflect the additional variance process in the double Heston model. In each scheme, it is possible to apply a martingale correction to improve the accuracy of the scheme, but these are not covered.

Simulation of the Stock Price

Rather than simulating the log stock price $\ln S_t$, Gauthier and Possamaï (2010) suggest simulating the discounted log price $\ln(e^{-rt}S_t)$ and applying the Predictor-Corrector scheme. This scheme is given in terms of two standard Brownian motion $W_{1,t}$ and $W_{2,t}$ as

$$\begin{aligned}\ln\left(e^{-r(t+dt)}S_{t+dt}\right) &= \ln\left(e^{-rt}S_t\right) + K_0^1 + K_1^1 v_{1,t} + K_2^1 v_{1,t+dt} \\ &\quad + \sqrt{K_3^1(v_{1,t} + v_{1,t+dt})}W_{1,t} + K_0^2 + K_1^2 v_{2,t} \\ &\quad + K_2^2 v_{2,t+dt} + \sqrt{K_3^2(v_{2,t} + v_{2,t+dt})}W_{2,t}, \qquad (12.19)\end{aligned}$$

where the constants are, for $j = 1, 2$

$$\begin{aligned}K_0^j &= -\frac{\rho_j\kappa_j\theta_j}{\sigma_j}dt, \quad K_1^j = \frac{dt}{2}\left(\frac{\kappa_j\rho_j}{\sigma_j} - \frac{1}{2}\right) - \frac{\rho_j}{\sigma_j} \\ K_2^j &= \frac{dt}{2}\left(\frac{\kappa_j\rho_j}{\sigma_j} - \frac{1}{2}\right) + \frac{\rho_j}{\sigma_j}, \quad K_3^j = \frac{dt}{2}(1 - \rho_j^2).\end{aligned}$$

Note that the Brownian motions $W_{1,t}$ and $W_{2,t}$ are independent, but the discretization scheme preserves correlation through the constants K_i^j. The stock price is then found by exponentiating $\ln(e^{-r(t+dt)}S_{t+dt})$ and multiplying the result by $e^{r(t+dt)}$.

Euler Scheme for the Variance

This is a straightforward extension of the univariate case. Under the full truncation scheme, for example, each variance $v_{j,t+dt}$ is generated independently of the other using the current value $v_{j,t}$ as

$$v_{j,t+dt} = v_{j,t}^+ + \kappa_j(\theta_j - v_{j,t}^+)dt + \sigma_j\sqrt{v_{j,t}^+}\sqrt{dt}Z_{j,V}, \qquad (12.20)$$

for $j = 1, 2$ and where $Z_{1,V}$ and $Z_{2,V}$ are independent Brownian motions. The current and updated values $v_{j,t}$ and $v_{j,t+dt}$ are then fed into Equation (12.19), and the process is repeated. Note that $v^+_{j,t} = \max(0, v_{j,t})$ so that in (12.20), negative variances are avoided. It is also possible to use the reflective scheme instead, by replacing $v^+_{j,t}$ in (12.20) with $|v_{j,t}|$.

Alfonsi Scheme for the Variance

Gauthier and Possamaï (2010) adapt the second-order discretization scheme of Alfonsi (2010) to the double Heston model. The adaptation is straightforward. Hence, for example, K_2 becomes

$$K_{2,j} = \exp(\kappa_j dt/2)\left[\left(\frac{\sigma_j^2}{4} - \theta_j\kappa_j\right)\Psi_j + \left(\sqrt{e^{\kappa_j dt/2}\left(\frac{\sigma_j^2}{4} - \theta_j\kappa_j\right)\Psi_j + \frac{\sigma_j}{2}\sqrt{3dt}}\right)^2\right], \tag{12.21}$$

for $j = 1, 2$.

The VBA function DHEulerAlfonsiSim implements the Euler and Alfonsi schemes.

```
Function DHEulerAlfonsiSim(scheme As String, ...) As Double
' Required quantities for j=1
K01 = -rho1 * kappa1 * theta1 * dt / sigma1
K11 = dt / 2 * (kappa1 * rho1 / sigma1 - 1 / 2) - rho1 ...
K21 = dt / 2 * (kappa1 * rho1 / sigma1 - 1 / 2) + rho1 ...
K31 = dt / 2 * (1 - rho1 ^ 2)
' Required quantities for j=2
K02 = -rho2 * kappa2 * theta2 * dt / sigma2
...
' Starting values for the variance and stock processes
For j = 1 To NS
    S(1, j) = S0          ' Spot price
    V1(1, j) = v01        ' Heston v0 initial variance
    V2(1, j) = v02        ' Heston v0 initial variance
Next j
' Generate the stock and volatility paths
For i = 1 To NS
    For j = 2 To NT
        If scheme = "Euler" Then
            V1(j, i) = V1(j - 1, i) + kappa1 * (theta1 - V1(j - 1, i)) ...
            V2(j, i) = V2(j - 1, i) + kappa2 * (theta2 - V2(j - 1, i)) ...
            V1(j, i) = Max(0, V1(j, i))
            V2(j, i) = Max(0, V2(j, i))
        ElseIf scheme = "Alfonsi" Then
            V1(j, i) = AlfonsiV(params1, V1(j - 1, i), dt)
            V2(j, i) = AlfonsiV(params2, V2(j - 1, i), dt)
        End If
        ' Predictor-Corrector for the stock price
```

```
        B1 = NormSInv(Rnd())
        B2 = NormSInv(Rnd())
        logS = Log(Exp(-r * j * dt) * S(j - 1, i)) ...
        S(j, i) = Exp(logS) * Exp(r * (j + 1) * dt)
    Next j
Next i
' Simulated price
DHEulerAlfonsiSim = Exp(-r * Mat) * Vmean(Payoff)
End Function
```

The algorithm to update v_t is implemented in the VBA function AlfonsiV. This function is identical to that presented in Chapter 7 and is not presented here.

Zhu Scheme for the Transformed Variance

We saw in Chapter 7 that one way to avoid negative variances is to simulate the volatility instead of the variance, and then square the volatility before using it as an input to the stock price process. It is straightforward to apply this approach to the double Heston model also. Recall from Chapter 7 that an application of Itō's Lemma produces the process for the volatility $\omega_{j,t} = \sqrt{v_{j,t}}$, and that Euler discretization of the volatility, produces

$$\omega_{j,t+dt} = \omega_{j,t} + \frac{\kappa_j}{2}\left[\left(\theta_j - \frac{\sigma_j^2}{4\kappa_j}\right)\frac{1}{\omega_{j,t}} - \omega_{j,t}\right]dt + \frac{1}{2}\sigma_j\sqrt{dt}Z_{j,V}, \tag{12.22}$$

for $j = 1, 2$. Hence, we first simulate $(\omega_{1,t}, \omega_{2,t})$ and then obtain the variances as $v_{1,t} = \omega_{1,t}^2$ and $v_{2,t} = \omega_{2,t}^2$. These are then fed into the Predictor-Method of Equation (12.19) to obtain S_{t+dt}. Note that this method suffers the same problem of numerical instability as the univariate version, due to the fact that the mean levels $\theta_{\omega,j} = [\theta_j - \sigma_j^2/(4\kappa_j)]/\omega_{j,t}$ are stochastic.

We saw in Chapter 7 that the remedy proposed by Zhu (2010) to this numerical instability is the transformed volatility scheme. Gauthier and Possamaï (2010) show how to apply this scheme to the double Heston model also. The transformed volatilities are defined analogously to those in Chapter 7, except with the additional "j" subscript on the parameters and variances.

The VBA function DHTransVolSim implements the Euler or the transformed volatility scheme.

```
Function DHTransVolSim(scheme As String, ...)
' Generate the stock and volatility paths
For i = 1 To NS
    For j = 2 To NT
        Zv1 = NormSInv(Rnd())
        Zv2 = NormSInv(Rnd())
```

```
        If scheme = "ZhuEuler" Then
            ' Euler volatility scheme
            w1(j, i) = w1(j - 1, i) + 0.5 * kappa1 ...
            w2(j, i) = w2(j - 1, i) + 0.5 * kappa2 ...
        ElseIf scheme = "ZhuTV" Then
            ' Zhu (2010) process for the transformed volatility
            m11 = theta1 + (w1(j - 1, i) ^ 2 - theta1) ...
            m21 = theta2 + (w2(j - 1, i) ^ 2 - theta2) ...
            m12 = sigma1 ^ 2 / 4 / kappa1 * (1 - Exp(-kappa1 * dt))
            m22 = sigma2 ^ 2 / 4 / kappa2 * (1 - Exp(-kappa2 * dt))
            beta1 = Sqr(Max(0, m11 - m12))
            beta2 = Sqr(Max(0, m21 - m22))
            thetav1 = (beta1 - w1(j - 1, i) * Exp(-kappa1 * dt / 2)) ...
            thetav2 = (beta2 - w2(j - 1, i) * Exp(-kappa2 * dt / 2)) ...
            w1(j, i) = w1(j - 1, i) + 0.5 * kappa1 ...
            w2(j, i) = w2(j - 1, i) + 0.5 * kappa2 ...
        End If
        ' Predictor-Corrector for the stock price
        logS = Log(Exp(-r * j * dt) * S(j - 1, i)) ...
        S(j, i) = Exp(logS) * Exp(r * (j + 1) * dt)
    Next j
Next i
' Simulated price
DHTransVolSim = Exp(-r * Mat) * Vmean(Payoff)
End Function
```

Quadratic-Exponential Scheme

The last simulation scheme we cover in this chapter is the quadratic-exponential (QE) scheme developed by Andersen (2008) and adapted to the double Heston model by Gauthier and Possamaï (2010). Again, the adaptation to a double variance process is straightforward.

As in the univariate case, we use the value of $\psi_c = 1.5$, recommended by Andersen (2008). The QE simulation scheme for the double Heston model is implemented using the DHQuadExpSim VBA function. The function calls the normICDF function presented in Chapter 7, for inversion of the standard normal distribution function, which applies the algorithm of Wichura (1988) and leads to a considerable reduction in simulation time.

```
Function DHQuadExpSim(...) As Double
' Generate the stock and volatility paths
For i = 1 To NS
    For j = 2 To NT
        ' First variance process
        m1 = theta1 + (V1(j - 1, i) - theta1) ...
```

```
        s1 = V1(j - 1, i) * sigma1 ^ 2 * Exp(-kappa1 * dt) ...
        phi1 = s1 / (m1 ^ 2)
        p1 = (phi1 - 1) / (phi1 + 1)
        u1 = Rnd()
        If phi1 < 0.5 Then
            B1 = Sqr(2 / phi1 - 1 + Sqr(2 / phi1 * (2 / phi1 - 1)))
            a1 = m1 / (1 + B1 ^ 2)
            Zv1 = normICDF(u1)
            V1(j, i) = a1 * (B1 + Zv1) ^ 2
        ElseIf phi1 >= 0.5 Then
            If u1 <= p1 Then
                V1(j, i) = 0
            ElseIf u1 > p1 Then
                beta1 = (1 - p1) / m1
                V1(j, i) = Log((1 - p1) / (1 - u1)) / beta1
            End If
        End If
        ' Second variance process
        m2 = theta2 + (V2(j - 1, i) - theta2) ...
        s2 = V2(j - 1, i) * sigma2 ^ 2 * Exp(-kappa2 * dt) ...
        ...
        ' Predictor-Corrector for the stock price
        logS = Log(Exp(-rf * j * dt) * S(j - 1, i)) ...
        S(j, i) = Exp(logS) * Exp(rf * (j + 1) * dt)
    Next j
Next i
' Simulated price
DHQuadExpSim = Exp(-rf * Mat) * Vmean(Payoff)
End Function
```

To illustrate the different simulation schemes covered in this chapter, we use the same settings as those in Gauthier and Possamaï (2010) that were used to generate Figure 12.1, with a maturity of one year. We use 5,000 simulations and 90 time steps per simulation. The results are shown in Figure 12.6.

Even with a small number of simulations, the quadratic-exponential and transformed volatility schemes produce results that are reasonably accurate.

The VBA code and examples for the double Heston simulation schemes are in the Excel file Ch12Simulation.xls.

It is instructive to plot the effect of double variances on a single simulated stock price path. This is illustrated in Figure 12.7. The stock price starts at $S_0 = 100$ and is represented by the black line. The high variance path (green line) uses $\sigma = 0.2$, $\rho = -0.9$, and starts at $v_{01} = 0.05$, while the low variance path (red line) uses $\sigma = 0.1$, $\rho = 0.9$, and starts at $v_{02} = 0.03$.

Figure 12.7 is generated using the VBA code in the Excel file Ch12PathSim.xls.

B	C	E	F	G
Double Heston Price, Gauthier and Possamai Table 3				
		Simulation Results with 5000 Simulations and 90 Time Steps		
Option Features		**Method**	**Price**	**Error**
Spot Price (S)	61.9000	Closed Form	19.4538	--
Strike Price (K)	61.9000	Alfonsi-Euler	20.0438	0.5900
Risk free rate (r)	0.0300	Alfonsi	15.7437	-3.7101
Maturity (τ)	1.0000	Zhu-Euler	20.8153	1.3615
Dividend (q)	0.0000	Zhu-Transformed Volatility	19.1141	-0.3397
PutCall ("C" or "P")	C	Quadratic-Exponential	19.4794	0.0257
Double Heston Parameters		**Trapezoidal Rule Settings**		
kappa1 (κ)	0.9000	Lower Limit	1.00E-10	
theta1 (θ)	0.1000	Upper Limit	150.00	
sigma1 (σ)	0.1000	Number of Abscissas	1000	
v01	0.36			
rho1 (ρ)	-0.5000	**Simulation Settings**		
kappa2 (κ)	1.2000	Number of Simulations	5000	
theta2 (θ)	0.1500	Number of Time Steps	90	
sigma2 (σ)	0.2000			
v02	0.49			
rho2 (ρ)	-0.5000			

FIGURE 12.6 Simulation Schemes for the Double Heston Model

AMERICAN OPTIONS IN THE DOUBLE HESTON MODEL

In the previous sections, we covered a number of simulation schemes adapted to the double Heston model by Gauthier and Possamaï (2010). We can use these schemes along with the Least-Squares Monte-Carlo (LSM) algorithm of Longstaff and Schwartz (2001) to obtain the prices of American options, in the same way that the LSM algorithm was applied to the univariate Heston (1993) model in Chapter 8.

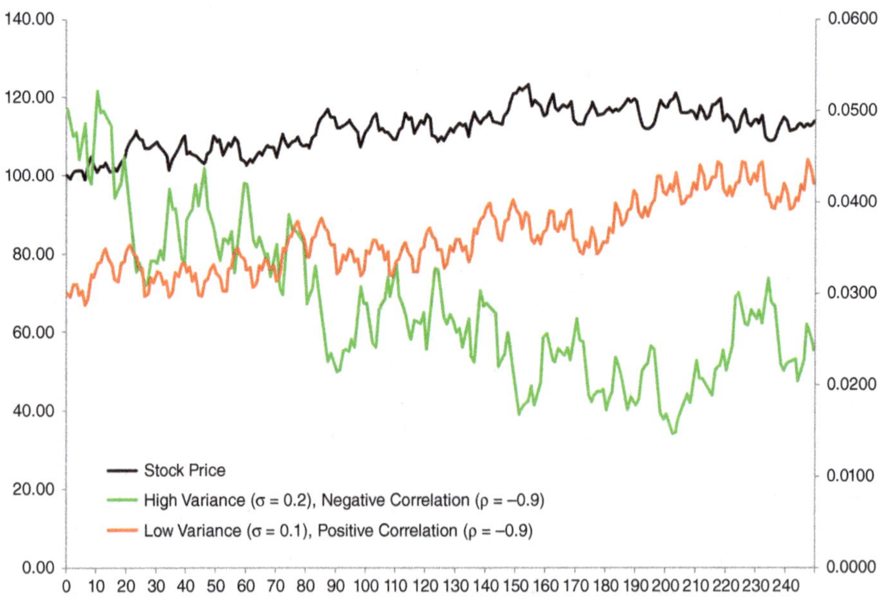

FIGURE 12.7 Simulated Stock Price and Variances with the Double Heston Model

We can also apply the control variate technique described by Hull and White (1988) and used by Beliaeva and Nawalkha (2010) in their bivariate tree, which we encountered in Chapter 8 also. The control variate price of the American put is

$$\text{American Put}_{\text{True}} = \text{European Put}_{\text{True}} + (\text{American Put}_{\text{LSM}} - \text{European Put}_{\text{LSM}}).$$

We use the closed form of the double Heston model to calculate the true price of a European put.

To implement the pricing of American puts with the LSM algorithm and the double Heston model, we first choose a simulation scheme among those covered in this chapter to generate a set of stock price paths. We then feed these stock price paths into the LSM functions to obtain the simulated prices of American and European puts. Finally, we apply the control variate technique to obtain the price of the American put. The required functions for the LSM algorithm are those described earlier in this chapter and in Chapter 8, and are not presented here.

For example, suppose we use $N_S = 50{,}000$ simulations along with $N_T = 1{,}000$ time steps per simulation to obtain the price of an American put price, using the same settings as those used to create Table 12.1. This is accomplished with the following C# code:

```
// Simulation settings
string PutCall = "P";
int NS = 50000;
int NT = 1000;
// Select the simulation scheme
string scheme = "QE";
double LSMEuro,LSMAmer,Premium,CVPrice;
DHSim Soutput = new DHSim();
if((scheme == "Alfonsi") || (scheme == "Euler"))
    Soutput = DHEulerAlfonsiSim(scheme, ...);
else if((scheme=="ZhuEuler") || (scheme=="ZhuTV"))
    Soutput = DHTransVolSim(scheme, ...);
else if(scheme == "QE")
    Soutput = DHQuadExpSim( ...);
double[,] S = Soutput.S;
double SimEuro = Soutput.EuroPrice;
// LSM algorithm
double[] LSMoutput = new double[2];
double[,] St1 = MTrans(S);
LSMoutput = HestonLSM(St1,K,rf,q,Mat,NT,NS,PutCall);
LSMEuro = LSMoutput[0];
LSMAmer = LSMoutput[1];
Premium = LSMAmer - LSMEuro;
// Control variate American price
double TrueEuroPrice = DoubleHestonPriceGaussLaguerre(...);
CVPrice = TrueEuroPrice + Premium;
```

TABLE 12.1 Double Heston Prices of an American Put

Method	Price	Exercise Premium
Closed-form European	17.6244	—
Euler	17.8278	0.2034
Alfonsi	17.8095	0.1851
Zhu-Euler	17.8068	0.1824
Zhu transformed vol	17.8372	0.2128
Quadratic-Exponential	17.8185	0.1941

The closed form European price is 17.6244, and the American prices obtained under the simulation schemes covered in this chapter are in Table 12.1.

The schemes all point to an early exercise premium of roughly \$0.20 and a price of roughly \$17.82 for the American put using the control variate technique.

CONCLUSION

The double Heston model is a convenient way to introduce flexibility in the model by allowing for additional parameters. The characteristic function of the double Heston model is a natural extension of its univariate counterpart. As such, obtaining the call price and Greeks in the double Heston model is only slightly more complicated than in the original Heston (1993) model. Moreover, simulation schemes specifically designed for the original model translate easily to the double version. With these simulation schemes, it is straightforward to obtain American option prices with the LSM algorithm of Longstaff and Schwartz (2001).

Other investigations of the double Heston model, or multifactor volatility versions of the model, include the double-lattice approach of Costabile et al. (2012), the multifactor volatility Wishart process of da Fonseca et al. (2008), and the variance curve approach of Buehler (2006).

Bibliography

Afshani, S. (2010). "Complex Logarithms and the Piecewise Constant Extension of the Heston Model." Working Paper, Standard Bank.

AitSahlia, F., M. Goswami, and S. Guha. (2012). "Are There Critical Levels of Stochastic Volatility for Early Option Exercise?" Working Paper, University of Florida.

Aït-Sahalia, Y. (2002). "Maximum Likelihood Estimation of Discretely Sampled Diffusions: A Closed-Form Approximation Approach." *Econometrica*, 70(1):223–262.

Aït-Sahalia, Y., and R. Kimmel. (2007). "Maximum Likelihood Estimation of Stochastic Volatility Models." *Journal of Financial Economics*, 83:413–452.

Albanese, C., and G. Campolieti. (2006). *Advanced Derivatives Pricing and Risk Management: Theory, Tools, and Hands-On Programming Applications*. London, UK: Elsevier Academic Press.

Albrecher, H., P. Mayer, W. Schoutens, and J. Tistaert. (2007) "The Little Heston Trap." *Wilmott Magazine*, January, 83–92.

Alfonsi, A. (2010). "High Order Discretization Schemes for the CIR Process: Application to Affine Term Structure and Heston Models." *Mathematics of Computation*, 79:209–237.

Andersen, L. (2008). "Efficient Simulation of the Heston Stochastic Volatility Model." *Journal of Computational Finance*, 11(3):1–42.

Andersen, L. B. G., and R. Brotherton-Ratcliffe. (2005). "Extended Libor Market Models with Stochastic Volatility." *Journal of Computational Finance*, 9(1):1–40.

Andersen, L. B. G., and V. V. Piterbarg. (2007). "Moment Explosions in Stochastic Volatility Models." *Finance and Stochastics*, 11(1):29–50.

Atiya, A. F., and S. Wall (2009). "An Analytic Approximation of the Likelihood Function for the Heston Model Volatility Estimation Problem." *Quantitative Finance*, 9(3):289–296.

Attari, M. (2004). "Option Pricing Using Fourier Transforms: A Numerically Efficient Simplification." Working Paper, Charles River Associates, Boston, MA.

Backus D., S. Foresi, and L. Wu. (2004) "Accounting for Biases in Black-Scholes." Working Paper, Stern School of Business, New York University.

Bagby, R. J. (1995). "Calculating Normal Probabilities." *The American Mathematical Monthly*, 102(1):46–49.

Bakshi, G., C. Cao, and Z. Chen. (1997). "Empirical Performance of Alternative Option Pricing Models." *Journal of Finance*, 52(5):2033–2049.

Bakshi, G., and D. Madan. (2000). "Spanning and Derivative-Security Valuation." *Journal of Financial Economics*, 55:205–238.

Bams, D., T. Lehnert, and C.C.P. Wolff. (2009). "Loss Functions in Option Valuation: A Framework for Selection." *Management Science*, 55:853–862.

Barone-Adesi, G., and R. E. Whaley. (1987). "Efficient Analytic Approximation of American Option Values." *Journal of Finance*, 42(2):301–320.

Beerends, R. J., H. G., ter Morsche, J. C. van den Berg, and E. M. van de Vrie. (2003). *Fourier and Laplace Transforms*. Cambridge, UK: Cambridge University Press.

Beliaeva, N. A., and S. K. Nawalkha. (2010). "A Simple Approach to Pricing American Options under the Heston Stochastic Volatility Model." *Journal of Derivatives*, 17(4): 25–43.

Benaim, S., and P. Friz. (2008). "Smile Asymptotics II: Models with Known Moment Generating Functions." *Journal of Applied Probability*, 45(1):16–32.

Benhamou, E. (2002). "Smart Monte Carlo: Various Tricks Using Malliavin Calculus." *Quantitative Finance*, 2(5):329–336.

Benhamou, E., E. Gobet, and M. Miri. (2010). "Time Dependent Heston Model." *SIAM Journal on Financial Mathematics*, 1:289–325.

Bollerslev, T., M. Gibson, and H. Zhou. (2011). "Dynamic Estimation of Volatility Risk Premia and Investor Risk Aversion from Option-Implied and Realized Volatilities." *Journal of Econometrics*, 160(1):235–245.

Borak, S., K. Detlefsen, and W. Härdle. (2011). "FFT Based Option Pricing." SFB Discussion Paper 2005-11, Humboldt University.

Breeden, D. (1979). "An Intertemporal Asset Pricing Model with Stochastic Consumption and Investment Opportunities." *Journal of Financial Economics*, 7:265–296.

Breeden, D., and R. Litzenberger. (1978). "Prices of State-Contingent Claims Implicit in Option Prices." *Journal of Business*, 51:621–651.

Brigo, D., and F. Mercurio. (2006). *Interest Rate Models—Theory and Practice: With Smile, Inflation, and Credit*. Second Edition. New York, NY: Springer.

Broadie, M., and P. Glasserman. (1996). "Estimating Security Price Derivatives Using Simulation." *Management Science*, 42(2):269–285.

Broadie, M., and Ö. Kaya. (2004). "Exact Simulation of Option Greeks under Stochastic Volatility and Jump Diffusion Models." In R. G. Ingalls, M.D. Rossetti, J. S. Smith, and B. A. Peters, eds. *Proceedings of the 2004 Winter Simulation Conference*, pp. 1607–1615.

Broadie, M., and Ö. Kaya. (2006). "Exact Simulation of Stochastic Volatility and Other Affine Jump Diffusion Processes." *Operations Research*, 54(2):217–231.

Brunner, B., and R. Hafner. (2003). "Arbitrage-Free Estimation of the Risk-Neutral Density from the Implied Volatility Smile." *Journal of Computational Finance*, 7(1):75–106.

Buehler, H. (2006). "Consistent Variance Curve Models." *Finance & Stochastics*, 10(2):178–203.

Burden, R. L., and J. D. Faires. (2010). *Numerical Analysis*. Ninth Edition. Boston, MA: Brooks Cole.

Carr, P. (2004). "Implied Vol Constraints." Working Paper, Bloomberg.

Carr, P., and D. Madan. (1999). "Option Valuation Using the Fast Fourier Transform." *Journal of Computational Finance*, 2(4):61–73.

Carr, P., and D. Madan. (2005). "A Note on Sufficient Conditions for No Arbitrage." *Finance Research Letters*, 2:125–130.

Carr, P., D. Madan, and E. C. Chang. (1998). "The Variance Gamma Process and Option Pricing." *European Finance Review*, 2:79–105.

Chacon, P. (1991). "Applications of the Fourier Transform to Probability Theory and Stochastic Processes." *International Journal of Mathematical Education in Science and Technology*, 22(5):695–708.

Chan, J. H., and M. S. Joshi. (2010a). "Fast and Accurate Long Stepping Simulation of the Heston Stochastic Volatility Model." Working Paper, University of Melbourne.

Chan, J. H., and M. S. Joshi. (2010b). "First and Second Order Greeks in the Heston Model." Working Paper, University of Melbourne.

Chensey, M., and L. Scott. (1989). "Pricing European Currency Options: A Comparison of the Modified Black-Scholes Model and a Random Variance Model." *Journal of Financial and Quantitative Analysis*, 24(3):267–284.

Chernov, M., and E. Ghysels. (2000). "A Study towards a Unified Approach to the Joint Estimation of Objective and Risk Neutral Measures for the Purpose of Options Valuation." *Journal of Financial Economics*, 56:407–458.

Chiarella, C., and A. Ziogas. (2006). "Pricing American Options under Stochastic Volatility." Working Paper, University of Technology, Sydney.

Choudakis, K. (2005). "Option Pricing Using the Fractional FFT." *Journal of Computational Finance*, 8(2):1–18.
Chriss, N. A. (1996). *Black-Scholes and Beyond: Option Pricing Models*. New York, NY: McGraw-Hill.
Christoffersen, P., S. Heston, and K. Jacobs. (2009). "The Shape and Term Structure of the Index Option Smirk: Why Multifactor Stochastic Volatility Models Work So Well." *Management Science*, 55:1914–1932.
Christoffersen, P., and K. Jacobs. (2004). "The Importance of the Loss Function in Option Valuation." *Journal of Financial Economics*, 72:291–318.
Christoffersen, P., K. Jacobs, and K. Mimouni. (2010) "Volatility Dynamics for the S&P 500: Evidence from Realized Volatility, Daily Returns, and Options Prices." *Review of Financial Studies*, 23(8):3141–3189.
Clarke, N., and K. Parrott. (1999). "Multigrid for American Option Pricing with Stochastic Volatility." *Applied Mathematical Finance*, 6:177–195.
Cohen, H. (2011). *Numerical Approximation Methods*. New York, NY: Springer.
Corrado, C. J., and T. Su. (1997). "Implied Volatility Skews and Stock Index Skewness and Kurtosis Implied by S&P 500 Index Option Prices." *Journal of Derivatives*, 4(4):8–19.
Costabile, M., I. Massabò, and E. Russo. (2012). "On Pricing Contingent Claims under the Double Heston Model." *International Journal of Theoretical and Applied Finance*, 15(5):1–27.
Cox, J. C., J. E. Ingersoll, and S. A. Ross (1985). "A Theory of the Term Structure of Interest Rates." *Econometrica*, 53(2):385–408.
Da Fonseca, J., M. Grasselli, and C. Tebaldi. (2008). "A MultiFactor Volatility Heston Model." *Quantitative Finance*, 8(6):591–604.
Davis, M. H. A., and M. P. Johansson. (2005). "Malliavin Monte Carlo Greeks for Jump Diffusions." Working Paper, Imperial College.
Demeterfi, K., E. Derman, M. Kamal, and J. Zhou. (1999). "A Guide to Volatility and Variance Swaps." *Journal of Derivatives*, 6(4):9–32.
Derman, E., I. Kani, and J. Z. Zhou. (1995). "The Local Volatility Surface: Unlocking the Information in Index Option Prices." Goldman Sachs Quantitative Strategies Research Notes, December.
Dréo, J., J.-C. Nunes, and P. Siarry. (2009). "Metaheuristics for Continuous Variables." In P. Siarry, ed. *Optimization in Signal and Image Processing*. Hoboken, NJ: John Wiley & Sons.
Duffie, D., J. Pan, and K. Singleton. (2000). Transform Analysis and Asset Pricing for Affine Jump-Diffusions. *Econometrica*, 68:1343–1376.
Duffy, D. J. (2006). *Finite Difference Methods in Financial Engineering: A Partial Differential Equation Approach*. Hoboken, NJ: John Wiley & Sons.
Duffy, D. J., and J. Kienitz. (2009). *Monte Carlo Frameworks: Building Customisable High-Performance C++ Applications*. Hoboken, NJ: John Wiley & Sons.
Dupire, B. (1994). "Pricing with a Smile." *Risk*, 7:18–20.
Elices, A. (2009). "Affine Concatenation." *Wilmott Journal*, 1(3):155–162.
Eraker, B. (2004). "Do Stock Prices and Volatility Jump? Reconciling Evidence from Spot and Option Prices." *Journal of Finance*, 59(3):1367–1403.
Fang, F., and C. W. Oosterlee (2008). "A Novel Pricing Method for European Options Based on Fourier-Cosine Series Expansions." *SIAM Journal on Scientific Computing*, 31(2):826–848.
Fengler, M. (2009). "Arbitrage-Free Smoothing of the Implied Volatility Surface." *Quantitative Finance*, 9(4):417–428.
Forde, M., and A. Jacquier. (2009). "Small-Time Asymptotics for Implied Volatility under the Heston Model." *International Journal of Theoretical and Applied Finance*, 12(6):861–876.

Forde, M., A. Jacquier, and A. Mijatovic. (2010). "Asymptotic Formulae for Implied Volatility in the Heston Model." *Proceedings of the Royal Society*, 466(2124):3593–3620.

Galiotos, V. (2008). "Stochastic Volatility and the Volatility Smile." Working Paper, Department of Mathematics, Uppsala University.

Gatheral, J. (2006). *The Volatility Surface: A Practitioner's Guide*. Hoboken, NJ: John Wiley & Sons.

Gauthier, P., and D. Possamaï. (2010). "Efficient Simulation of the Double Heston Model." Working Paper, Pricing Partners (www.pricingpartners.com).

Gauthier, P., and P.-Y. H. Rivaille (2009). "Fitting the Smile: Smart Parameters for SABR and Heston." Working Paper, Pricing Partners (www.pricingpartners.com).

Geske, R., and H. E. Johnson. (1984). "The American Put Option Valued Analytically." *Journal of Finance*, 39(5):1511–1524.

Gil-Pelaez, J. (1951). "Note on the Inversion Theorem." *Biometrika*, 38(3–4):481–482.

Gilli, M., and E. Schumann. (2011). Calibrating Option Pricing Models with Heuristics. In Brabazon, A., O'Neill, M., and D. Maringer, eds. *Natural Computing in Computational Finance*, Volume 4. Berlin: Springer-Verlag.

Glasserman, P. (2003). *Monte Carlo Methods in Financial Engineering*. New York, NY: Springer.

Guillaume, F., and W. Schoutens. (2012). "Use a Reduced Heston or Reduce the Use of Heston?" *Wilmott Journal*, 2(4):171–192.

Haug, E. G. (2006). *The Complete Guide to Option Pricing Formulas*. Second Edition. New York, NY: McGraw-Hill.

Heston, S.L. (1993). "A Closed-Form Solution for Options with Stochastic Volatility with Applications to Bond and Currency Options." *Review of Financial Studies*, 6:327–343.

Hogg, R. V., and S. Klugman. (1984). *Loss Distributions*. New York, NY: John Wiley & Sons.

Hull, J. C. (2011). *Options, Futures, and Other Derivatives*. Eighth Edition. New York, NY: Prentice Hall.

Hull, J. C., and A. White. (1987). "The Pricing of Options on Assets with Stochastic Volatilities." *Journal of Finance*, 42:281–300.

Hull, J. C., and A. White. (1988). "The Use of the Control Variate Technique in Option Pricing." *Journal of Financial and Quantitative Analysis*, 23(3):237–251.

Ikonen, S., and J. Toivanen. (2008). "Efficient Numerical Methods for Pricing American Options under Stochastic Volatility." *Numerical Methods for Partial Differential Equations*, 24(1):104–126.

In 'T Hout, K. J., and S. Foulon. (2010). "ADI Finite Difference Schemes for Option Pricing in the Heston Model with Correlation." *International Journal of Numerical Analysis and Modeling*, 7(2):303–320.

Itkin, A. (2010). Pricing Options with VG Model Using FFT. Working Paper, Department of Mathematics, Rutgers University.

Janek, A., T. Kluge, R. Weron, and U. Wystup. (2010). FX Smile in the Heston Model. SFB 649 Discussion Paper 2010-047, Humboldt University, Berlin. Also in Cizek, P., W. K. Härdle, and R. Weron, eds. *Statistical Tools for Finance and Insurance*. New York, NY: Springer.

Jarrow, R., and A. Rudd. (1982). "Approximate Option Valuation for Arbitrary Stochastic Processes." *Journal of Financial Economics*, 10:347–369.

Johannes, M. S., N. G. Polson, and J. R. Stroud. (2009). "Optimal Filtering of Jump Diffusions: Extracting Latent States from Asset Prices." *Review of Financial Studies*, 22(7):2759–2799.

Jondeau, E., S.-H. Poon, and M. Rockinger. (2007). *Financial Modeling under Non-Gaussian Distributions*. New York, NY: Springer.

Jones, C. S. (2003). "The Dynamics of Stochastic Volatility: Evidence from Underlying and Options Markets." *Journal of Econometrics*, 116:181–224.

Joshi, M. (2008). *The Concepts and Practice of Mathematical Finance*. Second Edition. Cambridge, UK: Cambridge University Press.

Kahalé, N. (2004). "An Arbitrage-Free Interpolation of Volatilities." *Risk*, May: 102–106.

Kahl, C. (2008). *Modeling and Simulation of Stochastic Volatility in Finance*. Published by Dissertation.com.

Kahl, C., and P. Jäckel. (2005). "Not-So-Complex Logarithms in the Heston Model." *Wilmott Magazine*, September: 94–103.

Kahl, C., and P. Jäckel. (2006). "Fast Strong Approximation Monte-Carlo Schemes for Stochastic Volatility Models." *Quantitative Finance*, 6(6):513–536.

Kahl, C., and R. Lord. (2010). "Fourier Inversion Methods in Finance." Working Paper, Commerzbank, and Cardano.

Kilin, F. (2007). "Accelerating the Calibration of Stochastic Volatility Models." Working Paper, Frankfurt School of Finance and Management.

Kloeden, P. E., and E. Platen. (1992). *Numerical Solution of Stochastic Differential Equations*. New York, NY: Springer.

Kluge, T. (2002). "Pricing Derivatives in Stochastic Volatility Models Using the Finite Difference Method." Diploma Thesis, Chemnitz University of Technology, Chemnitz, Germany.

Kutner, M. H., C. J. Nachtsheim, J. Neter, and W. Li. (2004). *Applied Linear Statistical Models with Student CD-ROM*. Fifth Edition. New York, NY: McGraw-Hill Education.

Kwok, Y.-K. (2008). *Mathematical Models of Financial Derivatives*. Second Edition. New York, NY: Springer.

Lee, R. (2004a). "Option Pricing by Transform Methods: Extensions, Unification, and Error Control." *Journal of Computational Finance*, 7(3):51–86.

Lee, R. (2004b). "The Moment Formula for Implied Volatility at Extreme Strikes." *Mathematical Finance*, 14(3):469–480.

Leisen, D. (2000). "Stock Evolution under Stochastic Volatility: A Discrete Approach." *Journal of Derivatives*, 8(2):9–27.

Lewis, A. L. (2000). *Option Valuation under Stochastic Volatility: With Mathematica Code*. Newport Beach, CA: Finance Press.

Lewis, A.L. (2001). "A Simple Option Formula for General Jump-Diffusion and Other Exponential Levy Processes." www.optioncity.net.

Lin, S. (2008). "Finite Difference Schemes for the Heston Model." MSc Dissertation, University of Oxford.

Lipton, A. (2002). "The Vol Smile Problem." *Risk*, February: 61–65.

Longstaff, F. A., and E. S. Schwartz. (2001). Valuing American Options by Simulation: A Simple Least-Squares Approach. *Review of Financial Studies*, 14(1):113–147.

Lord, R., F. Fang, F. Bervoets, and C. W. Oosterlee. (2008). "A Fast and Accurate FFT-Based Method for Pricing Early-Exercise Options under Lévy Processes." *SIAM Journal on Scientific Computing*, 30(4):1678–1705.

Lord, R., and C. Kahl. (2007). "Optimal Fourier Inversion in Semi-Analytical Option Pricing." Working Paper, Rabobank International and ABN AMRO.

McNamee, J. M. (2007). *Numerical Methods for Roots of Polynomials, Part I*. Studies in Computational Mathematics 14. Amsterdam, the Netherlands: Elsevier.

Medvedev, A., and O. Scaillet (2010). "Pricing American Options under Stochastic Volatility and Stochastic Interest Rates." *Journal of Financial Economics*, 98(1):145–159.

Mikhailov, S., and U. Nögel. (2003). "Heston's Stochastic Volatility Model: Implementation, Calibration, and Some Extensions." *Wilmott Magazine*, July: 74–79.

Milstein, G.N., Platen, E., and H. Schurz. (1998). "Balanced Implicit Methods for Stiff Stochastic Systems." *SIAM Journal on Numerical Analysis*, 35(3):1010–1019.

Musiela, M., and M. Rutkowski. (2011). *Martingale Methods in Financial Modelling*. Second Edition. New York, NY: Springer.

Nelder, J. A., and R. Mead. (1965). "A Simplex Method for Function Minimization." *The Computer Journal*, 7(4):308–313.

Nykvist, J. (2009). "Time Consistency in Option Pricing Models." Doctoral Thesis, KTH Royal Institute of Technology.

Pan, J. (2002). "The Jump-Risk Premia Implicit in Options: Evidence from an Integrated Time-Series Study." *Journal of Financial Economics*, 63(1):3–50.

Platen, E., and D. Heath. (2009). *A Benchmark Approach to Quantitative Finance*, Volume 13. New York, NY: Springer.

Press, W. H., S. A. Teukolsky, W. T. Vetterling, and B. P. Flannery. (2007). *Numerical Recipes: The Art of Scientific Computing*. Third Edition. New York, NY: Cambridge University Press.

Raible, S. (2000). "Lévy Processes in Finance: Theory, Numerics, and Empirical Facts." PhD dissertation, Albert Ludwig University of Freiburg.

Reiss, O., and U. Wystup. (2000). "Efficient Computation of Option Price Sensitivities Using Homogeneity and Other Tricks." Working Paper, Commerzbank.

Rouah, F. (2013). *The Heston Model and Its Extensions in Matlab and C#*. Hoboken, NJ: John Wiley & Sons.

Ruckdeschel, P., Sayer, T., and A. Szimayer. (2013). "Pricing American Options in the Heston Model: A Close Look at Incorporating Correlation." *The Journal of Derivatives*, 20(3):9–29.

Rudin, W. (1986). *Real and Complex Analysis*. Third Edition. New York, NY: McGraw-Hill.

Schmelzle, M. (2010). Option Pricing Formulae Using Fourier Transforms: Theory and Applications. www.pfadintegral.com.

Schoutens, W., Simons, E., and J. Tistaert. (2004). "A Perfect Calibration! Now What?" *Wilmott Magazine*, March: 66–78.

Scott, L. O. (1987). "Option Pricing When the Variance Changes Randomly: Theory, Estimation, and an Application." *Journal of Financial and Quantitative Analysis*, 22:419–438.

Singleton, K. J. (2001). "Estimation of Affine Asset Pricing Models Using the Empirical Characteristic Function." *Journal of Econometrics*, 102(1):111–141.

Shephard, N. G. (1991). "From Characteristic Function to Distribution Function: A Simple Framework for the Theory." *Economic Theory*, 7:519–529.

Shimko, D. (1993). Bounds of Probability. *Risk*, 6(4):33–37.

Singleton, K. (2001). "Estimation of Affine Asset Pricing Models Using the Empirical Characteristic Function." *Journal of Econometrics*, 102(1):111–141.

Smith, R. D. (2007). "An Almost Exact Simulation Method for the Heston Model." *Journal of Computational Finance*, 11(1):115–125.

Stein, E. M., and J. C. Stein, (1991). "Stock Price Distributions with Stochastic Volatility: An Analytic Approach." *Review of Financial Studies*, 4:727–752.

Storn, R., and K. Price. (1997). Differential Evolution—A Simple and Efficient Heuristic for Global Optimization over Continuous Spaces. *Journal of Global Optimization*, 11: 341–359.

Stroud, A. H., and D. Secrest. (1966). *Gaussian Quadrature Formulas*. Upper Saddle River, NJ: Prentice Hall.

Stuart, A. (2010). *Kendall's Advanced Theory of Statistics*. Three Volume Set. Hoboken, NJ: John Wiley & Sons.

Tavella, D., and C. Randall. (2000). *Pricing Financial Instruments: The Finite Difference Method*. New York, NY: John Wiley & Sons.

Tzavalis, E., and S. Wang. (2003). "Pricing American Options under Stochastic Volatility: A New Method Using Chebyshev Polynomials to Approximate the Early Exercise Boundary." Working Paper 488, Queen Mary, University of London.

Van Haastrecht, A., and A. Pelsser. (2010). "Efficient, Almost Exact Simulation of the Heston Stochastic Volatility Model." *International Journal of Theoretical and Applied Finance*, 13(1):1–43.

Vellekoop, M., and H. Nieuwenhuis. (2009). "A Tree-Based Method to Price American Options in the Heston Model." *Journal of Computational Finance*, 13(1):1–21.

Vollrath, I., and J. Wendland. (2009). "Calibration of Interest Rate and Option Models Using Differential Evolution." Working Paper, FINCAD Corporation.

Whaley, R. E. (2006). *Derivatives: Markets, Valuation, and Risk Management.* Hoboken, NJ: John Wiley & Sons.

Wichura, M. J. (1988). "Algorithm AS241: The Percentage Points of the Normal Distribution." *Applied Statistics*, 37(3):477–484.

Wiggins, J. B. (1987). "Option Values under Stochastic Volatility: Theory and Empirical Estimates." *Journal of Financial Economics*, 19:351–372.

Wu, L. (2008). "Modeling Financial Security Returns Using Lévy Processes." In J. R. Birge, and V. Linetsky, eds. *Financial Engineering.* Volume 15. Amsterdam: North-Holland Elsevier.

Zhu, J. (2010). *Applications of Fourier Transform to Smile Modeling: Theory and Implementation.* Second Edition. New York, NY: Springer.

Zhylyevskyy, O. (2010). "A Fast Fourier Transform Technique for Pricing American Options under Stochastic Volatility." *Review of Derivatives Research*, 13(1):1–24.

Zwillinger, D. (1997). *Handbook of Differential Equations.* Third Edition. Orlando, FL: Academic Press.

About the Website

All the calculations for the implementation of the models covered in this book are done in VBA code that resides in Excel files. All of the Excel files are available on the book's companion website: www.wiley.com/go/hestonvba (password: rouah15).

Files are arranged in directories that correspond to the chapters in which they're used. The files are then arranged in subdirectories that correspond to the type of analysis for which the files are used.

See sections "About This Book" and "VBA Library for Complex Numbers" in the front matter of this book for more information.

Index

Alfonsi scheme for variance, 161–165, 302–303
Alternating Direction Implicit (ADI) schemes, 251–255
American options, Heston model for, 169–208
  Beliaeva-Nawalkha bivariate tree, 178–190
    combining trinomial trees, 182
    implementation in VBA, 182–190
    trinomial tree for stock price, 180–181
    trinomial tree for variance, 179–180
  Chiarella and Ziogas American call pricing method, 200–207
    American call price, 200–204
    early exercise boundary approximation, 200
    estimating early exercise boundary, 204–207
  explicit method, 174–178
  Least-Squares Monte Carlo (LSM) algorithm, 169–174
  Medvedev-Scaillet expansion, 191–199
    for Black-Scholes, 191–195
    for Heston, 196–199
Attari representation, 47–49

Balanced implicit method, 155–157
Beliaeva-Nawalkha bivariate tree, 178–190
  combining trinomial trees, 182
  implementation in VBA, 182–190
  trinomial tree for stock price, 180–181
  trinomial tree for variance, 179–180
Benhamou-Miri-Gobet model, 223–231
  constant parameters, 225–227
    implied volatility from, 227
  piecewise constant parameters, 228–231
Bivariate characteristic function, 210–211
  linking with general Riccati equation, 212–214
Black-Scholes derivatives, 231–232
Black-Scholes model, xiii, 14
  Medvedev-Scaillet expansion for, 191–195
  as a special case, 10–12

Call prices
  comparison of, 69, 75
  using the volatility expansion, 80
Carr and Madan representation, 49–61
Carr-Madan formulations, Greeks under, 273
Carr-Madan integrands, 55
  for OTM options, 56

Chiarella and Ziogas American call pricing method, 200–207
  American call price, 200–204
  early exercise boundary approximation, 200
  estimating early exercise boundary, 204–207
Christoffersen, Heston, and Jacobs (CHJ) loss function, 119
Contour variations and call price, 72–75
Craig-Sneyd scheme, 252
  modified, 252–253
Crank-Nicolson scheme, 242

Damping factor
  optimal, 51–52
  and optimal value, bounds on, 50–51
Delta, 258–260
Density, effect of correlation on, 20
Derivation of Gatheral, 46
Differential Evolution (DE), 128–132
Dividend yield and put price, 8
Double Heston model, 287–308
  American options in, 306–308
  call price, 288–292
  Greeks, 292–297
  multidimensional Feynman-Kac theorem, 288
  parameter estimation, 297–300
  simulation in, 301–306
    Alfonsi scheme for variance, 302–303
    Euler scheme for variance, 301–302
    quadratic-exponential scheme, 304–306
    stock price, 301
    Zhu scheme for transformed variance, 303–304
Douglas scheme, 252
Dupire local volatility, 29–34

Elices model, 219–223
  implied volatility from, 224
Euler scheme, 146, 152, 301–302
European Greeks, analytic expressions for, 258–263
  delta, gamma, rho, theta, and vega, 258–260
  vanna, volga, and other Greeks, 260–263
European options, Heston model for, 1–12
  Black-Scholes as a special case, 10–12
  consolidating integrals, 9–10
  dividend yield and put price, 8

European options, Heston model for (*Continued*)
  Heston European call price, 2–8
  model dynamics, 1–2
Explicit method, 174–178, 248–251
  American Greeks using, 281–283
  call price using, 251

Fast Fourier transform (FFT), 84, 106–108, 119
  Greeks using, 276–279
Fat tails, xiii
Feynman-Kac theorem, multidimensional, 288
Finite differences, methods for, 235–256
  Alternating Direction Implicit (ADI) schemes, 251–255
  boundary conditions for PDE, 240–241
  building grids, 236–238
  explicit scheme, 248–251
  finite difference approximation of derivatives, 239–240
  PDE in terms of an operator, 236
  weighted method, 241–248
Fourier transform, derivations using, 45–61. *See also* Fast Fourier transform (FFT); Fractional fast Fourier transform (FRFT); Numerical integration schemes
  Attari representation, 47–49
  Carr and Madan representation, 49–61
    damping factor and optimal value, bounds on, 50–51
    numerical implementation and illustration, 52–54
    optimal damping factor, 51–52
    OTM options, representation for, 57–58
    OTM representation, generalization of, 59–61
    puts, representation for, 54–57
  derivation of Gatheral, 46
Fractional fast Fourier transform (FRFT), 108–113, 119
  Greeks using, 276–279
Fundamental Theorem of Calculus, 83
Fundamental transform for pricing options, 63–81
  Parseval's identity, option prices using, 70–75
    contour variations and call price, 72–75
    for the Heston model, 71–72
  payoff transform, 64–69
    call price using fundamental transform, 67–69
    fundamental transform for the Heston model, 66–67
    fundamental transform and option price, 65–66
  volatility of volatility series expansion, 75–80

Gamma, 258–260, 264, 268, 292
Gatheral, derivation of, 46
Gauss-Laguerre integration, 6–7, 56, 75, 95, 217, 265, 274
Gaussian quadrature, 84, 90–98
  for double integrals, 97–98
  Gauss-Laguerre quadrature, 91–93, 201, 292
  Gauss-Legendre quadrature, 93–95, 201, 203
  Gauss-Lobatto quadrature, 96–97
Greeks, 257–286, 292–297
  American
    from Medvedev and Scaillet, 284–285
    using the explicit method, 281–283
    using simulation, 279–281
  double Heston model, 292–297
  European, analytic expressions for, 258–263
    delta, gamma, rho, theta, and vega, 258–260
    vanna, volga, and other Greeks, 260–263
  finite differences for, 263–264
  numerical implementation of, 264–267
  under the Attari and Carr-Madan formulations, 267–273
  under the Lewis formulations, 273–276
  using the FFT and FFRT, 276–279

Heston integrand and maturity, 8
Heston model
  for American options, 169–208
    Beliaeva-Nawalkha bivariate tree, 178–190
    Chiarella and Ziogas American call pricing method, 200–207
    explicit method, 174–178
    Least-Squares Monte Carlo (LSM) algorithm, 169–174
    Medvedev-Scaillet expansion, 191–199
  for European options, 1–12
    Black-Scholes as a special case, 10–12
    consolidating integrals, 9–10
    dividend yield and put price, 8
    Heston European call price, 2–8
    model dynamics, 1–2
  simulation in, 143–167
    Alfonsi scheme for variance, 161–165
    balanced, pathwise, and IJK schemes, 155–157
    Euler scheme, 146, 152
    general setup, 144–146
    Implicit Milstein scheme, 149–152
    Milstein scheme, 147–149
    moment-matched discretization scheme, 165–167
    quadratic-exponential (QE) discretization scheme, 157–161
    transformed volatility scheme, 152–155
  time-dependent, 209–233
    Benhamou-Miri-Gobet model, 223–231
    bivariate characteristic function, 210–211
    Black-Scholes derivatives, 231–232
    Elices model, 219–223

linking the bivariate CF and general Riccati equation, 212–214
Mikhailov and Nögel model, 214–219
Riccati equation, generalization of, 209–210
Heston parameters, effect of, 20–26
Black-Scholes prices, comparison with, 21–24
correlation and volatility of variance, effect of, 20–21
implied volatility, 24–26
terminal spot price, 20
Heston terminal spot price, 20
Hundsdorfer-Verwer scheme, 253

IJK schemes, 155–157
Implied volatility mean error sum of squares (IVMSE), 117, 119, 128
Implied volatility root mean squared error (IVRMSE), 139–140, 297, 298
Implied volatility slope, bounds on, 40–42
Integrals, consolidating, 9–10
Integration
contours of, 73
limits, 98
multidomain, 99–101
Integration issues, parameter effects, and variance modeling, 13–43
characteristic functions, 14–16
Heston parameters, effect of, 20–26
Black-Scholes prices, comparison with, 21–24
correlation and volatility of variance, effect of, 20–21
implied volatility, 24–26
terminal spot price, 20
implied volatility slope, bounds on, 40–42
integrand, problems with, 16–18
discontinuities in, 17
oscillations in, 17
"Little Trap" formulation, 13, 18–20
moment explosions, 38–40
variance modeling, 26–38
approximate local volatility, 35–36
Dupire local volatility, 29–34
local volatility with finite differences, 34–35
numerical illustration of local volatility, 36–37
variance swap, 26–29

Kahl and Jäckel transformation, 101–103, 104
Kurtosis, xiii, 20, 23

Least-Squares Monte Carlo (LSM) algorithm, 169–174, 279–281, 306–307
Legendre polynomials, 94
Lewis formulations, Greeks under, 273–276
"Little Trap" formulation, 13, 18–20, 31–32, 46, 290
Lord and Kahl optimal alpha function, 55
Loss functions, parameter estimation using, 116–120
Nelder-Mead algorithm in VBA, 120–122
starting values, 122–126

Maximum likelihood estimation, 132–135
Mean error sum of squares (MSE), 116, 298
Medvedev-Scaillet expansion, 191–199
American Greeks from, 284–285
for Black-Scholes, 191–195
for Heston, 196–199
Mikhailov and Nögel model, 214–219
Milstein scheme, 147–149
implicit, 149–152
Moment explosions, 38–40
Multidomain integration, 99–101

Nelder-Mead algorithm in VBA, 120–122
Newton-Cotes formulas, 84, 85–90
midpoint rule, 85–86
Simpson's rule, 88
Simpson's three-eighths rule, 88–90
trapezoidal rule, 86–88
for double integrals, 87–88
Numerical integration schemes, 83–114
fast Fourier transform (FFT), 84, 106–108
fractional fast Fourier transform (FRFT), 108–113
Gaussian quadrature, 90–98
for double integrals, 97–98
Gauss-Laguerre quadrature, 91–93
Gauss-Legendre quadrature, 93–95
Gauss-Lobatto quadrature, 96–97
illustration of, 103–106
integrand in, 84–85
integration limits, 98
Kahl and Jäckel transformation, 101–103, 104
multidomain integration, 99–101
Newton-Cotes formulas, 84, 85–90
midpoint rule, 85–86
Simpson's rule, 88
Simpson's three-eighths rule, 88–90
trapezoidal rule, 86–88

Parameter estimation, 115–141, 297–300
Differential Evolution (DE), 128–132
in the double Heston model, 297–300
maximum likelihood estimation, 132–135
risk-neutral density (RND) and arbitrage-free volatility surface, 135–140
speeding up, 126–128
using loss functions, 116–126
Nelder-Mead algorithm in VBA, 120–122
starting values, 122–126
Parseval's identity, option prices using, 70–75
contour variations and call price, 72–75
for the Heston model, 71–72

Partial differential equation (PDE) in terms of an operator, 236
Pathwise adapted linearization quadratic method, 155–157
Payoff transform, 64–69
  call price using fundamental transform, 67–69
  fundamental transform for Heston model, 66–67
  fundamental transform and option price, 65–66
Puts, representation for, 54–57

Quadratic-exponential (QE) discretization scheme, 157–161, 304–306

Relative mean error sum of squares (RMSE), 116–117, 127–128, 298
Rho, 258–260
Riccati equation, generalization of, 209–210
  linking with bivariate CF, 212–214
Risk-neutral density (RND)
  and arbitrage-free volatility surface, 135–140
  from double Heston model, 300

Simpson's rule, 88
Simpson's three-eighths rule, 88–90
Simulation in the Heston model, 143–167
  Alfonsi scheme for variance, 161–165
  balanced, pathwise, and IJK schemes, 155–157
  Euler scheme, 146, 152
  general setup, 144–146
  Implicit Milstein scheme, 149–152
  Milstein scheme, 147–149
  moment-matched discretization scheme, 165–167
  quadratic-exponential (QE) discretization scheme, 157–161
  transformed volatility scheme, 152–155
Skewness, xiii, 20
Stochastic differential equations (SDEs), 144, 288
Stochastic volatility models, xiii

Theta, 258–260, 264, 268, 293
Time-dependent Heston models, 209–233
  Benhamou-Miri-Gobet model, 223–231
    constant parameters, 225–227
    piecewise constant parameters, 228–231
  bivariate characteristic function, 210–211
  Black-Scholes derivatives, 231–232
  Elices model, 219–223
  linking the bivariate CF and general Riccati equation, 212–214
  Mikhailov and Nögel model, 214–219
  Riccati equation, generalization of, 209–210
Transformed volatility scheme, 152–155
Trapezoidal integration rule, 5, 9, 86–88, 201, 203, 274
  for double integrals, 87–88

Vanna, 260–263, 294, 296–297
Variance modeling, 26–38
  approximate local volatility, 35–36
  Dupire local volatility, 29–34
  local volatility with finite differences, 34–35
  numerical illustration of local volatility, 36–37
  variance swap, 26–29
VBA code, xvii
VBA library for complex numbers, xix–xxiii
Vega, 258–260, 265, 285, 293, 296–297
  Black-Scholes, 298
Volatility, xiii
  approximate local, 35–36
  Dupire local, 29–34
  implied, 24–26
    from double Heston model, 300
    at extreme strikes, 43
  local
    with finite differences, 34–35
    numerical illustration of, 36–37
  of volatility series expansion, 75–80
Volga, 260–263, 265, 293–294, 296–297

Weighted method, 241–248
  call prices using, 248

Zhu scheme for transformed variance, 303–304

www.ingramcontent.com/pod-product-compliance
Lightning Source LLC
LaVergne TN
LVHW080021210926
848481LV00011B/3077